SBC

In July 1992, 77 years after the subject's death, the Commonwealth War Graves Commission took the unusual and newsworthy action of erecting a headstone in St Mary's Advanced Dressing Station CWGC Cemetery, Loos, with the caption

'LIEUTENANT
JOHN KIPLING
IRISH GUARDS
27TH SEPTEMBER 1915 AGE 18'

on a grave previously attributed to

'A LIEUTENANT
OF THE GREAT WAR
IRISH GUARDS'

Lieutenant John Kipling was hitherto – *and still is* – commemorated on the Loos Memorial to the 'Missing with no known grave'.

HAM
3
D1076833

BY THE SAME AUTHORS

Picture Postcards of the Golden Age: A Collector's Guide

Till the Boys Come Home: the Picture Postcards of the First World War

The Best of Fragments from France by Capt Bruce Bairnsfather

In Search of the Better 'Ole: The Life, Works and Collectables of Bruce Bairnsfather

Revised edition 2001

Picture Postcard Artists: Landscapes, Animals and Characters

Stanley Gibbons Postcard Catalogue: 1980, 1981, 1982, 1984, 1985, 1987

Germany Awake! The Rise of National Socialism illustrated by Contemporary Postcards

I'll be Seeing You: the Picture Postcards of World War II

Holts' Battlefield Guidebooks: Normandy-Overlord/Market-Garden/Somme/Ypres

Visitor's Guide to the Normandy Landing Beaches

Battlefields of the First World War: A Traveller's Guide

Major & Mrs Holt's Concise Guide to the Ypres Salient

Major & Mrs Holt's Battle Maps: Normandy/Somme/Ypres/Gallipoli/MARKET-GARDEN

Major & Mrs Holt's Battlefield Guide to the Ypres Salient + Battle Map

Major & Mrs Holt's Battlefield Guide to the Normandy Landing Beaches + Battle Map

Major & Mrs Holt's Battlefield Guide to Gallipoli + Battle Map

Major & Mrs Holt's Battlefield Guide to MARKET-GARDEN + Battle Map

Violets From Oversea: Reprinted 1999 as Poets of the Great War

My Boy Jack: The Search for Kipling's Only Son: Revised limpback edition 2001

Major & Mrs Holt's Concise, Illustrated Battlefield Guides to the Western Front – North and South

Major & Mrs Holt's Pocket Battlefield Guide to Ypres & Passchendaele

Major & Mrs Holt's Pocket Battlefield Guide to the Somme 1916/1918

'MY BOY JACK?'

The Search for Kipling's Only Son

by

Tonie and Valmai Holt

Pen & Sword
MILITARY

First published in Great Britain in 1998 by Leo Cooper
Re-printed in 2001 and 2007
Re-printed in this format in 2008 and 2009 by
PEN & SWORD MILITARY
an imprint of
Pen & Sword Books Ltd
47 Church Street
Barnsley
South Yorkshire
S70 2AS

Copyright © Tonie and Valmai Holt, 1998, 2001, 2007, 2008, 2009

ISBN 978 1 84415 7 044

The right of Tonie and Valmai Holt to be identified as authors of this
work has been asserted by them in accordance with the
Copyright, Designs and Patents Act 1988.

A CIP catalogue record for this book is
available from the British Library

All rights reserved. No part of this book may be reproduced
or transmitted in any form or by any means, electronic or mechanical
including photocopying, recording or by any information storage and
retrieval system, without permission from the Publisher in writing.

Printed and bound in Great Britain
By CPI UK

Pen & Sword Books Ltd incorporates the imprints of
Pen & Sword Aviation, Pen & Sword Maritime, Pen & Sword Military,
Wharncliffe Local History, Pen & Sword Select,
Pen & Sword Military Classics and Leo Cooper.

For a complete list of Pen & Sword titles please contact
PEN & SWORD BOOKS LIMITED
47 Church Street, Barnsley, South Yorkshire, S70 2AS, England
E-mail: enquiries@pen-and-sword.co.uk
Website: www.pen-and-sword.co.uk

CONTENTS

FOREWORD

by
Michael Smith
Honorary Secretary of the Kipling Society

In 1992 the Commonwealth War Graves Commission announced that as a result of examining old documents in their archives their Records Officer had established, beyond reasonable doubt, that Lieutenant John Kipling's final resting place had been located. As a human interest story the media soon broadcast the details of the discovery to a wider public, for it was well embedded in folk consciousness that John's grief-stricken parents had taken enormous trouble to establish the truth of their loss. Since that time there has been even more widespread coverage, including a dramatization of the events in a play by David Haig called, after Rudyard Kipling's poetic *cri de coeur, My Boy Jack.*

Now a really authoritative account is presented to a readership eager to find out more about the events leading up to a loss which typified the experience of millions of Britons during the fight for survival that was the First World War. Perhaps, because hardly any family was untouched by the death and destruction, many could identify with the heartbreak experienced by one who for long had been the voice of the man in the street, the one who tried to get due recognition for the soldier, to advance the cause of naval men and who was aware of the potential of an air arm in its infancy.

It would be difficult to find authors more tailor-made for so daunting a task. A search for truth among the embers which had, for decades, grown cold; with many cross-winds to disturb what was still to be found; and in which prejudice had left an impression on the motives of those closely affected. Tonie and Valmai Holt have, for many years, been recognized as having a single-minded determination to research war and the consequences of war, and to place their findings before those who needed to know the why, when and wherefore, the locations and the conditions of battles in which their closest had given their lives or their sanity or their health in the service of the Empire. They proved outstanding in doing so and now, with a fresh challenge raised in 1992, they set about the new task with the same meticulous attention to detail to sieve and to sift the facts from regimental documents and the memories, written or oral, from those closer to the action than we can ever be.

The result is as compellingly readable as one could wish and is as memorable as the best of other Kipling biographers. The Holts' part of that story has never before been subjected to such an intricate appraisal or such meticulous searching. For that, those who are moved by the work of such an extraordinary Englishman, or for those whose interest might primarily be in military history, or for those who admire the indomitability of the human spirit, all must remain indebted. Having read the manuscript with growing interest, I am sure that *My Boy Jack?* is a major contribution to the Kipling canon and its authors deserve congratulations, both on their exceptional research and on their ability to present the results in such an attractive fashion.

ACKNOWLEDGEMENTS AND SOURCES

We have to admit to an antipathy to the traditional method of annotated footnotes which constantly force the reader to turn to the back of the book for enlightenment on sources. Instead we have indicated our references throughout the text, either in square brackets [e.g. 'Carrington'] or by indicating 'letter from Carrie to her mother', 'Carrie to Lady Edward' etc. Our main primary sources are the Kipling Papers held in the archives in the University of Sussex Library (which include Carrington's transcript of Carrie Kipling's diary and letters from and to Rudyard Kipling and his wife, children and various friends and associates); the *Kipling Journal*; the Kipling-Balestier-Dunham Letters (letters from Carrie and Rudyard Kipling to her American relatives) a microfilm of which is also held in the archives in Sussex; *The Letters of Rudyard Kipling*, edited by Professor T. Pinney; the Cecil-Maxse MSS, held at the Bodleian Library (letters from Carrie Kipling to Lady Edward, wife of Lord Edward Cecil, and various documents pertaining to the deaths of George Cecil and John Kipling); the archives of the Commonwealth War Graves Commission; the archives of the Irish Guards at Wellington Barracks, Bird Cage Walk; the John Kipling file released to the public by the Public Record Office in February 1998. We wish to thank the CWGC, the Irish Guards, the P.R.O. and the National Trust for Places of Historic Interest or Natural Beauty, for permission to quote from his letters and from his work. Other sources are listed in the select bibliography at the end of the book.

We would also like to thank the staff – in particular Beverley Webb (now retired), Liam Hanna, Barry Murphy, Roy Hemington and Ian Small – of the Commonwealth War Graves Commission Head Office at Maidenhead for their hospitable and trusting attitude in allowing us access to their newly catalogued and computerized archives; the highly professional and patiently helpful Dr Elizabeth Inglis, curator of the Kipling Papers at the University of Sussex; the supportive staff in Room 132 of the Bodleian Library, Oxford; Wolcott B. Dunham, Jr for his personal permission to quote from the Kipling–Balestier-Dunham letters; Lieutenant Colonel Frank Groves (Retd), MBE and Mr Dominic M. Kearney, mines of information and constantly helpful custodians of the Irish Guards Archives; Tim Padfield and William Spencer of the P.R.O.; Peter Simkins and Brad King, Historians, Imperial War Museum; Terry

Pitt of the National Trust who opened Bateman's for us on a closed winter's day; Sian Wynn-Jones of the British Red Cross Museum and Archives; Mr J, Sworder, the Secretary of the Old Wellingtonian Society and the Wellington College Archivist; the Bursar's office at St Aubyns School at Rottingdean; Norm Christie of C.E.F. Books, Nepean, Ontario; the staff in the Reference sections of Canterbury and Dover Libraries; Captain David Horn, Curator, Guards Museum, who answered endless questions; Judge Anthony Babington, Howell Griffiths, J.P., and Michael Johnstone, Metropolitan Stipendiary Magistrate for their opinions; Dr Alan Gauld of the Department of Psychiatry, Nottingham University, Leslie Price of the College of Psychic Studies and Michael Colmer, author of many books on spiritualism and other subjects, for information about Trix Kipling in her guise of 'Mrs Holland'; Geoffrey Barwell for information about Kipling and Freemasonry; James Brazier of the WFA for information on Sir Charles Wheeler; Mr John Bushell for information on his relative Rupert Grayson; Rosalie Young for information on Captain H.F.D'A.S. Law; Gareth and Sam Holt for extensive research at the Public Record Office; Louise Hooper, B.B.C.; Philip W. Guest and the Wilfred Owen Association; Christopher Walker, Oliver Baldwin's biographer, for permission to quote from letters in his possession; Charlotte Zeepvat for early initial research; Mr Andrew Kirk of the Theatre Museum; Mr Max Tyier, Historian of the British Music Hall Society, Dollond & Aitcheson, Opticians, Deal; and most of all to those supremely omniscient officers of the Kipling Society, Mrs Lisa Lewis, George Webb and, in particular, Michael Smith for painstakingly reading our draft manuscript and making many helpful suggestions and for whom no question seemed too simple nor too complicated to attempt to answer. Finally our grateful thanks go to all the long-suffering staff at Pen & Sword, Barnsley and especially to our Editors, Leo Cooper's successor. Henry Wilson, Tom ('The Knowledge') Hartman and Miss M Holdsworth for spotting some literals..

The authors acknowledge with gratitude permission to reproduce the photographs used in this book: The National Trust for Places of Historic Interest or Natural Beauty, Nos 1, 2, 3; Irish Guards Archives, Nos 4, 5, 13; Collection Viollet, No 6; the Commonwealth War Graves Commission, Nos 8, 9, 10, 11,

2007 Edition

We acknowledge the continuing assistance of Roy Hemington at the CWGC and the Loos Museum for photos of the Lt Jacob's name and of Puits 14 in 1905.

My Boy Jack

'Have you news of my boy Jack?'
Not this tide.
'When d'you think that he'll come back?'
Not with this wind blowing, and this tide.

'Has any one else had word of him?'
Not this tide.
For what is sunk will hardly swim,
Not with this wind blowing, and this tide.

'Oh dear, what comfort can I find?'
None this tide,
Nor any tide,
Except he did not shame his kind –
Not even with that wind blowing, and that tide.

Then hold your head up all the more
This tide,
And every tide:
Because he was the son you bore,
And gave to that wind blowing and that tide!

INTRODUCTION

Few lives have been so thoroughly examined and analysed as that of Rudyard Kipling, despite the fact that biographical and archive material was jealously guarded and censored, first by his wife, Carrie, and then by his daughter, Elsie. The Internet book shop, Amazon (amazon.com), for example, lists over 250 Kipling entries.

Kipling's autobiography, *Something of Myself*, published in 1936, had lived up to its title. It was indeed 'something' but by no means 'all' that there was to know about this prolific author, whose personal life had been so full and varied. It is immensely readable, however, and certainly reveals a far more human side to the great man than his detractors could have imagined. His work, as we shall see, is often far more self-revelatory than his autobiography.

It seems impossible to be lukewarm about Kipling. The pendulum of reaction to him swings from the almost sycophantic 'Kipling-ite', for whom he could do nothing unworthy, to the hostile 'detractor', for whom he could produce little of merit.

He intrigued and sometimes irritated many famous writers and historians. T.S. Eliot wrote in the Introduction to *A Choice of Kipling's Verse* in 1941, 'There is always something alien about Kipling, as of a visitor from another planet . . . Kipling is the most elusive of subjects: no writer has been more reticent about himself.' As for his poetry, Eliot decided that on the whole it is more accurately described as 'verse'. In reviewing Eliot's anthology, George Orwell launched a searing attack on Kipling, claiming that 'During five literary generations every enlightened person has despised him . . . Kipling *is* a jingo imperialist, he *is* morally insensitive and aesthetically disgusting.' Yet he grudgingly admitted that he wrote 'good bad poetry', which 'is a graceful monument to the obvious'. Henry James saw in his much-admired output of 1889–90 'almost nothing of the complicated soul or of the female form or of any question of *shades*'. But writing to Robert Louis Stevenson in 1890, when Kipling left on a world tour, James referred to Rudyard as 'a little black demon of a Kipling . . . [who] publicly left England to embrace you many weeks ago carrying literary genius out of the country with him in his pocket.' Stevenson awaited a visitation from what he deemed 'the most promising young man who has appeared since – ahem – I appeared'. Unfortunately Kipling ran out of time and did not manage to visit Stevenson in Samoa.

The first authorized biography was Charles Carrington's *Rudyard*

Kipling: His Life and Work, published in 1955, followed by Lord Birkenhead's *Rudyard Kipling* in 1978. Although Rudyard's daughter, Elsie Bambridge, gave Birkenhead encouragement and access to family papers when he started the work in the late 1940s, to his utter surprise and horror she condemned the final manuscript and the book was not published until after the deaths of both Lord Birkenhead and herself.

Both these accounts were accurate but somewhat predictable, lending credence to the theory that there lurked a 'dark secret' yet to be unearthed in Kipling's life. They were followed by Kingsley Amis's *Rudyard Kipling And his World*, 1975, and Angus Wilson's *Strange Ride of Rudyard Kipling* (the title borrowed from Kipling's 1885 short story *The Strange Ride of Morrowbie Jukes*) in 1977, which are more thought-provoking but still contain no scandalous revelations. This was 'remedied' by Martin Seymour-Smith's controversial *Rudyard Kipling* which burst on a shocked literary world in 1989. In it he maintained that Rudyard Kipling had engaged in a homosexual relationship with his wife's brother, Wolcott Balestier, in 1890. '*Sex-slur on Patriot "Ludicrous Nonsense"*' was a typical tabloid reaction.

Yet the theory was reinforced by what we consider to be among the most informative and most intelligently researched recent studies of Rudyard Kipling, *East and West*, by the American M.D. Thomas N. Cross, published in 1992. Dr Cross's clinical and psychological approach seems to get right under Kipling's often impenetrable skin as no other biographer has hitherto. The fact that he is American and has used many new American sources necessarily gives a greater insight into Kipling's years spent in the States, for instance. While confirming in a rational manner Seymour-Smith's theory of Kipling's (at the least latent) homosexuality, his main contention is that Kipling's life and works were coloured by the dilemma of whether he was a child of India or of England: was his true mother his coloured *ayah* or his white biological mother? A secondary theory is that Kipling was forever obsessed by his deficient eyesight (a complaint that was to be an important factor in the death of his son).

An August 1997 BBC1 *Omnibus* programme on Kipling, whose principal theme was the search for the missing manuscript of Kipling's unpublished novel *Mother Maturin* (convincingly explained five years before in Cross's biography) proposed another 'dark secret'. It was that Kipling had had a hidden marriage – or at the least a passionate liaison – with an Indian girl during his second stay in India from 1882 to 1889. This, too, is a plausible theory, given the young Rudyard's solitary nocturnal wanderings in *The City of Dreadful Night* in Lahore where he immersed himself in the seductive patchwork of Indian life in all its mysteries and squalor. Much of Kipling's work had biographical references. *Without Benefit of Clergy, Lispeth, Kidnapped* and *Beyond the Pale* all deal with liaisons between coloured girls and white men. They all end in unhappiness or tragedy. Could this have been the unfound secret in Kipling's life that Carrie, his widow, would later try so hard to cover up? Could there even have been a child of the liaison? Kingsley Amis regards 'the rumours, still current, that he left India littered with small brown Kiplings' as being 'not impossible', but clearly doubts them as, 'If there existed real evidence . . . some of it would have been sure to come out. There's no fire without smoke, and in this case there's no smoke.'

Such questions and detailed analysis of the great man's life are beyond the scope of this book, other than when they impact on Rudyard's behaviour as a father and his reaction to his son's death. Yet it is Kipling's very fame and renewed popularity that make the story of the short life and death of what has hitherto generally been acknowledged to be a fairly unexceptional young man, John Kipling, of general interest. Without it this book would have no *raison d'être*.

Rudyard Kipling bestrode three reigns as a literary and human colossus: a mighty name, linked with the essence of Empire, of Britishness, even Englishness, as did Chaucer and Shakespeare, or, in the musical field, Elgar and Vaughan Williams. Like them he was a 'household name'. Generations of British children were brought up on the *Just So Stories*, and *The Jungle Books*, on Mowgli and Rikki-Tikki-Tavi, on *Kim*, *Puck of Pook's Hill* and the moral code of *If*.

The jingoistic patriotism and nationalism apparent in *Plain Tales from the Hills*, *Soldiers Three*, *The White Man's Burden*, *Barrack Room Ballads* and the like made him for many years, to the superficial reader, rather a figure of fun, the outmoded and politically incorrect spirit of the Raj, whose day died when the Phillips' Atlas was no longer predominantly red: the Orwellian view of Kipling.

Never good at games himself, Kipling's derisory phrases in *The Islanders* 1902, 'the flannelled fools at the wicket or the muddied oafs at the goals', for instance, which drew attention to England's military unpreparedness, attracted much opprobrium. Forgetting his 1882 poem, *Ave Imperatrix!* rejoicing at Victoria's escape from an assassination attempt and written in a most 'laureate' style, the perceived irreverence towards Queen Victoria in *The Widow at Windsor*, 1890, was popularly (but almost certainly erroneously) believed to have led to her denying him the Poet Laureateship on Tennyson's death in 1892. Yet when Kipling appeared to be dying of pneumonia in New York in January 1899, the Hotel Grenoble where he lay was besieged by a horde of reporters and fans anxious to hear of his progress. 'If sympathy could cure a man, Mr Kipling would have been well by now,' exclaimed the *Tribune*. T.N. Cross records that 'Prayers were offered in many churches that Sunday and people at the hotel were seen kneeling and praying for his recovery.'

At some stages in his life Kipling the man sometimes drew more love and admiration than Kipling the writer. Certainly he was complex and often paradoxical both as a writer and as a man. The strain of bigotry and cruelty that often emerged in his work, the extremism that made patriotism more of a vice than a virtue, the apparent anti-semitism and racism, the perhaps more understandable virulent anti-Germanism of the Great War period contrasted strongly with the frequent tenderness and sensitivity of this creator of insistently unforgettable lines and characters. Kipling has been responsible for more memorable phrases that have crept into everyday English usage than any other writer with the exception of Shakespeare and Oscar Wilde. As H.G. Wells wrote in 1911, 'He got hold of us wonderfully, he filled us with tinkling and haunting quotations . . . he coloured the very idiom of our conversations.' One has only to look in the *Oxford Book of Quotations: The female of the species is more deadly than the male; East is East and West is West, and never the twain shall meet; You're a better man than I am, Gunga Din; And the Glory of the Garden it shall never pass away!; And a woman is only a woman, but a good cigar is a Smoke; We get the Hump; The Law of the Jungle; Oh, it's Tommy this, an' Tommy that; a rag a bone and a hank of hair; But that is another story; east of Suez; Lest we Forget* (a phrase much used in Remembrance ceremonies) and *If* in its entirety. *If* was even voted the Nation's favourite poem in a poll conducted by the BBC in the politically correct environment of 1996.

It was the culmination of a process of rehabilitating Kipling that had perhaps been started by Marghanita Laski with her sympathetic 1987 biography, *From Palm to Pine* (a phrase from *Recessional* that Kipling borrowed from Tennyson's poem *The Daisy*, 'In lands of palm and southern pine'), and her series of BBC broadcasts extolling his verse. Now it is quite acceptable to admit to admiring Rudyard Kipling.

The more serious and perceptive student cannot fail to recognize the two deep strains that run through the prolific works – poetry and prose alike – of this man who was often described as 'enigmatic', or 'misunderstood', and who was not universally loved by his fellow writers, as shown above, or by the general public. The two strongly flowing creative sources that permeate his writing are his deep love and understanding of, his sympathy for and with, what he perceived as almost a special race: the British soldiery, warts and all, and the separate race that was 'children'. These two streams of love crossed paths and burst their banks of emotion on one traumatic day in Kipling's life.

It occurred on 27 September 1915 when his own soldier child, his only son John, was killed in the Battle of Loos, just after his 18th birthday. It was to change Rudyard's life and works for ever more.

The boy was posted as wounded and missing. Locating John's whereabouts and, when it became apparent that he could no longer be alive, his grave, became a tragic and obsessive crusade for Rudyard and his wife,

Carrie. Despite extensive enquiries, searches and travel, both private and in his capacity as a Commissioner of the Imperial War Graves Commission, Kipling never found his son's grave. If anyone had the burning desire to discover it and access to relevant information that might have revealed it, then surely it was Rudyard Kipling.

Yet in July 1992, 77 years on, and 54 years after Rudyard's death, the Commonwealth War Graves Commission took the exceptional action of replacing the headstone of an unknown Lieutenant of the Irish Guards in St Mary's Advanced Dressing Station Cemetery on the Loos battlefield with another, which bears the name Lieutenant John Kipling.

Up to that time the Commission had rarely undertaken such identification and then only on what they considered to be watertight evidence. The Commission's Charter requires them to commemorate each of the dead within their care by name, either on an individual headstone or on a memorial. The former is regarded as infinitely preferable, especially by the deceased's family. Of the 1914–1918 war dead, 472,469 are listed as identified burials, 415,325 (a horrifying near 50% of the total) as being commemorated only on memorials. Since the high-profile case of John Kipling's supposed identification, with all the publicity attendant on the finding of such a famous man's missing son, a more 'open' attitude exists at the Commission's HQ and, most significantly, their considerable records have been computerized. The result is that identifications are becoming more and more frequent – there are now 20 or 30 per year and a new 'addenda' panel has had to be placed on the Thiépval Memorial to cope with all the alterations on that one memorial alone. It is a measure of the humanity with which this admirable organization approaches its ongoing task that identifications are now being actively sought.

In the Kipling case the certitude of the identification rests on the premise that, of the three 2nd Battalion Irish Guards subalterns who went missing on 27 September 1915, John Kipling was the only full lieutenant. The map reference where the body was found on 23 September 1919 is also of importance. It was deemed to have been wrongly recorded at the time.

In this book we examine the factors in Rudyard's early life which were to affect his behaviour as a father; John's short life; the relationship between the famous father and his beloved son, which may have indirectly led to John's death: the father's feelings of remorse and sorrow and the influence on his subsequent work.

The title of the book comes from Kipling's anguished poem of grief at the loss of his manchild, *My Boy Jack*, and his hopeless search for his body. Although Rider Haggard referred to Kipling's 'boy, Jack', in our extensive research we have come across no use of this name within the family. As Wolcott B. Dunham Jr, grandson of Carrie Kipling's sister Josephine, wrote to us, 'My father spoke of his first cousin as "John"', and confirmed that this was 'the name used in the family'. Whatever he was called, what emerges is a picture of a far brighter, more humorous character than has hitherto been represented. John's story is that of a typical product of his class and age: a public school boy with a classical education who enjoyed to the full the privileges that money and fame brought, whilst still preserving a refreshing modesty and sense of fun. The trauma that entered that innocent life in the form of the Great War: the desire to enlist, the hard training, the loss of many close friends, his own inevitable death, all make an interesting story in its own right. That one of the principal characters in the brief drama of John's life was a world-famous figure makes it doubly so.

Finally we re-examine the meticulous detective and research trail that led to the official identification of John Kipling's grave by the Commonwealth War Graves Commission in 1992, assemble evidence old and new, and attempt to resolve the question, was the body identified 'beyond reasonable doubt'.

Tonie and Valmai Holt
Sandwich, March 1998

Postscript

In researching this book we have had the privilege of reading many original letters and other documents which have given us a deeper knowledge and insight into the Kipling family and the appalling effect upon them of the deaths of their children, Josephine and John.

Carrie Kipling, and later her daughter, Elsie Bambridge, destroyed all but a careful selection of Rudyard and John Kipling's letters. Most that is generally known of Rudyard's wife and companion of 44 years originates in the scrappy transcript Carrington made of her diary, the original of this, too, later being destroyed. The picture we have of Carrie from the major Kipling biographies is remarkably consistent: a pathologically controlling, domineering, humourless, cold, snobbish woman. Fortunately, in the Kipling–Balestier-Dunham letters and in the Cecil-Maxse Mss many letters from and about Carrie exist which portray her in a more rounded fashion. Whilst, occasionally, the normally perceived characteristics emerge and her hypochondria is more than confirmed, one also gets to know a loyal and faithful, admiring wife, a multi-capable manager and an adoring mother who was in turn deeply loved by her husband and children. Her heartbreak at the two fearful losses is vividly and eloquently poured out in the stream of letters she wrote to her mother (to whom she corresponded twice a week for the 27 years of their separation) and her ever closer friend, Violet, Lady Edward Cecil (later to become Lady Milner) to whom she sometimes wrote twice a day. To most outsiders the

Kiplings closed ranks and licked their painful wounds in private. Carrie could talk to Violet in such a soul-baring fashion because she, too, had lost an only son, first declared 'wounded and missing' in the War. The Kiplings had left no stone unturned in their attempts to help the Cecils locate their son, George. Ironically this was to be a dress-rehearsal for their own frantic search for John and, as such, is followed in depth in this book. Carrie could allow herself to express her hopes, her fears and her bleak despair in such an uncontrolled way to Violet, firstly because the latter was in the Kiplings' emotional debt and secondly because she would perfectly empathize with Carrie's feelings.

These voices from the past ring out clearly from the now fragile and precious material their words are written upon: thin blue paper, thick grey or fading white; brittle buff telegrams, heavy white cards; printed addresses and two digit telephone numbers; headed notepaper from Army Camps and Orderly Rooms, from the Savile or the Garrick, from the smartest London addresses and the country mansions of the powerful and privileged. Often the paper is edged in black as a sign of mourning. The Kiplings never had a telephone at Bateman's, so were prolific letter and 'wire' [telegram] senders. Some are brief and testify to the efficiency of the Edwardian postal system – '. . . will drive over to see you this afternoon . . .'. Others run to many pages of close, spindly, sometimes almost indecipherable handwriting, occasionally with added lines written at the diagonal over the original letter. Sometimes the words get bigger, the lines shorter and further apart as emotion overtakes the writer. Some are typewritten and corrected by hand. Spelling and punctuation are often erratic and inspirational – especially in Carrie Kipling's case. In quoting from her letters we have made no attempt to correct her idiosyncracies.

The letters were written in an age before information technology killed the art of letter writing (although the Internet has, in a curious way, revived it and the authors were able to locate the provenance of a biblical quotation because a young American wanted the whole world to know that his wife, Judith, had a price far above rubies who would 'do him good and not evil all the days of her life', as Rudyard wrote of Carrie in 1897.) Not only were letters written, but they were carefully kept as well. John must have been required to bring home from school all his parents' letters (for one reason because Carrie forbade any items bearing Rudyard's signature to remain out of her jurisdiction). Lady Milner kept virtually all the letters she received, as did the Balestier-Dunham family if they were from the Kiplings. Among these collections are many letters from the bereaved parents, widows, brothers, sisters and children of men who were killed in the war that is called 'Great'. Their raw grief, whether expressed in educated words or in an almost illiterate fashion, still seems so immediate that reading them transported the authors back to the dreadful days of '14–'18 and often reduced them to tears. Equally heartrending was the Kiplings' progression from pride, to anxiety, to downright fear as John enlisted, trained and then reached the front – by this stage they secretly knew that his death was inevitable – and the subsequent emotional seesaw of hope, disappointment and final acceptance of that death.

Chapter 1

RUDYARD'S CHILDHOOD:

India. The House of Desolation.
Westward Ho! and Stalky.

'Give me the first six years of a child's life and you can have the rest.'
A quotation generally attributed to the Jesuits, reinforced in principal by
Diderot, Montaigne and Bernard Shaw, and quoted by Kipling as
the heading to Chapter 1 of *Something of Myself.*

The first five years of Joseph Rudyard Kipling's life were so happy and
satisfyingly secure that they bolstered him through the misery and cruelty
of the next six and gave him the outward confidence, sometimes interpreted as 'cockiness', that saw him through the rest of his eventful and
often tragic life.

He was born on 30 December 1865 in Bombay to John Lockwood
Kipling, a short (5'3''), pleasant, intelligent craftsman and artist from a
stolid Yorkshire family and his wife Alice. Alice was born to the brilliant
and talented Macdonald family. Three of her sisters wed outstanding
achievers in their field: Georgiana married the pre-Raphaelite painter
Edward Burne-Jones (later to be knighted); Agnes married the artist
Edward Poynter (also to be knighted) and Louisa married the MP Alfred
Baldwin and gave birth to the future Prime Minister, Stanley Baldwin.
Alice, too, was intelligent, but her wit and charm were occasionally
barbed.

The story goes that they had become engaged after a picnic at Lake
Rudyard, now a reservoir near Leek in Staffordshire, and romantically
named their first-born son after this spot of sentimental memory to them.
The Kipling family tradition was to alternate the names Joseph and John,
and Joseph was Rudyard's first given name. It was the name, in its other
form Yussuf, that he would use as one of his many pseudonyms.
Lockwood and Alice's second son, born in 1870, who suffered the fate of
so many Anglo-Indian children and lived only long enough to be christened, was called John. Following the pattern, Rudyard was to name his
only son John. A daughter, christened Alice like her mother, but always
known as 'Trix', had been born on 11 June 1868.

Ruddy, as he was affectionately called, was brought up, as was the

1

custom, by an *ayah* who taught him Hindustani as his first language and fed him on stories of native myth and legend. He had been told that his mother's difficult labour when giving birth to him had been relieved by making a sacrifice of a kid to the cruel godess Kali. Thus to Kali he owed his existence and, perhaps, his continued compliance to dominant women (his mother, 'Antirosa' his child minder in *The House of Desolation* and later his wife, Carrie.) A small tyrant in this enclosed and comforting kingdom, with occasional interludes with his delightful parents, young Ruddy's cup of happiness was overbrimming.

When Ruddy was five and a half and Trix was three and a half their parents, in keeping with the traditions of expatriate families, took their children to England for schooling, but the way in which they did it was extraordinary. The practice of sending one's children home was wide-spread and considered not only normal but essential for the child's very survival: infant mortality was frighteningly high in the Anglo-Indian community in the heat and disease of India. What is more, the Kiplings, who were obviously loving parents in the arm's length fashion of their age and class, had already experienced the death of one child. What was abnormal was their lack of preparation and explanation to the two little children of what was happening to them, and why. Initially it was left to his *ayah* to tell Rudyard that he was going away. For this information we have to rely on the short story *Baa Baa, Black Sheep*, a truly terrible account of the mental and physical torture of those nightmare years. This harrowing story, with the first chapter of *Something of Myself* and the opening chapter of the story *The Light that Failed*, paint a picture of unbearable childhood misery. Much literary debate has taken place over the accuracy of these three word pictures. The verity of some details is irrelevant: the experience scarred the child and forever influenced the adult creative artist and future father.

It happened when, as Kipling related in *Baa Baa, Black Sheep*, the children, called Punch and Judy, were roused by their parents 'in the chill dawn of a February morning [actually it was in December] to say Goodbye', and then they were gone. No word of for how long, or how necessary it was, simply 'Don't forget us . . . Oh, my little son, don't forget us, and see that Judy remembers too.' Trix later wrote, 'We had no prep-aration or explanation; it was like a double death or rather, like an avalanche that had swept away everything happy and familiar . . . We felt that we had been deserted, almost as much as on a doorstep, and what was the reason?'

No East-end London child, evacuated to the country in deepest Dorset in 1940 to escape the German bombers, could have felt more alienated. From being the bossy little Sahib, master of his own small kingdom of warmth and light and a myriad of sensual pleasures, Ruddy was projected into the abyss of the cold, dark 'House of Desolation', as he called it, where food was so sparse that servants were forced to steal and where he was bullied and beaten. The actual hardships in Lorne Lodge, Southsea, at the hands of Mr and Mrs Holloway (known as 'Uncleharri' and 'Antirosa' or 'the Woman' in *Baa Baa, Black Sheep*) and their malevolent son, Harry (called the Devil-Boy), are well documented in Rudyard's writings: the attempt to alienate his only ally, Trix, the accusations of lying, of 'showing off', of being 'the black sheep' of his family (hence the title of the story), the solitary confinements in his room or in the dank basement, the beatings, and, worst of all, being forbidden to read the books that were his only salvation and escape. Antirosa's Calvinist religiosity did, however, give Rudyard a knowledge of the Bible that was to stand him in comforting stead throughout the bad times of his life, and even influence his style. The Book of Ecclesiasticus, in particular, provided him with reassuring and resonant phrases that he would use, some 40 years later, in his capacity as a Commissioner of the Imperial War Graves Commission.

The most relevant outcome of Rudyard's stay at Lorne Lodge to the story of John Kipling is that the received pattern of abused child becoming a child abuser simply did not occur in the case of Rudyard Kipling. One of the mitigating factors was obviously his first stable five years. Then it must be acknowledged that most abuse of children occurs in deprived and uneducated households, neither of which conditions strictly prevailed in Lorne Lodge. To read Rudyard's accounts, the Lorne Lodge household was, however, spartan, (although Rudyard admits to being 'adequately fed') and there is no doubt that he was mistreated there. Trix confirmed and even reinforced many of Rudyard's claims to Birkenhead when he was researching for his Kipling biography in the 1940s. Antirosa 'drank wine'; she had 'the power to beat him with many stripes'; according to *Baa Baa, Black Sheep*, in which it is often impossible to distinguish fact from fiction, she went on holiday with her son Harry and young 'Judy' (Uncleharri, Ruddy's only ally, having died) leaving him alone in the house for a month with a servant girl who 'had many friends' and 'went out daily for long hours'; she tied a placard with the word 'Liar' on his back and forced him to wear it to school; she threatened him with 'all the blinding horrors of Hell'; she segregated him from his sister, his only link with home, and failed to notice that he was nearly blind. Thankfully, though distanced from his loving parents, Rudyard was in regular contact with his mother's family during his years at Lorne Lodge. 'For a month each year I possessed a paradise which I verily believe saved me,' he wrote in *Something of Myself*.

This haven was 'The Grange', at North End Road in Hammersmith, home of his mother's sister, Georgiana and her husband, Edward Burne-Jones. 'At "The Grange" I had love and affection as much as the greediest, and I was not very greedy, could desire,' wrote Rudyard. 'Best of all, immeasurably, was the beloved Aunt herself reading us *The Pirate* or *The Arabian Nights* of evenings . . . Often the Uncle, who had a "golden voice", would assist in our evening play.' He also had the company of his lively cousins Margaret and Philip Burne-Jones and their friends May and Jenny, the daughters of William Morris (known as 'Uncle Topsy'). This meeting place for the Pre-Raphaelite painters and members of the Arts and Crafts Movement was an intellectually stimulating environment for the knowledge-thirsty young Ruddy. He adored 'the beloved Aunt', the feisty Georgie, for the rest of her life.

In *Three Houses*, 1931, Margaret's daughter, who was to become the famous novelist Angela Thirkell, described her grandparents, and the 'open house' that they kept for friends and relatives every Sunday at 'The Grange'. 'There can be few granddaughters who were so systematically spoiled as I was,' she wrote. That affection was also shown to their virtually orphaned nephew and niece from far-off India. One wonders how they did not sense Rudyard's unhappiness. 'Often and often afterwards, the beloved Aunt would ask me why I had never told anyone how I was being treated. Children tell little more than animals, for what comes to them they accept as eternally established,' Rudyard explained in *Something of Myself*. But eventually, when 'some sort of nervous breakdown' occurred, Georgie must have been informed, for she sent for 'Inverarity Sahib', the doctor who had delivered Rudyard as a baby in India and who would now deliver him from Antirosa.

'Good God, the little chap's nearly blind!' he exclaimed. It was a momentous revelation. Rudyard's 'lovely Mamma' was summoned, arrived unexpectedly to the bewildered Rudyard ('I do not remember that I had any warning'), bathed him in kisses and tears of guilt and remorse and took the children away from the House of Desolation.

Spectacles were quickly prescribed for the neglected eyesight and so began one of Rudyard's lifelong fears: that he would become blind. The poor eyesight was another link that was to bind him to his son John, who also had deficient eyesight and had to wear spectacles. As we shall see this was a significant factor in John's premature death.

That he was physically able to read again, and do so without any restraint, was a key to Rudyard remembering the next few months as among the most enjoyable in his life. They started in the relaxed environment of a farmhouse at Loughton near Epping Forest, joined occasionally by their cousin Stanley Baldwin, sealing a lifelong friendship. There 'I was completely happy with my Mother,' he wrote in *Something of Myself*. No wonder: any display of love and kindness must have seemed like heaven to the two deprived children. But, despite Alice's efforts to re-ingratiate herself with her son, it was his father to whom Ruddy would feel closer in later years.

The next important episode in Rudyard's life, and one which was later to affect his attitude as a father with a son at public school, was the period of his own schooldays at the United Services College at Westward Ho! It was an experience that gave him the material for the series of short stories that were later collected under the name *Stalky & Co.*

The establishment was designed to produce officer material for the British Army or the upper echelons of the Civil Service. Rudyard was never destined for either. The choice of school was made purely on its cheapness and the strength of the family's friendship with the nonconformist Headmaster, Cormell Price, who had taught at Haileybury, after which establishment he, to a certain extent, modelled Westward Ho! At Oxford Price had been a member of the pre-Raphaelite/Arts and Crafts set, but he veered away from them, first to study medicine and then to become a tutor in Russia. He was an exceptional man who early recognized the potential of his nonconformist pupil. In later conversations 'Uncle Crom' revealed to Kipling how he had deliberately tested and stretched him and encouraged other masters to do likewise. During his final weeks at the school, as Kipling recounts in the *Stalky & Co* story *The Last Term*, and in *Something of Myself*, he was given the run of the Head's personal Library Study as editor of the school magazine, *The United Services College Chronicle*. 'Many of us loved the Head for what he had done for us, but I owed him more than all of them put together and I think I loved him even more than they did,' he recorded. Cormell Price was to remain a well-loved mentor until his death in 1910.

Though credit must be given to Price for nurturing the fish-out-of-water child, it must also devolve on Rudyard for not only surviving, but triumphing in his own way in what was for him a hostile environment. Kipling was bookish (a 'swot') and hopeless at sport (with the exception of swimming) in a society where sporting achievement was revered. He came from an artistic, rather than a military background. He was odd-looking where physical beauty was admired: he was small – full-grown he would reach no more than 5'6" – hirsute, had to start shaving at an early age, sported a moustache by the age of 15, had thick dark eyebrows, and above all he had to wear glasses – the only boy in the school to do so. It led to his nickname of 'Gigger', for gig (carriage) lamps, which was a term he would use himself for glasses in later years. Yet he was popular with his peers and his friendship with the originals of the main characters of the *Stalky* saga, Lionel Charles Dunsterville (Stalky) and George C. Beresford (M'Turk), was to remain steadfast throughout all their lives.

The main lessons that Rudyard learned at USC that he would endeavour to pass on to his own son can be summed up in the code of *Kim*. One should be manly at all times, calm in adversity, and survive, and be strengthened by, the testing and character-building situations that life meted out. One should also guard against 'beastliness' – Kipling's euphemism for juvenile homosexuality. In the light of the suggestion of his own homosexual feelings (in particular in regard to his brother-in-law

Wolcott Balestier), Rudyard may have protested a little too much about the 'cleanliness' of Westward Ho! 'I remember no cases of even suspected perversion,' he wrote in *Something of Myself*, and even discussed this rare absence of homosexuality in the Public School of the age with Cormell Price after he left school. Price's antidote was to send the boys to bed 'dead tired.' That it did exist in the school might be indicated by a claim made by M'Turk in *Slaves of the Lamp, 1*, that 'The Head never expels except for beastliness or stealing.' As described by Seymour-Smith, Kipling had also been moved during his last term, by his housemaster, M.H. Pugh, from the dormitory he shared with Beresford. Pugh (who appears as 'Prout' in the *Stalky* saga) obviously suspected 'impurity and bestiality', indicating that homosexuality *did* exist in the school.

Kipling also urged John to endeavour to become a prefect. It was a position that, in part because Rudyard left school early and also because 'in large part to their House-master's experienced distrust, the three [Stalky, M'Turk, and Beetle, one of Kipling's own nicknames at school because of his hunched and dark appearance] for three consecutive terms had been passed over for promotion to the rank of prefect', Rudyard would never attain himself. It was another example of him wishing to achieve through his son. 'I want you to be a pre before I die,' he wrote on 24 May 1913. 'I think with your knowledge of mixed human nature you'd make a good pre. I never was one.' Ironically he also warned John not to try 'scoring off a beak. He may stand it a dozen times but sooner or later you'll hit on a time when his liver is annoying him or he is otherwise short in the temper and then you'll have to pay for your past performances. I've been there and I know,' Rudyard wrote to John on 21 October 1913. Yet many of the *Stalky* stories are about just that – and the three companions usually win the day.

Although in retrospect Rudyard loved and admired Cormell Price for stretching his abilities and building his character, often in seemingly hurtful and painful ways, at the time he felt that 'Westward Ho! was brutal enough . . . my first term . . . was horrible . . . My first year and a half was not pleasant.' The experience helped him to identify with John's occasional unhappiness at Wellington College. When John wrote a letter which Rudyard described (on 19 February 1913) as 'a cross between a whine and a snarl', he went on to say, 'But I sympathise. I know what that infernal Easter term is like – I've gone through many of 'em. It isn't nice but its part of one's portion of life. It is helped out and it must be eaten.' Like John, Rudyard wrote a stream of unhappy letters to his parents which caused his mother to write to Cormell Price (whose letters were auctioned at Sotheby's in 1964). 'It is the roughness of the lads he seems to feel most . . . This lad has a great deal that is feminine in his nature, and a little sympathy from any quarter will reconcile him to his changed life more than anything.' It was an extraordinary statement for a Victorian mother to make to the headmaster of a Victorian Public School. It certainly explains why he was the butt of bullying.

It was not, as he wrote, until 'after my strength came suddenly to me about my fourteenth year, there was no more bullying', and he 'found me two friends [Dunsterville and Beresford] with whom, by a carefully arranged system of mutual aids, I went up the school on co-operative principles,' that Kipling began to enjoy school. Choosing the right friends was important. 'Lowther don't look much of a person somehow. Why d'you barge about with him?' Rudyard demanded in a letter to John of 2 June 1913.

Above all, Rudyard left his school with a joy in reading and learning, in literature, art and the classics. His often terrifying classics master William Crofts (who appeared as 'King' in the *Stalky* story, '*Regulus*') taught Rudyard 'to loathe Horace for two years; to forget him for twenty, and then to love him for the rest of my days.' This joy was not a gift that Rudyard was able to impart to his son. Academic achievement did not come easily to John. 'Does 13th in your form mean that you have pulled up several places,' wrote Rudyard hopefully to John on 19 February 1913.

During Rudyard's second year at USC a 'tide of writing set in' and Lockwood and Alice, obviously in close consultation with Cormell Price, decided it was timely for him to leave at the end of his fifth form year to pursue a literary career. Obviously he would not go into the Army or the Civil Service, as would many of his friends: Stalky went on to Sandhurst, M'Turk to Cooper's Hill (the Royal Indian College of Civil Engineering). University was not an option: 'Oxford we can't afford,' wrote Lockwood to Crom. (It is intriguing to speculate what effect the stimulating creative environment of an Oxford College would have had on Rudyard's life and works.) So Lockwood obtained a post for his young aspiring writer son on *The Civil and Military Gazette* in Lahore at £100 per annum.

Rudyard sailed for India on 20 September 1882 on the SS *Brindisi* from Tilbury. He left England with mixed feelings. Most of his pangs were caused by the thought of leaving Florence ('Flo') Garrard. Surprisingly, after their realization of the way in which the Holloway household had treated their children, Lockwood and Alice still left Trix in Mrs Holloway's care once Ruddy had gone to Westward Ho! Going to Lorne Lodge to fetch Trix out for the holidays at the age of fourteen and a half in July 1880, Rudyard met Florence, a year or so older than he, also a boarder there with her sister, and fell head over heels into adolescent love.

He had reached puberty early and was proud of his youthful maturity. 'I was physically precocious,' he claimed in *Something of Myself*, and describes being forced to shave by Pugh and given 'a written order on a Bideford barber for a razor etc', Stalky and 'Turkey' were invited to join in the ceremony. 'Why [they] did not cut their throats experimenting with the apparatus I do not understand,' he added. Kipling regarded shaving as a significant manly ritual and one he was to share with John, to whom he wrote on 14 April 1915, with echoes of this incident, accusing John, who had purloined Rudyard's razor, of trying to cut his father's throat as he had altered the tension to suit his 'own hide. I used it without, naturally, suspecting this and the result was that I scraped large flakes off my throat and chin and bled like a pig. Kindly consider yourself disinherited.'

Rudyard certainly considered himself man enough for his declarations of love to be taken seriously. To Flo Rudyard penned immature, romantic verses, collected in a notebook he entitled *Sundry Phansies*, not printed until 1986 in *Early Verse by Rudyard Kipling*. Flo felt that she was destined to become an artist (she did indeed later attend the Slade) and rejected him. T.N. Cross deduced that he loved Flo because his relationship with her bore some of the elements of 'helplessness, submission and pain' that he experienced in his relationship with Mrs Holloway (and his mother, and later his wife). By and large his fun and pleasure would be spent in the company of men or, ever a Peter Pan figure, of children – especially his own. 'Frankly I miss you awfully,' he was to write to John (then aged 17) on 14 April 1915 from the Bath Spa Hotel where Carrie was taking the waters, 'as there is no one to play with here.'

Despite her coolness, when Rudyard left for India in September 1882, not yet seventeen, he considered himself engaged to Flo.

Chapter 2

RUDYARD'S YOUNG MANHOOD

India and Family Life Again. The Apprentice Journalist and Author. Return to England. The Young Husband. America.

'Have done with childish days'.
From *The White Man's Burden*, Rudyard Kipling, 1899.

Rudyard had many lessons to learn or to relearn about relationships when he returned to the family home in Lahore in October 1882. In the eleven years since he left India he had seen his father only once. Surely there were some awkwardnesses in the first meetings, joyful as they must have been. The pain of the long separation was to make Kipling determined never to leave his own son for any longer than necessary. Even when John was at Warley Barracks at the beginning of the Great War, fulfilling his father's ambition for him to become a service officer, Rudyard could not bear to be parted from him for more than a few days. On 14 April 1915 he was to write to John, in the typical light-hearted, bantering, mate-ish style that cloaked the strength of his love, 'I awfully miss the little middle-week glimpses that we used to have of you and I fear that, deprived of my valuable moral and elevating conversation you may go headlong to ruin – night gambling halls, harlotry etc etc.' Again on Sunday 30 May 1915 in a letter to John after a recent stay at Bateman's, he complained, 'It seems the deuce and all of a time since you left but we are still smacking our lips over the good time that we had. It <u>was</u> good! . . . We are thinking of coming up to town on <u>Wednesday</u>.' He pleaded that if Wednesday was out of the question, then could it be Thursday? Parted from his own father for more than a decade, he longed for his son after only a couple of days' absence.

When in December 1883 Alice brought the fifteen-year-old Trix back from England 'The Family Square' was reformed after the traumatic sundering of 1871. 'Not only were we happy but we knew it,' Rudyard somewhat self-consciously proclaimed. Once again he had a position as the respected Lockwood's son: his own room and servant, horse, cart and groom and, most of all, his own job. It was grinding work – 'Seven Years

Hard' is how he described his apprenticeship as a journalist of *The Civil and Military Gazette* of which he 'represented fifty per cent of the "editorial staff"'. He learned his lessons as a journalist so well that for some he would forever be categorized and limited as such.

Respite from the oppressive heat of Lahore was to be found in the hill station of Simla, the summer seat of the British Raj. There Kipling made lasting friendships that were often to stand him in good stead in later life. The most significant was with General Roberts, newly awarded the title Lord Roberts of Kandahar after his famous relief of the Afghan town of that name in September 1880. In 1885 he had been appointed Commander-in-Chief, India, and one of his A.D.C.s was Ian Hamilton with whom Kipling became friendly. Hamilton was unusually literary for an Army Officer, recognized Kipling's genius and took some of his stories back to London to show to magazine editors of his acquaintance.

In 1884 Flo Garrard had finally broken off their tenuous engagement, and if one takes at all literally the hints of light-hearted liaisons and repeatedly broken hearts that abounded in the verses collected under the title *Departmental Ditties*, which would be published in 1888, he soon found consolation. A warning not to take him at face value in his compositions, however, was made at the beginning of the poem *La Nuit Blanche*,

> A much discerning Public hold
> The Singer generally sings
> Of personal and private things,
> And prints and sells his past for gold.
>
> Whatever I may here disclaim,
> The very clever folk I sing to
> Will most indubitably cling to
> Their pet delusion, just the same.

His determination not to reveal too much of himself in his writing and his conviction that his readers were avid to penetrate his veil were obsessions that stayed with Kipling all his life.

It is a curious coincidence that one of the light-hearted and delightfully told poems in *Departmental Ditties*, entitled *The Post That Fitted*, tells the story of Sleary who 'Ere the steamer bore him Eastward . . . was engaged to marry [as was Kipling] An attractive girl at Tunbridge, whom he called "my little Carrie"' [the name of Kipling's future wife].

Simla social life, with its many illicit relationships and intrigues (one feature of the main thoroughfare, The Mall, was actually called 'Scandal Point'), gave him the inspiration for many of the 39 short stories first published in *The Civil and Military Gazette* during 1886 and 1887 which appeared under the collective name *Plain Tales from the Hills* in 1888.

10

The most interesting character to emerge from the tales is the scheming, manipulative, attractive woman of a certain age, Mrs Lucy Hauksbee. Once he had got Flo Garrard out of his system, strong, older women began to attract Rudyard more and more. He was continually fascinated by his mother. The poem *My Rival* was probably inspired by his mother and his sister. It is narrated by a gauche girl, who, although pretty, is continually up-staged by a mature woman who draws the attention of all the young men,

> And that's because I'm seventeen
> And She is forty-nine.

The young girl will get her revenge, however—

> Just think, that She'll be eighty-one
> When I am forty-nine!

Plain Tales is dedicated 'To the wittiest woman in India' and Trix later maintained that Rudyard gave a copy of the book to Alice inscribed with the words, 'To the lady of the dedication from her unworthy son'. It is usually accepted, however, [*Kipling Journal*, June 1959] that it was actually the wife of Major F.C. Burton, with whom Rudyard had often acted on the stage of the theatre of Simla and who is thought to be the inspiration for Mrs Hauksbee, to whom he gave this accolade.

Between the welcomingly cool intervals at Simla, it was at Fort Lahore and the Mian Mir Cantonments which lay five miles outside the city walls of Lahore that Kipling first encountered the military whom he came to love and with whom he would always be associated. He could never join them professionally. His eyesight was too poor. But he could learn their language, their *modus vivendi*, their motivation and ideals, their ethos and their language. He soon became their self-appointed minstrel and chronicler. In that same brilliant year of 1888 *Soldiers Three* was published, establishing the characters of the lovable, feisty rogues, Mulvaney, Learoyd and Ortheris, his three most famous and enduring characters. Once the highly professional Kay Robinson had replaced Rudyard's first exacting editor, Stephen Wheeler, at the *Civil and Military*, the young journalist began to enjoy his working life. In what little spare time he had he started work on the mysterious novel of Indian life that he never finished, but for which he had such high literary hopes – *Mother Maturin*. There is little doubt that he later returned to the manuscript and expanded its horizons to become the glorious picaresque story of *Kim*.

By the end of 1887 Rudyard's industry was rewarded by promotion to the more important *Pioneer* newspaper based in Allahabad. There he was introduced to an American couple, Professor Aleck Hill and his 29 year old wife Edmonia, known as 'Ted'. The 22-year-old Rudyard, fast maturing and with a growing reputation as a writer, was entranced by her forthrightness and strong opinions and soon they built up a close relationship. When the Hills decided to return to the States, Rudyard, who had been encouraged by Kay Robinson to return to England to enlarge his opportunities, was persuaded to sail with them, and thence to London. He considered the voyage a great adventure. In Burma they visited Moulmein, where a 'Burma girl' inspired one of his most famous poems, especially in its musical form – *Mandalay*. Then it was on to San Francisco, via Singapore, Hong Kong and Japan. During a whirlwind tour of the United States, Rudyard transferred his affections to Ted's young sister, Carrie, and she accompanied the Hills and Rudyard to England. It was generally acknowledged that the young couple were engaged, but in October 1889 the Hills and Carrie left for India, leaving Rudyard in London.

At first feeling lonely and once more abandoned, he was soon introduced by Andrew Lang, the leading literary critic of the period (who had been sent a copy of *Departmental Ditties* to review in his capacity as contributor to the *Longman's Magazine*) to the Savile Club. There he met the literary giants of the day, many of whom were to become regular acquaintances, even friends, such as Henry James, Thomas Hardy, H.G. Wells and the man to whom, relatives apart, he probably grew closer than any other, Rider Haggard, ten years his senior. They were billed as competitors. 'Rudyard Kipling – your nascent rival . . . has already killed one immortal – Rider Haggard,' wrote James to Robert Louis Stevenson in Samoa. [*Rider Haggard and the Lost Empire*, Tom Pocock.] They were often somewhat scathingly grouped together by magazines with literary pretensions, such as *Harpers*. But Rudyard referred to him as 'Rider Haggard, to whom I took at once, he being of the stamp adored by children and trusted by men at sight; and he could tell tales, mainly against himself, that broke up the tables.' As time passed they were to find more and more in common: in their views on politics, on land management, on story-telling and, most importantly in later years, in their domestic circumstances. At that time Haggard was already a family man. 'His own hope and his principal comfort was his son, Jock [christened John]. Now aged eight, the boy [had] . . . "a nature of singular sweetness". Haggard was fond of his two little daughters and of his practical, if unimaginative, wife, but the boy was reflective and affectionate and his father saw him not only as his heir, who would carry their name through the twentieth century, but as the next step in founding a Haggard dynasty of strong, brave men with lively minds,' wrote Pocock. The parallels between the Kipling and Haggard families, as we shall see, increased to an extraordinary degree.

Firstly, in January 1891, the Haggards left the precious Jock with their friend, Edmund Gosse, who had a son of about the same age, when they sailed to New York. Rider had a dreadful presentiment that he would never see the boy again. Fearing that he himself would die on the journey, he even put all his finances in order before sailing. By the time they reached Lake Tezcuco in Mexico on 9 February, he wrote, 'My presentiments had returned to me with terrible strength and persistence.' Sadly they were all too well-founded. Jock contracted measles, rapidly deteriorated and died of complications. 'He was my darling,' anguished Haggard, 'for whom I would gladly have laid down my life.' His feelings of despair so exactly mirrored Rudyard's when, 24 years later, he, too, would suffer a similar tragedy, that Haggard was then uniquely able to empathize with and to comfort his friend. He even experienced the susceptibility to 'flu and digestive problems that beset Rudyard after his losses.

Kipling soon made other friends and literary associates as his reputation as a young literary lion grew. 'There was an evident demand for my stuff. I do not recall that I stirred a hand to help myself. Things happened to me,' he wrote in *Something of Myself*. His political interests and prejudices were already beginning to set, as was his affinity with Haggard. They were jointly lampooned by J.K. Stephen in the *Cambridge Review* of February 1891,

> Will there never come a season
> Which shall rid us from the curse . . .
> When the Rudyards cease from Kipling
> And the Haggards Ride no more?

Kipling's writing reflected his experiences and, much to his secret pride (he even mentioned it in *Something of Myself*), Rudyard was hailed as a new Dickens. He was taken on by the literary agent who was to look after his affairs for the rest of his life and whose firm still acts for his literary estate, A.P. Watt. For the first time Kipling was beginning to make serious money from his writing and was amazed to discover that he had £1,000 in the bank.

Soon after his return to London he was introduced to Wolcott Balestier who had come to Europe representing an American publishing company in a search for promising British authors. Soon the two young men felt powerfully drawn towards each other. From all accounts Wolcott was a fascinating and attractive personality, as well as a highly talented man and, extraordinarily in view of the strong personalities and ambitious literary pretensions they both shared, Kipling agreed to collaborate with him on a novel. It was to be called *The Naulahka* (a corruption of the Hindustani for 'nine lakhs' of rupees, the value of a fabulous Indian jewel, a lakh being 100,000). Work started on it before Kipling took off for Italy in the autumn of 1890 and they resumed it on his return. Kipling had also been working on his first attempt at a full length novel, *The Light That Failed*, which had many autobiographical allusions, notably that the hero, Dick Heldar, goes blind and that the heroine, Maisie, had many affinities with his lost love Flo Garrard (whom he had briefly met again by accident in London). Wolcott also influenced the unusual decision to publish *The Light That Failed* with two different endings. One was tragic, with Dick committing suicide. The other was happy, ending with Dick and Maisie planning to marry. The latter was aimed at a commercial market with popular sales in mind. During the writing of *The Naulahka*, Wolcott's family visited him. Caroline, his well-born mother, descendant of a signatory of the Declaration of Independence, had high social aspirations. Though she never penetrated into the aristocratic London circle she so desired, she was impressed by meeting the likes of the artists Whistler and Sergeant, the critic Sir Edmund Gosse and Henry James, the American author living in London – all part of the milieu in which her son and his friend Kipling moved. Her youngest son Beatty, the black sheep of the family, behaved in character and soon had to be packed off home to Vermont. She and her younger daughter, Josephine, considered to be the sweeter and prettier girl of the family, soon moved on in their travels, while the elder daughter, also Caroline but universally known as Carrie (the third young lady of that name to interest Rudyard), stayed on to act as housekeeper for her brother. Her letters to Josephine show the bossy side of her nature that was to manifest itself so strongly once she had Rudyard well and truly in thrall. Ironically one of her first letters to her sister berates her, 'You certainly dropped your molasses jug when you did not answer my question about autographs for now I have about decided to become an autograph collector myself.' During her marriage, autograph hunters were to become anathema to her and she would go to extraordinary lengths to prevent would-be collectors from getting their hands on Rudyard's signature. Her first mention of Rudyard refers to him as 'Kippling' and complains that everyone is trying to get in touch with him through Wolcott. The three young people soon obviously developed a close relationship and Carrie adopted the role of slave master. She tells Josephine that Wolcott is 'at the book in the morning', but she has to compete with the attractions of the hard-drinking clique the two young authors mix with. 'Whistler had a little too much wine at a recent dinner,' she reported reprovingly, 'and rather stumbled down the stairs and when he reached the bottom he looked back and said some —— tetotler [sic] of an architect built those stairs.' By Christmas-time of 1890 Carrie had learned how to spell her future husband's name and tells Josephine how she took him 'a popper and some corn I got at Fullers but it was a fraud of the worst sort was the corn and did not pop for a cent.' The Gosses, she gleefully reported, were 'wildly jealous of our intimacy with Kipling though of course I never mention his comings and going to them.' The

14

Balestiers had totally ingratiated themselves with Rudyard, who was missing his own family, and Carrie wrote to Josephine on 31 December 1890, 'Mr Kipling said last night "Can't we make the mother come?" But he can't make his mother [come] either and so he has a sympathy, for she is selfish about it.' She and Alice didn't get on. 'That woman is going to marry our Ruddy,' Alice is said [by Carrington] to have remarked when first they met, and Lockwood was also not enamoured. 'Carrie Balestier was a good man spoiled,' he commented, immediately recognizing her business acumen and organizational skills.

But when Kipling set sail for India in August 1891, after spending July with the Balestiers in their house on the Isle of Wight, he certainly had no apparent plans to marry Carrie. He reached Lahore the week before Christmas of 1891 and there he received the shocking telegram from Carrie informing him that Wolcott had died in Dresden of typhoid. His mother and sisters, then in Paris, had arrived in time to see him before he died and were devastated. Carrie soon showed her mettle and, as she was to do through so many personal crises and tragedies in the future, took command of the situation. When Rudyard received the devastating news, he immediately set off for London, sailing to Trieste and thence back overland, arriving in London on 10 January. Within eight days he and Carrie were married. Why?

There is now little hard evidence left to help unravel this complicated conundrum. Firstly one must examine the nature of Rudyard's friendship with Wolcott. Carrington uses veiled speech to say that Wolcott's 'personal conquest of Rudyard Kipling was an event in the history of literature' and 'No man ever exercised so dominating an influence over Rudyard Kipling during the eighteen months of their intimacy'. Was that last word as loaded with sexual connotations in 1950 when Carrington wrote it as it is today? Other biographers skate over the question. Hilton Brown says, 'Wolcott Balestier . . . enthralled and enchanted Kipling for reasons which no one has ever been able to discover.' Birkenhead tries to understand Wolcott's 'extraordinary magnetism, so evanescent, and now impossible to capture' as he ensnared Henry James, Edmund Gosse and then Rudyard Kipling with whom an 'intimate friendship' followed. Again that word 'intimate'. But Birkenhead later quotes a letter from Rudyard to his Aunt Louie (Louisa Macdonald who married Alfred Baldwin) written the day before his marriage to Caroline in which he says, 'The affair has been going on for rather more months than I care to think about in that they were sheer waste of God's good life . . . That I am riotously happy is yet more true, and I pray that out of your own great store of happiness you will bless us, because we have gone through deep waters together.' This would imply that he had been thinking of marrying Carrie for some considerable time and that after some profound soul-searching he had come to the conclusion that he was very much in love with her. The 'deep waters' may refer to their joint sorrow at Wolcott's death; on the other hand it could possibly mean that Carrie was aware of the nature of Rudyard's relationship with her brother and the two of them had suffered agonies in resolving their own. Perhaps a sudden voyage that he had made to America in May of 1891 with his uncle Fred Macdonald had been an attempt to sort out his mixed emotions. Even Carrington describes the trip as 'a mystery', and Cross is convinced that during it Rudyard actually managed to evade the pursuing reporters to visit Ted Hill, his purpose to discuss with his old confidante the dreadful dilemma he felt himself to be in – torn between his love for Wolcott and his growing love for his sister. For Cross subscribes to Seymour-Smith's theory that Rudyard and Wolcott had a deep homosexual relationship, although he has no proof that it was consummated. Cross interestingly found two more sentences omitted by Carrington in the letter quoted above from Henry James to Edmund Gosse, 'One thing, I believe, the poor girl could not meet – but God grant . . . that she may not have to meet it – as there is no reason to suppose that she will. What this tribulation is – or would be, rather, I can indicate better when I see you.' Cross points out that both Gosse and James had homosexual tendencies. Perhaps they both had affairs with the seductive Wolcott and James was indicating that he knew that Kipling had also, but he was hoping that he could keep it from Carrie.

What is indisputable is that Kipling had a pathological horror of homosexuality (for which he used the euphemism 'beastliness') in a public school context and was to make strenuous efforts to guard his son against it. But whatever the nature of Kipling's love for Wolcott, there is no evidence to show that he was ever anything but totally faithful to his sister once he had married her.

It was a strange wedding. It took place on a cold and foggy 18 January in a London 'in the thick of an influenza epidemic, when the undertakers had run out of black horses and the dead had to be content with brown ones. The living were mostly abed,' described Rudyard gloomily in his autobiography. Henry James gave Carrie away in the ceremony which took place in All Souls Church, Langham Place. 'She is a hard, devoted, capable little person, whom I don't in the least understand his marrying. It's a union of which I don't forecast the future though I gave her away at the altar in a dreary little wedding,' he wrote. Also present were Edmund Gosse and his wife and son and William Heinemann, Wolcott's publisher partner. Rudyard's cousin Ambrose Poynter was the best man. All the bride and groom's immediate family were laid low with 'flu and after the ceremony Carrie had to rush off and tend her mother while Rudyard and Ambrose enjoyed the wedding breakfast at Brown's Hotel. The bride joined him there later for their wedding night and it was to become 'their' hotel, enjoyed by the couple and later their children on many happy occasions, until Rudyard died on the 43rd anniversary of their wedding, after which Carrie could no longer bear to enter its doors.

The next day she confided dryly to the diary that she was to keep assiduously throughout her wedded life, 'We continue to be married.' On 3 February they sailed from Liverpool on SS *Teutonic*, 'the magic carpet' that was take them on a planned round the world honeymoon. Their first stop was New York and then it was on to the Balestier family home at Brattleboro in Vermont where Rudyard was entranced by the crisp and sparkling snow, the cloudless sky, the white velvet hills, the forests and the wide open vistas. He also delighted in his baby niece, Marjorie, daughter of Beatty and his wife Mai. The newly-weds made the fateful decision to buy some building land from Carrie's feckless brother Beatty, though leaving him the mowing and other rights over it.

From New York the honeymoon continued into Canada and from Vancouver they sailed on the *Empress of India* to Japan. In Yokohama a most significant set-back occurred that was to change their relationship. When they set off on their wedding trip, Kipling very much felt himself the head of the family, the wage-earner with a couple of thousand pounds in the bank, the organizer. After an earthquake which he in retrospect took to be an omen (which he ignored) Kipling discovered to his horror that his bank had failed. Here he was, stranded in the most foreign of countries, with but a little cash and a wife who by now they had discovered to be pregnant. Luckily Thomas Cook's came to the rescue and refunded the money for the next planned leg of their journey and they still had their return tickets to Vancouver. They would be all right. But Kipling was shaken and the young couple immediately formed the 'Committee of Ways and Means, which advanced our understanding of each other more than a cycle of solvent marriage'. Carrie was obviously the senior partner and would remain so. From now on she would hold the purse strings and make the financial decisions. It was an arrangement that suited them both, leaving Rudyard the luxury of being able to devote himself to his writing without having to worry about the responsibility of managing the family affairs.

From Vancouver they returned to Brattleboro and a rented cottage that Carrie's mother found for them called, felicitously, Bliss Cottage. There they stayed, enjoying little Marjorie's company and making plans for the house they were building on the land acquired from Beatty. It was a happy time. 'We were extraordinarily and self-centredly content,' glowed Rudyard. Between playing at keeping house with his new wife in their simple and somewhat primitive cottage, Rudyard was working gently. Money was coming in from articles he had written about his travels, notably from *The Times*. He completed the poems he had started on their trip to Japan, *The Rhyme of the Three Sealers* and *Judson and the Empire*. In November 1892 he started work on the *Just So Stories*. As the birth of his first child became imminent his mind went back to his own happy early days in India, to the folk stories and myths recounted by his indulgent servants. The result was to be *The Jungle Book* and more tales for the *Just So Stories*.

Rudyard's cup of happiness was full to overflowing when 'My first child and daughter was born in three foot of snow on the night of December 29th, 1892.' She was christened Josephine after her young aunt and sometimes referred to as 'Joss'. When she was three weeks old the proud father wrote to his cousin Margot (Margaret Burne-Jones). Carrie, he told her, 'is walking though new worlds, wild with happiness,' while baby Joss was 'wickedly and uncannily, like me in profile'. Parenthood inspired him. 'I am more full of tales than I can hope to be empty,' he crowed. Margot was given frequent bulletins on 'the sweetest infant in all the world'.

Meanwhile the construction of their own house was renewed once the winter snows had melted, with brother Beatty engaged as the contractor (and this would prove another fatal mistake). The house was called Naulakha, after the book that Rudyard wrote with Wolcott, though the book title had been mis-spelt, probably by the latter, as *Naulahka*. But as his fame – and his fortune – grew, so the public and the press felt they had a right to encroach on the privacy which he now began, with Carrie as its protective doorkeeper, jealously to guard. To their warm-hearted and outgoing American neighbours the couple were soon perceived as snobby, superior and aloof. Beatty, his money-spinning contractual opportunities having dried up as Naulakha was completed, and often the worse for alcoholic wear, started to become an embarrassment and an annoyance.

In the spring of 1894 Rudyard and Carrie took a long holiday. First they sailed to Bermuda and en route they met a Mrs Catlin and her two daughters, Julia and Edith (known as 'Tommy') with whom they became instant bosom pals. Indeed their friendship with Julia would last all their lives, but on returning to Brattleboro they were horrified to find that Beatty, left in charge, had run their account into debt and Carrie had a great deal of sorting out to do before they could embark on the second part of their vacation, this time to visit the parents in England. Surprisingly the precious Josephine was left with her nurse Susan Bishop (with Beatty supposedly supervising) during both these trips. Lockwood and Alice had taken a house in Tisbury and Rudyard and Carrie rented a nearby house for three months. There, in the company of his inspirational father, Kipling worked on *The Jungle Books*. It was a happy time, but they were missing Josephine and were nervous about what Beatty might be doing in their absence.

When they returned in August Rudyard fell head over heels in love all over again with his adorable little daughter. Josephine was now 20 months old, walking, talking, curious, inventive, amusing, lively, incredibly bright, as advanced as her cousin Marjorie who was twice her age. She was also extraordinarily beautiful with fair hair and blue eyes. Her father was her adoring slave, playing with her at every available moment, stretching her comprehension, her imagination and her vocabulary with the stories he invented for her or remembered from his own childhood in India. 'Flat-curls' (his current pet name for her), he wrote to Tommy Catlin, 'is in enormous form, learning a new word every ten minutes, playing with the coal scuttle, eating pencils, smearing herself, bumping her head, singing, shouting, bubbling from dawn till dark.' Kipling, though not at all musical, always had a tune in mind when he was composing poetry. Soon Josephine could distinguish between what she called the 'howly-growly' ones and the 'tinkley-tinky' ones. In February 1895 Kipling wrote to his father's Harvard Professor friend, Charles Eliot Norton, whose daughter Sallie became a lifelong friend. 'The baby (glory be) keeps her rude health and becomes to us daily more charming. But what can we do with a small impudence who stops the coachman and enquires magisterially after the health of each horse by name?'

During a pleasant interlude in Washington in 1895 Rudyard met Theodore Roosevelt and a life-long friendship began, but, in Brattleboro, Beatty, now building a tennis court for the Kiplings, had overspent and was drinking heavily and publicly. Relations deteriorated and the families only communicated through notes. Had Carrie not been pregnant again, Rudyard may well have upped sticks and returned to England for good. Carrie was attended by the local doctor, James Conland, 'the best friend I made in New England,' as Kipling asserted. Conland, who had been to sea as a young man, inspired Rudyard to write the novella he called *Captains Courageous*, which brims with maritime technology and terms and established Kipling's penchant for all things naval. The Kiplings' second daughter, christened Elsie, was born on 2 February 1896. 'A very fat and healthy she-girl-babe, ridiculously like her mother,' Rudyard described her to Norton.

Then, in March, Beatty filed for bankruptcy. Things went from bad to worse and, on 6 May, in a fit of pique following Rudyard's assertion that he had been obliged to 'carry him for the last year' Beatty tipped Rudyard off his bicycle by swerving in front of him in his buckboard. Rudyard took Beatty to court, but local opinion swung strongly against the Kiplings and the media took a vicarious interest in the saga, destroying the privacy which the family so valued. It was time to leave and, with mixed feelings of regret and relief, the family set sail for England on 2 September.

They took a house at Maidencombe near Torquay which they soon found to be unwelcoming and oppressive. 'It was the Feng-shui – the Spirit of the house itself – that darkened the sunshine and fell upon us every time we entered, checking the very words on our lips.' Rudyard wrote ominously in *Something of Myself*. He never appeared to rapturize over

Elsie as he had over Josephine and he was to do over John. 'Elsie eats and sleeps, and sleeps and eats,' seemed all he could manage to say about her. His main consolation was nearby Dartmouth. Still obsessed with all things naval and maritime as a result of his research for *Captains Courageous*, he delighted in visiting the naval training ship *Britannia* and was thrilled to meet up again with his old friend Captain E.H. Bayly, R.N., who invited him to visit the Channel Fleet. And so the winter and the spring of 1897 passed, enlivened with visits by various relatives and friends such as Ambrose ('Ambo') Poynter, the beloved parents and his old headmaster Crom Price. Intellectual excitement came from Kipling's association with his artist cousin, Philip Burne-Jones. Rudyard wrote a set of verses for the picture that Burne-Jones exhibited at the Royal Academy called *The Vampire*. It may have been triggered by the publication that year of Bram Stoker's *Dracula* and it is said that the female figure was inspired by Philip's passion for the actress Mrs Patrick Campbell. Together, the picture and the verses caused a sensation, with the shocking opening lines, seen as a vicious indictment on women in general,

> A fool there was and he made his prayer
> (Even as you and I!)
> To a rag and a bone and a hank of hair
> (We called her the woman who did not care)
> But the fool he called her his lady fair—
> (Even as you and I).

Nevertheless, Rudyard was elected to the Athenaeum Club and dined with Alfred Milner and Cecil Rhodes. He dined at Balliol College, attended the Royal Academy banquet and rubbed shoulders with men as famous and stimulating as himself. He began to enjoy life once more.

But Carrie was pregnant again and they were determined to move from the uncongenial Maidencombe house before the new baby was born. Once again the beloved Aunt came to the rescue.

Chapter 3

JOHN'S BIRTH AND EARLY CHILDHOOD:

The Elms. The Woolsack.

'There was a man sent from God, whose name was John' (St. John 1:6)
Written by Rudyard, in the Burne-Jones's visitors' book,
on the birth of his son.

Early in the morning of 17 August 1897 Carrie Kipling gave birth to a
healthy male child in the Burne-Jones's North End House, Rottingdean,
as, according to *Something of Myself*, 'The Aunt and Uncle had said to
us: "Let the child that is coming to you be born in our house"' They had
'effaced themselves till my son John arrived on a warm August night of
'97, under what seemed every good omen.'

Extraordinarily, this is the only mention of John in Rudyard Kipling's
autobiography, but the word 'seemed' is laden with significance because
John's life was to end in tragedy. By the end of his life, when the book
was written, Kipling had perhaps learned how to sublimate his grief about
John, or perhaps the grief remained ever too raw to talk about, hence the
lack of reference to him in it, but at the glorious moment of the arrival of
the longed-for manchild, he wanted to tell the world about his joy.

To W.J. Harding Rudyard, over-brimming with pride in his fatherhood
of a boy, described his absorption with 'one small craft recently launched
from my own works'. He gave its weight '(approx.) 8.957 lbs', its h.p.
'(indicated) 2.0464', and its fuel consumption 'unrecorded but fresh
supplies needed every 2½ hours. The vessel at present needs at least 15
years for full completion but at the end of that time may be an efficient
addition to the Navy, for which service it is intended'.

The choice of name was dictated by the Kipling tradition of alternating
John and Joseph. From the moment of his birth Rudyard intended John
for the services, the Navy being the first choice. It so happened that
Kipling, whose love affair with the Army was giving way to a flirtation
with all things naval, had to refuse an invitation to attend 'torpedo-boat-
destroyer trials' to be at home with Carrie during the birth and in the
weeks prior to it he had been working on some verses about 'Destroyers'.

21

In Carrie's diary Rudyard recorded 'The boy John is born at 1.50 a.m. this day. C. and he doing well . . . inundation of letters, cables, p.c.s and advertisements. I think she is more cheerful than ever before and the boy John he says nuffin' and takes his vittals.'

Rudyard's letters to family and friends at this time all glowed with his delight, ill-concealed under jokingly derogatory remarks about his little son's appearance. 'Reserved young person, John; but considerably better looking than he was two days ago,' he said to Sallie Norton. To his Uncle Alfred Baldwin he wrote, 'John, the beetle-browed John does nothing but grunt and yawn. He is getting a shade more presentable and in a week or so will be fit to look at.' His cousin Margaret Burne-Jones was informed. 'He has ferocious eyebrows and doesn't say grace before meals . . . There'll be performances when Josephine returns to discover him.' It is interesting that in describing John, Rudyard commented on his own physical characteristics – the bushy eyebrows that came to be his trademark – and used the word that was one of his own nicknames, 'Beetle'. Soon after John was born, Kipling was to be seen wheeling his son's perambulator up and down across The Green 'and was rather proud of it', as he wrote to a friend Dora Clarke [*The Rottingdean Years*, Michael Smith].

A month later Rudyard designed a visiting card for Baby John and proudly took him, wearing his first 'boy's hat' and his new card, round to visit Aunt Georgie. She kept the visiting card in her purse, wrapped in a piece of paper, until the day she died.

Once Carrie had recovered from the confinement, the family moved into the house that they had rented (for 3 guineas a week) across The Green called 'The Elms'. It wasn't ideal, being sprawling, rambling and difficult for the meticulous Carrie to housekeep, but the great advantage was its propinquity to the stimulating Burne-Jones and Baldwin families – Rudyard's cousin Stanley often stayed at 'The Dene', his wife's family home, which flanked one side of The Green. 'One could but throw a cricket ball from any one house to the other,' Rudyard was pleased to observe. There were jokes and intellectual banter and affection aplenty. It was a happy time, the more so because 'my people [his parents] had left India for good, and were established in a small stone house near Tisbury, Wilts'. The proud grandparents were able to visit the new boy in the family and Rudyard enjoyed not only the filial pleasure of their presence, but also the artistic and literary communication he shared with his father.

Before John's birth the Queen's Diamond Jubilee, on 22 June, had been the big event of the year. It inspired Kipling to return to a phrase which haunted him, and which he would use in his later work as literary adviser to the Imperial War Graves Commission, 'Lest we forget'. Around it he wrote the majestic poem, *Recessional*, to the tune of the hymn *Eternal Father, strong to save*. Encouraged by Carrie, Aunt Georgie and Sallie Norton, who was staying with them at the time and who suggested the repetition of the sonorous phrase as a refrain running through the poem, he completed it and sent it to *The Times* who published it on 17 July. It was to become one of his most popular and most memorable works. When he had settled down after the excitement of the arrival of a son, Rudyard returned to the work set in India that had its roots in the abandoned manuscript that had begun as *Mother Maturin* and was busy transforming it into the story that was to become the masterpiece *Kim*. 'In a gloomy, windy Autumn *Kim* came back to me [he had toyed with the idea of it whilst in Vermont] with insistence, and I took it to be smoked over with my Father,' wrote Rudyard. 'Under our united tobaccos it grew like the Djinn released from the brass bottle.' Now that he had a boy of his own he more than ever appreciated the special relationship between father and son and perhaps it was the presence of a boy child in his household that inspired him to delve into his childhood memories to create such an attractive hero as Kim. As he grew up John would be introduced into the mysteries of 'the Great Game' (the workings of the Secret Service) and 'the Way' (Kim's Lama mentor's code of life).

A succession of visitors came to The Elms, including Crom Price and his fellow author J.M. Barrie. Christmas of 1897 was a joyful family occasion. The parents came to stay and Rudyard ended the year with an entry in Carrie's diary. The sixth year of our life together. In all the ways the richest to us two personally. "She shall do him good and not evil all the days of her life."' [Proverbs 31:12.] By and large she probably did, but this year she had given him a son: there could be no doubt about her value to him.

During all this domestic bliss, Kipling's restless mind had been pondering on foreign affairs 'At the back of my head there was an uneasiness, based on things that men were telling me about affairs outside England . . . It was this uneasiness of mind which led us down to the Cape in the winter of '97, taking the Father with us,' he wrote in *Something of Myself*. In fact it was on 8 January 1898 that the entourage, including Josephine, Elsie and the baby John, set sail for Cape Town, setting a pattern for future winters, bar the following fatal one. The Indian-born Kipling yearned for the stimulation of travel, preferably to a warm climate. America seemed out of the question since the Brattleboro fiasco and, in addition to satisfying his curiosity about what was causing the 'sound of a going in the tops of the mulberry trees' [II Samuel 5:24] after which 'thou shalt then bestir thyself'. South Africa seemed to fit the bill.

In the event it was an even better choice than Kipling could have imagined for during the three-month stay in the Cape he again met two men who were to become close to him until their respective deaths: Sir Alfred Milner, the newly arrived Queen's High Commissioner, and the legendary Cecil Rhodes. Kipling found himself at the centre of policy-forming in the wake of the controversial Jameson Raid and went on a fact-finding mission for Rhodes to Rhodesia. Jameson himself became a close friend and, Rudyard maintained, the inspiration for *If*. Young John learned early how 'to walk with Kings'.

Margaret Burne-Jones's children, Angela Mackail (later the novelist Angela Thirkell) and her brother Denis, spent idyllic holidays with the grandparents in North End House playing with 'our cousins at The Elms' who were about the same age. A great source of envy was that the Kipling children were allowed to go barefoot for most of the year, while the young Mackails could only take off their shoes and stockings during the summer holiday. This hardened the little Kiplings' feet so 'that they could run over the tops of the downs without feeling the little thistles which lie spread out quite flat and close to the ground in that short herbage.' The soft-footed Mackails 'could only move with hops and shrieks of agony and were ignominiously reduced to putting on the sand-shoes which we usually carried slung round our necks for emergencies,' she wrote in *Three Houses*. The dispensation to go barefoot was a prized concession and featured largely in the *Puck of Pook's Hill* stories to come. Angela also remembered the newly erected Drill Hall which Rudyard Kipling had 'imperially' given to the village with its 25-yard shooting range, and where they sometimes continued their boisterous games when wet weather prevailed. Kipling had also started a Boys' Social Club in the village and took a particular interest in the shooting range set up on the far flanks of East Hill and the butts across Lustrell's Vale.

'Josephine, very fair-haired and blue-eyed, was my bosom friend and ... we both adored her father,' she commented, recalling the lively games, instigated by Rudyard, of 'Cavaliers and Roundheads'. The Kiplings' nurse, Lucy, who looked after the younger children, was another favourite. She was 'given to song' as was Josephine's governess, and during the fortnight when a new governess overlapped with the old, 'they sang Mendelssohn duets together all over the downs, much to Josephine's delight and mine.' During those long warm summers Rudyard used to try out the *Just So Stories* on a nursery audience. 'Sometimes Josephine and I would be invited into the study, a pleasant bow-windowed room [in actual fact it was a 'bay' window – Michael Smith], where Cousin Ruddy sat at his work-table looking exactly like the profile portrait Uncle Phil (Philip Burne-Jones – a much-reproduced portrait) painted; pipe always at hand, high forehead, baldish even then, black moustached, and the dark complexion which made gossip-mongers attribute a touch of Indian blood to him.' She actually believed that his dark complexion came from his mother's Highland forebears from the Isle of Skye, and 'two at least of them could have passed as natives anywhere in Southern Europe.' So much for the persistent rumours of a 'touch of the tar-brush' in Kipling's genes. Angela also remembered the *Just So Stories* as poor things in print 'compared with the fun of hearing them told in Cousin Ruddy's deep unhesitating voice. There was a ritual about them, each phrase having its special intonation which had to be exactly the same each time and without which the stories are dried husks.' Others too remembered his 'inimitable cadence', his way of emphasizing certain words and exaggerating phrases 'which made his telling unforgettable'.

One thing that irritated Angela, however, was the occasional 'American-ness' of her cousins. Only baby John was English through and through. Both Josephine and Elsie were born in Vermont and learned to talk with their American mother and relatives. Even Rudyard returned to England speaking with a noticeable (and, it is said, somewhat jarring) American accent. On the question of manners, Angela considered they had an 'odious habit of breaking their boiled breakfast eggs into a glass and stirring them up with a spoon'. That the glass was pink 'somehow made matters worse, and with the complete candour of the nursery we stigmatized the whole proceeding as disgusting.'

Expeditions to the beach were complicated rituals, with nursemaids in control of the perambulators and older children alike. When it wasn't fine enough to go to the beach the cousins played in the sand garden which, remembers the Rottingdean girl Lucy Hilton, Rudyard, who was 'at his best with his children and their playmates', made 'for their delight'. Carrie grew gourds for them and 'cut the initials of each child upon a different gourd, and each day they would watch to see whose initials had grown the largest. They were so happy and safe in that high walled garden.'

It is obvious from personal accounts by family members and letters to them and from his letters to his children (best studied in Elliot L. Gilbert's collection *O Beloved Kids*) that Kipling was far removed from the conventional Victorian, or even Edwardian, father. His hands-on, intimate relationship more resembled the enlightened attitude of a 1990s 'new father' than an 1890s one. Indeed his behaviour with his children was perhaps even more like that of a modern grandfather. In a family where there were nurses and governesses, there was always someone to whom one could hand the children back when they became over-excited. Yet Rudyard, and Carrie too, were intensely involved in every facet of their offsprings' lives: their illnesses (and they were a profoundly hypochondriacal family and were perpetually nursing each other through a succession of heavy colds, influenza, grippe, swollen glands et al) their dental hygiene, their eating habits, their reading matter and education, their morals, their games, many of which Rudyard invented. Not for them the production of scrubbed and polished children by Nanny for a strained daily half hour with their undemonstrative parents. The word 'doting' may have been coined for them.

One of Kipling's talents was his ability to move from the trivia of domestic life – which he found infinitely attractive and into which a lesser genius may well have been sucked – into the world stage of statesmanship and politics, to which he gained access from his acclaim as a writer. The prolific strain continued throughout 1898: more work on *Kim*; *Stalky* stories; and the brilliant, but controversial and oft misunderstood *The White Man's Burden*, written in reaction to the United States' involvement in the war with Spain. This sparked a lively correspondence with Theodore Roosevelt. In September Rudyard was thrilled to take part in naval manoeuvres on board *HMS Pelorus*, the guest of Captain Norbury, off the Irish Coast. His love affair with the navy was cemented and with it his hopes for John's career in the senior service.

One fly in the ointment of this happy summer was the unwanted attention of Kipling's fans. Angela Thirkell (who Carrie described in her diary as 'a nice child') recalled the habitual knot of sightseers who would gather outside the high white gate which screened the house, peering through its little hole with a sliding shutter, and how throughout the summer charabancs would 'disgorge loads of trippers at the Royal Oak and as there was little for them to see in the village besides my grandfather's house and the church, they spent a good deal of time round Cousin Ruddy's gate.' Often Carrie had 'to ask a kneeling crowd of sightseers to move aside and let her go into her own house.' Angela and her cousins took 'a perverse pleasure in lingering near the gate and deliberately misleading anyone who asked us questions.' Another Rottingdean resident, the formidable Mrs Ridsdale, whose daughter Lucy married Stanley Baldwin, would demand of the 'Kipling-hunters' when they asked, 'Can you tell me where Rudyard Kipling lives?' 'Have you read anything of his?' and if she received a negative answer she would reply. 'Then I won't tell you.'

Autograph hunters too were a menace and it was at this time that Rudyard stopped paying his bills with cheques that he had signed as they were being sold on by the tradesmen to whom they were written. When Kipling wrote to the local bus company complaining of a driver who always pointed him out with a flourish of his whip to his fares and who broke the branch of an overhanging tree, he got no reply and had to write again several times. Eventually he got so exasperated that he called on the proprietor who was 'all smiles. "I wish you'd write me a letter every day, Mr Kipling. It's better than bus-driving."' The autographed letters were sold in The White Horse [Michael Smith].

The family was rocked by the sudden death of 'dear Uncle Ned' (Sir Edward Burne-Jones) on 17 June 1898. His ashes were interred in Rottingdean church, further binding the family to this small Sussex seaside village. His widow, Aunt Georgie, who had sustained the young Rudyard during the terrible years in the 'House of Desolation', became more dependent upon her nephew. Further upset for the family ensued when Rudyard's sister Trix returned from India with her new husband John Fleming, her mind unbalanced. This was due to a combination of a possible congenital mental disorder and a late reaction to those early years of separation from her parents in Lorne ('Forlorn') Lodge and the strain to which she and Rudyard had been subjected. Although better treated than her brother, it was still a traumatic experience for so young a child. She was entrusted to the care of her mother at Tisbury.

Affected by the intrusive attention of the tourists and family concerns, 'Rud does not work,' noted Carrie in her diary, 'the children amuse him a bit, but he is very anxious.' She herself, surrounded by the somewhat overwhelming Kipling/Macdonald/Burne-Jones and Baldwin relatives, longed for her own family – especially her mother – and to show them the new baby John. She persuaded Rudyard (against his own mother's strong advice) to spend the winter in America. They left a foggy, frosty Liverpool on 25 January 1899 and, after an appallingly rough passage, arrived, the two little girls complete with heavy colds, in New York on 2 February. They checked into the Hotel Grenoble where the girls were declared to have whooping cough. Carrie's mother and her sister Josephine with her new doctor husband, Theodore Dunham, joined them. Carrie succumbed to a fever, then rallied, and she and Rudyard managed to complete some business with Rudyard's publisher and friend, F.N. Doubleday (known, of course, as 'Effendi') and to try to sort out the fate of their Brattleboro house, Naulakha.

Then on 20 February Rudyard, too, developed a fever and his brother-in-law diagnosed 'inflammation in one lung'. Two days later little Josephine started to run a high temperature. Carrie moved her to the house of friends, the de Forests, on East 35th Street, and, still weak from her own illness, was left not only to look after Rudyard, but also the three-year-old Elsie and eighteen-month-old John, both of whom now had whooping cough. Day and night nurses were engaged. Josephine's condition deteriorated into pneumonia and Dr Conland, their Brattleboro physician who had brought her into the world, tended her. Rudyard declined rapidly and became delirious (and, extraordinarily, he later dictated what Birkenhead called 'the rambling adventures that he had experienced in the land of shadows' and which he reproduced as an Appendix to his biography of Kipling). He was attended not only by his brother-in-law but by a specialist, Dr Janeway, called in by Dunham. Elsie too seemed to be developing pneumonia, but thankfully John's condition settled at 'slight bronchitis'. Only a woman of underlying steel could have coped in the way Carrie Kipling so magnificently did. Often suffering from ailments (whether real or imaginary) herself, throughout her life as a wife and mother she always managed to subjugate her own ills to look after her loved ones. During this crisis the first signs of her propensity to be a 'control freak' became apparent. Kipling was a world famous figure in an age when writers were revered and lionized, and the world's press, hearing of the gravity of his illness, flocked to the lobby of the Grenoble. Carrie wrote the terse bulletins that she herself distributed to the press.

They clamoured for more information and employed all the ferreting and prying tactics so vilified of the press of the 1990s, hounding the hotel and medical staff. Telegrams poured in: ironically even the Kaiser sent one. Rudyard nearly died and all the while Carrie, much sustained by Doubleday, managed to carry on. By 5 March Rudyard had reached – and survived – his crisis and was sleeping deeply. But the next day Carrie had to make the terrible entry in her diary, 'Josephine left us at 6.30 this morning'.

If Carrie had been brave up to this point, now she had to become almost superhuman. For she deemed Rudyard still not strong enough to hear the news and had to carry the burden of it alone. She told Sallie Norton that these were 'dreadful' days. Only she knew the devastating effect it would – and assuredly did when he was finally told – have on him, for both Kiplings were extraordinary in the way that they could bind themselves together in their grief while hiding it from even their nearest and dearest. Indeed, when she visited him on 30 March Sallie Norton felt that 'that blessed English temperament' was equipping him to cope with the loss. How wrong she was. The inner turmoil was never stilled.

Angela Thirkell glimpsed some of it when she wrote, 'Much of the beloved Cousin Ruddy of our childhood died with Josephine and I feel that I have never seen him as a real person since that year.' Though the 'same charm, the same gift of fascinating speech, the same way of making everyone with whom he talks show their most interesting side' remained, she sensed that 'one was only allowed to see these things from the other side of a barrier.'

Josephine's death placed a heavy burden on the remaining two children. They had now been reduced to a family square and Rudyard and Carrie closed ranks, becoming even more jealous of their privacy. Elsie could never replace her adorable elder sister as the apple of Rudyard's eye. She could not match Josephine's star-like looks, described by Hilton Brown as having 'sapphire-blue eyes, hair of the true gold but dark brows and lashes – surely a beauty was lost to the world when death carried Taffimai [the character from the *Just So Stories*, undoubtedly based on Josephine] away ungrown'. Elsie had, perhaps, too much of her mother in her character, but her parents leaned on her more and more as she grew up until, eventually, she was looking after them. John was another matter. He was sunny and humorous: as a boy he could not be unfairly compared to his dead sister, he was the longed-for son and heir, and into him Kipling could pour all his own thwarted hankering for a service life. He began to take an almost obsessive interest in his education.

The return to Rottingdean on 24 June was painful beyond description. 'We come quietly to The Elms to take on a sort of ghost life,' wrote Carrie in her diary. The faraway expression in Rudyard's eyes in the portrait painted by his cousin Philip is explained when one knows it was begun

28

the following month, when he wrote to his old friend 'Ted' Hill, 'I don't think it likely that I shall ever come back to America. My little Maid loved it dearly (she was almost entirely American in her ways of thinking and looking at things) and it was in New York that we lost her.' His father wrote to Sallie Norton that the house and garden were 'full of the lost child' and the grieving grandfather saw visions of Josephine 'when a door opened, when a space was vacant at table, coming out of every green dark corner of the garden.' One wonders what effect the suffocating burden of this tragedy must have had on the young Elsie and her baby brother – try as their parents did to suppress it – and what in heaven's name Carrie and Rudyard told them. Most small boys adore their elder sisters and it is inevitable that John, coming up to three, would have repeatedly asked for his sister in whatever toddler-speak he could manage for 'Josephine'.

Some small consolation came that autumn when Kipling blazed a trail by acquiring (by hiring) the first of his succession of motor cars, starting a lifelong passion for the automobile that he passed on to John, although, unlike his son and daughter, he never learned to drive. Angela Thirkell described her first sight of the Kiplings' motor 'pawing the ground before the door . . . When we saw the Kipling children dancing round it, we were consumed with longing to go and dance too.' Disappointingly, promised rides never actually materialized as 'the monster' always refused to start and 'we sat and sat in it while the chauffeur tinkered at its inside and then had to get out with a promise for a real ride some day.'

Another consolation was the understanding of Rider Haggard, who had also lost his most favoured child. 'Both suffered a grief that they knew would be with them for the rest of their lives,' wrote Pocock. He believed that they had other factors in common: 'Neither was married to the love of his life' – in Kipling's case this was Flo Garrard, in Haggard's Lily Jackson, whom he had to leave when his father found a post for him in Natal, just as Kipling had had to leave Flo to take up the post found for him by Lockwood in Lahore. Finally, continued Pocock, 'each valued the company of other men . . . There was a shared interest in South Africa.'

New writing was difficult. Only the *Just So* story, *The Elephant's Child*, written in August whilst convalescing in Andrew Carnegie's house in the Highlands, and first told to John and Elsie, was recorded in Carrie's diary. *Stalky & Co* was published on 6 October 1899, to mixed reviews. But Kipling's fascination for politics was fanned by the outbreak of the Boer War on the 11th of that month. He became involved with the raising of volunteers and Carrie wrote that he was 'absorbed with excitement and anxiety about the troops in Africa'.

On 31 October the *Daily Mail* published his extraordinary poem *The Absent-Minded Beggar* which Kipling, in an unusual gesture for this publicity-shunning man, milked for all the exposure and fund-raising potential it was worth. The money (and it eventually raised the vast sum in those days of a quarter of a million pounds) went to support the families of soldiers who had gone out to South Africa – 'the girl that Tommy's left behind him'. Sir Arthur Sullivan set it to music and it was illustrated by the famous artist Caton Woodville and reproduced, as Bruce Bairnsfather's *Fragments From France* cartoons were to be in the following war, on all manner of souvenirs from hankies to tobacco jars. Birkenhead calls it 'a rhymed invitation of singular vulgarity'. Nevertheless it touched the jingoistic chord of the moment and on 14 December Kipling was offered a knighthood. Of course he refused, although Carrie noted, 'We are much pleased to be offered it, however.'

Christmas was dismal: the whole family had 'flu, were still grieving and couldn't wait to get out of the country and back to the sunshine of South Africa, in spite of (or even because of, in Rudyard's case) the war that now raged there. The 1899's year-end message from Rudyard in Carrie's diary simply said, 'One year ended and I owe my life to Carrie.'

On 20 January 1900 Rudyard, Carrie, Elsie and John, plus nursemaid and governess, set sail for the Cape. They stayed at the Mount Nelson Hotel, the hub of military and political gossip, patronised by many of the foremost journalists covering the conflict. Kipling was soon gratified to be asked by Lord Roberts to write for the new army newspaper *The Friend*. 'Bobs' now owed him a favour which he was to collect, with fateful results for John, in August 1914. He visited the troops at the front and in hospitals, and experienced military action for the first time in his life. Rhodes offered the Kiplings the opportunity to build a house on his Groote Schuur estate, and Herbert Baker (who was to become one of the principal architects of the Imperial War Graves Commission) designed it with Carrie, while Rudyard was covering the engagements at the Modder River. He flung himself into his war correspondent assignments with gusto, enjoying the company of his fellow journalists. Some of them, such as the American Julian Ralph writing for the *Daily Mail*, whose son Kipling tenderly nursed through typhoid in Bloemfontein, H.T. Gwynne of Reuters and Perceval Landon of *The Times*, would remain lifelong friends. Yet he still found time to write verses, such as his tribute to the Boer General Joubert, who had defeated his friend Jameson in 1896 and who died on 27 March 1900. Meanwhile Carrie, feeling herself abandoned with the children, unable to control Rudyard as she wished, and, as seemed habitual, feeling ill, chafed. Rudyard returned to Cape Town on 3 April and by the 28th they had arrived back in England.

Back in Rottingdean Kipling found his attitude to the war at odds with his feisty yet beloved Aunt Georgie, her daughter Margaret and her husband Jack Mackail, who drew the shutters of North End House when Kipling rattled tin cans for joy at the relief of Mafeking. *Kim* was completed that year and Rudyard also wrote two of the few overt tributes to his little lost daughter. They were the *Just So* stories, *How the First*

Letter was Written and *How the Alphabet was Made* in which the principal character was Taffimai ('Taffy'), the 'Best Beloved' girl-daughter of
her father, Tegumai Bopsulai. Taffy is bright and strong-willed and the
bond between her and her father comes over strongly: 'As soon as Taffy
could run about she went everywhere with her Daddy.' Equally apparent
was their conspiratorial relationship to the mother, Teshumai
Tewindrow, who would say, 'Where in the world have you two been to,
to get so shocking dirty?' Substitute the names Josephine, Rudyard and
Carrie and there is no doubt that a typical real-life situation is being
described. As was Kipling's habit, he wrote a poem called *Merrow Down*
to accompany the story. It ends with the almost unbearably poignant
lines,

> But as the faithful years return
> And hearts unwounded sing again,
> Comes Taffy dancing through the fern
> To lead the Surrey spring again.
>
> Her brows are bound with bracken-fronds,
> And golden elf-locks fly above;
> Her eyes are bright as diamonds
> And bluer than the skies above.
>
> In mocassins and deer-skin cloak,
> Unfearing, free and fair she flits,
> And lights her little damp-wood smoke
> To show her Daddy where she flits.
>
> For far – oh, very far behind,
> So far she cannot call to him,
> Comes Tegumai alone to find
> The daughter that was all to him.

They felt they had to get away from the painful memories that infused
The Elms and began house-hunting. The expeditions were undertaken in
a series of eccentric motor or steam vehicles by 'the Committee of Ways
and Means', together with the intrepid and determined beloved Aunt.
After many tiring and abortive trips, when the motor let them down and
they had to take the train to Etchingham and then the local 'Fly', they
finally arrived at a large Jacobean house in Burwash. 'That's her! The
Only She! Make an honest woman of her – quick,' they unanimously
declared at their first glimpse of Bateman's. Her Feng-shui was good.
Sadly the house was let and it was another twelve months before she came
on the market again.

In 1900 the Kiplings went to South Africa in December, arriving on Christmas Day. By now their Dutch colonial gift house from Rhodes, which they called The Woolsack, was completed. Carrie loved it and John, now three and a half, was old enough to enjoy the warmth, the freedom and the glorious beaches – an idyllic setting for a young boy to grow up in. Kipling wrote in *Something of Myself*, 'To this Paradise we moved each year-end from 1900 to 1907 – a complete equipage of governess, maids, and children, so that the latter came to know and therefore as children will, to own the Union Castle Line – stewards and all.' The children were 'regularly and lovingly spoiled; the large smile of the Malay laundress, and the easy pick-up-again of existence,' wrote their indulgent father.

Elsie added to these happy recollections in her *Epilogue* to Carrington's biography, 'The *Just So Stories* were first told to my brother and myself during those Cape winters, and, when written, were read aloud to us for such suggestions as could be expected from small children.' Many of these delightful stories must have been influenced by the contact that the family had with the wild animals that surrounded them. 'The children . . . had all the beasts on the Rhodes estate to play with. Uphill lived the lions, Alice and Jumbo, whose morning voices were the signal for getting up. The zebra paddock, which the emus also used was immediately behind The Woolsack.' There were also 'an aged lawn mower pony', a 'spitting llama, whose peculiarity the children learned early' and 'a bull-kudu of some eighteen hands.' Imagine the delight of the two children at such intimate contact with animals. All this and the most entertaining father in the world and a mother (though sometimes, perhaps over-fussy), whose unstinting love was never in question. What a perfect childhood John and Elsie enjoyed. They particularly loved the voyage out each year but once at The Woolsack their education continued despite the sun and the fun. In the evenings Rudyard would recite poetry to the children 'by the hour . . . Wordsworth, Longfellow, the *Sagas* of King Olaf, the *Lays of Ancient Rome*, Percy's *Reliques* and *Border Ballads* became so familiar to the two small eager listeners that quotations from them became part of their every-day talk. Misquotations were frowned upon.' Later Carrie wrote her mother that 'Rud reads through the Psalms as poetry and they love them also.'

Elsie also recalled some of the illustrious personages who travelled out with them to the Cape or visited them at The Woolsack: Baden-Powell, 'Dr Jim' (Jameson) and, of course, their benefactor Cecil Rhodes among them. The children from birth had been surrounded by clever, influential and powerful people, not least by the sparkling members of their own family.

The Summer of 1901 started pleasantly, with a visit from their American friends, the Catlins, with whom they paid a visit to Paris. Carrie, however, was feeling ill and there were some hysterical outbursts in her diary in July at being left alone and desperately ill when Rud went to stay with his parents at Tisbury and then on to play at 'sailors' in the Naval Manoeuvres. As often happened when she was feeling unwell, Rudyard took over the correspondence with her mother, and, perhaps feeling guilty at leaving her, wrote, 'You have no notion what a sweet and winning little woman your Carrie has grown into. Her face gets more beautiful year by year, and her character deepens and broadens with every demand upon it. She is near an angel, but her Puritan conscience which she has inherited from her New England forbears still makes her take life too blame seriously.' There was no doubt of his devotion to her, but there was, nevertheless, a slight sting in the tail of this eulogy. On the literary front the publication in *The Times* of the long poem *The Islanders* caused a furore – as it was meant to do. In it Kipling criticized Britain for not taking national military service as seriously as she took the playing of sports, and for putting into the field in South Africa 'a remnant . . . When your strong men cheered in their millions while your striplings went to the war.' The lines 'then ye contented your souls With the flannelled fools at the wicket or the muddied oafs at the goals' (which could surely only have been written by an Englishman as bad at, and indifferent to, the nation's favourite games as Kipling. His schoolfellow, G.H. Malcolm, wrote in the *Kipling Journal* of September 1935 that 'Kipling hated cricket and football and the other compulsory games and all the to-do there was over them') were particularly irritating, especially as there happened to be a Test Match in progress in Australia when the poem appeared.

When the Kiplings returned to The Woolsack on 7 January 1902 a young reporter called Edgar Wallace (who had taken John Ralph's place on the *Daily Mail*) was waiting to interview him about the poem and its sensational effect. Kipling encouraged him to take up a career in writing. On 28 January he wrote to Rider Haggard, 'I ought to have written hired fools instead of flannelled. That might have made my meaning clearer.'

In a contrasting vein – ever the versatile – Rudyard continued the *Just So Stories*, completing *The Cat that Walked by Himself* and *The Butterfly that Stamped*. Then on 26 March Rhodes died after a long illness. On 2 April Rudyard recited the obituary verses that he had hastily written and which were carved on Rhodes's memorial which end,

> Living he was the land, and dead,
> His soul shall be her soul.

At long last negotiations for peace in South Africa were started on 9 April and the Kiplings sailed for home a week later in the company of Jameson. They returned to The Elms where the ghost of Josephine lingered, the tourists continued to gawp and Carrie suffered increasing bouts of depression. It was to be their last summer there before, with great relief, they could move to 'The Very-Own House'.

Chapter 4

GROWING UP:

Bateman's. Puck of Pook's Hill. School Days. Engelberg.
Letters to and from 'Daddo'.
Training to be a Man.

If you can fill the unforgiving minute
With sixty seconds' worth of distance run,
Yours is the Earth and everything that's in it,
And – which is more – you'll be a Man, my son.

If, Rudyard Kipling, 1910.

Rudyard had long ago decided that Sussex was the county in which he wished to settle. He had written the poem *Sussex*, which celebrates the typical downlands which surrounded Rottingdean, at The Woolsack before returning home earlier that year (1902). It ends,

God gives all men all earth to love,
    But, since man's heart is small,
Ordains for each one spot shall prove
    Belovèd over all,
Each to his choice, and I rejoice
    The lot has fallen to me
In a fair ground – in a fair ground –
    Yea, Sussex by the sea!

It was a new-found and deep love of the English countryside that he was to impart to his children.

At last negotiations for Bateman's were successfully concluded and, in September 1902, they moved into the house that was to be John's base for the rest of his life – and Rudyard and Carrie's too.

Much has been written of the gloomy nature of Bateman's, its fortress-like quality. Kingsley Amis found its interior 'chilly, damp, and dark even on the south side . . . I soon decided that I should very much dislike spending as much as 24 hours in [it].' He also refers to the house as 'an overground dungeon'. Seymour-Smith agrees with him, though admits that 'It is a lovely house in itself, but melancholy'. Despite Carrie's inevitable grumbles at the amount of work there was to do to lick it into liveable shape as she moved into what she confided to her diary were 'chaos and black night', the whole family soon came to love the house. There certainly was a great deal of work to do, not the least being the installation of electricity by the harnessing of the River Dudwell (that became such a well-loved feature of life at Bateman's) at the old mill that was to be the setting of the story *Below the Mill Dam*, written soon after they moved in. This they did with the help of no less an authority than Sir William Willcocks, who had installed the hydro-electric system at the Aswan Dam. The Kiplings decorated their 1634 house in a pleasing but idiosyncratic blend of the unavoidable Pre-Raphaelite with elements of their Indian and American days and suitable Jacobean furniture. 'It is a good and peaceable place,' wrote Rudyard to C.E. Norton on 30 November. 'We coveted the place for two and a half or three years, and have loved it since our first sight of it.'

Soon the Kiplings were playing the game of Lord, or Squire, and Lady of the Manor. They farmed and gardened with enthusiasm, learning on the job, Carrie as always approaching it in a business-like manner (soon she was making Bateman's farm the only profitable farm in the area), Rudyard in more dilettante fashion. Rider Haggard had written a book called *Rural England* on the decline of traditional English farming, published in November 1902, Rudyard wrote to him, 'I have been reading *Rural England* with deep joy. I take off my hat to you deeply and profoundly because it is a magnum opus . . . I – alas! hold land now . . . an old house and a 25-acre farm of good hop land and fruit and a mill (water) that dates from 1196. The farm is let down and neglected . . . Now you see why your book touches me.'

On the literary front the *Just So Stories*, so long practised on his children and appreciative friends, and with Rudyard's own illustrations, were published. In reviewing them G.K. Chesterton called Kipling 'a most extraordinary and bewildering genius'. Interspersed with the stories were some of Rudyard's most amusing and memorable verses. Among them is 'The Camel's hump is an ugly lump . . .', which gives the English language the phrase 'getting the hump'. Famous again in the 1970s, when it was often used in self-development courses, was the poem for *The Elephant's Child*:

> I keep six honest serving-men
> (They taught me all I knew);
> Their names are What and Why and When
> And How and Where and Who,

Elsie explained that it was written for her, known as 'Elsie Why' because of her endless 'stream of enquiries', to which her father's patience in answering was 'immense'. To Elsie and John these were not the works of a famous man, but the habitually amusing conversation of a beloved Daddy.

Now well-settled in his own home which gave him the privacy and stability he craved at that time, this was another prolific period for Rudyard, notably of the short story. There was *A Deal in Cotton* (not published until 1907), *With the Night Mail* (published in 1905), generally categorized as a science-fiction story, and *Mrs Bathurst* (published in March 1904), one of his most remarkable, currently acclaimed and latterly criticized, stories. Its theme is the destructive power of obsessive love, and in it Kipling coined the word 'It' for sex appeal, picked up in 1927 in the film *It* and by its star, Clara Bow. The fourth story from this era was another cry of pain for the loss of Josephine, *They*. Its autobiographical theme is strong. A motorist driving through Sussex Downsland happens upon a beautiful Elizabethan house to the north. It is run by a blind woman and peopled with shadowy children whose laughter tinkles behind a hedge, who wave from a window but who will not approach the motorcar brought into the grounds to amuse them. When the narrator tells the blind woman (Miss Florence) that he had 'never seen the faces of [my] dead in any dream', she replies, 'Then it must be as bad as being blind.' On a second visit the children venture out of the woods to peek at the intriguing tools he spreads out around the car which had broken down. The narrator then goes with the butler, Madden, to fetch a doctor to a neighbour's ill child. Madden, too, had a daughter who died who would now 'have been close on ten'. So would Josephine. On a third visit the narrator is invited inside the house and sits in a room frequented by the children when a tenant, obviously terrified by the strange atmosphere of the house, comes to see Miss Florence. He put his hands behind his back and 'felt my relaxed hands taken and turned softly between the soft hands of a child . . . The little brushing kiss fell in the centre of my palm – as a gift on which the fingers were, once, expected to close; as the all-faithful half-reproachful signal of a waiting child not used to neglect even when grown-ups were busiest – a fragment of the mute code devised very long ago.' This is pure personal experience. The tender description is of himself and Josephine: he would *always* find time for her, even in the midst of grown-up affairs, and the bestowing of a kiss on the palm was her special token of love to him. At this magical encounter the narrator suddenly understands the nature of the little fleeting inhabitants of the house: they are ghosts, come because Miss Florence, who had neither borne nor lost a child, yearned to give them love.

Writing this original story, with its delicate touch which could so easily have fallen into bathos or whimsy, must have had a cathartic effect on Kipling. It was the last overtly identifiable reference to Josephine in his works and was published in August 1904. It also shows that Kipling had an interest in the paranormal, which he was to suppress after the death of his son when urged to contact him through a medium.

It is interesting to note the parallel between Rudyard Kipling and Victor Hugo at this point. Both were writers who inspired the extremes of adulation and loathing at various points in their careers; who had a high public profile and political persona as well as a literary one; who adored children and wrote tenderly of them; who both lost a son and a daughter. First Hugo lost his son, Victor, and his dead son's children lived with him through the seige of Paris in 1870. He told them stories much as Kipling told his children the *Just So Stories* and the tales from *The Jungle Book*. Then his newly married, adored daughter, Léopoldine, drowned in the River Seine before the eyes of her husband, Charles Vacquérie, who plunged into the water after her and also died. Hugo's charming poem, *Elle avait pris ce pli . . .*(She got into this habit . . .) is very reminiscent of the intimate passage described above from *They*. He recalls the happy times when she was little when his daughter had formed the habit of coming into his room each morning, taking up his pen, opening his books, disturbing his papers, sitting on his bed and laughing, disrupting his work and yet inspiring his best verse (*mes plus doux vers*). *Quand nous habitions tous . . .* (When we all lived together . . .) also describes how his heart cried out 'My God' when his little girl called him *Mon père*, so deeply did he love her. At last in the bleaker poem, *A Villequier*, Hugo finally reconciles himself with a God whom he at first blamed and abandoned for his loss, but reminds God that '*nos enfants nous sont bien nécessaires, Seigneur*' ('our children are necessary to us, Lord'). Kipling would certainly have agreed and the grief felt by these two literary giants for the loss of beloved children is strikingly similarly expressed in their work and their lives. Another link was that Hugo's youngest daughter, Adèle, lost her mind, much as Rudyard's sister Trix was to do from time to time. They would have had much in common had they met.

A distraction to Rudyard was the continuing passion for motoring. A Lanchester was delivered by Mr Lanchester himself and in June 1904 Carrie wrote to her mother, 'A specialist came from Birmingham to see to the motor. He and John are great friends. John got his rubber apron and spent a happy hour cleaning the car and only left to plant potatoes in his garden.' She also reported that a new governess, Miss Blaikie, had arrived.

Despite an awakening interest in national politics – of the far right variety – Kipling refused several offers (notably from Edinburgh) to stand as a Member of Parliament that year. His popularity was now somewhat on the wane. His virulent anti-Liberalism, culminating with his reaction to the Liberal landslide of 1906, tolerated when he triumphed as the people's minstrel of war, came to be regarded as bigotry in some quarters. Despite his increasing political activity, Rudyard, as always, continued to write.

By September of that year he was working on the stories that were to reinforce his reputation as a children's writer (though, like all his juvenile tales, they were cleverly 'layered' and could be read at more than one level), collectively known as *Puck of Pook's Hill*. Kipling did nothing by halves. When he lived in India he immersed himself in the colourful culture and myths of India. Now he considered himself a Sussex man he became steeped in the history and folklore of his adopted 'foreign' land. But the catalysts that produced stories of such charm were his own children and three triggering factors.

These were the enacting by the children of their own simplified version of *A Midsummer Night's Dream* in the open air, their being given a boat and sailing off on adventures on the Dudwell and the fact that there was a distinct fairy ring in one of the water meadows. Rudyard felt it was fate: 'You see how patently the cards were stacked and dealt into my hands?' he asks in *Something of Myself*. The opening paragraphs of the first story, *Weland's Sword*, are a delightful account of that performance, with Elsie becoming Una and John changed into Dan. They inadvertently summon up the real Puck, who lives, of course, on nearby Puck's (Pook's) Hill. With his ancient catch-phrase 'By Oak, Ash and Thorn,' Puck, 'the last survivor in England of those whom mortals call Fairies', then guides the children back through time to meet some of the previous inhabitants of the land. *Puck of Pook's Hill* was followed by another series of Puck, Dan and Una stories, called *Rewards and Fairies*. The title came from a 17th century poem by Bishop Corbet, *The Fairies' Farewell*. The story *The Wrong Thing*, set in a builder's yard, was written especially for John and *Marklake Witches* was written for Elsie, using a real incident when she was taught to milk a cow.

As in the *Just So Stories*, the tales are interspersed with poems, giving us some more of Kipling's most timelessly resonant verses. *Puck of Pook's Hill* ends with *The Children's Song*, which immediately became popular as a sort of school anthem and was to become one of the banes of John's young life. On 28 September 1909 Rudyard wrote to John, 'Sorry to hear about the "Children's Song" – for which I feel I ought to apologize deeply. All your fault for having a poetical pa!' But things didn't change: 'Of course we had the "Children's Song" in Church this morning. I do get sick of it,' he wrote to his parents on returning to school on 30 January 1910. Rudyard replied, 'Sorry about the "Children's Song." You know that I didn't write the darn thing with the faintest idea it would be so cruelly used against the young.' John was equally fed up with *If*. Demonstrating the fact that he was a mischievous boy, always getting into trouble at school, he wrote to Rudyard, 'Why did you write that stuff? I've had to write it out twice as an impot.' Kipling described the poem as a set of verses 'which escaped from the book, and for a while ran about the world'.

They were drawn from Jameson's character and contained 'counsels of perfection most easy to give. Once started, the mechanization of the age made them snowball themselves in a way that startled me,' he pretended to complain. What would he have made of his verses being faxed around the globe or transmitted through the Internet? 'They were printed as cards,' he continued, 'to hang up in offices and bedrooms; illuminated text-wise and anthologized to weariness. Twenty-seven of the Nations of the Earth translated them into their seven-and-twenty tongues, and printed them on every sort of fabric.'

Writing these books 'loaded with allegories and allusions . . . was glorious fun,' recalled Kipling, for the 'Daemon' which drove him to write 'was with me in the *Jungle Books, Kim* and both *Puck* books.' It is interesting to note that this muse, which almost made him feel that he was doing automatic writing at times, was at its strongest when he was writing for his children.

In June 1906 Rudyard laboriously penned the spoof 'Dudwell Charter' that granted his children the right 'at all times' to be 'free to come and go and look and know – whether shod or barefoot' along the family stretch of the Dudwell River. They were granted rights over 'all Birds, Beasts, Reptiles, Fishes and Insects' thereon. It is significant that, although Elsie was the elder, the 'charter' named 'John Kipling and Elsie his sister'. The son and heir took precedence. Poor Elsie was always the also-ran.

Life continued in the felicitous pattern of spending six months at Bateman's, six months at The Woolsack. The last South African winter was in 1906/07 when one of the first of the letters between Rudyard and his children published in O *Beloved Kids* was written. Dated 15 March 1907, this letter describes his attendance at the unveiling of a monument to the Cape Town Volunteers who died during the Boer War. It sets the style for many subsequent letters. It is jokey, contains several amusing and skilful sketches and ends with heavy parental instructions to bathe, wash behind the ears, dry thoroughly and wear flannel next to the skin. Several of Kipling's biographers completely misunderstand the tone of Kipling's letters to his children. Even Marghanita Laski, normally so sympathetic to him, agrees with the poet Craig Raine that 'though Kipling was a master at writing for children he was less good at writing *to* children'. She herself says, 'It cannot have been easy being Kipling's children [and this is indisputable], even though we do not know that John and Elsie ever resented the dreadful screen of hilarity through which their father addressed them. "Oh you Awful Kid" one letter to Elsie begins, though it contains perhaps the nearest expression of direct affection in any of them – "I too sometimes, want to see you – most dreffle! You see, I love you!"' In fact the letters *over-brim* with love and affection and the bantering, humorous tone was that used by the whole family and many others of their class and generation.

At Bateman's the garden and farms thrived – with much advice from Rider Haggard – and there were many visits from the extraordinary variety of celebrities and eccentrics who attracted Kipling and must have amused the children enormously. One of the most bizarre was their neighbour, a certain Colonel Wemyss Feilden who had served in the Black Watch during the Indian Mutiny and ran the blockade in the American Civil War. Colonel Feilden became a close and much loved friend of the whole family and his failing health and his offers to help with John's stamp collection feature in several letters to the lad at school. Lady Edward Cecil, whom they had first met in South Africa during the Boer War, had taken a house called Great Wigsell at nearby Bodiham when her husband's career took him to Egypt (a country she disliked) in 1901. Her two children, George and Helen, were ideal companions for Elsie and John. Occasionally she brought her old friend Clemenceau to see the Kiplings. She had studied art in Paris and got to know the fiery old politician well through her father, General Duff Maxse. Other regular visitors were Crom Price's son and daughter, 'Teddy' and Dorothy, Julia Catlin, now married to Chauncey Depew and living in France, and her daughter Frances. The families were so close that the young Kiplings called her 'Aunt Julia' and Frances called Kipling 'Uncle Rud'. Later [in the *Kipling Journal*] Julia recalled, 'They had three children: Josephine, their first and she was a fairy child. When she was taken from them at a very early age, Rud never seemed to become reconciled to her loss. The second child, Elsie, "Ladybird" [usually shortened to "Bird"], as Rud called her, was so full of life, so intelligent and attractive . . . John was a bit younger and such a dear. He bade fair to be very brilliant.' Jameson was another favourite visitor with whom they could reminisce about South Africa. Young John must have been force-fed with heroic tales of political and military prowess from a very early age. That he would be able to emulate them was becoming doubtful. Although he loved nothing more as a little boy than to strut around with his beautifully plaited naval lanyard, his eyesight had already become a worry. On 10 May Carrie recorded in her diary that they were making a visit to town as there was anxiety about John's eyes. He was only nine.

In this year, 1907, Kipling having refused all the national honours he had been offered, accepted a series of academic honours. The first was from Durham University in June, quickly followed by Oxford. There they were accompanied by Sir William and Lady Osler. Osler, a famous Canadian physician, was Regius Professor of Medicine at Oxford and Lady Osler was related to Carrie's family, the Balestiers. (They, too, would lose their only son, 2nd Lieutenant Edward Revere Osler serving with A Battery, 59th Bn RFA near Poperinghe on 30 August 1917, during the Battle of Passchendaele.) Rudyard wrote to John describing the solemn ceremony, during which many there were dying for a smoke. 'A fine person in a gown' indicated where they could light up and 'Mark Twain came with us and three or four other men followed and we had a smoke like naughty boys under a big archway.' This is typical of the lively and human word pictures with which Rudyard regaled John in his letters. Also frequent are affectionate references to Carrie. In this letter of 27 June 1907 Rudyard described allaying his nervousness when 'I looked about and saw Mummy looking very sweet and beautiful and then I didn't mind'. Later they went out to dinner and 'Mummy wore her blue silk dress and looked simply *lovely.*'

Governesses continued to provide education for both the children until it was deemed time for the son and heir to go to school. The school that was chosen for him reinforced the Rottingdean links. It was St Aubyns prep school situated in Field House, just down the High Street from The Green that was so familiar to John as a small child. It had been established in 1895 by Vaughan Lang and C.E.F. Stanford. John entered in September 1907 at the age of ten, motoring there with a father who obviously had mixed feelings about leaving his young son for the first time. Memories of his own abandonment at the House of Desolation and of his own first day at school must have come flooding back. John was bolstered up for the occasion by a '*specially* large tea' with Aunt Georgie. Her comforting closeness had been a factor in choosing the Rottingdean school, even though she was getting rather old and forgetful and sometimes referred to John as 'Ruddy'. Then Rudyard and John walked round the school together 'till we examined every apartment thereof'. Rudyard returned in misery: 'No – it was not a cheerful drive,' he admitted. Carrie and Elsie, meanwhile, waited anxiously at Bateman's to know how it had all gone.

Then began the preparations for Rudyard and Carrie's trip to Canada, where Kipling had finally agreed to receive an honorary degree from McGill University in Montreal, perhaps as a result of McGill Professor Stephen Leacock's visit to Bateman's in May and because Kipling had become convinced that Canada was the land of future promise. That he had chosen to go to Canada rather than to the United States was a measure both of the continuing antipathy he felt to all things American in the wake of the Brattleboro fiasco, and because he could not bring himself to visit the country where his dearest daughter had been taken from him. Rudyard undertook a gruelling tour of lectures and receptions, covering vast distances, yet he promised to write to John twice a week. This was a heavy commitment considering his busy schedule and is a measure of the loving bond that existed between father and son. For the letters were not merely perfunctory notes and must have taken a considerable chunk out of each tiring day to complete. Those that survive are so amusing and vivid that the children must have been able to imagine every step of their parents' exciting trip: their posh private railway car (particularly enjoyed by Carrie who liked to be treated as a VIP) and the 'Noble Nigger'

41

assigned to take care of them; the whales 'spouting and blowing in every direction' seen from the steamer from Victoria to Vancouver, and they would particularly have enjoyed Rudyard's description of their own bossy mummy meeting '*her* Mummy'. (Carrie's mother had to travel from America to Canada to see her daughter and son-in-law because of Kipling's refusal to set foot in the country.) 'In less than ten minutes Grandmother was ordering Mummy about like anything and called her "Child", ("Come here, child! Don't do that, child!") while I laughed to see Mummy taking it all so meekly.' Letters arrived back from the children and Rudyard replied to John that he was 'very pleased to know that you like school – I feel sure that you will like it more and more as time goes on and you settle down and make your own friends. But I know exactly how homesick you feel at first. I can remember how I felt when I first went to school at Westward Ho! But my school was more than two hundred miles from my home – my Father and Mother were in India and I knew that I should not see them for years . . . and the grub was simply beastly.' The lessons in manliness and stiff-upper-lipness continue. 'I am rather pleased with you about one thing. You know I never mind jumping on you when you have done something I don't like – the same way I generally tell you when you have behaved decently. Well from all I can discover, you behaved yourself like a man when you felt homesick. I understand you did not flop about and blub and whine but carried on quietly. *Good man.* Next time it will come easier to you to keep control over yourself and the time after that easier still.'

The year of the academic or literary honours continued with one of the greatest it was possible to receive: the Nobel Prize for Literature. Kipling was the first English writer to win this prestigious award. Unfortunately the award ceremony took place in December and Rudyard and Carrie had a dreadful crossing from Denmark to Sweden (which he described in some detail to his sister-in-law Josephine Dunham). The impressive ceremony was rather low key because of the recent death of the old King Oscar. They were however, met by the new King, Gustav V, and the crown Prince (later to become Gustav VI) and Princess. The Princess was the eldest daughter of Arthur, Duke of Connaught, Queen Victoria's third and favourite son. This meeting was significant, as the Princess would re-enter his life after John was posted missing in 1915.

The entire ceremony and the journey, in 'Cinderella's glass coach', to the Academy of Music where it was held was described in great detail in a letter to Elsie and John, complete with sketches of Rudyard being surrounded by large hands that jostled to shake his and of the gold medal which 'weighs about half a pound'. An endearing trait in Kipling's character was his lack of self-importance and his honesty to his children. The awe-inspiring ceremony made him feel, he reported to them, 'like a bad boy up to be caned'.

Although the family move to Burwash and John being at school all term slightly distanced the Kipling family from the Rottingdean clan, family gatherings still continued in the holidays. Lorna Baldwin (later Lady Lorna Howard) wrote in the *Kipling Journal* of September 1985 of her fond memories of her 'dear, funny' cousin John, whose image as 'slow' or 'unintelligent' she was anxious to dispel. The John she recalls was 'a witty fellow, and he was very quick on the uptake'. The anecdote she chose to illustrate her point is set in St Aubyns. John had the embarrassment of falling flat on his face when visiting the room of the Under-Master, who quipped, 'Embracing Mother Earth?' 'No Sir, kissing Cousin Carpet,' riposted John. The tale was soon recounted to a delighted Great-Aunt Georgie. The incident may well have inspired a limerick and sketch at the end of his father's letter to John of 17 May 1910,

> There was a fat person of Zug
> Who was found on all fours on the rug.
>   When they said:- 'You've a fit!'
>   He said:- No! I've been bit –
> And I'm morally sure it's a bug!

Lady Howard also remembers John's facility with the hybrid family in-language that would now be called 'franglais'. The Kiplings and the Baldwins were all practically bilingual and they delighted in translating slang phrases literally, such as; *'Ne fussez-pas vouse-même, vieille fève'* (Don't fuss yourself, old bean) or *'Venez-ici, old collez-dans-la boue'* (Come here, old stick-in-the-mud). Talking in Arabian Nights-speak was another of John's specialities: 'We would salute with an upraised arm the morning appearance of Uncle Ruddy, "Ho! Son of the eldest Daughter of my Grandmother's Father".' John's closeness to his young cousin Oliver Baldwin was strengthened when the latter followed him to school at St Aubyns in 1908. 'Remember me to the cheeksome Oliver,' wrote Rudyard to John at school on 18 May 1908. In that same letter John was praised for having the guts to venture downstairs at the dead of night when his pal Beresford (and Kipling had already commented on the coincidence of John having a chap called Beresford in the next bed in his dormitory – just as he had had at Westward Ho!) thought he saw a ghost. 'That's the sort of thing that a man who means to get into the navy ought to do. Don't you bother too much about your eyes. They will come all right,' wrote Rudyard blithely; he would make sure that they did.

The main topic in the letters at the time was John's new watch: 'Maybe I shall bring a gunmetal hunter with me [on his next Saturday visit to John]. I believe you wanted a hunter'. On 14 May 1908 Carrie duly told her mother of the planned visit to Rottingdean to see John and that 'We are taking him over a watch which he has much wanted having.' On 18

May Rudyard went to London to 'try on a lot of beastly new clothes' but also to buy John a leather watchguard for his new treasure. During this trip to town Rudyard met his old friend Jameson, who then returned to Bateman's in the motor. On 21 May Kipling asked his son if he had received the watchguard. 'The swivel on it is real silver.' Again on 26 May he wrote, 'You didn't tell me whether you had received the watchguard which I got for you in London. Next time you write let me know if it came safely.' By 2 June John had still not acknowledged the precious gift and he was chastised, 'You never told me whether you got the watchguard: so please remind me to kick you when we meet.'

Now that John could not be swept off to warmer climes for six months of the year the family pattern changed. The winter holidays from now on would be spent ski-ing in Switzerland. The chosen resort was Engelberg. There Rudyard picked up the ski-ing he had learned in Vermont, and fellow author Jerome K. Jerome, also staying in the resort, remembered the whole Kipling family with affection that particular holiday. 'Engelberg is too low to be a good sports centre,' he wrote in *My Life and Times*. 'We had some muggy weather and to kill time I got up some private theatricals. Kipling's boy and girl were there. They were jolly children. Young Kipling was a suffragette and little Miss Kipling played a costermonger's donah. Kipling himself combined the parts of scene-shifter and call boy. It was the first time I had met Mrs Kipling since her marriage. She was still a beautiful woman, but her hair was white. There had always been sadness in her eyes, even when a girl.' As they had first met soon after she married Rudyard, the initial sadness would have been for her brother Wolcott's death. Now it was a legacy of Josephine's. It is interesting to note that when Jerome first describes Carrie in 1892 he calls her Kipling's 'secretary, a beautiful girl with a haunting melancholy in her eyes'. Jerome is virtually unique in describing Carrie as 'beautiful'. That he should consider her thus might help to explain her attraction to Rudyard.

Other friends at Engelberg were the Hornungs, whose only child Oscar became John's closest friend. Oscar's mother, Constance, or Connie, was Conan Doyle's sister. Dr Alfred Fröhlich of the Neurological Institute at Vienna also remembered the Kiplings at Engelberg, as he recounted in the *Kipling Journal* of June 1936. They first met on the day of the great earthquake at Messina, on 28 December 1908, when Fröhlich had the temerity to attend the fancy dress ball as Rudyard Kipling. 'I donned his well-known skating costume and a theatrical wig-maker converted me into a second Rudyard Kipling, while the original posed as the model. He owned to having experienced an uncanny feeling when he saw his "double" gradually evolving under the hands of the skilful hairdresser.' Carrie entered into the spirit of the deception and swept into the ballroom on the Fröhlich-Kipling arm. Rudyard then followed as himself, giving the other guests quite a shock. Typically, he and Carrie were under the weather:

Fröhlich continues, 'Both Mr and Mrs Kipling caught a slight chill at this ball, and I, their friend, was naturally appointed their family doctor.' He might have known it would be a mistake: the Kiplings disagreed with his treatment, demanding pills 'to relieve the liver'. But Rudyard recovered his humour sufficiently to send Fröhlich his representation of 'an enormous bacillus with the designation "Bacillus Tusis Engelbergensis, var. Frolich".' Fröhlich might have been somewhat surprised to know that Rudyard referred to him as 'the Golliwog' when he recounted this same incident and other 'Professor' stories to John, already back at school in January 1909. The friendship, however, continued through many sporting winters as did their correspondence. 'I also have bought skis,' Rudyard wrote one year to Fröhlich, 'a pair for John and a pair for me. We will wallow in the snows together . . . We have had the Zurich match – in which John played.' Carrie had told her mother that John was very good at ski-ing and was having skating lessons. Winter-sporting was thoroughly enjoyed by the whole family, Rudyard and the children taking an active part in the outdoor activities, Carrie enjoying the social life of fancy dress balls, thought-reading demonstrations and the time to play patience.

In January 1910 John travelled back philosophically to school, leaving the other three to continue to disport themselves. Back at Rottingdean he and Oliver went to their usual pre-school blow-out tea with Aunt Georgie, while Oliver's parents joined Rudyard, Carrie and Elsie in Engelberg. 'Uncle Stan has gone mad about skis,' wrote a delighted Rudyard in a letter that reported the extraordinary event of Carrie (known occasionally as 'the Bear') putting on skates, skating for twenty minutes, lunching in the open and going down the monastery slope on her luge. He also compared John's first letter from school unfavourably with Oliver's, which 'gives *heaps* more news'. The Kiplings and Baldwins obviously showed their offsprings' letters to each other. John could sometimes write a good narrative, for example, 'After we had got home we all went out to see the "Comet" which was quite plain to see. I hope you have had good weather out at Engelberg. It was raining hard on Friday. We [he and Oliver] got a "four wheeler" on that day in Brighton to take us here but the Horse would not go up the hill as it had been very ill and laid up for 3 weeks and this was his first time it had been out since then so we had to go back and get another "four wheeler" but we had to give the other chap 3 shillings,' he reported in January 1910. At other times he and Oliver had resorted to space-filling rather than news. 'You've taken a leaf out of Oliver Baldwin's book – you young villain! D'you remember when he sent Mother the complete score of a county cricket-match? Your two page time-table of your studies rather reminded me of it,' complained Rudyard on 5 October 1909.

Although Oliver was younger than John, they were in the same form at

St Aubyns and seemed to vie with each other for bottom place. In the 4th Form (in June and July 1908) John was often 8th and Oliver 9th out of a class of 10. At times, however, the younger of the two cousins attained a higher place than John. The 'great sunshine' in their young lives, as Oliver described it, was that every other Sunday during term-time they lunched with Aunt Georgie.

Far from the gloomy picture that is often painted of them, the Kiplings were an active, demonstrably affectionate and fun-loving family, who nevertheless suffered a succession of ailments, real and imaginary, which at times seemed overly to concern them. The practice of taking 'the waters', or 'cures', at various spas was still fashionable and at the end of the Swiss holiday that year they went on to Vernet-les-Bains for Carrie to take a cure. It was so successful that the process was repeated annually. One year they met Lord Roberts and his daughter Aileen here and Elsie remembers her father acting as interpreter 'at a formal meeting between the aged Field-Marshal (very worried because he was in plain clothes), the commander of the area garrison (very much in uniform) and the local Archbishop.'

While the rest of the family gadded about the Continent – sometimes the Swiss trip was followed by visits to Julia Depew (née Catlin) at the Château d'Annel at Compiègne, or to other parts of France (Kipling was well-regarded there) – John remained at school and the letters flowed to him from his over-anxious but indulgent father. In February 1910 he was given yet another watch – not a half-hunter 'because they are out of fashion', but 'not a cheap watch. *Au contraire c'est un montre très expensif!* Therefore do not brutalize it – on no account look into its stomach to behold its works.' John's academic prowess – or sometimes lack of it – features strongly in the letters of this period, as does his somewhat delicate health. That month he was third in his form and 'second in Arith'. On 28 May he had been taken to the doctor and got a lecture on eating properly, repeated on 3 June. These clean your teeth/eat properly/wash behind your ears/spell properly instructions were interspersed with *If-Just So-Jungle Book*-Bible-type homilies, e.g. 'You are now getting on in life . . . and I want your behaviour to correspond with your years. Therefore, O my Son, do all that you can to win, honestly and fairly, the events for which you have entered. If you win, shut your head. Exalt not yourself nor your legs nor your wind nor anything else that is yours. To boast (not that you are given to it) is the mark of the Savage and the Pig. If you lose remember that you have lost. It doesn't matter one little bit but it matters a great deal if you go about jawing about your handicap being too heavy or your having had a bad start or your being tripped or put off,' etc, etc, etc. It was a heavy burden for this young white man to carry. That he made a good stab at it is evident in Rudyard's proud letters to his sister-in-law Josephine (familiarly known as 'Jay') Dunham. In September

Rudyard wrote, with the inimitable Kipling knack of making the most mundane details seem fascinating. 'The little chap has reached the first division of the school which means he is in a select class of twelve (there are 84 in the whole school) who have special privileges and I suppose look down on the other 72 with awful scorn. One of his privileges he tells me in his letter is "We are allowed to help ourselves to vegetables. This is a great advantage." Now why should it be a great advantage? I suppose the common herd have thier [sic] vegetables – greens and potatoes – dumped onto their plate out of a spoon. Another of the privileges is to give out the school mail about once a week. Would it make you proud if you were an amateur post mistress? But the ways of boys are past finding out.' On 21 October he continued the saga of John, who was 'getting quite a man as the English reckon manhood', as the distributor of mail. 'He writes me that the other day he handed a letter written to one of the matrons to a schoolmate who bore the same name. The boy read half of it before he realized that it wasn't for him and the matron was extremely wrath. Indeed the only person amused by the mistake appears to have been John who thought it comic! Glad it wasn't any of my letter.' Though he was doing well at school and gaining in confidence, John's eyes still caused concern. On 2 November Carrie wrote to her mother saying they had received a report on John's eyes, which were deteriorating. The previous month she and Rudyard had been to Wellington College to give it a thorough vetting as it was their choice of school for John. Like Westward Ho! Wellington had a strong military image. It had been founded by public subscription in 1859 in memory of the famous Duke and its pupils were destined for the services, especially the Army. On 3 October, the day after the visit, Rudyard wrote a long letter extolling the virtues and attractions of the school to John. 'I was very delighted with the whole thing,' he summarized, 'It seemed to me quite like an Oxford College in miniature. Now you must buck up and go in with flying colours!

That year saw several deaths that affected Rudyard deeply. First there was his old headmaster and friend, Crom Price, for whom he wrote the inscription for the Westward Ho! memorial window, 'Who with toil of his today Bought for us tomorrow'. This was echoed by John Maxwell Edwards in one of his 1916 epitaphs for World War One, 'When you go home tell them of us and say "For your to-morrows these gave their to-day"'. Another version of this couplet, suggested by Major John Etty-Leal, was inscribed on the Kohima War Memorial in 1945. Crom was not a wealthy man by any means and after his death Rudyard took a close interest in the welfare of his young children, contributing to their education. Price had married late and Teddy (Cormell Edward William) had been born on 28 February 1898. He and his younger sister Dorothy became even more regular visitors to Bateman's, especially over the period of John's birthday.

Then the King, Edward VII, died. There was a memorial service for him in Burwash on 20 May (and a school service at Rottingdean attended by John) and all the Kipling staff were given time off to attend, the Boer War veterans among them sporting their medals. Colonel Feilden read the lesson. On 22 November Rudyard's mother, Alice, exhausted by her devotion to Trix in her period of mental instability, died at Tisbury. Trix had recovered sufficiently to return to her husband, John Fleming, and they were both with her when she died, as was Rudyard. His father, John Lockwood, survived his companion of 45 years by less than two months. Rudyard was recalled from Engelberg in January 1911, when his father was taken ill whilst staying with the Wyndham family at their Salisbury home, Clouds. He was too late to see the man who had been not only a parent, but friend, collaborator and counsellor. The children had lost a beloved grandfather for whom they had great affection and who adored them. Among the Kipling Papers at Sussex University are two charming books, hand-written and beautifully illustrated by John Lockwood, probably in 1903, one for Elsie (stories and rhymes involving members of the family) and one for John (an animal Alphabet).

John, too, was a worry. 'We have been having an awful time with John,' wrote Carrie to her mother from Engelberg, just before they were recalled to his dying grandfather's side. He had a bad chill and swollen glands and it was thought unlikely he would go back to school at the beginning of term on the 25 January 1911. Added to this concern, organizing two funerals for two such dear people in such a short time had debilitated Rudyard. 1910 had also been an exhausting year on the political front. He spent much time with MPs like his cousin Stanley Baldwin and his friend, the Canadian-born Andrew Bonar Law, sometimes attending debates in the House. He took a strong interest in the crises which led to Parliament being twice dissolved. In both cases the Liberals only just scraped back, much to the chagrin of Kipling who was part of the right-wing group known as the 'Die-hards'. After his father's funeral, Rudyard took off with Carrie to Vernet-les-Bains and this time Rudyard, too, bathed in the hot sulphuric water, enjoyed the local food, wine and fishing and, reinvigorated, returned to exchange the Daimler that had replaced the Lanchester for what would become his trade-mark Rolls Royce. Although often portrayed as a Toad of Toad Hall-like figure, Kipling was never more than a back-seat driver. There was always a chauffeur at the sharp end of his succession of motors.

John's impending move to public school and the perennial problem of his failing eyesight were the family's greatest concern that summer. Carrie had reported to her mother in May that John's eyes were still getting worse. Though Admiral Sir John Fisher had offered to nominate him for a naval cadetship and Rudyard had set his heart on a naval career for his son, it was now obvious that his eyesight would debar him from it. He would still go to Wellington in September 1911, however, into Pearson's house which had so impressed his parents. 'I liked Pearson,' Rudyard had pronounced. 'The boys in the house didn't seem to be a bit in awe of him.' On John's fourteenth birthday, the month before he went to Wellington, Aunt Georgie sent him and Oliver (due to go to Eton) a copy of her son-in-law John Mackail's *Sayings of the Lord Jesus Christ*, bound in red morocco. 'I have dearly liked your little visits to me these last three years,' she wrote, 'and am glad to have seen you both as child and boy . . . Yes, it will be fourteen years tomorrow . . . and I am looking across from the green writing-table in the studio to the little room where you first drew breath.' Oliver wrote in his autobiography, *The Questing Beast*, 'When John was killed at Loos in 1915 I asked for his copy and his parents gave it me. I have the two books to-day.'

John was occasionally addressed as 'William' by his father, and one wonders if the 1911 poem *Mary's Son* was a coded message to John who was at this stage beginning to dither between a naval and army career:

> If you stop to find out what your wages will be
> And how they will clothe and feed you,
> Willie, my son, don't you go on the Sea,
> For the Sea will never need you.

Christmas that year was marked by John's favourite present – a gramophone with 24 records. 'You can imagine how lively the house has been ever since,' wrote Rudyard to his mother-in-law on Christmas Day as Carrie was not feeling up to writing her regular letters. John's love of his gramophone is movingly recalled by Kipling in the 1917 poem, *A Recantation (To Lyde of the Music Halls)*. Before John's death Kipling found his son's music hall pin-up, 'Lyde', not to his taste:

> Ere certain Fate had touched a heart
> By fifty years made cold,
> I judged thee, Lyde, and thy art
> O'erblown and over-bold.
>
> But he – but he, of whom bereft
> I suffer vacant days –
> He on his shield not meanly left –
> He cherished all thy lays.

But when Lyde's own son is also killed in France, Kipling admires her determination that 'the show must go on', despite her grief. It is a trait that Kipling understood well and he also identifies with a fellow artist who makes her living by the word and is sometimes vilified for it.

Never more rampant rose the Hall
  At thy audacious line
Than when the news came in from Gaul
  Thy son had – followed mine.

But thou didst hide it in thy breast
  And, capering, took the brunt
Of blaze and blare, and launched the jest
  That swept next week the Front.

This poignant poem, which appeared in the 1919 collection *The Years Between*, is rarely anthologized or interpreted, but is one of Kipling's most touching tributes to John. On the subject of the identity of 'Lyde' there has been much debate. The concensus is that she is an amalgam of Marie Lloyd (who certainly fits the bill as 'O'erblown and over-bold' and whose surname phonetically resembles 'Lyde') and Sir Harry Lauder (also similar to 'Lyde') who did indeed lose a son in the war. Lauder's son (also called John) was killed on 28 December 1916 at Ovillers on the Somme and the old music hall trooper made a pilgrimage to see his son's grave in June 1917, during which he gave a series of concerts to entertain the troops. As Kipling wrote *My Boy Jack* to express his grief, Lauder wrote *Keep Right on to the End of the Road*. However, Julian Moore of Flinders University, Australia, and an expert on *The Years Between* proposes the Australian music hall artiste, Florrie Forde, as the inspiration.

Continuing his letter to his mother-in-law, Rudyard drew one of the most vivid word pictures of John that exist: 'John has come home from school growing like a cornstalk with a deep cracked voice and great taste for clothes. This is very comic. He talks about his school with the greatest love and pride, not to say swagger, and is really a humorous chap. Now and then he reminds me of Wolcott in the speed and accuracy of his ripostes.' It is interesting that Rudyard makes this favourable comparison between the two males that he loved most in his life: his wife's brother Wolcott and his son John. T.N. Cross feels that physically John actually resembled his roguish uncle, Beatty. His sister Elsie agreed. She described 'My brother, John, who took after his American forbears in looks, with brilliant hazel eyes dark eyebrows and hair, and a slim figure. A quick and vivid personality of much charm was evident.'

The portrait of the amusing but unassuming John continues: 'He has just discovered that his father is a sort of public man – a fact that he didn't realize before and he is very funny about it. They ask him at school whether he has read any of his father's works and when he, quite truthfully, says "No", they don't believe him.'

John's short period at Wellington was undistinguished as far as academic or sporting prowess was concerned and seemed somewhat to deteriorate as time went on: for on 11 February 1912 Rudyard added a *'Private'* note to his letter from Engelberg to John in which he expresses his joy on receiving a letter from 'Pompey' (the nickname for John's house-master, John Pearson) saying that John had been top of his form the previous week. Sadly this achievement would not continue long. In his correspondence to relatives Kipling attributes a passion for his school to which John may not have wholeheartedly subscribed. His days there were always overshadowed by his father's over-anxiety for him to achieve.

After the family holiday in Engelberg, Rudyard, Carrie and Elsie went on to Italy, visiting Florence and Venice. As they would not be home in time to pick John up for the Easter vacation, they arranged for Moore (the current chauffeur) to transport him to old Colonel Feilden's house. The family arrived home on 25 March and after the holidays Rudyard wrote John a rather curious letter in which he says, 'What really bothered me most was not being able to have a last jaw with you. I wanted to tell you a lot of things about keeping clear of any chap who is even suspected of beastliness. There is no limit to the trouble possible if one goes about (however innocently) with swine of that type. Give them the widest of wide berths. Whatever their merits may be in the athletic line they are at heart only sweeps and scum and all friendship or acquaintance with them ends in sorrow and disgrace. More on this subject when we meet.' One cannot help but conjecture that the lack of an opportunity to have a face-to-face chat about the dangers of public school homosexuality was not accidental at all, but that Kipling, like many a parent before and since, lacked the courage for it. He certainly would have found it hard to use such 'over-the-top' language to his son's face. Was there actually 'more on this subject' when next they met, one wonders? Perhaps there was, as in his letter of June 5 Rudyard was to say 'I can't tell you what a joy it was to me to have that time with you. I hope I didn't bore you with good advice but it *is* good advice.' The letter ends with the stricture to 'flee from the contaminating swine!', but more probably the advice was about general achievement, for he went on to say, 'Oscar Hornung who is only 17 is now on the edge of having a house to manage and I'd give a deal if some day I could see you head of your house.' It was not to be.

On 25 May 1912 Kipling probably caused his son, who was easily embarrassed by his father's fame, considerable discomfort when he gave a lecture to the Wellington College Literary Society on the subject of 'The Uses of Reading'. John had to admit, however, that the talk had 'not been badly received'. Another thing that made life at Wellington difficult was the fact that two of his best friends, Oscar Hornung and his cousin Oliver Baldwin, went to Eton. Later that year Rudyard, Carrie and Elsie attended the annual 4 June celebrations at Eton and as they drove up in the latest Rolls, the 'Green Goblin', 'Oliver in white or yellow waistcoat, huge buttonhole and immaculate topper suddenly appeared on the foot-board.

His hawk-eye had discovered us and he piloted us to a great yard roaring full of more parents and kids and glossy toppers.' There they met Oliver's parents and Oscar and his parents. [That year Oscar's father, the novelist E.W. Hornung and author of *Raffles, the Gentleman Burglar*, had written *Fathers of Men*, the story of a working class boy who is sent to a public school.] Oscar then took over as their 'pilot' and they had tea in his rooms. Kipling was obviously trying to play down the attraction of Eton as opposed to Wellington in this letter – which must have made John rather jealous at the jollity of it all. 'The form-rooms tho' old struck me as pretty frowzy and full of germs . . . On the whole the houses didn't strike me as being specially clean and the lavatory accommodation was not extra special.' Rudyard almost seems proud (in his letter of 2 July) that John had had a beating 'for larking on a Sunday'. Carrie was 'awfully excited' – a euphemism for 'upset' about it, but Kipling, 'having been beaten much and often' was 'not unduly agitated'. He was more agitated at the prospect of John not doing well in the end-of-year exams and being 'in danger of being hung up among the lumps and louts of the IVth form and of getting the reputation of being a fool'. By November Rudyard was trying to convince himself that John was '*much* cleverer than you make out to be. You have an ungodly gift of "jaw" and a faculty of putting arguments together which ought to be useful to you in after life.' For once, however, John had obviously upset his doting Mother with this gift of the gab and was encouraged to approach his father next time he wished 'to blow off steam'. A 'giddy time' with Oscar Hornung and Charlie Law (Bonar Law's son) was recalled with pleasure. Charlie was pronounced 'much nicer than I had ever seen him before. He wasn't playing up to anything.'

One thing that pleased Rudyard was John's eager participation in the Wellington Officers' Training Corps (OTC). On 25 June Rudyard praised him (calling him 'Dear Warrior') for his part in the war games, reported in *The Times*, when public school opposed public school. 'I am much delighted by your field-day. It shows that you are getting tougher.' Later Carrie was to put great faith in the fact that John's school OTC training would have given him good preparation for the real game of war.

Another beating was reported in November – this time for going to the school tuck shop, 'Grubby's', when he obviously wasn't supposed to. Rudyard was 'only *very* glad that you didn't show it hurt'. On 1 November Rudyard, ever anxious to foster John's interest in all things martial, took him to see the 'flying machines at Aldershot', as Carrie noted in her diary. There was no doubt in anyone's mind that John was destined to serve his country in uniform. The whole family was then thrilled in December when John won the Young Cup for running in a House competition. 'Wait till *you* have a son of your own (God help the poor little kid!) and you'll know how you feel when your son does well,' gloated the proud father to his prize-winning son. The prize was to be a trip to

London to look at the motorbike John was promised for Easter.

After Engelberg as usual during the Christmas holiday, for which they left on Boxing Day, praying for the snow that was particularly scarce that year, Rudyard, Carrie and Elsie went on to Paris. There the parents left Elsie with Dorothy Ponton and proceeded to Marseilles where they boarded the P & O steamer *Persia* en route for Port Said and a tour of Egypt. The letters that Rudyard wrote over the duration of their 1913 tour to Elsie in Paris and John at Wellington are a superb account of their travels and experiences, complete with sketches. One highlight was meeting Lord Kitchener whom he pronounced 'a fatted Pharoah in spurs' who had 'gone to seed physically' and who was 'garrulously intoxicated with power'. He also dined in Cairo with Captain Flower who ran the Cairo Zoo. 'He was a Wellington man of course (every one out here seems to be Wellington) and of course knew Pompey,' wrote Rudyard, forever wanting to make his son feel proud of his school. But John was going through an unhappy period and could not be cheered up. He was berated for the misery of his letters and warned not to write depressing letters to Elsie in Paris. There was a measles epidemic at school and John succumbed; added to this, his parents' chatty letters from Egypt were not getting through to him and his well-loved housemaster was away. When a less than glowing half-term report caught up with Rudyard and Carrie as they arrived back in Europe on 20 March 1913, they were prepared to accept that 'the term seems to have been too vile for anyone to be able to do justice to himself and I don't propose to count it. You were off your feed half the time: the masters were sick: the school disorganized and what else could you expect . . . I am pleased that Pompey said your conduct was "very satisfactory". You know how proud I am of you secretly – or if you don't you may have guessed it by now – and I was cheered to find that a Hellish term hadn't lowered your house morale. You've got no end of character, my son. I don't care how much or how often or how fully you grouse or curse to me – I know and I understand and I sympathise, as you know: but it pleases me that you have carried on decently and quietly thro' heavy burdens of wet, discomfort and indifferent health.'

There was a joyful family reunion at Bateman's in April and on the 7th Carrie recorded in her diary the momentous words, 'John has a motor bike'. One can imagine the laddish delight of the engine-mad father with his equally motor-mad son. Back at school the question of pince-nez and how to wear them cropped up. On April 14 he was advised to get a chain (or cable) for them as soon as possible. 'Swimming is *not* what the optician built 'em for, but I expect if some sort of thing was attached to 'em you might be able to save one pair of three. Never mind the breakages. Go on wearing 'em. They give you a <u>distingay</u> air, and may help your eyes, which is much more important.' John had obviously been whizzing around the countryside on his motor bike and Rudyard encouraged him to look at the ground 'from a military point of view'. A lecture followed: 'I don't like your frivolous report on your form-master. Even if he is a worm, for goodness sake buck up and work.' What was worrying Kipling was the possibility of John being 'superannuated' (or 'supered'), ie his not being moved up a form with his peers when the new school year started: 'though it isn't morally disgraceful, one's contemporaries remember the little fact twenty and thirty years afterwards.'

On 2 May Rudyard and Carrie went to Wellington to discuss John's progress with Pearson. During this visit John told them that, despite his father's ambitions for him to pursue a naval career, he had decided that he wanted to go into the Army. Wellington was, after all, an Army-orientated school and John belonged to its Officers' Training Corps which trained boys to become Army officers and it was inevitable that he would be influenced by that culture. Rudyard then threw his energy and influence into helping him to fulfil that desire.

On 5 May he wrote to John saying that he had met Sir Edward Ward, the Under-Secretary for War and discussed John's wish to join the Army. Ward agreed to write to the head of the Physical Examining Board on his behalf. On 15 May Rudyard confirmed to John that he had 'applied to the War Office for a prelim. exam on you which, they tell me, will take place at Aldershot before a Medical Board. This means you'll be looked over by an Army doctor there. Word will be sent when that examination is to take place and I will come over in the car and take you to it. So be prepared for the summons . . . Meantime keep yourself as fit as possible and for goodness sake don't smash up all your available pincenez so that you can sport a pair before the Board.' The next day Rudyard wrote to confirm the meeting with the Medical Board at Aldershot on Monday next at 12.45. He would be at the College at 12.30 in the car to pick John up. He was advised to be 'dressed in your best kit' and 'It will be rather a rag,' said Rudyard, playing down the importance of the interview. In reality this test had Rudyard on tenterhooks: so much was riding on it, all his hopes and fears that his son would fulfil the military ambitions that he had been incapable of pursuing himself. On 19 May Carrie wrote in her diary, 'Rud and John go to Aldershot for John's medical. His eyesight found below standard.' This understated entry belies the disappointment and gloom that must have descended on Bateman's at this news. Rudyard was not prepared to lie down and accept it. On 25 May Carrie wrote, 'Sir Edward Ward from the War Office promises he will do what he can about John'. Superannuation was looming even stronger, provoking sterner and sterner homilies about bucking up. Rudyard and John had enjoyed a boys' own day out together a couple of days earlier, which Rudyard conspiratorially called 'our stolen afternoon among the aeroplanes' when John had missed two lessons and they had enjoyed a lunch together. Poor John. The pressure on him must have been enormous at that time: Rudyard's pride in him, his love and hopes for him approached the obsessive and stifling. At times Rudyard's whole world seemed to revolve about him. In June Rudyard wrote to him about the visit of Lord Edward Cecil's son, George, to Bateman's. George was now at Sandhurst and an obvious desirable role model for John, who was invited to tea with him at the Academy.

By July John appeared to be cracking under the strain. It was very hot and exams were looming. He wrote letters that 'grieved Mother a good deal' and was encouraged to 'take a pull on yourself for the last few days of term'. His wretched glands were playing up yet again. The promise of 'a good talk between us' which would 'clear up many of our present difficulties' in the hols could not have been a totally pleasurable prospect. The fact that a new motor bike had been ordered may have eased the situation, as did the new squash court built earlier that year at Bateman's. On the down side the poor chap had mumps.

He was pronounced well enough to return to Wellington in September with the usual exhortations to work, and his Uncle Edward (Poynter), then President of the Royal Academy, came to Bateman's to do a water-colour of the house. Rudyard described him as 'an industrious old bird' as he worked from 10 to 1 and then from 2 to 4.30 without a break. He was dreading, however, having to sit for Poynter who had been commissioned to do a 'drawing' of him. This news was imparted in a significant letter of 27 September, which continued, 'You will have seen, I fear, that I had to attend a National Service meeting at Burwash. I'm awfully sorry, for your sake, that I couldn't get out of it. [In fact Kipling enthusiastically shared Roberts's views on the need for National Service.] Lord Roberts asked me and as I want to keep solid with him for your sake, you ungrateful little devil, I agreed. 'Twasn't a bad meeting and I always like speaking to a crowd in the dark. But I thought of you and was brief.' The dread subject of 'supering' raised its uncomfortable head again and for once Rudyard threatened John with one of the drawbacks of being the son of a famous father: 'It may not be a disgrace but it's not nice and there will, in your case, probably be a heap of publicity about it. Don't say damn! I'm only telling you the cold facts of our case.' John was also most upset that, for health reasons, he had been debarred from running that term. 'I do most deeply sympathise with you, old man . . . but what can I do? I'd sooner have you well not running than sick even tho' you ran like three bloody hares. See how your literary style has corrupted mine.'

John's health did not improve: he was in and out of the sanitorium and eventually he was taken to see the family physician, Sir John Bland-Sutton (known as the 'small specialist'). Thyroid troubles had been diagnosed and the family was 'greatly distressed' (Carrie's phrase) when it was thought that Switzerland would have to be barred that winter.

By half-term in October John had recovered sufficiently for two dancing mistresses to come to Bateman's to teach him and Elsie the Tango. The young people's social life was hotting up and on 22 November Elsie attended her first grown-up house party. It was at Taplow Court, the home of the Desboroughs. Carrie recorded in her diary that the Asquiths were also there. They were moving in rather rarified social circles. The Desboroughs and the Asquiths were part of the set known as 'The Souls', whose male children, known as 'the Coterie', were to be virtually wiped out during the war. The Desboroughs (family name Grenfell) would lose sons Julian and Billy, and twin cousins Francis and Riversdale. The Asquiths would lose their pride and joy, the brilliant Raymond.

On 26 November came a reprieve from Bland-Sutton. 'We are to go to Switzerland for Christmas,' crowed Carrie to her diary. It was to be their last family visit to the much-loved Engelberg, now as familiar as The Woolsack and where they met many friends each year. For John it was marred by having to be coached by the current governess Dorothy Ponton (especially in maths) because of his poor end-of-term results. On 20 January he returned to England and Wellington for what was to be his last term at the school. At one time (in March 1913) he had flirted with the idea of going on to University. His choice of Cambridge and Clare College was thoroughly squashed by Rudyard. 'Whence has come the new idea of going to the Varsity and why – oh why – Clare? Cambridge is sad enough [Oxford, which had honoured Kipling, was infinitely to be preferred] but Clare – C-L-A-R-E-!!!' Now he openly talked of leaving school as soon as he could. With his deficient eyesight and low academic achievement there was no way he would cruise into Sandhurst as was expected of many a Wellingtonian. The decision was made to send him to a 'crammer' in Bournemouth to help him pass the entrance exam. He duly started there on 4 May 1914.

On Sunday 19 July the family attended an unusual event. Much to their surprise John had made his own decision to be baptized. Carrie wrote, 'John lunches with us and we go directly after to St Peter's Church to see him baptised and be his witnesses.' It showed an admirable initiative. The Kiplings were not particularly religious in a conventional sense – hence John not having been baptized as a baby, as would have been expected at that time, and he was often teased about his love of the church. On 3 October 1913 Rudyard had written to him, 'I know you love the clergy so you will be glad to know that His Grace the Archbishop of Canterbury is coming to Bateman's next week. *This is true*! I wish you were here to make him welcome.'

Ten days after his baptism John graduated from his crammer 'with a good report', his schooling over, but his carefree days were short-lived. On 4 August *The War that will end War*, to quote the over-hopeful title of H.G. Wells's book, broke out.

Chapter 5

THE GREAT WAR:

Rudyard's Involvement. The Manchild Attempts to Enlist.
Rudyard's Influence. The Irish Guards. The Search for
George Cecil. Training at Warley Barracks. Anxiety
Grows. To the Front.

> *For all we have and are*
> *For all our children's fate,*
> *Stand up and take the war.*
> *The Hun is at the gate!*
>
> Rudyard Kipling, 1914.

Throughout 1913 and the first half of 1914, Kipling had been concerned
with politics and the impending war that he knew and loudly proclaimed
to be inevitable and the lack of preparedness for which caused him
immense anxiety. On his return from Egypt the Irish question was his
greatest worry. He strongly felt that Ulster should force the Government
to abort the proposed Irish Home Rule Bill. Prophetically he wrote to
H.A. Gwynne, now Editor of the *Morning Post* and with whom he
frequently corresponded, 'The South Irish have no passion for Home Rule
as such. They realize it would be against their business interests; their
leaders know that the money to finance a new revolt could not come from
Ireland, but must come from the U.S.' Lord Roberts, Lord Milner, Sir
Edward Elgar, Gwynne and Bonar Law shared his concerns and they all
pledged allegiance to the Ulster Covenant to prevent the Catholic south
from taking control of the Protestant north. They became known as 'the
Covenanters' and Roberts was elected their first president. There is a story
that Kipling himself made a substantial financial contribution to its funds.
He certainly wrote an inciting, Cassandra-like poem, entitled *Ulster*,

> The dark eleventh hour
> Draws on and sees us sold
>   To every evil power
> We fought against of old.
>   Rebellion, rapine, hate,
> Oppression, wrong and greed
>   Are loosed to rule our fate,

By England's act and deed.
What answer from the North?
One Law, one Land, one Throne.
If England drive us forth
We shall not fall alone!

This was followed by a rabble-rousing anti-Government speech by Kipling on 16 May 1914 on Tunbridge Wells common attended by a reported 10,000 Unionists. It was an unusual act for him: he always professed to hate public speaking, but in this case the subject matter riled him into action. The speech was widely reported and not well received. The *Manchester Guardian* called it a 'wild outburst'. Even Carrie was swept up in the whirlwind and became an active member of the ladies' committee to provide relief to loyalist refugees from Ulster.

In July Rider Haggard lent the Kiplings his house, Kessingland Grange, on the Suffolk coast near Lowestoft. The house had been threatened by the erosion prevalent on that part of the coast and Haggard constructed elaborate earthworks to protect it. His daughter Lilas described the house as resembling 'a large, stationary ship, which perhaps gave Rider the idea of naming every bedroom . . . after a British Admiral'. No wonder it appealed to Rudyard, who confirmed that staying there was indeed like living on board ship. At the beginning of the month Haggard was only fifteen miles away at Ditchingham which added to Kipling's pleasure. They all seemed very remote from the drama that was playing out in Middle Europe. On 28 June the heir to the Austro-Hungarian throne, the Archduke Francis Ferdinand, and his wife were assassinated in Sarajevo by the Serbian nationalists Princip and Cabrinovic. The event triggered a fateful game of dominoes whereby Austro-Hungary, Germany, Russia, France, Belgium and Great Britain were gradually knocked into a state of war.

The Kiplings were first aware of the crisis when Helen Cecil, who had been staying with them at Kessingland Grange, was sent for to join her father, Lord Edward Cecil, who had been recalled from leave 'because of the war' on 31 July. The Kiplings stayed on in Suffolk and on that momentous day of 4 August, when Britain finally declared war on Germany, Carrie wrote in her diary, 'My cold possesses me'. Rudyard, seeing the significance of the wider picture, added, 'incidentally Armageddon begins'. He also wrote to his old Burwash friend Colonel Feilden, 'I feel like Jonah or whoever it was who went about saying: I told you so.' From Kessingland he had been observing the 'sea and all the drama of the skirts of war laid out before us. Destroyers going up and coming down in twos and fours – then a gunboat or so,' as he described in a letter to R.D. Blumenfeld of the *Daily Express*.

John, naturally, was swept up in the general youthful euphoria that prevailed: the feeling that it would all be over by Christmas and that one must get a slice of the action before it was all over. He was itching to enlist. On 10 August he left Bateman's for London set on volunteering for a commission in Kitchener's New Army. He failed. His eyesight was too bad. By the time that Rud, Elsie and Carrie reached Brown's Hotel John had already left to stay the night with Colonel Feilden and to lick his wounds. A week later, on his 17th birthday, he tried again and set off with Rud to Hastings and then to Maidstone. Once more he failed. Carrie noted in her diary, 'They will not have him on account of his eyesight'. There was now talk of him enlisting as a private soldier. As revealed by the release of a number of WW1 soldiers' records at the Public Record Office in February 1998, John's 'Application for a Temporary Commission', dated 19 August 1914, included the information that his right eye had 6/36 vision – with glasses 6/9 – and his left eye 6/36 – 6/6 with glasses. According to the authors' optician this means that without glasses he would have had difficulty in making out any of the letters on the second line of a standard eye-test chart and even with glasses would not have got anywhere near the bottom. His moral character was attested to by Colonel Feilden and by his Wellington housemaster, though the best Pearson could find to say was that John had been 'in the middle school and reached no position of responsibility'.

Rudyard wrote to Julia Depew on 28 August, 'John is trying very hard to get a commission but as he is only seventeen and his eyes are not what they should be, it is somewhat difficult.' Later [in the *Kipling Journal* of October 1943] she wrote, 'Lord Roberts was an intimate friend of Rud's and John insisted so much that I believe Lord Roberts rather overlooked the calendar.' On 2 September Carrie, too, noted that Rud had decided to ask Lord Roberts for a nomination for a commission for John. He was calling in his debt from Vernet and for his support for Roberts' campaign for National Service. On 3 September Carrie wrote to her close friend Lady Edward Cecil, 'I wanted badly to write to you yesterday, but I practically sat at the end of a telegraph wire the whole day. Rudyard was in town trying to arrange about John's commission. The Coldstreams is impossible, there is a tremendous waiting list of reserve officers, and now we are trying for something else with a nomination. With the greatest difficulty Rudyard was persuaded to ask Lord Roberts for one, and I hope that it will go through . . . They want Rudyard to speak at a recruiting meeting in Brighton next week, but I do not know whether he is going to be able to manage it with the other things he has undertaken to do. The best recruiting agents are the Germans, if we just wait a bit they may be depended upon to do their job!' In fact on 7 September Rudyard gave an impassioned recruiting speech at Brighton, which he had to repeat as so many people had come to listen to him.

On 10 September Rudyard drove up to town to meet Lord Roberts at the Irish Guards HQ at Wellington Barracks. It seemed the height of irony that after all his virulent anti-Irish rantings, Kipling should be pleading for a commission for his son in this crack Irish Regiment. It had been formed in April 1900, as 'Her Majesty the Queen [Victoria], having deemed it desirable to commemorate the bravery shown by the Irish regiments in the recent operations in South Africa, has been graciously pleased to command that an Irish regiment of Foot Guards be formed. This Regiment will be designated "The Irish Guards"' [Army Order No. 77]. The new regiment had its first public service as the guard of honour at the reception by HRH the Prince of Wales, at Paddington, of Lord Roberts, the Commander-in-Chief, on the occasion of his return from the field of operations in South Africa. He was soon appointed their Colonel. In 1914, at the age of 82, 'Bobs' was still energetic and enthusiastic, ready to do his bit. He had hinted to Kitchener, somewhat surprisingly rushed back from Egypt to become Secretary of State for War and, thanks to Alfred Leete, soon to become the most famous recruiting poster of all times, that he would dearly love to serve under him as C-in-C Home Forces. But Kitchener, in view of the old soldier's frailty, merely gave him the consolation prize of Colonel-in-Chief of Overseas Forces.

Bobs still had influence, however, and Rudyard was able to return with the exciting news that John was to report for duty almost immediately. 'I write to say I will gladly nominate John for the Irish Guards if that Regiment will suit him. I ask because I am not sure whether you would like to have him [in] the guards. If you would rather not no doubt I could get him nominated for some other Regiment. Kindly let me know,' he wrote to Rudyard. The offer was gladly accepted and two days later the longed-for commission arrived, back-dated to 16 August.

The next day the whole family escorted him to town for a last binge together after visiting some of the estate workmen in the village to say goodbye. The current secretary, Miss Chamberlain, was 'working hard to put John's affairs in order'. In London John had a haircut and visited his tailor for an hour to work on his uniform. The family then planned to lunch together before John left for Brentwood where his regiment was training. There 'He has a small room for himself a cot bed and mattresses, brings his sheets and blankets and, says the Colonel, a pillow if he cares for such things. I hope he will prove strong enough for the job. Rud thinks it may be a good thing for him. At any rate he goes from the stiff life of a public school which means much. I hope we shall be able to see him from time to time when he can get leave and come to town. He is only 40 minutes from London,' Carrie told her mother. She hoped that he would not 'go on foreign service until after Xmas'. The day after John reported to Warley Barracks in Essex (14 September) Carrie wrote to her mother, 'We sent John away yesterday to his new life with outward good spirits and inward misery, but it must be born and after all every mother I know has had to do the same.' Her solidarity with others in the same position was to help her later. John was immediately plunged into the frenetic life of a raw subaltern in training. 'He had no voice left when he wrote as he had been put to drill 20 recruits and his voice was not up to the strain,' wrote his concerned mother, but she reassured herself, 'you see he has done a lot of very real soldiering at school where they are trained properly in army drill and shooting by Army men and he did it every term for his four years so he had a start at his new trade.'

Meanwhile Rudyard had been watching the news from Belgium as the Germans swept through this supposedly neutral country, over-running the fortified towns of Liège and Namur, forcing the surrender of Brussels. Feelings of support for 'Poor Little Belgium' were running hysterically high. The recruiting offices were beseiged by young men who were as eager as John to do their bit. The mobilization machine cranked into gear, faithfully following the section in the War Book entitled, 'In the Event of War with Germany'. The British Expeditionary Force (B.E.F.), under the command of Sir John French, was rushed out just in time to meet the advancing German mass at Mons on the Franco-Belgian border. There the two armies clashed head-on on 23 August. At Bateman's Rudyard was completing his call-to-arms poem, *For All We Have and Are*, which ends,

> No easy hope or lies
> Shall bring us to our goal,
> But iron sacrifice
> Of body, will and soul.
> There is but one task for all –
> One life for each to give.
> What stands if Freedom fall?
> Who dies if England live?

The life that Kipling had to give was, of course, John's.

The poem was published on 1 September in *The Times* and on that day the war came unhappily close to the Kiplings for the first time. Their young friend George Cecil had passed out from Sandhurst in January 1914 and joined the 2nd Battallion, the Grenadier Guards. He was a frequent visitor at Bateman's and had come to stay on 13–14th July. His friend John Manners, the son of Lord and Lady 'Hoppy' and 'Con' Manners and a cousin of the dazzling Manners sisters, Violet, Marjorie and Diana, (who, confusingly, also had a brother John) the children of the Duke and Duchess of Rutland with whom the Kiplings occasionally stayed, served with him in the regiment.

They were due to go out to France with the B.E.F. on 12 August 1914. They were very close and, like John Kipling, were typical products of their age, class and schooling, carefree and dedicated to pleasure. Cecil felt somewhat protective of John Manners and wrote to his father that he was not liked 'because he was frightened'. John had another protector at school (Eton) in the form of Duff Cooper, two years his senior. 'Imaginative boys of seventeen,' wrote Duff Cooper in his autobiography, *Old Men Forget*, 'who read poetry demand some outlet for sentiment, and if they are surrounded during the greater part of the year by their own sex, as our public-school system decrees, and if the remainder of their time is spent in the narrow circle of their own family, as it was in my case, it is not surprising that masculine friendships should become infected or sublimated by a spirit of romance. It would be foolish to disregard the danger that attends such relationships, but it can easily be exaggerated. Normal young men with broad interests and healthy appetites can afford to gild their masculine friendships with a little of the gold they will lavish on their first love affairs and there is nothing in my life upon which I look back with less remorse than the almost passionate affection I felt for my greatest friend. John Manners combined personal beauty and athletic prowess with a love of literature.' What Rudyard Kipling would have thought of this unashamed confession of probable 'beastliness' concerning a friend of a friend of his son one can only shudder to contemplate. A curious irony is that, just as Rudyard had married the sister of the man he loved and who died, so Duff Cooper would marry John Manners' cousin, the beautiful siren, Diana Manners.

From the moment a nervous George Cecil and his friend set off for the front on 12 August their story unfolded in a manner that would be repeated in an extraordinarily similar way the following year by John Kipling. Like John they were to be thrown into the deep end of warfare – in their case in the exhausting Retreat from Mons. They, too, wrote graphic letters home to their families describing their experiences. The Grenadiers' withdrawal took them to the thick forest of Villers Cotterets to a circular clearing called the Rond de la Reine where on 1 September, in a bayonet charge in support of the Irish Guards (John Kipling's Regiment), Manners was killed and Cecil was reported missing, all their men being killed, wounded or taken prisoner.

Knowing his love for John Manners, Lord Congleton of the 2nd Bn the Grenadiers – who was to be sent out on 19 September with a small group of officers to replace the losses of 1 September, but who would only last until 10 November when he was killed near Ypres – wrote to Duff Cooper, describing the heroic action of the Grenadiers and saying, 'Cecil and John were shot dead'. Although Duff had at first heard rumours to the effect that Manners was missing, Congleton's letter killed his hopes. He passed the letter on to Lady Manners and she in turn sent it to Lady Edward.

The news that George was missing at Villers Cotterets had already reached Lady Edward. On 5 September she received a letter from Brig-General the Hon W. Lambton, Military Secretary to Sir John French and a personal friend, 'I am afraid that by now you must have got the bad news that your boy is wounded and missing!' At this stage Lady Edward employed all the power of an influential, wealthy and privileged family to find out what had happened to George. It is an interesting case from several points of view. Firstly it showed exactly the sort of undemocratic process that was made possible by that privilege which, as we shall see, Fabian Ware was dedicated to eliminating when he created the Imperial War Graves Commission. Secondly, as the Kiplings were among the first to be approached for help, it was to give them a complete run-through of what they would have to do when they found themselves in a similar position. Lastly, it is interesting to note that in both cases Kipling was quite prepared to pull all the strings he could, though later he was to subscribe completely to Ware's principles of equality of treatment in death. In a letter to her mother, which contains some impressive name-dropping, Carrie was concerned that poor Lady Edward still had no news of her boy 'but Mr Roosevelt is asking the Kaiser to give him a list of our wounded'.

Lady Edward had two distinguished brothers. One was Frederick Ivor Maxse ('Freddy') who was in command of 18th Division. The other, Leo James Maxse, was editor of the *National Review*, an outspoken crusader for human rights and justice who had campaigned for national awareness of the 'German menace' before the war broke out. He joined in the family's search for news of George and on 9 September he wrote to his sister Violet, 'I have just seen a man who crosses to Paris to-night with instructions to get hold of the fastest car he can find and make his way to Compiègne to collect any possible news. It is much the best chance but of course there is a doubt about his getting through as we don't know whether there are Germans at Compiègne or not.' In fact there were, as Carrie confirmed in her letter to Violet of 3 September: 'Our friends who started their hospital at Compiègne – Chauncey and Julia Depew who lived at Château d'Annel – had to flee to Havre as they were in the firing line on the 31st.' If there were, Maxse considered that an American – they were still neutral at this stage – might get through. 'You may rely on everything being done,' he reassured. 'Northcliffe [Lord Northcliffe, the newspaper magnate, who was to lose his nephew, Val Harmsworth, with the Royal Naval Division in 1916] is splendid and a most kind-hearted man.' A second letter written by Leo that day advised applying to the family's old friend, Clemenceau, then between terms as French Prime Minister, as it was 'most difficult to get any wires through'. This Lady Edward would do.

In London her next port of call was to Sir Edward Goschen, Ambassador in Berlin before the War. Goschen it was who had delivered the fateful ultimatum to the German Chancellor, von Bethmann-Hollweg, not to violate Belgian neutrality or Britain would have to consider herself at war with Germany. The two men had been good friends and

Bethmann-Hollweg professed his astonishment that Britain was prepared to take this drastic action, all for the sake 'of a scrap of paper' (the Treaty of 1839 which guaranteed Belgian neutrality). Feelings ran so high in Berlin that the British Embassy had been stoned and the Ambassador and his staff had to be escorted to a special train which took them to the Hook of Holland and thence back to London. Goschen wrote to Lady Edward from Portman Square, where he was staying with a friend who had a nephew with the 3rd Hussars who was also missing, to say that they too had received no answer from the American Embassy in Germany. He recommended she try the *'Bureau Central* of the *Croix Rouge* in Geneva'. Meanwhile Carrie, anxious to help, was trying her American connections and had wired Myron Herrick, the American Ambassador in Paris. Then came a comforting letter from Lord Roberts to say that 'several army medical officers are reported missing and if your son is wounded I trust they would be able to attend to him'.

Now Lady Edward played her trump card. She somehow got herself out to Paris and from the Hotel France et Choiseul she wired Clemenceau, now in Bordeaux. He immediately used his considerable influence with the English Ambassador and the French Minister of War to get her authorization to go to Villers Cotterets. The American Ambassador lent her his car and once there Violet met the Mayor, Dr Mouflier, and his wife, a nurse at the local hospital, thus starting a warm acquaintance that would last for 44 years until the Moufliers were both dead.

Lord Robert Cecil, her brother-in-law, had already been to nearby Vivières. Few families could have afforded, or could have pulled strings, to make such a journey, yet it resulted in little comfort or concrete news for the Cecils.

Lady Edward returned to find conflicting accounts of her son's last seen movements, exactly as would happen to the Kiplings. One comfort to her was that Con, Lady Manners shared her feelings and they communicated frequently with each other, clutching at mutual straws, even though Con had already been told that her son was dead. It was a syndrome that was to be repeated by Carrie Kipling a year later. Now she and Rudyard were still beavering away. 'Rud has contacted the American Ambassador in Berlin who will be glad to do something for him,' reported Carrie on 2 November, searching for crumbs of comfort to dispense. They had been following news of the recent fighting and were 'so thankful George is out of it. The earlier work was in quite a different spirit – the sort of thing George would have imagined war to be perhaps. Now it's all quite different.'

Though an intelligent and worldly woman, Violet Cecil, despite mounting evidence to the contrary, was clinging on to the straws of hope that George might not be dead. She was soon forced to abandon the last, unlikely embers that kept that spark alive. For on 17 November a Red

Cross Enquiry Department party that included Lord Killanin, brother of Colonel Morris of the Irish Guards, visited Villers Cotterets to exhume the bodies that had been hastily buried after the 1 September engagement. He identified his brother's body from the gold watch on his wrist and George's body from initials on his uniform. They and other officers were reburied in the village cemetery; Dr Mouflier helped throughout and for the rest of his life and, after he died, for the rest of her life, his wife, continued to cherish all the British graves in their commune.

Lord Robert Cecil, George's uncle, who, as an officer of the Red Cross, had accompanied the party, sent Killanin's report to Violet. His only comfort for her was that 'terribly sad as it was I can honestly say that it was in a way deeply consoling – somehow the great beauty of the place . . . made one see a little that even war with all its horrors was consistent with the Divine government of the world . . . It is impossible to grieve for him – a wonderfully perfect life – so affectionate, so upright so true so innocent – followed by a painless and glorious death.' Today one would not imagine that these sentiments would console a bereaved mother. But in 1914, the war still a few months old, the concepts of chivalry, patriotism, honour and glory were still very much alive, the legacies of wars fought in distant lands whose news was filtered by the long journey home into heroic deeds by heroic men. Parents still felt obliged to be proud to sacrifice their sons for such high principles. Certainly the Kiplings felt this obligation to encourage John to serve his King and country. This attitude was epitomized by a famous letter printed in the *Morning Post* and reproduced by an appalled Robert Graves in *Goodbye to All That*. It was 'A Message to the Pacifists. A Message to the Bereaved. A Message to the Trenches. By a Little Mother' and was in answer to a soldier, who, fed up with the horror of the trenches, felt that it was time to sue for peace. 'We the women, who demand to be heard, will tolerate no such cry as "Peace! Peace!" where there is no peace,' was the Mother's reply. 'The corn that will wave over land watered by the blood of our brave lads shall testify to the future that their blood was not spilt in vain . . . We women pass on the human ammunition of "only sons" to fill up the gaps, so that when the "common soldier" looks back before "going over the top" he may see the women of the British race at his heels, reliable, dependent, uncomplaining . . . Women are created for the purpose of giving life, and men to take it.' So in tune with the current white heat of fervour was this battle cry that the newspaper was forced to reproduce it in pamphlet form and 75,000 copies sold in less than a week. Its sentiments were echoed by the bands of women who issued white feathers to any men not wearing uniform and by the virulent and blithely insensitive poetess, Jessie Pope, to whom Wilfred Owen addressed his bitter poem *Dulce et Decorum Est*.

Kipling, too, on visiting Villers Cotterets later, felt that the 'one long rustic-fenced grave' was 'perhaps the most beautiful of all resting places in France, on a slope of the forest off the dim road, near the Rond de la Reine' [*Irish Guards History*]. The discovery of George's body did not stop his considerable efforts to chart for Violet the last moments of her son's short life. His passionate love for his own son contrasted strongly with that of Lord Edward Cecil, who had been a remote and absentee father for many years. 'Beloved V,' he wrote to his wife when the news of George's death came through, 'I cannot tell you how awfully I feel for you. There is nothing in the world so terrible as this must be for you. In comparison my own seems so much less. I have my work and though I love George as much as any father loves his son yet of course I know that a mother's love is like nothing else on earth.' All the letters to John that remain surely demonstrate that Kipling felt that his fatherly love was just as strong and demonstrative as Carrie's motherly love. He sympathized strongly with Violet, and Carrie repeatedly wrote saying that he was doing everything he could. Mostly it involved a careful tracking down of the surviving Grenadiers and Irish Guardsmen who had been in the Villers Cotterets fight. There were several letters from Carrie to Violet in early December about the arrangements to go to Gatcombe House and other hospitals. There he interviewed three witnesses, James, Barker and Titcombe. He then meticulously pieced together the probable jigsaw of George's last hours and wrote them up in a report. A further witness, Snowden, who had to go to Brown's to meet Rudyard, was then interviewed. 'Now, and as far as you will ever get it from a soldier present at the fight, I think you have the whole story,' he wrote to Violet on 8 December. The family was grateful to Kipling and felt that his account to be 'as clear as one could expect'. Colonel Smith of the Grenadiers was less enthusiastic. 'I am afraid private soldiers' stories are generally misleading.' This Rudyard was to find when he repeated the interviewing process that he had now refined in the later search for news of his own boy.

Whilst Rudyard and Carrie were so involved in their friends' tragedy, the Kipling family's involvement in the war and, in particular, John Kipling's short career, were progressing.

Once Rudyard had gone through the frenetic and emotionally charged process of getting John nominated into the Irish Guards he suffered a powerful reaction and a physical collapse. Already he had had to absorb the fear engendered by George Cecil's disappearance. The news from the front was disturbing. Their old friend Julia Depew, managing to get across the Channel to visit them, told harrowing tales of German atrocities. At her château near Compiègne, converted into a hospital, she insisted that she had seen an English surgeon with his hands cut off so that he could not help his own wounded and had spoken to Belgian friends who had been 'ravaged four times in an hour'. 'Rud is ill,' commented Carrie to her diary on 21 September. She reported that he was suffering from acute toothache from the stump of a tooth cut to fit his new plate. Rudyard, in a letter to Elsie, who was staying with Mrs Bonar Law at Castle Menzies in Scotland, called it a 'variorum mixture of neuralgia, toothache and temperature . . . Mummy was more different sorts of an angel to me than even she had ever been before,' he continued pathetically, 'and you can guess how much that meant!' In addition there were new worries about his sister Trix and her husband, whom Carrie pronounced to be 'pig-headed' and 'himself rather off his head'. She went on to say that Rud only recovered when John arrived for a weekend's leave on 26/27 September, 'already much set-up . . . He looked so nice in his uniform. Nothing impresses me as much as to see English officers in uniform in the streets,' she continued in true 'Little Mother' mode. Rudyard told Elsie that he felt John 'very much becomes his uniform . . . It was a changed John in many respects but all delightful. A grave and serious John with an adorable smile and many stories of "his" men . . . The Irish Guards I gather are racially and incurably mad – which of course suits J. down to the ground' – a comment which shows that John was by no means the stolid character that is often portrayed. More down to earth, Carrie felt that the effect of the 'general sadness means that John and Elsie look 25 instead of their real age.' She thought that, although 'Rud is gaining slowly . . . in his happiness to have John yesterday [he] did a little too much.' Elsie was 'over-tired from grief of loss of friends . . . She says very soon she won't know anyone who is alive.' To bolster everyone's confidence John was indulged with a motor car. It was a Singer: 'I don't think, honestly, that there's a better car in the market. It's her amazing strength, speed and handiness that attracts me,' raved the motor enthusiast Rudyard. The car had to be given the name of some eminent singer, of course. Patti and Car-uso were suggested, as was 'Dépêche Melba'!

Already Carrie was beginning to worry about John going to the front. Rudyard had been more philosophical in a letter to his publisher Frank Doubleday of 11 September, 'We are all settling down to the business of war now. John goes off in a day or two to join his battalion at Warley in Essex, and – the rest is as God shall dispose.' On 16 October Carrie wrote to her mother that John was well, in good spirits and 'posted for picket duty'. 'A new draft of six officers and a number of men went from his regiment to the front last week and one day it will come John's turn: but we hope it won't before Spring.' The war was coming ever closer to them at Bateman's and Carrie was concerned about 'a Belgian family of refugees just come to this part two such delightful pretty girl children 6 and 8 without hands. The Germans cut them off.' Stories of such outrages were rife at the time: babies used for bayonet practice, women raped and their breasts cut off, civilians used as human shields in front of columns of German soldiers, wholesale massacres of civilians. It was always considered after the war that tales of German atrocities had been grossly exaggerated in order to stoke the fires of recruiting fervour and a 1922 enquiry set up by the Belgian Cardinal Mercier to investigate such incidents found no substantiation or any real supporting evidence. Yet intelligent, responsible people like the Kiplings and the Depews described them in vivid detail and new research in the 1990s gives credence to the findings of the Committee set up during the war by Viscount Bryce, former Ambassador at Washington. It concluded that the rules and usages of war had indeed frequently been broken and that 'murder, lust and pillage prevailed over many parts of Belgium on a scale unparalleled in any war between civilised nations during the last three centuries'.

Rudyard was still in correspondence with Theodore Roosevelt, whom he regarded as a kindred spirit and whose son Kermit and his wife had come to stay at Bateman's just before the war broke out, in July 1914. He wrote to him and to Doubleday in anger at Belgian women and girls being publicly raped (the stories he had heard from Julia Depew) by German officers' order, 'I know it must be difficult to give you any idea of it, but – believe me – it is true, and the half of the truth has not yet been revealed – for obvious reasons. And so this Hell-dance goes on: and the U.S. makes no sign,' he wrote to the latter, exhorting him to be as neutral as he liked but not to let the brutalities be passed over in silence. His anger spawned the story *Swept and Garnished* which tells of a German woman who in her illness-induced delirium sees the child victims of atrocities described to her by her soldier son serving in Belgium.

In his desire always to be at the nub of things, Kipling made visits to nearby military hospitals, already full of the wounded of Mons, Le Cateau, the Retreat and the Battle of the Marne. He visited training camps, gathering material for his booklet, *The New Army in Training*, delighting in mingling once more with 'the brutal and licentious', renewing acquaintance with the modern versions of Mulvaney, Ortheris and Learoyd. At Salisbury Plain and Larkhill, at Portsmouth and at the south coast camps, he talked to men from Devon and Scotland, Canada and South Africa and, to his great pleasure, from his beloved India.

One young man chafing at the bit at not being able to join them was Oliver Baldwin. Now that his big cousin John had joined the Irish Guards, he couldn't wait to follow him, but at only fifteen and a half had to be content with training at Trinity College, Cambridge, where he was visited by Carrie and Rudyard on 18 October. On the 31st the Kipling family wrote to him during one of John's 24-hour leaves at Bateman's. Rudyard thanked him for his letter 'which I observe is occupied mainly with John'. John himself added that 'we have pretty stiff training in the Brigade but it is great fun. With luck I ought to be out at the front in eight weeks.' He promised that if he were to be stationed at Windsor he would come over 'and have tea some day and we will "gas" about the dirty German'. Elsie exhorted him to work hard 'like a good boy!' and added, 'We are all very busy knitting socks making shirts and looking after wounded Belgians, as well as refugees.' Finally Rudyard wrote out the following advertisement:

<table>
<tr><td>✝ Burwash
🚂 Etchingham</td><td></td><td>Bateman's
Burwash
Sussex</td></tr>
</table>

C KIPLING & C0.

SHIRT-MAKERS TO H.M. REGIMENT OF IRISH GUARDS

1914 *established* 1914

HIGHEST STANDARD OF NEEDLE-WORK AND FINISH
GUARANTEED
PRE-WAR MATERIAL ONLY EMPLOYED

Individual Attention given to each Order

TERMS CASH

CUSTOMERS SENDING FIRST ORDER WILL FIND IT MOST SATISFACTORY TO FORWARD
OLD WELL-FITTING SHIRT FOR PATTERN

Socks - double heel and ditto secret French pattern toe -

a speciality. Orders must be given well in advance.

No note from Carrie appeared in the letter. She was preoccupied with John who she described as 'looking rather pale and tired'. On 5 November he was involved in a court martial, always a testing experience for a young officer. And then on 13 November his recent benefactor, Lord Roberts, died in St Omer, exhausted and chilled to the marrow by a gruelling visit to the front. Kipling, who hated 'writing to order', felt obliged to dash off an appropriate tribute in verse. Entitled *Lord Roberts*, it starts,

> He passed in the very battle-smoke
> Of the war that he had descried

and goes on to comment on the fact that 'Bobs' had been visiting the Indian troops who meant so much to him the day before he died,

> But, before his eye grew dim
> He had seen the faces of the sons
> Whose sires had served with him.

> He had touched their sword-hilts and greeted each
> With the old sure word of praise.

Kipling had fiercely identified with Roberts's disregarded plea for National Service.

> Never again the war-wise face,
> The weighed and urgent word
> That pleaded in the market-place–
> Pleaded and was not heard!

he wrote with affection and regret.

'Rud has known him since he was our John's age,' wrote Carrie to her mother. 'His death is a great personal loss.'

And so life went on: a series of snatched meetings with John, many of them at Brown's, reports of his exercises and training, route marches and trench digging; the knitting of socks and the packing of parcels for the Red Cross, the research on behalf of Lady Edward, until the first Christmas of the war arrived and it was obvious that the show wasn't going to be all over by 25 December. The situation at the front was such that by 2 December all officers had been recalled from leave and John was told that he had to stay within a certain distance of Warley. Christmas was spent, together with the Bonar Laws, at the Aitkens' (Sir Max, later Lord Beaverbrook) house near Leatherhead, as it was within what Carrie described as the 'prescribed' distance from the Barracks, which Bateman's was not.

The new year of 1915 dawned with the usual Kipling round of ailments. One cannot but help comparing the family to the entertainer Paddy Roberts's 'Englishman with his usual bloody cold' (a spoof translation of *sang-froid habituel*). On 5 January Carrie wrote to Lady Edward to say that she had been in bed since Christmas Day and was trying to get up sufficient strength to go to London to visit Sir John Bland-Sutton. 'It is a bother to me because it prevents my seeing John,' she complained, 'but we have very nice letters from him, and I think I shall be able to persuade Rud [it was a letter typewritten by her secretary, as Carrie maintained that she could not write herself, and she had crossed out the typewritten 'Mr Kipling' and written in 'Rud'] to leave me and go up to town this week, at any rate for a day and bring me word as to how he is.' She went on to explain that they often went to London only to find that John was unable to meet them. Although she felt that John would not be sent out at once, he was impatient to go and had to be calmed down. 'He has done four months' training now, and of the sort, of course, unknown before the war, and other months that he adds to that will be a great gain,' she attempted to reassure herself. By 14 January she was pronounced 'very ill' and recommended to rest in a dry climate with no anxiety! As she was unpacking at Brown's after her visit to Bland-Sutton, 'John who was not expected until 5.30 came in looking dreadfully ill. I got him into a hot bath gave him a pill and some hot tea and got him into bed in short order and there he spent Tuesday and as I could not discover what was the matter and he was still feeling slack I sent for a doctor who said a mild form of influenza (gripe) and exhaustion and advise our taking him home. This we did and put him to bed early last night and for the second night he slept 11 hours and looks better today.' Carrie could have had no better cure for her own ailments than to be called upon to fuss over John. When he recovered, John and Elsie went to his old prep school at Rottingdean and saw the growing Roll of Honour in the school church. 'That list will be a long one before it is finished,' commented Carrie with dread, as 'almost every boy who had been at the school since it started is either in the new Army or belonged to the regular services.' She was still hoping against hope that John would be 'considered too young to be sent to France before early summer except in case of an unexpected shortage of officers in his regiment.' An additional worry was Zeppelin raids. Although Carrie professed 'we don't think too much about them', nevertheless blackout curtains were made for Bateman's. Invasion was another fear. As early as the previous October Carrie had packed up many of Bateman's most treasured possessions and 'sent car loads of stuff useful and good away'.

On 1 March John was sent on a signalling course in London and the Kiplings moved into Brown's to see as much of him as possible. After the war one of John's fellow officers on this course wrote an amusing account, a version of which was published as *A Man at Arms* by Francis Law (Captain H.F.D'A.S. Law). He wrote of their riotous games in the Guards Club at Marlborough House where Stephen (his friend Lieutenant S.E.F. Christy, who had passed out of Sandhurst with Law in January when they had together entered the Irish Guards and who was to be killed in action on 12 July 1916) 'being large and strong was splendid on these occasions and little Johnny Kipling [his height on his service record was recorded as just 5'6½''] very small, a useful ally who fitted neatly under a table shooting out a leg neatly with admirable timing to leave attacking giants sprawling on the floor. There they looked foolish and were easy meat!' John, Francis and Stephen at Warley appear in the photo at Plate 4.

Law recalled the course they all attended at Chelsea Barracks when 'One morning as I debouched afoot from Lower Sloane Street Johnny Kipling did so too, but at speed in his little yellow Singer car and charged into a Battalion of Scots Guards taking them in the flank. Very sensibly those threatened scattered like starlings before continuing on their way, affronted no doubt, but happily undamaged. Next day came a complaint, fully justified, from Birdcage Walk calling for disciplinary action. We were all interviewed and all denied responsibility and were promptly confined to barracks until one of our number owned up. When a day or too had passed with no relief in sight we tended to look rather sourly at one another and it was time to search out Johnny. It happened that he had been laid up at home and off duty for two days [yet again!]. As soon as he was told of our plight he lost no time in informing authority that he alone was responsible and we were all set free.' No mention of this escapade appears in any of the Kipling Papers. There were some things that even John didn't tell his parents.

The question of why John was in an Irish Regiment was raised when Carrie and Rudyard went to St Leonards where both Rider Haggard and John and Elsie's old governess, 'Mademoiselle', were recuperating. Mademoiselle asked, 'But *why* is he in the Irish Guards?' Rudyard fudged a curious reply: that 'our family blood was "prudently mixed" in view of all international contingencies and that there was some Irish in the strain.' Then she couldn't understand why he was in the Army at all. '*If* there is no compulsion,' she said, 'why should John enter the Army?' 'Precisely *because* there is no compulsion,' was the Kiplingesque reply.

After the visit Rider Haggard noted in his diary on 23 March that 'Neither of the Kiplings look so well as they did at Kessingland. He is greyer than I am, and, as he says, his stomach has shrunk, making him seem smaller. I expect that anxiety about the war is responsible. Their boy John, who is not yet eighteen, is an officer in the Irish Guards, and one can see that they are terrified lest he should be sent to the front and killed, as has happened to nearly all the young men they know . . . I asked him what he was doing to occupy his mind amidst all these troubles. He answered – like myself – writing stories, adding, "I don't know what they are worth. I only know they ain't literature".'

One of the stories he had been working on was *Sea Constables* subtitled *A Tale of '15*. In it Rudyard showed off his technical knowledge of the navy, gained from his attendance at naval manoeuvres, laying himself open to the charge of obscurity that is often levelled at the story. The theme of retribution and revenge, taken to its ultimate in *Mary Postgate*, on which he was also working, is apparent in this story of four naval officers who pursue a neutral ship which they knew to be carrying oil to the enemy. Eventually the skipper, seriously ill with pneumonia, 'threw in the sponge', his engines were smashed with a hammer and he agreed to offer his oil to the Admiralty agent. The naval officers refuse his pleas to be taken to England to see his doctor and he dies. This Carrington found 'ethically deplorable'. The story certainly expressed the venom Kipling felt about the war for which, had his warnings been heeded, the country would have been, at the least, better prepared.

Lighter moments occurred when the amusing Rupert Grayson, a fellow officer of John's in the Irish Guards, became a frequent visitor to Bateman's with John. He wrote [in *Voyage not Completed* – his autobiography] a vivid and affectionate description of the house and its inhabitants with none of the gloomy impressions that met Kingsley Amis. He noted, 'The odour, so deeply satisfying, of old furniture that has stood for a lifetime on parquet floors, and of ash logs burning in a giant fireplace will always take my mind back to Bateman's.' He described it as 'a mellow sandstone house, gabled, with mullioned windows and high sixteenth-century brick chimneys,' where Rudyard loved to play at being an Englishman and a farmer to the extent of having 'R. Kipling, Bateman's, Burwash' painted on his farm-carts and had 'all the things that he had longed for, even to an English river wandering through his land'. Even so, Rupert perceived that at heart he was always a wanderer, 'who was never more than a man who lived in Sussex, though I think in his heart he longed to have been a Sussex man'. Much as Grayson liked and admired Kipling himself, he considered that 'he was essentially a man of the cities. In the village he was never popular' – an impression born out by Martin Seymour Smith.

By March 1915 Bateman's was full of keen officers of the 10th Bn the Loyal North Lancs who were billeted there whilst their men were practising digging trenches, posting sentries and outposts in the vicinity. Elsie had chicken-pox and John was advised to keep away as 'An ensign with chicken-pox is ridiculous'. Meanwhile John was given the daunting task of being sent to Dublin over the period of St Patrick's Day to bring back thirty-four recruits to Caterham. 'Can the "front" present a worse prospect than this little "Dublin Stunt"? *"Je pense que non"*,' he wailed. What relieved the 'most bloody trip' was staying at 'the best hotel in Ireland' – the Shelbourne – even though he moaned, 'By gad Dublin is a frowsy hole, all slums and stinks but the faces are all the same, just like Warley . . . I think I will go to a Music Hall tonight, it ought to be good fun.' He and Rudyard often went to the Alhambra and other music halls together. It was a shared manly pleasure which Carrie and Elsie were not always allowed to enjoy with them.

Rudyard's passion for the popular theatre and the heady atmosphere around it dated from his bachelor days in London in 1889/90, and C.B. Cochran in one of his autobiographies, *Cock-A-Doodle-Do*, quotes Kipling's reminiscences of the glory days of the old Pavilion theatre, 'One recalls the pious bobbies, and the virtuous chuckers out, on the peaceful occasions after the Army exams when Leicester Square and Piccadilly Circus used to fizz with young gentlemen, and ladies in yellow satin, who preferred sherry and lemonade to other drinks.' He certainly imparted this excitement to John. On 14 April he wrote to him from Bath where Carrie was taking one of her interminable cures and asked him to 'pick out a good show for Saturday night – something really amusing.'

John, who was currently on his signalling course, was finding it hard to maintain the fast life that he was now living and complained to his parents about his 'limited allowance'. Rudyard wrote back: 'I was looking over various trifling accounts for motor bikes, Singer cars and such like and find that I have expended within six months close on £300 for various forms of ironmongery with wheels. Not bad for a man who can't weigh more than 10.2 at the outside.' Despite the banter and the light-hearted outings, apprehension in the Kipling family was mounting. John was ill yet again – one wonders if there ever was a period when all four of them were fit – and had to be brought home, not returning to Warley until 30 April. He was then 'warned for the next draft' as Carrie wrote in her diary. On 2 May she told her mother that she was convinced that 'The Guards Brigade will be in the next fight. Their reserves are at their base in Harve [sic]. Meanwhile we wait and everything changes in a day.' She was concerned that capacity in all military hospitals was being increased to take the wounded from the next big battle. She had sent her mother photos of the children and was delighted that her family, so far away in America in this anxious time for her, were pleased with them. 'John is certainly a very smart well set up soldier and a nice boy into the bargain,' she preened with motherly pride. On the 24th John was at home yet again, 'with a serious attack of influenza. The doctor says he's "over-worked in mind and body". He rests and takes a tonic,' only getting up to take a long chair in the garden. He hoped to be back Thursday for work on Friday morning as 'they need him as soon as he is fit to go . . . Any day or hour the summons may come and one has to be ready in one's mind to face it.' An additional fear was the rumour Carrie had heard that Germans infected with plague were poisoning the rivers.

Nothing had happened by 30 May when Rudyard (after telling John that Max Aitken's brother had been wounded in the Dardanelles) wrote, 'We should most deeply appreciate a line from you to let us know how matters stand in the Irish Guards and what the prospects are of additional drafts being sent out.' This crossed with a racy letter from John: 'I went on the "Razlle-Dazlle" [sic] last night. Dinner at Princes, Alhambra and Empire next, then supper at the Savoy, then Murays [sic] and two other night-clubs of lesser repute. I left Town in the Singer at 10 past 3 a.m. and got here at 7 minutes to 4 (43 mins); that is "going some". I only met 2 taxies a cart on the way down being broad daylight I could move like hell.' One can almost hear Rudyard chuckling, 'That's my boy!' There was a more worrying section in the letter, however: 'We had 18 casualties in one day out there, and 15 officers were sent out whilst I was sick – just my luck. I have been warned to be ready to go out at 5 minutes notice, so it won't be long now. I have got the last of my kit together and am waiting.' Carrie would have inwardly cried, 'Not my boy!'

But still nothing happened. On 2 June Carrie confirmed to her mother that 'John's Regiment suffered more than I knew' and repeated his figures. He was under orders for the front. 'Of course that does not mean he will go . . . Only it does mean the arrangement for field kit and so on and I am so uncertain and anxious.' John's training intensified. 'We perspired sympathetically with you at every step of your route march,' wrote Rudyard on a hot 10 June. It was cooler on the 16th, but the route marches were still going on. On the 26th John was allowed leave and the

Rolls arrived at the barracks at 1200 to take him to Burwash where Rudyard was 'yearning for billiards', knowing that John 'doubtless wants strawberries'. As he returned to Warley Carrie wrote to her mother, 'John went back yesterday to start work this morning. A big draft has gone out in his absence and left them v short of officers and yesterday's casualty list had 11 junior and 4 senior officers in his battalion, 7 of them being officers of John's rank. Only 2 however killed so the rest may very well rejoin but it was a bad note for John to return on and the shortage of officers means ever harder work for him and of course increases the chance of his going out to France in spite of his age. We are all delighted in John's visit and he was so happy for the rest and quiet and good food all things he would have taken for granted this time last year.'

On 5 July the uncertainty was finally quelled. John wrote that Kerry (Lieutenant Colonel Henry William Edmond, Earl of Kerry, commanding the 2nd Battalion at Warley) had promised him that he 'would be the first ensign to go out to France after the 17th August [his 18th birthday] and I would have been too young then if I hadn't had a year's service in the Brigade. So going in early was a damned good move after all . . . I feel so bucked that the fatigue of the march does'nt [sic] trouble me a bit.' Rudyard was over the moon, but questioned Kerry's statement about his year's service being the reason why he would be allowed to go to France. 'It is because you deliberately went into it for a purpose and gave yourself up to the job of becoming a good officer. (I have heard indirectly from another source that you are considered to be "damned smart"),' he opined. John had told him that he had decided to sell the Singer, which was in want of repair. Had our daredevil young driver had an accident, returning to barracks early one morning from one of his nightclub sprees? Rudyard would have promised him anything at the moment, so full of pride and fear was he. 'Don't bother to sell the Singer,' he advised. 'Turn her in to the makers and tell 'em to repair her. I'll allow you £100 for her as she stands (you told me she was worth about that much). If you want the £100 I'll pay it into your account. If you don't, I'll let it stand over and put it aside towards a new car when you come back. Of course I'll pay for having the Singer repaired.'

The decision not to let John go to France until his 18th birthday meant that the Kiplings' readily granted permission to allow him to go overseas whilst still officially under-age was not actually needed.

John's excitement at the prospect of going to the front was brought short by the death of another close friend, Oscar Hornung, killed in the Ypres Salient where he was serving with the 2nd Bn the Essex Regiment on 5 July, the very day that John heard he was to go to France. A nephew of Conan Doyle, neighbour of the Kiplings, his body was never found and he is commemorated on the Menin Gate at Ypres. 'There is another of the "old Brigade" gone,' commented John. But life had to go on and John went to town to be fitted with new 'specs' for the great adventure. The next weekend he took Rupert Grayson with him to Bateman's and a jolly weekend was spent by all. This may have been the time when Rupert recalled how he 'had a sudden longing to see a little dancer I knew'. He sent her a telegram arranging to meet in London and departed, telling the Kiplings he had an appointment with his dentist. On his return the next day 'Rudyard Kipling handed me an open telegram. His eyebrows were raised and his eyes were twinkling. "I hope the dentist didn't hurt too much, old man," he said. The telegram he handed me read: "Meet me at stage door 5.30 love Irene".' Rupert also recalled how 'In London the Kiplings kept open suite in their old-fashioned rooms at Brown's in Dover Street. Since his first visit to London he had never stayed at any other hotel; he had grown old with it, with the servants and with the wine in its cellars.' Carrie certainly recorded Rupert's visit in her diary and mentioned various trips to music halls.

On 20 July John wrote to his parents excitedly telling them that his battalion had been officially sanctioned by His Majesty the King. They were no longer a '(res) Battln': the Irish Guards now had two regular battalions. What's more, the newly qualified young signaller was detailed by the Adjutant, Captain the Hon Thomas Eustace Vesey, to get sixteen trained signallers ready to go out with him in ten days time. The excitement was building. Preparations began in earnest. At Warley the Secretary of State for War, Lord Kitchener, who had succeeded Lord Roberts as the Irish Guard's Colonel-in-Chief, was expected any day to present the newly formed battalion with its colours and to inspect them. Rudyard had written to John on 23 February, just after 'K''s appointment, 'Dined at the Marlborough with Sir Reginald Braid [in fact 'Brade', the Permanent Under-Secretary of State to the War Office]. He told me with his own lips that K is "as pleased as Punch at being made Colonel of the Irish Guards".' Route marches continued – 19 miles in one day was reported, with men fainting like flies in the heat and falling out with cramp. There was a memorial service at St Paul's and a night march of 20 miles.

At Bateman's the Kiplings persuaded their dentist, Mr Norris, to see John at Brighton the following Sunday, it being thought, as Rudyard told John, 'very important that you should be overhauled as to your teeth'. Carrie bought him 'a perfect duck of a little electric lamp' and the shirt factory worked over-time. A letter to her mother on 6 August shows the terror she was feeling inwardly, a terror she would have tried hard to hide from her husband and children. It starts by recounting more bereavements for close friends. First there was 'Bobbie Longbotham, [actually 2nd Lieutenant Robert Longbottom of the King's Royal Rifle Corps, a Wellingtonian, killed on 31 July] killed yesterday, age 20. 3 months in France.' Then 'Another of our friends the Desboroughs with whom we have often stayed has been killed this week. A second son in 6 weeks.' The two sons were Julian Grenfell, author of the famous war poem *Into Battle*, and his brother Billy. Julian had been mortally wounded near Ypres and died in hospital at Boulogne on 26 May. His sister Monica was working as a VAD in nearby Wimereux and she was joined at Julian's deathbed by their parents – another example of the privileged, even in this second year of the war, still managing to travel to France. A telegram arrived from the hospital informing the Desboroughs of Julian's wound and invited them to 'Use this as permit'. This they did, travelling on an ammunition boat that got them to Boulogne the next morning. Billy was also killed in the Ypres Salient, on 30 July, but his body was never found and his name is recorded on the Menin Gate Memorial. 'There is one left,' continued Carrie,' aged 17 [Yvo] who is to start his training after Xmas. You write you don't see where one finds the courage to send a boy but there is nothing else to do. The world must be saved from the Germans . . . One can't let one's friends' and neighbours' sons be killed in order to save us and our son. There is no chance John will survive unless he is so maimed from a wound as to be unfit to fight.' At this stage, after writing these dreadful words, Carrie's writing and the spaces between lines became larger and larger. 'We know it and he does. We all know it but we all must give and do what we can and live in the shadow of a hope that our boy will be the one to escape.' There is none of the Little Mother's raucous jingoism here, simply an heroic and desperately sad fatalism.

About this time John wrote (in an undated letter) on the notepaper of the Royal Automobile Club in London. It was posted 'in a mourning envelope as it looks smarter'. An arrow, with the proud comment 'Some note paper'. Pointed to the heading. He had 'become a member of this pot-house for the payment of £3 (temporary war member). It is the most luxurious and palatial place you ever saw. You must come and dine with me here soon.' Whilst staying at his posh new club John had 'been buying the last little things'. He was particularly excited about the small 'Kukri' he had bought at Holtzappel, as 'nearly everyone takes out a sheath-knife. I thought this was the very thing, as one can cut wood & Boches with it equally (I think it will mostly be used for wood).' The shopping expedition had been provoked because 'I think Vesey's application about me has been passed by Frankie [possibly Major-General Sir Francis Lloyd, commanding London District, who was to inspect the battalion on 10 August, when he informed them that they were due for France in a few days] all right but stand by for old K [Kitchener] in case there is a hitch. I am going out if I have to dress as a drummer boy,' he added with deter-mination. The regimental gossip was all about the appointment, which became official on 27 July, of Major (Brevet Lieutenant Colonel) the Hon L.J.P. Butler as the Battalion's commanding officer whilst 'Jerry' (Major G.H.C. Madden) was appointed '2nd in command a post which will suit him very well as there is no responsibility, but he is furious at being brought back to be ragged about the CO-ship.' The blasé young officer ended his letter by requesting the Bateman's shirt factory to produce twelve collars similar to the one he was enclosing. More shirts were requested as 'Taylor [his servant] sent that shirt to the wash like a fool and it is the only one I've got, so carry on with the shirts as per instructions.'

On 11 August father and son met, unknowingly, for the last time. John was staying at the Bath Club in Dover Street and Rudyard, off to France the next day to visit the front to gather material for a series of articles for the *Daily Telegraph* under the title *France at War*, lunched with him. Then John, excited about his imminent departure, spent two hours with the manager at Harrods 'arranging for feeding the mess for which he is President', as Carrie wrote to her mother.

Lord Kitchener finally arrived at Warley to inspect his new battalion on 13 August. The review started at 8.30 and Rupert Grayson describes how, as usual, 'John was superbly smart, for he was meticulous about his appearance. Kitchener was seated between Lord Kerry and our commanding officer, the Hon. L.J.P. Butler. Unfortunately John, from his superior height, had noticed a grease-spot on the Field-Marshal's cap, which he immediately pointed to; and in the intense hush which precedes the taking of a photograph, his resonant voice broke the silence: "I told you, Rupert, that Kitchener would never have made a guardsman." After the photograph had been taken we made a quick getaway; we expected an immediate summons to the Orderly Room. Unwittingly, by speaking my name, John had involved me too; but fortunately the Kiplings' Rolls was waiting to take us down to Bateman's . . . I stayed for an hour, then made my farewells to these dear people who had been so kind to me. I too was going home to say even more poignant farewells; but it never occurred to me that for John this was the last night he would ever spend in the old house with those he loved so well.'

Carrie told her diary on 15 August that John was off to the front. 'He looks very smart and straight and grave and young as he turns at the top of the stairs to say, "Send my love to Daddo".'

Chapter 6

THE BATTLE OF LOOS:

*John Goes to France. Background and General
Description of the Battle. The involvement of the
2nd Battalion, the Irish Guards.*

*You have no idea what enormous issues depend on the next few days.
This will be my last letter most likely for some time.*

John Kipling, 25 September 1915.

Even while he was waiting to sail for France on the SS *Viper* John found time to write to his parents from Southampton on 16 August. His excitement was mounting: 'The men are behaving splendidly and the weather is top hole,' and he requested, importantly, that his 'first parcel of goods' should be sent to him at '2nd Btln 1 Gds Div. B.E.F.' The battalion sailed overnight and he landed at Le Havre on the very day that he was 18, the first birthday he had spent away from his family. Again he found time to describe the crossing to his 'Dear Old Things'. He had been chosen for Picquet Officer and spent the night patrolling the ship and posting sentries, so only got 4 hours' sleep in the last 48 hours. He requested '1 pair roomy carpet slippers 2 towels seize [sic] of face towel but rough 2 pairs of civilian black socks 1 pair brigade braces' and finished, in pure Julian Grenfell style, 'This is the life'. Carrie was so thrilled with the letter that she immediately relayed its contents to Lady Edward, commenting 'He is happy and serious, bless him.'

On the same day Rudyard, still in France on his war correspondent's work, wrote to John from Verdun equally boyishly excited about his trip, obviously unaware that his son was now also in France. He was having 'rather a good time. Been to several nice places including a bombarded town; had a squint at the Crown Prince's Army in the Argonne; seen Rheims (they weren't bombarding it for the moment) and have greatly admired French artillery. The men I saw in the trenches were mostly Saxons.' He actually got to see the enemy before his soldier son. Rudyard was also writing to Carrie. On 13 August he was staying in the Ritz in Paris and complained that, as he was dining at the next table to Maurice Baring, Private Secretary to Hugh Trenchard, first commander of the RFC, 'I saw one waiter playfully kick another man's behind right in the middle of the dining room.' He had received Carrie's letter 'with the news of John's final inspection and the success of it and K's remark to him. I am very proud.' He told her that on the 15th he would be in Soissons, in Rheims and Verdun on the 16th and in Toul and Nancy on the 17th.

On John's 18th birthday, a worried Carrie wrote from Brown's to Lady Edward, 'John left here at noon Sunday and I have no idea when they sailed. His servant, who came with some of his luggage last night, only wanted to say he "called Mr Kipling at 1.45 a.m." so I left it at that. Today is his birthday and I allow myself to feel its a bit of bad luck he is neither here or as far as I know there, at any rate he is not where a word can reach him . . . Rud writes constantly . . . The only real news is the strong impression he gathers of the entire failure of the Germans as a people to ever contemplate another winter in trenches. So we shall have an active time I take it up to November.' It was also active on the home front. 'They write from Bateman's of a "Zepp" over Tunbridge Wells last Thursday and a [sic] explosion. Have you heard?' Elsie was also feeling the strain and Carrie was concerned about her too. 'I think I shall send her to Scotland for a bit. She is young to live on the raw edge all the time and the change will perhaps divert her, though she don't know she wants it.'

Rudyard told Carrie that 'I wrote a line to John at le Havre before I left Verdun this morning and had it expressed and passed by the military so he ought to get it without delay.' The urgency was that it was a birthday letter. He was desperately hoping to meet up with his son as he embarked on his great journey. 'I can't see John at Havre unless he comes to the railway station as I go through and I can't stay a night in Havre because that isn't allowed. Beside,' he added understandingly, 'he wouldn't like to have me tracking after him yet. So I shan't see him now . . . Afterwards when I visit the English lines I may accidentally like run across him.' But it was not to be.

John had left le Havre and was getting nearer to the front. His letter of 18 August showed an inherited sense of observation as he described the day's progression, starting with the dramatic line, 'I am writing this in a train proceeding to the firing line at 15 m.p.h.' He was a caring young officer and he was worried that his men had been cramped. The whole battalion, 73 horses, 50 carts and 1100 men, had been packed into the one train with one engine to pull the lot. 'We are due at our destination at 11 a.m. tomorrow; till then we Black Hole of Calcut.' John was appreciative of the three 'quite pretty English ladies who had succoured the men with tea or coffee and great slabs of bread and butter' from their stall at one of the frequent stops. The approaching danger caused the adrenalin to course through the veins of the subalterns who had 'great fun', sticking their bare feet out of the train window, singing, smoking, eating bread, sardines and jam, drinking whisky and water – 'A-1!!'

Rupert Grayson remembered how 'from the ship's decks we watched the Channel waters swishing by. We knew nothing except that we were sure "to see the fun" before it was over, and that on the approaching shore there would be wine awaiting us and romantic encounters with lovely French girls.' Reading these innocent, hopeful words eighty years later in the knowledge of what these boys – they were scarcely young men – were headed towards makes one want to shout out 'STOP! TURN BACK' in a futile Canute-ish hindsighted gesture. Carrie's appalling, resigned words, that John would only survive if he was so dreadfully maimed that he wouldn't be able to fight any more, also ring in the ears. He, apparently, was oblivious to these fears and demanded an Orilux service lamp for officers, plus a refill. Touchingly he enclosed a cutting from a newspaper which reported Rudyard's progress in France, 'I follow his movements in the paper,' he said.

Grayson described how the battalion detrained at Lumbres, the railhead, and set out to march to battle along the never-ending French *pavé*. 'The only transport then considered fit for the infantry was one pair of hob-nailed ammunition boots per man. Only field officers were mounted and the transport was mule-drawn. As we marched we sang soldiers' bawdy songs, mile after mile, day after day.' John's letter to his 'Dear F—' of 20 August described their comfortable billet in Acquin (complete with 'a very pretty daughter – Marcelle – who is awfully nice and we get on very well') and the fact that Grayson's hope of compliant French girls was already fulfilled, as he 'has discovered a French girl who rather resembles Gaby [their favourite Gaiety Girl, Gaby Deslys] in appearance and very much so in morals so he is quite happy.' The men, too, were managing to fraternize successfully: 'talking French they are screamingly funny, but they manage to get on very well with the French girls.'

Despite all their training at Warley, the march to their first billets was gruelling for the rookie troops. 'At the end of each day's march I could have dropped exhausted wherever the halt was made and slept for ever,' wrote Grayson, 'but I had to see to it that my men were fed, inspect their feet – it was our pride that no man should fall out – and install them in what-ever shelter was available. They were even wearier and more footsore than I. They squatted on their packs with drooping heads like winded horses.' This concern to see to the men's comfort before their own was standard practice for junior officers of the B.E.F. and largely accounts for the excellent relations between the two elements.

One thing was guaranteed to buck the tired men up, however. This was the news, as Grayson related in a delightful and vivid cameo, 'that Alex was to dance'. At this news, 'the entire battalion would be seated round the platform, some with bottles of unaccustomed vino, but all quietly as became men who had marched their twenty-five miles. Each knew that a man they loved, their commander who marched with them footsore step for step, was ready to dance for their delight. His performance had an electrifying effect on them, for Alex was always the complete individualist. He wore a hat with the upper part elevated and pressed back a la Russe and beneath it his fair moustache.' Expecting some exotic Cossack dance, 'it was only with the discordant wail of the squeeze box and the cries of the men that one realised that the dance was the nostalgic jig and the music was the music of the defiant Gael. There Alex would be "steppin" on an improvised wooden platform, head erect, arms and body rigid, and feet tapping and lifting and leaping and crossing and clicking like objects with a life of their own, as the lads in rural Ireland jig at the cross-roads after Mass on Sundays. And the men would sit enthralled, their weariness cast off, stamping their feet and clapping their hands and uttering wild Gaelic yells and battle-cries to the tap of their feet.' This precursor of the Lord of the Dance in *River Dance* was none other than Harold Alexander, the future Field-Marshal, later Earl Alexander of Tunis, then commanding a company as a Captain. Alex had originally gone out with the 1st Battalion but got a 'Blighty one' on 1 November 1914 at Zillebeeke Wood. He had recovered sufficiently to come out again with the 2nd Battalion.

On 22 August Rudyard set off from Troyes to stay at the Hotel Brighton in Paris, where the family used to stay in calmer times. He wrote to Carrie – he only missed writing one day, whilst he was in the trenches at Alsace: 'Dearest Heart . . . just a line to tell you how I love you. This hasn't in the least prevented me from falling in love with a very beautiful V.A.D. (I think) orderly in the Scottish Women's Hospital 2 kilometres down the road – the Hospital run by French's sister [Charlotte Despard, sister of Sir John French, Commander of the B.E.F.].' Despite the affectionate and bantering tone he was lost without her to organize him; 'I wired you . . . to ask your views about what we ought to do with the letters for France. The pressure for my views etc. is simply awful. Hurry up and let me know your Royal Mind, my Queen.' Just as he was missing her, he knew how Carrie would be missing him, alone in the dreadful aftermath of John's departure. He continued with tender support, 'Yes, dear. It is worth all and more that we have kept the unit [the family four] intact until now and that you have made that unit what it is. D'you suppose I didn't think of that all his birthday? . . . And now my dearest dear I'll write a line to John. Oh those last tearing days. What they must have meant to you! I don't suppose ever was a girl more loved than you by your family and a million-fold more by your Boy.' Later he said, 'I have sent John an account of my experience in the trenches for his instruction and guidance.'

Carrie had sent on John's letters from Southampton and le Havre. Rudyard picked them up from the Ritz, with Carrie's letters of 13, 15, 16, 17, 19 and 20 August and he responded to John's account of his picket duty with tales of watching 'the Boche' in their trenches, seeing a batch of fifty German prisoners, driving along a road that might be shelled and walking '2 hours in the dam trenches'. As during his period of being under fire in the Boer War, he was exhilarated by the experience and already considered himself an expert in trench warfare. 'Don't forget the beauty of rabbit netting overhead against hand grenades,' he warned. 'Even tennis netting is better than nothing.' He was writing to John from Room 315, 'Just opposite your old suite No. 301 with the bath that you had when last here' [in the Hotel Brighton].

John's letter of the same day bears witness to the efficiency of the military postal service. He had already received a parcel of the supplies he had requested. 'You sent me enough kit to carry on with for a long time.' Sharing his parents' interest in farming, he described how the crops were being 'brought in by old women and girls entirely. An old lady thinks nothing of cutting a 2 acre field of wheat with a sickle. They all work like horses as they have to get the crops in somehow. One old soul told me that this was the best year for crops since 1906.' His other news, proudly imparted, was that, as he was the 'only Ensign or Subaltern with a year's service' available, he was detailed to sit on a court martial. Using 'veiled speech', a technique that employs asides and oblique references to refer to places or events that cannot be mentioned for security reasons, he managed to impart where this was taking place: '20 miles away in some town where a regiment of guards that has no bearskin plume are stationed'. This was the Scots Guards. Knowing that Rudyard would want more military detail than the censor would allow in his letters, John wondered where his father's old journalistic colleague Landon (for whom the Kiplings had refurbished a cottage called Keylands at Bateman's and who was currently in France with Rudyard) was, as he could 'take back a far more interesting letter than any of these'.

As Rudyard's letter of the following day showed, Landon was in fact in Paris with him and the two dined at the Café de Paris. This letter was full of praise of the French: their infantry, their well-made trenches (not a view shared by the British Tommies who hated taking over trenches from the French), their latrines – 'Any god's quantity of chloride of lime and no flies'; the way they buried their dead 'outside the rear trenches if they can and plant oats over 'em'; their 'pom-poms' and trench mortars. Rudyard, now seeing himself as a seasoned campaigner, offered his son much advice – how to interrogate prisoners, a reminder not to forget the overhead rabbit netting and to use a man with a whistle to warn of the first *minenwerfer* – all of which John was invited to let his 'C.O. or O.C. or anyone you think fit hear what I have written.'

This was followed by a letter of the 24th from Rudyard who was still 'held up in Paris because Joffre wants to see me'. Unusually, he urged John to namedrop: 'I'm *awfully* wondering where you are likely to be sent. If it is anywhere outside our present front – in the direction of the Argonne or that way, west of Soissons (which may be possible) I think you'll find it useful to chip in with my name among the French. This isn't swank but they all seemed to know me.' The Kiplings were a particularly fastidious family and just as John had complained in his letter of the 20th that 'The French here are the dirtiest I ever saw, their ideas of hotels are simply unspeakable!!', so Rudyard now complains, 'I'm going out in a French taxi. They are burning petrol mixed with pee. At least that's how it smells.' Kipling was furious with Joffre, who was keeping him kicking his heels: 'D——d impertinence, isn't it,' but consoled himself with visits to the Palais Royal Music Hall, which he described in minute and hilarious detail to John, down to the 'flamingly indecent red and green drawers' worn by the 'indelicate female' representing the Irish. He was still in Paris on the 26th, though just off to Boulogne to take a boat back to Folkestone, and quivering with anticipation at the thought that submarines might be 'on the rampage'. He wrote again from the train en route to the port, chuffed at John's happy billet and his liaison with the landlord's daughter, Marcelle and advising that the 'best dictionary for French is a dictionary in skirts'. After the war Kipling visited Acquin in search both of information about John's last days and also in his capacity of researcher for his History of the Regiment. He described the 'little village on a hill-side a few miles from St Omer, in a fold of the great Sussex-like downs', obviously feeling that this similarity to his familiar home countryside would have been a comfort to John. 'The men were billeted in barns forty and fifty at a time . . . But it was to be their first and only experience of comfort for any consecutive time, and of French life a little untouched by the war. They most deeply enjoyed the simple kindliness of the village-folk . . . and the French men and women upon whom they were billeted liked them well and remembered them long. Said one, years after, with tears in the eyes: "Monsieur, if you drew a line in the air and asked those children not to cross it, it was a wall to them. They played, monsieur, like infants, without any thought of harm or unkindness; and then they would all become men again, very serious – all those children of yours."' No doubt one child in particular was discussed.

During the train journey Kipling and Landon were disgusted by a 'damned Yankee' who bored them noisily with his experience on the *Lusitania* as she sank and had been even more irritated in the Hotel Brighton by 'a round hairy pinkish Canadian who told me he was the son-in-law of "Mr Ellis of Burwash". It takes a fair amount to surprise me nowadays but I own I was a little bit astonished. He had come over, he said, to sell arms to the French and was disgustingly prosperous.' The prosperity of American arms dealers particularly infuriated Kipling, who was outraged that America was still sitting on the fence. On a lighter note, he commented on the resemblance between Rupert Grayson and the French Colonel's orderly who had showed him round some trenches. 'He had exactly Grayson's slow way of trickling out his sentences and rolling his eyes.'

John's next letter was also written on the 26th, complaining that parcels were only delivered every four days. Nevertheless he was being inundated with underclothes, collars, shirts and handkerchiefs from the Bateman's shirt factory and begged them to desist. Chocolate was another matter, however, as the food – 'what there is – is *rotten*'.

On 20 August they reached their somewhat cushy billets at Acquin and the battalion settled in. On the 24th the diary records that orders were given to fall in ready to march as a 'practice alarm'. They took over an hour to respond, however, as the orderlies were too far from HQ and there was some confusion over the orders – not a good omen for the battle ahead. From 25–27 August there was training, with shooting practice for the worst shots.

Meanwhile Rudyard had returned to Bateman's, from where he wrote that 'Ollie is about fed up with Eton and refuses to stay on. At any rate Stan talks about getting him a tutor for the next six months, with an eye to coaching Ollie for the Diplomatic. This, I think, will be "all my eye" for Stan added that as soon as he was old enough Ollie wants to go into the Guards – Grenadier for choice as Stan knows a lot of old Grenadiers. Well, everyone to his taste. I expect that Ollie may have written to you about it.' There was little chance that Oliver would be fobbed off with the Diplomatic Service now that his cousin and hero, John, was nearing the front, as later correspondence proved. Rudyard also passed on the news with pride that Baldwin had been told by the Earl of Kerry that his nephew 'young Kipling' was 'a very good boy and he's done very good work'. The letter finished with yet another exhortation to use rabbit wire over the trenches, complete with detailed sketch, and greetings to Grayson.

On 29 August John's long letter showed how he was thriving on the hard work and that, despite the heat and the flies, they were all 'lean and bronzed', like 'the heroes in the *Daily Mirror* serials'. He felt that his father's 'tips for the trenches' were 'rather quaint' and continued, 'Surely you know it is a standing order never to have any thing over the top of a trench, even rabbit wires. If the Bosch comes, he has you like rabbits underneath it.' The young warrior was now feeling confident enough to crow over his famous father and to remind him that 'Our C.O. was 7 months on a "Brigade" staff what he doesn't know about the game isn't worth knowing.' Rather hurtfully he rubbed salt in the wound – 'Of course you were only allowed to see specimen trenches, not those which a French battalion had made in one night, the great test of Trench digging.' Even Carrie got another reprimand for her continuing flow of undies, 'Please don't send any more underclothes, shirts, collars,' he pleaded once again, repeating at the end of the letter, 'I am really rolling in shirts good things here'. Instead he asked for chocolate and biscuits ('not Digestive'), writing paper, a refill for his Orilux lamp, some Colgate tooth powder and shaving powder, tobacco 'in 2 oz tins', a portable glass in a strong case for travelling and some 'literature' [magazines] – a list that would keep Carrie and Elsie occupied and distract them from shirt-making. On the military front he reported, 'There is ceaseless drill here all day & route marching; the dust is simply unspeakable'. He boasted that, 'You never saw anything as smart as the men are now, & by Gad the discipline!' The excitement of the moment was the formation of the battalion's own 'drums': 'We have a lot of drummers and & players in the ranks so it won't take long. When the Colonel in Chief [Kitchener] comes out we are going to have the massed drums of the Division that will be a grand sight.'

On the next day, 30 August, the two battalions of the Irish Guards met up for the first time at St Pierre. 'We both marched out to meet each other halfway & had a great picnic,' wrote John. The 1st Battalion had reached le Havre on 13 August 1914, arriving at Mons on the 23rd, just in time to take part in the gruelling retreat and the action at Villers Cotterets in which they lost their Commanding Officer, Colonel the Hon G. Morris, and in which George Cecil and John Manners of the Grenadiers had been killed, as we have seen. In the intervening year they had fought on the Aisne, in the First Battle of Ypres, at Cuinchy in February 1915, Neuve Chapelle in March and Festubert in May. By this time their losses were considerable and in his History of the Battalion Kipling wrote, 'There is no hint of the desperate hard work of the 2nd, Reserve, Battalion at Warley, which made possible the supply at such short notice of so many officers of such quality. These inner workings of a Regiment are known only to those who have borne the burden' – a reference to John and his fellow officers.

No wonder that John said 'The men looked very strained . . . & it was hard to recognize the ensigns. Some realy [sic] looked like animated corpses.' Kipling noted that 'There are few records of this historic meeting; for the youth and the strength that gathered by the cookers in that open sunlit field by St Pierre has been several times wiped out and replaced. The two battalions conferred together, by rank and by age, on the methods and devices of the enemy, the veterans of the First enlightening the new hands of the Second with tales that could lose nothing in the telling, mixed with practical advice of the most grim. The First promptly christened the Second "The Irish Landsturm", and a young officer, who later rose to eminent heights and command of the 2nd Battalion [Alexander], sat upon a table under some trees, and delighted the world with joyous songs upon a concertina and a mouth-organ. Then they parted.' Though this was a story common to both parts of his History, Kipling added in the 2nd Battalion account, 'when the merry gathering under the trees in the field was at an end, after dinner, the 2nd Battalion fell in and marched off the ground "before the critical eyes of their older comrades, and the 1st followed." No fault was found, but it was a breathless business, compared, by one who took part, to the performance of rival peacocks.'

In the same letter John described the court martial in which he participated. 'It was a "Field General Court Martial" which holds the power of "life and death",' wrote this boy of barely 18. 'One man came very near the extreme penalty and I didn't like it at all.' Nevertheless John felt he had acquitted himself 'Comme Monsieur Edoward Carson' [the current Attorney General and Rottingdean neighbour]. As no lorry was available to take him to the court, nine miles distant, John rode on 'a horse, a streamline one with "bulbous stern and disc wheels", also raked steering.' No wonder he complained, 'By gad I was stiff the next day!'

To his great amusement, Rudyard's "fruity" letter of Wed 25th arrived with a big notice over the flap "Opened by Censor". 'A long addition to John's letter of the 30th, written the next day, talked of an expedition by motor bus to dig first line trenches to defend the seaports, of the "Divisional Field Day" which means Frightfulness', of 'moenuvres [sic]' – the 'sort of thing [which] brings the war right to your front door and drops you there with a bump'.

At this stage the weather broke. Up to now it had been extremely hot; John thought it was 'far hotter than the Cape'. Dust and flies had been the main irritations on the long marches and the digging of trenches. Now the heavens opened with a vengeance. According to the battalion diary the heavy rain had started during the afternoon of 1 September, and continued unabated for several days. On 2 September John wrote home with a long list of wants, from 'a coat carrier', to 'thick woolen gloves and that stocking cap Elsie made me. Also 2 pairs of <u>thick</u> underclothes not too thick but thickish and not long pants, just to the knee . . . I want really "medium weight" woolen underclothes.' The sudden rain was an added hazard. 'We marched 22 miles yesterday in the pouring wet. The G.O.C. London District "Frankie" reviewed us. It was a great sight as we were marching in one long line as a division, mile after mile of us. By gad but <u>it was</u> wet. We were soaked through and through but not a man fell out. We are off the day after tomorrow I believe. We are having a pretty slack day today as the mens clothes are still wet and they are a bit done up.' There was no abatement overnight. 'It keeps on raining like Hades. Will you send me an oilskin coat,' asked John the next day. He wanted a genuine navy oilskin as no '"Burbury" or Mac will stand up to these soaking rains,' even though it was 'a great "comedown" for me to utilize the kit of the Senior Service'. By 4 September the rain and constant movement of columns of men were making conditions even more unpleasant. 'Never in my life have I seen rain like this,' complained John, 'the roads are flooded. There are feet of mud.' He now required a nailbrush and the '2 rather light-coloured Khaki flannel ties I sent back from Warley. Pipe

87

cleaners tin box of matches (B & Ms [Bryant and Mays]) . . . chocolate and litereture [sic].'

Rudyard was tickled at the oilskin request. The current Bateman's secretary, Jerry, of whom John was very fond, was detailed to track one down. In jocular mood Rudyard enthused at the visiting Lady Aitken's *eight cylinder* Cadillac and opined that 'If the Censor opened my "fruity" letter, it probably cheered him up.' Lady Aitken was another favourite of John ('I much admire your taste in admiring her,' his father commented) and on 10 September John wrote that she had sent him 'a topping box of chocolates'. What he did *not* want, however, was socks: 'I have ample . . . so please don't sent out anymore till I write for them.' He also pleaded, 'No more *shirts collars or underclothes* till I write.'

Training was intensifying. On 3 September the battalion had a lecture on first aid to the wounded. On the 4th they practised taking a village and making good the ground gained, a process known as 'consolidation', and on the 6th the companies were issued with, and instructed in the care of, smoke helmets. The eye pieces of the helmets with which they had been issued at Warley had cracked and the new helmets had protective boards over the eyepieces. Later that day they marched to new billets at Avroult and early the next morning were out digging trenches again, before returning to the familiar billets at Acquin. John found time to describe this in vivid detail in a letter home, first admonishing, 'Don't put 2nd Brigade in address'. Thankfully the rain had stopped, 'but since then it has been awfully hot. We left this village on Monday at 1230 a.m. on a trench digging expedition. We marched 15 miles to a small village which we reached at about half past six in the evening. We went into billets there for the night (as there are only about four beds in the place I slept in a barn on some straw really quite comfortably except for the great amount of animal life in there.) Got up at 4.30 a.m. the next morning had breakfast at 5 paraded at 5.30 & marched off at 6 two miles to the place where we dug trenches. We dug from seven to half past one when we marched back to this spot again – 17 miles – arriving back at about seven in the evening (Tuesday). This morning we again got up at 4.30 a.m. & paraded at 5.30 marching off at 6 a.m. for a Brigade Field Day. [The diary records that this was at Tatinghem.] The rendez-vous was seven miles off. We started operations at about 9. It was a general "agony" as most Brigade Field Days are a rear guard sort of affair 3 miles across country. It took a long time and we got back at half past three, rather a long stretch without anything to eat or drink. Well that's the end of a rather strenuos [sic] three days. We covered 50 miles in it which is quite good considering it was very hot and the men are carrying very heavy kit only five men fell out and they were "done to the world".' He concluded with yet more requests to the 'Universal Provider' – 'a pair of sock suspenders like the ones I have on my evening socks at Brewins. Also a stick of Colgates

Shaving soap (in a tin case)'. He was receiving *Sketch, Tatler, Punch, S.Pictorial, Sunday Herald & London Mail* but wanted the 'IG [Irish Guards] cuff links' Taylor [his servant] had sent back in a shirt the last time he went to Bateman's.

The next two days were spent in general training and laying out trenches. John was beginning to feel a sense of destiny. 'Dad most likely knows what is going to happen out here in ten days. [Knowing Kipling's contacts, he almost certainly did.] That is what the Guards Division have been formed for. Sounds mysterious but I can't say what it is if you don't know. So we are moving up shortly,' he wrote on 10 September. The feeling of impending fate was compounded the next day by a careful check of company and next-of-kin rolls. The tension was relieved on the 12th when two inter-company football ties were played, there was an open air concert and a bonfire.

Training was now becoming so intense that John had no time to write home. By the 20th Carrie was worried and wrote to her mother, 'John has not written for a week and we are a bit troubled for fear he is not well at worst or overworked at best and are keen for the post.' During this period of silence the battalion had marched between Acquin and Dohem, digging yet more trenches, and on the 15th an impressive gathering took place at the HQ of the 1st Coldstream Guards at Lumbres. Here Lieutenant General Haking, C.O. of II Corps, addressed all the officers of 2nd Guards Brigade. He told them that the attack (which he billed as 'the greatest battle in the history of the world' – a phrase that Kipling would never let him forget) on the German lines was imminent and that they would be opposed by 40,000 of the enemy as against the allies' 200,000. The Germans, he reassured them had only six reserve divisions behind their firing line and supports, which had to serve the entire Western Front. The 2nd Battalion Diary noted that everything would 'depend on the platoon leaders and he instructed them always to push on boldly whenever an opportunity offered, even at the expense of exposing and leaving unguarded their flanks!!!' By the three exclamation marks the diarist made clear his opinion of the General's advice. In the History Kipling adds, 'The summary is set down in the Diary with no more comment than three exclamation points at the end.' Kipling allowed himself the indulgence of criticizing, 'From the civilian point of view the advice seems hardly safe to offer to a battalion of at least average courage a few days before they are to meet singularly well-posted machine-guns, and carefully trained bombers.' Interestingly enough, Kipling gets the date of this stirring address wrong in the History, recording it as the 5th, not as the 15th, which was correctly written in the Diary (perhaps a typographical error).

The next day there was a ceremonial drill of the whole of the 2nd Guards Brigade, when they were inspected by Major-General the Earl of

Cavan who 'complimented them on their appearance'. Another football match followed. On the 17th the battalion practised attacking through barbed wires in the Val de Lumbres and on the 18th joined the 14th Field Artillery and a Field Company of the Royal Engineers near Wisques for yet another field day, when they 'practised co-operation between infantry and artillery at wood fighting'.

John eventually found a moment to put pen to paper on the 17th, 'the first moment I have had time to write to you in the last 5 days as we have been very hard at it. Mostly from 4 a.m. to 8 p.m. which doesn't leave anything for writing letters.' The sock suspenders and books had arrived, but he now wanted a revolver lanyard 'as I have bust mine. I would like it of plaited leather if you can get such a one. I would love to see Phipps [Elsie's current nickname] driving the Singer,' he continued, obviously longing for his own little car, 'there are lots of them out here. Two at Divisional Headquarters. The weather is very uncertain out here at the present – one moment tremendous heat the next moment buckets of rain.' Then again using 'veiled speech', he tried to let Rudyard know some information about his new Division. 'The Guards Division is not allowed to be mentioned by the press as it is a "Flying Division" and its movements are not to be revealed. So we can't say much about it except like all Divisions it consists of 3 Brigades and that in each Brigade are 4 Gds battalions. George Cecil's old Battalion are in First Guards Brigade. We are in the second and Annabel Strachey's husband's regiment is in the Third Guards Brigade. Cuthbert's battalion is in our Brigade so that we see quite a lot of him he comes and dines with us sometimes. So now by putting two and two together you can roughly see the composition of the first Division in the B.E.F.' [Cuthbert was an Irish Guardsman whom John would have got to know at Warley and who was now seconded to the 1st Scots Guards.]

On the 19th John wrote what is an extremely important letter in regard to the uniform he was wearing when he was killed. He started by again enthusing about the Singer that Elsie had acquired. When she became proficient in driving, the Kiplings laid up the Rolls and dispensed with its chauffeur and Elsie and her little Singer became their only means of motor transport for the remainder of the war. John thought 'they *are* rather nice little things' and continued poignantly, 'if I live to get back I'm going to get myself the smartest 2 seater Hispano-Suiza that can be got'. Unusually for John, whose letters were normally full of enthusiasm and pride, he admitted to feeling heartily fed up with the tough life: 'We work like fiends . . . I've done enough marching the last month to sicken me of it for life; it is indescribable . . . Many is the time I've thought of a hot bath! evening clothes! dinner at the Ritz! going to the Alhambra afterwards!' In an uncharacteristic moan he railed, 'You people at home don't realize how spoilt you are. You don't realize what excessive luxury surrounds you.

90

Think of hot water tap alone.' It is not surprising that this somewhat delicate youth from a wealthy family, accustomed to travelling in comfort since he was a baby, staying in the best hotels and the smartest private houses, cossetted by his mother, indulged by his father, idolized by his sister and cousins, would find life at the front harder to bear than the tough Irishmen he led. Naturally the thought of the impending conflict, so hyped up by his senior officers, frightened him, hence the unusual 'if I live to get back' statement. He also asked for 'an Identification Disc as I have gone and lost mine. I think you could get one at the Stores' [Army and Navy].

It takes no great feat of imagination to visualize the conditions under which he was writing this letter. He was exhausted, nervous and felt convinced that he was, at the least, going to be badly wounded. Many of his friends had already been killed, some without trace. He carefully wrote out his rank – '2nd Lt', his name – 'J Kipling', his religion – 'C of E' (about which he had cared enough to organize his own confirmation) and his regiment – 'Irish 'Guards', so as to make sure that, if anything happened to him, his body would be properly identified.

The gruelling preparations for the battle continued. On 21 September each man had to fire ten rounds whilst wearing a smoke helmet, and a second one was issued. Then came musketry practice on the 22nd and at 7 p.m. the battalion assembled south-east of their now familiar home at Acquin and marched via Lumbres to Dohem. There they paraded in column of route and marched in a heavy downpour of rain via Estrée Blanche to more comfortable billets in Linghem, where they arrived at 10.50 p.m. on the 23rd. Here John was able to write to 'Dear Old F—'. It was, he explained, 'Just a hurried line to let you know what we are doing.' Continuing in the coded speech that Rudyard would have revelled in, he continued, 'We have begun what I said we were going to do; have been marching for the last two days.' In other words, 'We are approaching the front line and will soon be engaged in battle.' Now that the marching was for real rather than an exercise, 'We have had to chuck a good half of our Kits away as the waggons are very heavily loaded. I will write and tell you what to send later on. It made my heart bleed to leave a lot of my splendid Kit by the roadside.' Had the lovingly sewn shirts and underclothes, the Colgate tooth and shaving powder, the Orilux lamp, all had to be jettisoned? In their stead John's last request was for 'a really good pair of bedroom slippers (fluffy and warm with strong soles) (*not* carpet) also a good strong toothbrush'. Rudyard, meanwhile, had left again for France and on 23 September Carrie wrote to her mother that he was in Rheims 'doing articles'.

On 24 September General Haking repeated his 'we are on the eve of the biggest battle in the history of the world' battle cry to the Corps Commanders at Lillers, and stressed the necessity for speed and for the use of reserves. They then passed on the now familiar message to all their officers. The message was wearing thin. Kipling in his History wryly remarked that 'It may have occurred to some of his hearers that they were the reserves, but that speed was out of the question, for the roads were clotted with Cavalry, and there did not seem to be any great choice of those "parallel roads" on which they had been exercised, or any vast crush of motorbuses.'

25 September was a busy day. The Battalion left Linghem at 5.15 a.m. and joined the Brigade at Auchy au Bois. From there they marched to billets at Burbure, a message from Major-General Cavan wishing them 'God Speed' having been relayed en route. At 1.45 they marched on to Haquin through roads congested by cavalry, just as Kipling was to describe, and through the depressing sight of wounded who were already being brought back. They moved into their congested billets at about 1 a.m., 'very wet and very tired, ordered to be ready to move at 30 minutes notice'. Here John snatched the time to write his very last letter home. It was another 'very hurried line as we start off tonight. The front line trenches are nine miles off from here so it wont be a very long march.' With the prospect of the forthcoming battle so imminent, the culmination of all the gruelling training, the senior officers' motivational exhortations buzzing in his ears, all John's grumbles dissipated in the face of nervous pride in the importance of the test to come. 'This is THE great effort to break through and end the war,' he explained convincingly. 'We have to push through at all costs so we won't have much time in the trenches, which is great luck. Funny to think one will be in the thick of it tomorrow . . . They are staking a tremendous lot on this great advancing movement as if it succeeds the war won't go on for long. You have no idea what enormous issues depend on the next few days.' What a weight he and the other boy officers carried on their shoulders as they proceeded, untried and untested, into battle. Realistically, and with shielding understatement, he warned his parents and sister, 'This will be my last letter most likely for some time as we won't get any time for writing this next week.' Finally he bade them, 'Well so long old dears. Dear Love, John.'

THE BATTLE OF LOOS

The infantry assault that opened Haking's 'biggest battle in the history of the world' had actually begun at 0630 on 25 September while the 2nd Battalion Irish Guards were marching from Linghem to Auchy au Bois. They were part of the reserve forces held back in order to exploit any breakthrough. But there wasn't to be any breakthrough, only confusion.

The overall concept for the battle had been that of Joffre, the French Commander-in-Chief, who devised a two-pronged attack that 'could possibly end the war'. The main strike in Champagne, was to be an entirely French affair, while that in the north was to be a Franco-British offensive in Artois. The area allocated to the British 1st Army was that just north of Lens in front of a small town called Loos. (See map p.211).

Before the battle General Haig, commanding the 1st Army and responsible for the conduct of the British effort, had toured the area and declared that it was not suitable for an attack because the flat ground would be swept by gunfire from the enemy's front line trenches. Joffre remained adamant and Kitchener, visiting Sir John French, the British Commander-in-Chief in August, had told him that 'we may suffer heavy losses'. Haig, believing that he had insufficient forces to provide either the necessary weight of artillery fire or depth of infantry assault along the whole of his front, decided that in order to make up the deficiencies he would use gas – the first British attempt to do so. Even so, the final plan depended upon the wind being in the right direction and it was not until 0500 hours on the morning of 25 September, having watched the direction of the smoke from his ADC's cigarette, that Haig ordered the use of what had been called 'the accessory'.

North of the Vermelles–Hulluch road the wind refused to co-operate, one gas officer alongside the la Bassée canal deciding not to turn on the gas at all, but where it was used it blew back on to the British troops, causing many casualties and much confusion. Robert Graves, serving with the Welsh north of the road wrote later in *Goodbye to All That*, ' "What happened?" I asked. "Bloody balls up" was the most detailed answer I could get".' But south of the road and in front and around Loos the first day went well and it was time to bring up the reserves. Where were they? A long way back.

General French had nominated two new untried 'K' Divisions as his reserve. Both had arrived in France barely three weeks earlier. They had never been in battle trenches and had never been under fire, and, instead of giving them to General Haig for him to control and to employ as needed, General French kept them to himself many miles to the rear. It is not hard to guess at a reason. There was no love lost between the two men despite their mutual successes in South Africa, and Haig was covertly scheming against French. He wrote in his diary, 'I had come to the conclusion that it was not fair to the Empire to retain French in command. Moreover, none of my officers commanding corps had a high opinion of Sir John's military ability.' French, for his part, seeing the possibility that the use of the reserves in exploiting a breakthrough might be a decisive factor in the coming battle, may well have felt that by keeping them under his command any success that came from their use would be attributed to him and not to Haig. In any event the prevalent atmosphere during the Loos battle was that of confusion, both with regard to the command and use of the reserves and the precise situation on the battlefield.

On the afternoon of 26 September into that confusion marched the reserves, including the 2nd Battalion of the Irish Guards, part of the newly formed Guards Division. The day before the Irish had toiled for more than 15 hours along roads clogged with cavalry and wounded. At about 0100 hours on 26 September they 'moved into congested billets at Haquin . . . very wet and very tired . . . [and] . . . ordered to be ready to move at 30 minutes notice' [the War Diary]. At 1330 they moved out and marched towards Vermelles and the front, Captains Alexander and Hubbard going on ahead to reconnoitre the trenches that they were to take over. The confusion became evident. There was no one there to tell them which trenches they were supposed to take over, so the Captains discussed things with the 1st Scots Guards on their right and decided to occupy a line of captured German trenches between Le Rutoire and Lone Tree. It was midnight before the Battalion was settled in, some men having had less than four hours' sleep and none having had a true rest that day. Two and a half hours later they were on the move again to a line of trenches 500 yards ahead just short of the Loos–Hulluch road and it was broad daylight before the move was completed, with 3rd Company on the extreme right, then 2nd and 1st Companies, with 4th in reserve via a communication trench. John Kipling was with 2nd Company.

Ahead of the Irish, across the Loos–Hulluch road, and beside the la Bassée–Lens road, 600 yards away, could be seen the damaged mine head and buildings of 'Puits 14 bis' and to their left a scattering of small trees and bushes around chalk workings that became known as 'Chalk Pit Wood'. On the 25th this had been the area attacked and taken by 15th (Scottish) Division which captured Loos after all-night street fighting. A swift attack by fresh troops early on the next day, the 26th, could have been decisive. Instead, in the confusion on the ground and through the jealousies in command, there were no fresh troops available and the reserves that were called upon to make the key effort were tired and 36 hours late. The last hours of John Kipling's young life and those of many others began at 1000 hours on 27 September when the 2nd Guards Brigade was told to attack Chalk Pit Wood and Puits 14 bis.

Colonel Lesley Butler, commanding the Irish, gave clear orders as to the precise tasks for each company. 'No 2 Coy . . . were to advance on the left of No 3 straight at the centre of the wood and to continue No 3 Coy's line on the further edge of the wood, right up to and including the CHALK PIT' [War Diary]. The novice soldiers were given explicit instructions: they were to 'leave their trenches at 3.50 pm and get into position in front of their trenches, lying down and ready to rise and advance at 4pm. One platoon in extended order in front as line of skirmishers and the other three platoons each in column of four.' First there would be a preparatory bombardment by our artillery.

The orders were issued about an hour before the men had to go over the top and that last hour John Kipling and his fellow young officers would have spent talking to their men, lifting their spirits with optimistic words, checking their weapons, reassuring them that everything would be all right and among themselves have planned rendezvous at favourite clubs 'when this is over'. There was no time for their own fear. They were too busy seeing to their men, except – did John just briefly wonder if the coming fight was what his very existence was all about? Was this what 'Dear old F' had seen all along? Had his whole life been moulded for this moment? If so, then he would not let 'F' down, or his men, or his regiment.

At 1600 they rose to the attack, doubtless with the officers leading from the front as they had been taught and in a manner styled upon the brave drawings from South Africa of Caton Woodville. They were new to the game after all, and at first all went well. There had been a few casualties from shellfire while they had been lying out in the open, but Nos 2 and No 3 companies reached the far side of Chalk Pit Wood 'with small loss'. Soon, though, they lost their first officer. Second Lieutenant Pakenham-Law was wounded in the head and died later in hospital, and, seeing that the line had not extended as far as the Chalk Pit, Colonel Butler issued further orders to take the pit itself. Inevitably, although the attack had begun 'as ordered . . . rapidly, without hesitation,' confusion quickly set in. The Scots Guards, on the right of the Irish, attacked Puits 14, sweeping in a curve around the Irish flank and clipping off a number of the Irish as they did so. '2nd Lieuts Clifford and Kipling and some few Irish Guardsmen had also gone forward with this party and had reached a line just beyond the PUITS buildings. While there, according to the evidence of No 6846 Corpl ROSSITER (No 2 Co) and No 5824 PT POWER (No 2 Co), 2nd Lieut Clifford was shot and wounded or killed. Also while there, according to the evidence of No 5838 PT GREEN (No 2 Co), 2nd Lieut Kipling was wounded. These two officers were subsequently missing, for shortly before 5pm the men in and beyond the PUITS commenced to retire and fell back into and through CHALK PIT WOOD in some confusion.' [War Diary.] The language is economical. The Germans had considerable numbers of machine guns and, as General Haig had feared, almost flat fields of fire. The novice soldiers were out of their depth. Colonel Butler, seeing the confusion, went forward with the adjutant, Captain Vesey, hoping to stabilize the situation. Vesey was wounded and had to be carried off, while the stream of men stumbling back from Puits 14 and on into the wood could not be stopped. Not until the line of the Loos–Hulluch road could the men be halted and the CO had to call upon the 1st Coldstreams for support. It was a near rout. Tired virgin soldiers had been asked to do too much. As Rudyard put it in his history, 'Evidently, one and a half hour's bombardment against a countryside packed with machine-guns, was not enough to placate it. The Battalion had been swept from all quarters, and shelled at the same time, at the end of two hard days and sleepless nights, as a first experience of war, and had lost seven of their officers in forty minutes.' One of those officers was John Kipling. Two days later the Irish Guards were withdrawn.

Kipling's body had not been found. Was he dead, wounded and holing up somewhere or held prisoner by the Germans?

The fighting at Loos continued until the first week in October without significant results. The 'greatest battle in the history of the world' had been at best a failure and at worst a disaster. Lloyd George in his memoirs called it 'a futile carnage'. The generals, French and Haig, fearing recriminations about the conduct of the battle, began an overt argument about when the reserves had been available and to whom. Haig wrote to Kitchener on 29 September, 'No reserve was placed under me. My attack . . . was a complete success . . . We had captured Loos 12 hours previously and reserves should have been at hand THEN.' French had lost heart during the battle itself and wrote home to his mistress, 'My Darling Darling we've had such terrible losses which made me very depressed and sad'. It was to be the end of the war between the generals, for before the year was out Prime Minister Herbert Asquith wrote to Haig to say that French had resigned and 'I have the pleasure of proposing to you that you should be his successor'.

Haig won the contest with French, but in Rudyard's eyes he would always bear some responsibility for John's loss and years later Kipling showed his feelings in the way in which he made little reference to Haig's part in the King's Pilgrimage of 1922 (for which he was criticized) and had nothing laudable to compose for Haig's memorial cross at Dryburgh Abbey in June 1929.

In September 1915, however, there were more pressing things to do. Rudyard and Carrie had to find out what had happened to John. The search began.

Chapter 7

MY BOY JACK:

John Reported Missing. Attempts to Locate his Body.
Hopes Burn and Fade.

Is it well, is it well with the child?
For I know not where he is laid.

Rudyard Kipling, *A Nativity*, 1916

On 27 September 1915 John Kipling almost certainly died.

Blissfully unaware of this terrible fact, Carrie wrote that day to her mother, 'John has been in the firing line as far as we know since Saturday. We have this day a letter from him written Thursday evening I think . . . We think John is at La Bassée where the fighting is heaviest but the Guards Division is bound to be where the heavy work is being done.' She apologized that it was a 'dull' letter, but explained, 'one's mind can not easily be kept long away from Flanders'. Rudyard had returned from his trip to France – 'heavy with cold'.

On 2 October came the first mention that she and Rudyard had been informed that all was not well. In her diary she recorded, in typically understated and controlled fashion, masking the terror and turmoil within, 'A telegram from the War Office to say John is "missing".' When it arrived Isabel Law was with Elsie. 'We wait for Isabel to leave before telling Elsie.'

In his July 1992 report of the supposed identification of John Kipling's body, the *Daily Telegraph* reporter John Gaskell wrote, 'News of John's death, reputedly delivered by the then Conservative Party Leader, Bonar Law, caused Kipling to utter "a curse like the cry of dying man".' When asked by the authors for his source for this statement, Mr Gaskell said that unfortunately he had completely forgotten where he heard it and was unable to find his notes. Despite extensive research, no confirmation of the fact that Bonar Law was the bringer of the dreaded news has come to light. It has, however, an element of feasibility. Given Bonar Law's position, he may well have had prior access to such news; it was well known that he was close to the Kiplings. On that fatal day he could even have been collecting Isabel, who was visiting Elsie. What rings particularly true is Rudyard's awful curse.

That he and Carrie by now regarded John's death as inevitable, barring an injury so serious as to put him out of the rest of the war, is without doubt. That they considered it their duty to make this sacrifice, as so many of their friends and fellow countrymen were doing, is equally certain. What they had not prepared themselves for was the cruel uncertainty of whether their son was actually dead or not. That he was dearer to them than anything else on earth – poor Elsie came an undisguised second – was apparent to all who knew them. Now, in contrast to the stoical acceptance they had shown prior to the news, and perhaps because it was not final, they began to clutch at the flimsiest of straws. They knew what to do; they had meticulously explored every possible avenue that might lead to news in George Cecil's case. But this wasn't the dress rehearsal, it was the painful personal performance.

It is somewhat curious that their first action was not to use Rudyard's considerable influence to get themselves rushed out to as close to the Loos front as they could to start their investigation. After all Lady Edward had done so; so had the Desboroughs, Frances Horner, and many others of their acquaintance. Rudyard had only just come back from France. He would have had no problem in getting permission to return, yet seemed to make no attempt to do so. Rider Haggard obviously expected him to go as an entry in his diary entry will show.

The next day Carrie went to see to the one person whom she knew outside the family who shared her every emotion – Lady Edward. Now the roles were reversed: the comforter was in need of comfort. Sir Max Aitken rushed over from France 'to bring us what news he could collect about John, which is very little'. At first they were told that John had been wounded and left in a building surrounded a few minutes later by Germans. On 5 October they went to London and saw Viscount de Vesci at the Guards HQ. A professional soldier, de Vesci had joined the regiment as Ivo Richard Vesey in 1901, succeeded to his title in July 1903, and would go on to become Regimental Adjutant in July 1916 and then Director of Forestry in 1918, for which he was made a *Chevalier de l'Ordre de Mérite Agricole*. Despite his prestige and influence, he had less news than they had. Carrie recorded in her diary that John's Colonel, Butler, said that John was wounded fighting in the open with his men and that only nine returned from the attack.

On the 6th Gwynne of the *Morning Post* started enquiries on the news net and through the British Minister to the Vatican. A notice appeared in his and other papers with the 'heavy burden of announcing that Mr John Kipling of the Irish Guards is reported "missing believed killed." John Kipling was the child for whom his father wrote the "Just So Stories", the boy for whom Puck told immortal tales of the beloved land, for which this supreme sacrifice has now been made. Mr John Kipling was barely eighteen, a boy of delicate health but indomitable zeal and resolution. He had been nominated for the Irish Guards by Lord Roberts and was determined to take his share in the war. In assenting to his urgent pleas the father – and the mother also – offered the dearest of all possible sacrifices on the altar of their country – an only son, whose youth and health might have given them a good reason for evading the ordeal. The sympathy of the whole Empire will go out to Mr and Mrs Rudyard Kipling in their sorrow.' The report has a very personal feeling about it – Gwynne had known John since he was born – and gives the distinct impression that the sacrifice need never have been made – not the most comforting thing for his parents to read.

The stunned family was hit by an avalanche of messages of sympathy. Theodore Roosevelt, who was also to know what it was like to lose a son, was now able to tell them that 'there are so many things worse than death. Kermit [then serving with the British Army] and all my three other boys [Archie and Theodore Junior, both of whom were to serve with the 26th US Infantry Division and were seriously wounded, and Quentin, who became a pilot and was shot down on 14 July 1918 at Château Thierry] will feel exactly as I do.' Conan Doyle hoped 'May all yet be well'. Charles Beresford (M'Turk of the *Stalky* stories) expected that they would feel 'proud to have given such a noble son'. Jerome K. Jerome wrote, 'though I know it sounds trite – I cannot help remembrance of the gallant little lad with whom I once went ski-ing.' Princess Beatrice wrote from Carisbrooke Castle on the Isle of White, 'remembering how often we met at Vernet, I cannot remain silent in the face of the terrible misfortune that has befallen you in the loss of your only precious son. Alas! I know only too well what your grief must be, I beg you to believe how deeply I sympathise with you. I have still 2 dear sons spared to me, so I feel how much harder your trial is than mine.' Princess Beatrice, Queen Victoria's youngest daughter, had married Prince Henry of Battenberg who lost his life in the Ashanti campaign of 1896. Her youngest son, Prince Maurice, was killed in the Ypres Salient on 27 October 1914 and the two surviving sons were the Princes Alexander and Leopold.

Lord Curzon wrote of the 'cry of pain' they must have uttered at the loss of a dear and only son. Rider Haggard offered the '<u>earnest</u> sympathy of one who has gone through such a gate and knows what it means.' In his diary he recorded, 'John Kipling, Rudyard Kipling's son, whom I have known from a child, is wounded and missing, but there is little hope that he may be a prisoner as he was not severely hurt when last seen. Poor Kipling, I know how great have been his anxieties about this boy ever since he entered the Irish Guards about a year ago; now they must be terrible. I know too what view he takes of the world as a place of abode for mortals. I wonder what he thinks of it today! I wrote him a brief note from the Club, but perhaps he has gone to France. Personally I still hope that John may be alive. One wonders how he came to be abandoned in a wounded condition.'

The Attorney General, Edward Carson, remembered seeing John as a little boy on the shore at Rottingdean. 'Now I know that he was a hero and his death – great and noble – brought anguish to a loving father and mother.' Humphry and Mary Ward [the famous novelist] sent their 'deepest and most heartfelt sympathy.' Another famous novelist, the controversial Marie Corelli, remembered, 'When I was ill you wrote me a kind letter which I can never forget. Now that you are in deep trouble will you let me offer you my heartfelt sympathy.'

Anne Lay, wife of the American Consul General in Berlin, wrote as soon as she saw the announcement in *The Times*. 'Is it possible that dear John has been in the war and is missing? . . . I have phoned Julius to start at once on this side and see if we can hear anything. If we should trace him will send someone to see him if possible immediately and do anything needed. How very sad I feel for you both. Words cannot express it. I thought of him still as a young boy in school. Command us at all times if we can do anything.' This was encouraging. Carrie wrote at the bottom of the letter, 'If only she had put a date. The envelope has an English stamp (postmark Oct 15) so it must have come in the [diplomatic] bag.'

The Kiplings' distinguished and famous friends and acquaintances were not the only ones to express their sympathy. Complete strangers, like a certain James O. Hannay from County Dublin, wrote, 'As a stranger I have no right to intrude on your grief with any foolish words of sympathy. But the news of your son which appeared in this morning's papers touched us so nearly that I cannot refrain from telling you how deeply and sincerely we feel for you. Your son commanded No. 5 platoon. Mine No. 6. Your sorrow might well have been – may any day be – ours.' He enclosed 'a light-hearted mention of your boy' in an account of his time at machine-gun school at GHQ. James Hannay was fortunate. His son, Richard, although wounded on 29 July 1917 during the Third Battle of Ypres, survived to end the war as a Captain.

The following touching poem appeared in *The Globe* after the announcement that 'Mr John Kipling, of the Irish Guards, only son of Mr Rudyard Kipling, is reported "Missing, believed killed",

There was a singer of songs-o, a wonderful singer,
Son of the skalds who made valorous songs for our sires
And he speeded his song on the wings of the wave and the tempest,
    Calling a soul to the day of our slothful desires.

Bravely he sang – but they asked of him more than his singing,
    Asked of him more than his wonderful children of song,

And he gave with a heart that with joy healed the breaking of sorrow,
    And tendered his all that the arm of the King might be strong.

Bravely he sang-o, his song brings a solace to mourning,
Halving the tears that are sorrow's with tears that are pride's.
And the song in his heart shall o'ershadow the pain and the weeping
    As the glory of death gives proud men to the anguish it hides.'

It was signed 'R.F.W. Rees'.

According to Carrington there were also some hostile reactions to the news: 'Among his letters were some which reviled him with the brutal assumption that he deserved his loss because, in some way, he had provoked the war. One such letter that came through a neutral country from Germany was openly exultant.' He was also disturbed by letters from mediums, offering to "get in touch" with John by occult methods'. Both outright frauds and naive but genuine believers in the possibility of their being able to reach loved ones who had 'gone over' mushroomed in proportion to the casualty lists. Even educated and intelligent men like Conan Doyle and Sir Oliver Lodge, first principal of the University of Birmingham and a leading light in the Society for Psychical Research, joined the ignorant and the gullible. Lodge's son Raymond was killed on 14 September 1915 (just a few days before John) in the Ypres Salient, and he later wrote *Raymond, or Life and Death*, an account of his attempts to make contact with his son through the medium Mrs Osborne Leonard. Desperate as they were, there is no evidence that Rudyard and Carrie ever contemplated trying to reach John in this way and Rudyard's scorn for those who did was expressed in the poem *En-dor*, written the following year. The name of the poem came from his favourite source, The Bible, and has the sub-title, 'Behold there is a woman that hath a familiar spirit at En-dor,' 1 Samuel xxviii.7. The verses tell the tale of Saul travelling to En-dor and asking the woman to conjure up the spirit of the dead Samuel to help him overcome the threatening Philistines. Kipling's poem begins,

> The road to En-dor is easy to tread
>   For Mother or yearning Wife.
> There, it is sure, we shall meet our Dead
>   As they were even in life.

He then scathingly goes on to describe a typical seance – whispers in the dark, the touch of hands, the visions, the messages – all obtained 'at a price' from the 'alien lips' of mediums who 'twitch and stiffen and slaver and groan'.

Often, at first, what the dear one saith
    Is babble, or jest, or untrue.

Oh, the road to En-dor is the oldest road
    And the craziest road of all!
Straight it runs to the Witch's abode,
    As it did in the days of Saul.
And nothing has changed of the sorrow in store
    For such as go down on the road to En-dor!

There is little doubt that Conan Doyle, an active and vocal convert to spiritualism, would have tried to persuade his friend to try and find solace by attempting to reach John. But Kipling was adamant. There were strong family pressures, too. Kipling's mother, Alice Macdonald, and other members of her intuitive Celtic family, purported to be psychic. Angus Wilson claims that Kipling was too, 'but carefully avoided using his gifts or, at any rate, making them public'. His sister, Trix, then in one of her more rational periods, came to stay in a cottage on the Bateman's estate; she was also a strong believer in the psychic. The mother and daughter's interest in what Kipling called 'Theosophy' in *Something of Myself* had been aroused by the notorious Madame Blavatsky whom they met in Simla in the 1880s. Of Russian origin, she founded the Theosophical Society in 1875, bringing to India in 1879 her theory that all the major religions of the world were only different expressions of the same fundamental truth. This and other 'truths' were imparted to her by psychical communication and Lockwood Kipling called her 'one of the most interesting and unscrupulous imposters he had ever met'. Kipling was fascinated by the woman and her theories, but claims to have remained immune from them. But Trix remained a believer and in 1910, using the pseudonym 'Mrs Holland', she had worked with members of the Society for Psychical Research as a 'cross-correspondent'. This means that, through automatic writing, she and others received fragments of messages, which were then collated (by expert believers such as Sir Oliver Lodge) to form a complete picture. These messages were often prophecies, or other matters considered too sensitive or controversial by their senders to be entrusted to one person. Mrs Holland's writings were written up by Miss Alice Johnson and published in Volume 21 of the Society's papers in 1908/09 and made public in 1995. Other papers referring to Mrs Holland and cross-correspondence were published by W.H. Salter in 1934. It is unlikely that, given this background, Trix would not have pressed Rudyard to seek comfort in her beliefs.

But in *Something of Myself* Kipling reinforced his disdain for 'the road to En-dor', along which he had 'seen too much evil and sorrow and wreck of good minds . . . to take one step along that perilous track'. He described a strange experience he had while watching manoeuvres at Aldershot just before the war, where many of the officers taking part had been 'juniors' in the Boer War. In the heat haze, he 'conceived the whole pressure of our dead of the Boer War flickering and re-forming as the horizon shimmered in the heat; the galloping feet of a single horse, and a voice once well-known that passed chanting ribaldry along the flank of a crack battalion.' He told Gwynne, who was accompanying him, of this vision and of how he felt compelled to turn it into a story. 'But in cold blood it seemed more and more fantastic and absurd, unnecessary and hysterical . . . After the War I threw the draft away. It would have done no good, and it may have opened the door, and my mail, to unprofitable discussion,' he said, thinking of all the crank letters he was receiving. That he had written a story based on the paranormal in *They* seemed to have escaped his memory. But there had been no widespread flurry of desperate parents trying to communicate with their children after Josephine had died as there was in the period after John's death. Kipling did admit to once having passed 'beyond the bounds of ordinance' when he had a vivid dream of being present at a ceremony which he could not properly see 'because the fat stomach of my neighbour on my left barred my vision'. After the ceremony a man came up to him, 'slipped his hand beneath my arm, and said: "I want a word with you".' This scenario was repeated in reality and in exact detail six weeks or more later [on 19 July 1922] when 'I attended in my capacity of a Member of the War Graves Commission a ceremony at Westminster Abbey, where the Prince of Wales dedicated a plaque to "The Million Dead" of the great War.' A puzzled Kipling wondered, 'But how, and why, had I been shown an unreleased roll of my life-film? For the sake of the "weaker brethren" – and sisters [and here he might have meant the gullible likes of Trix] – I made no use of the experience.'

He had, however, used elements of the supernatural and the psychic in several of his short stories. The first was *The Sending of Dana Da*, published in 1888. It is the story of a 'miracle', confessed to be a fraud by Dana Da on his death bed, and probably inspired by his brush with Madame Blavatsky and her 'occult phenomena'. Then in 1909 came *The House Surgeon*. It is a psychic detective story with obvious borrowings from Conan Doyle and his famous characters, Sherlock Holmes and Dr Watson. The haunted house in which the story is set (said to have been based on Rock House, Maidencombe, Torquay, where Rudyard lived in 1896–7) is even called 'Holmescroft'. *In the Same Boat*, 1911, describes a brother and sister whose terrifying recurring nightmares are revealed to be caused by their mother's experience while carrying them. *The Dog Hervey*, published in April 1914 was felt by Carrington to be 'Kipling's most difficult tale . . . It abounds in literary, masonic, psychological and canine clues which lead nowhere.' Nevertheless, unless it was a case of the

103

gentleman protesting too much to hide a belief of which he was ashamed, Kipling appears to have stuck to his guns.

Whilst Rudyard was warding off the spiritualist faction, Carrie was distressed in case her mother first heard the news of John from the press because 'the telegrams come in hourly from India, Canada, Australia, S. Africa'. She sent her a copy of the Colonel's letter: 'You will like the letter from his Colonel. It's a nice picture – the gallant boy with his men leading and encouraging them and the Colonel under whom he was trained wrote Rud he was a most excellent officer.' Extraordinarily she maintained, 'We do not grudge him for a second. It would have been intolerable to have had him do otherwise than take his part but the anxiety is almost beyond bearing.' And then she voiced her main fear, 'One knows how the Germans treat prisoners only too well.' But enquiries were in motion: 'The PoW [Prince of Wales] who belongs to John's Division is going to help to sift the matter and we have asked the American Ambassador in Berlin to see if he can discover if he is in hospital but they have told us for a long time Gerrard [the Ambassador] is slack and a German sympathiser at heart so he may not bother though I believe Washington may ask him.' By the 11th she was reporting that there were 'thousands of letters which must in part be answered and the telegrams. Mrs Gladstone sent a cable. There was a telegram from General French looking as if the ground was retaken where John was wounded and if that is the case they may find some trace of him and the next days may bring us some news.'

The Prince of Wales connection came from Rupert Grayson, via Lady Edward. Rupert had received 'a Blighty one' in the 27 September attack. In his autobiography, *Voyage Not Completed*, he wrote a whole chapter entitled, 'My Friends the Kiplings'. When discussing his part in the battle he proudly quoted from Kipling's History of the Irish Guards, '2nd Lieutenants Sassoon and Grayson were wounded, the last being blown up by a shell.' As he came to in the Royal Free Hospital, having first been taken to base hospital at le Tréport and then by ship to Southampton, he heard that John had been reported missing. In the train of thought that followed, Grayson painted one of the most sympathetic word-pictures ever written of Carrie and Rudyard. 'As I lay in my hospital bed and closed my eyes I could at will seem to see Rudyard Kipling,' he reminisced, 'a short, wiry, alert man with steely blue eyes peering through his spectacles under bushy eyebrows and bald head, firm chin poked forward. His glasses were part of him, as headlights are part of a car. At school he was known as "gigs", after the lamps on each side of a gig. He was pedantically neat, with a butterfly collar and dark tie, pinned neatly beneath his high-buttoned waistcoat. Mrs Kipling chose his clothes, his ties, shirts and shoes as she chose his publishers, agents and bankers; and those who did not know whispered that she chose his friends as carefully. She was everything to him – the mother of his children, wife, secretary, nurse, banker and literary adviser – from the time they were married at All Souls', Langham Place (the pepperpot, he called it), until his death . . . Carrie was never far from his side and undoubtedly influenced him in everything he did. He rarely told a story that he did not call on her to finish. Added to her courage, she had an acute sense of humour, and together at table they passed the conversation from one to the other like a ball in a juggler's act. She invariably interspersed her talk, which never failed to be lively, with a neat little cough followed by a most infectious laugh.' Rupert was an acute observer and of Kipling he said, 'He gave his greatest attention to young people. The friends who came to Bateman's were rarely middle-aged. He liked the old if they were interesting, but the young he liked because they were young.'

Not long after experiencing this train of memory Rupert was visited by Lady Edward, 'a great friend of the Kiplings . . . she wanted to know about John, everything I could tell her. That was little because there was little to tell, and I was still suffering from the effects of concussion. But this was about the time I myself had first heard about John being missing. I was filled with a great sadness. I had lost a close friend and the regiment a grand officer. I was able to tell her only of how we awaited the grey dawn and of the casually tense trivialities before we went into action. It was little comfort to grieving parents. The next day Kipling came to see me himself, solely out of friendship and loyalty to John. He already knew I had nothing to tell him. He was holding himself under control, but the light had gone from his eyes' – this was something which struck many people who knew Rudyard well at this stage. Of the visit Carrie wrote to Lady Edward, probably not knowing that she too had visited Rupert, 'We saw a brother officer of John's on Tuesday who could I think have told us nothing even if we had asked but he was so shy of our trouble we did not talk of the advance but of their days in France. It was a delight to come near his life in those days and we seized it and let the other go. No news – a great darkness seems to be settling down on it all. But who should know better than you.'

But Rupert 'was able to make a suggestion that might give the family hope, or help them over the period of first shock. The Prince of Wales was attached to the Staff of Lord Cavan who commanded the Guards Division. He had a roving commission of which he took full advantage, moving among the troops from one end of our lines to the other. He was a familiar and much-loved figure. I suggested to Kipling that he was the one man who had the opportunity and authority to investigate the disappearance of one particular man in a battle where the dead and wounded were being counted in their thousands. The question was: would he do it? Nothing could be lost by asking him,' thought the intrepid Rupert. 'But the answer was really never in doubt; the Prince was a great-hearted man. A few days later I received this letter by hand-of-officer:

H.Q. Guards Div
October 15, 1915.

Dear Grayson,

Many thanks for your letter. I must apologise for the long delay of this answer, but it hasn't been easy to get hold of any information regarding Kipling. My answer is the enclosed note from Bird, who, I understand, was his company commander: I wrote to him as I thought he would know as much as anyone, and then I saw Father Knapp [the battalion's well-loved Catholic priest, who was awarded the DSO and the MC and was killed on 31 July 1917 during the Third Battle of Ypres] yesterday, whose story was much the same as Bird's in every detail. We can but trust he is a prisoner . . . I hope you are getting on well and will soon be out of hospital. I am sorry I can't tell you more about Kipling, but I have done my best.

Yours very sincerely,
EDWARD.'

Yet another avenue had opened only to lead to one more dead end, but the young Prince had tried, which would have pleased Carrie in particular.

Grayson reported a further strange example of the way Kipling was affected by John's situation. 'Valentine Castlerosse [Captain Lord Castlerosse, of the 1st Battalion, wounded at Villers Cotterets on 1 September 1914] unaware that John had that day been reported missing, happened to call in at Bateman's. The day passed pleasantly, for Valentine was a wit and a brilliant conversationalist, and Kipling was showing his usual grip of affairs and arriving at conclusions with his crystal-clear reasoning. Then the time came for Valentine to leave. "I'm off to France, so I'll be seeing John and I'll tell him that I've seen you." Kipling paused in his walk, looked Valentine straight in the face, and in a great voice that rang out like a trumpet, cried: *"He is missing".'* One shudders to imagine how the unfortunate Castlerosse felt at his blunder.

Rupert wrote to the Kiplings himself as soon as he was able, 'I wanted to write and tell you how worried and anxious I feel about old John. I was blown up by a shell myself and though I have not been wounded I have lost my memory and my nerves are a bit shattered. They tell me John is reported missing but I feel sure that it will all come right as everything was in a terrible muddle. I myself was officially reported missing, and have been in hospital here. Please remember me to Mrs Kipling, and tell her that we must still hope for the best in this anxious time. Dear old John, I have a feeling he'll turn up all right.'

Despite his grief, which was only occasionally allowed to be glimpsed,

Kipling found the time to reply to Rupert: 'I am sorry to learn – though it isn't in the least surprising seeing what you have gone through, that you are still a bit shaken up. However, I can assure you for your consolation that with your youth and temperament you will come through without damage ... So when you are feeling like "three penn'orth of tripe" as John used to say, remember that it isn't your weakness declaring itself but your strength coming back ... The serious matter seems to me the loss of your dog,' he continued in typical light-hearted Kipling fashion, 'A man has a feeling about a dog which is quite apart from other feelings. I only wish I had one that I could venture to recommend to fill the old one's place: but our animal Jack is rather a mongrel hound of reserved character and absolutely no morals. He began life as a poacher, under the able tuition of his sister, a brown and white rough-haired terrier bitch. And if ever that expressive word exactly expressed a lady, it did in her case.' Jack was the remaining terrier of the pair (the bitch was called Betty) bought for John and Elsie in 1910 and his name reinforces the fact that the family never referred to John as 'Jack' – for that was the name of his dog. Kipling went on to suggest that Rupert get a Sealyham; 'There isn't a wiser or more gentlemanly breed alive.' He was pleased that Rupert's mother had said that he would visit Bateman's when he felt fitter 'and that prospect is making us happy. There is a literary career open for you when you feel like it,' he ended, with a suggestion for some occupational therapy. It was 'the manufacture of scrap-books for the wounded in hospital. I do a bit at it myself.' It consisted of taking 'a mass of magazines, weekly papers, *John Bull, Life, Punch*, etc. – anything with fairly vulgar jokes. You cut out the pictures, from ads of motor bikes to beautiful females without clothes (the hospitals like this) and you mix in the vulgar jokes in the proportion of about 3 to 5. Then you take 12 sheets, not more, of brown paper and gum the resulting mixture on to 'em. Sometimes one makes a refined scrapbook – pretty girls and squashy verses – for a delicate soul. Otherwise one goes in for purely comic effects. Elsie invented this idea but they are called R.K. scrap-books. There is a great deal more art in making them than you would imagine. You'll probably have to make or help make some at Bateman's. If this disgusts you let me know.' Rudyard actually had some more serious therapy for himself: 'I've been among some of our ships lately – down in a submarine and so on and am now trying to write any impressions. It was a most interesting time.' An unusually sober postcript revealed his inner turmoil, 'Remember what I told you, the next time you feel more than usually wretched. "There are many liars but there are no liars like our own sensations." I forget where that comes from but it is true.' Rupert knew him well enough to deduce from this cryptic remark that 'Sorrow had eaten deep into Kipling's heart. He was quieter and seemed to lean more and more on his beloved Carrie.'

The R.K. scrapbooks were taken up by the Red Cross War Library which was established to supply free books and magazines to the sick and wounded in hospitals and hospital ships in the UK and abroad. The Joint War Committee Report 1914–1919, published by HMSO in 1921, reported, 'Scrapbooks were made in the first instance at the suggestion of Mr Rudyard Kipling for patients, especially those suffering from typhoid and dysentery, who were too weak, to hold or to read an ordinary book. They were made to a regulation size, 14 x 4 inches, and contained eight leaves of pictures, anecdotes, verse, etc. In response to an appeal a great number of such scrapbooks were made by the public. This was a branch of the work most required and appreciated by the patient.'

News about John soon started to pour in from many quarters, much of it conflicting and confusing. The Kiplings began tracking down men who were wounded in the same attack and who were now turning up in hospitals. Millicent Payne-Gallwey wrote from her Red cross hospital in Wantage that a Sergeant Davidson of the Irish Guards was there and that he told her that he had seen John 'fall wounded. It struck him as a leg wound and not very serious. He thinks there is no reason why he should not be safe. He speaks of him as a keen young officer, who bore all the hardships splendidly.' This sounded so hopeful that Carrie at once sent a telegram to the hospital, but she got the reply that, having gone ahead, Sergeant Davidson 'could not answer all your questions. He was wounded soon afterwards himself.' Carrie reported this exchange to Lady Edward, telling her that Lady Aitken had discovered three Irish Guardsmen in the Canadian Hospital at Beachborough, near Hythe. They rushed over to interview them but were somewhat disappointed to find 'only one of them from John's platoon . . . called Rafter, a delightful fellow over six feet. He was wounded on the Monday in the Chalk Pit Wood, two bullets and a shrapnel, and a fortnight from that was ready to go to a Convalescent Home. He said that he was wounded at 7 o'clock in the evening and that John was still at the Chalk Pit Wood then. Of course there is a mistake.' She meant as regards the timing; they were beginning to learn at first hand the inherent unreliability of soldiers' accounts, often coloured by a desire to be helpful and to offer a ray of hope. Carrie then referred to a long letter that she had received from a Mrs Cuthbert, the mother of 'Captain Cuthbert 1st Scots Guards with whom your dear son was when they were both "lost". My brother-in-law General Cuthbert says that my son went alone into the minehouse unwounded and wasn't seen again. Presumably he went to help or bring out your son, preparatory to falling back with his small force, too small, alas! and possibly was captured, your boy too, by an ambush of Germans in the building, and taken away by them when the body who attacked and defeated the unfortunate guardsman occupied it. My brother-in-law writes that patrols searched and brought away some wounded, but found no trace of Harold, nor, of course, your boy.' She then asked Rudyard's help in getting in touch with hospitals 'with 1st

1. *Left to right:* Elsie, John and Josephine Kipling in 1898.

2. Elsie and John Kipling, c.1900.

3. John Kipling in uniform, 1915.

4. John Kipling and friends, Warley, 1915.

H. A. Law
Lt. Langriske
J. Kipling
R.L.A. Close
S.S.7 Christie
J. B. Keenan

Warley.
1915

OFFICERS — 2ND BATTALION. WARLEY. JUNE. 1915.

LT R.S GRAYSON.　LT W.CLIFFORD　LT D.W.GUNSTON　LT D GRAYSON.　LT T.E.G. NUGENT.　LT A.R. PYM.　LT J.B. KEENAN.　LT R HANNAY.　LT LORD CASTLEROSSE.

LT D.C. PARSONS.　LT HON H. HARMSWORTH　LT J.B DOLLAR.　LT H. LAW.　LT H. BLOM.　LT G.WALTERS.　LT TISDALL.　LT B.B.WATSON.　LT T. PACKENHAM LAW.　LT R.E. SASSOON.

CAPT G.N. HUBBARD.　CAPT HON H. R. ALEXANDER.　CAPT E.B. GREER.　CAPT HON T VESEY.　LT COL THE EARL OF KERRY.　MAJ SIR J. HALL.　CAPT PACKENHAM.　CAPT J.B. BIRD　LT Q B J TINCKLER.

LT C.H. BREW.　LT J KIPLING.　LT H. LANGRISHE.　LT G.F.B. HINE.　LT C.F. PURCELL.

6. Rudyard and Carrie Kipling in Dud Corner Cemetery, Loos, 1930.

7. John Kipling's name on Memorial Wall, Dud Corner, Loos.

IRISH GUARDS

LIEUTENANT	LCE CORPORAL	PRI
KIPLING J.	O'ROURKE P.	DOY
SECOND LIEUT.	QUINLAN P.J.	DUN
CLIFFORD W.F.J.	PRIVATE	COU
		GRA
LCE SERJEANT	BANNON M.	CREE
	BEGLAN M.	GUIL
CASEY J.E.	BOLAND W.	HAR
DNEY B.	BULLEN R.	HIGG
EWIS C.	BURKE J.	HOL
	CAHILL M.	JOLL
CE CORPORAL	CLARKE T.J.	KEAT
OCHERTY M	CLARKIN P.	KEAT
ILMOUR B.M.		

8. Searching the battlefields for bodies.

9. Exhumation during battlefield clearance.

SHEET 44a.

CONCENTRATION OF GRAVES (Exhumation and Re-burials).

BURIAL RETURN.

Name of Cemetery of Re-burial — ST. MARY'S CEMETERY.   Map.Ref. G.17.B.8.9.   23.9.19

Plot	Row	Grave	Map Reference where body found.	Was Cross on Grave?	Regimental particulars.	Means of Identification.	Were any effect forwarded to Base?
D.	"	2	G.25.C.6.8.	No.	U.B.S. Officer Lieut. Irish Guards.		
"	"	3	"	"	U.B.S.		
"	"	4	"	"	U.B.S.		
"	"	5	G.25.C.9.9.	Yes *	2829 BLABER.P. 15th London Reg.Civil Service Rfs. K.I.A. 9.11.15.		
"	"	6	"	"	1802 Pte.McGee.P. 6th Royal Irish Reg.K.I.A. 6.6.16.		
"	"	7	"	No	U.B.S.		
"	"	8	G.25.C.6.8.	"	U.B.S.		
"	"	9	"	"	15th London Reg. U.B.S.	Numeral Found.	
"	"	10	G.25.C.9.9.	"	U.B.S.		
"	"	11	G.25.C.9.4.	"	U.B.S. Irish Guards.		
"	"	12	"	"	U.B.S.	Numeral Found.	
"	"	13	G.25.C.9.9.	"	U.B.S.		
"	"	14	"	"	U.B.S.		
"	"	15	G.25.C.25.	"	U.B.S.		
"	"	16	"	"	U.B.S.		
"	"	17	G.25.D.1.3.	Yes	633732 Pte.McPherson.T. 3rd Coy.		
"	"	18	G.25.G.2.5.	No	U.B.S.		
"	"	19	"	"	U.B.S.		
"	"	20	"	"	U.B.S.		

A.H. Domaille. 2/Lt.
For Lieut.O.C. 18th Labour Coy.

10. Burial return sheet 1. 23 September 1919. Note all map references begin with 'G'. Note also entries for Irish Guards and 2829 BLABER.P.

CONCENTRATION OF GRAVES (Exhumation and Re-burials).

BURIAL RETURN.

Name of Cemetery of Re-burial ST. MARYS CEMETERY.

Map Ref. G.N7B.8.9. 23.9.1919.

Sheet 44A.

Plot	Row	Grave	Map Reference where body found.	Was Cross on Grave?	Regimental particulars.	Means of Identification.	Were any effec[ts] forwarded to Base?
D	8	1.	G.25.C.2.5.	NO.	U.B.S. Irish Gds. Numeral found.		
		2.	"	"	U.B.S.		
		3.	"	"	U.B.S.		
		4.	G.25.C.9.2.	"	U.B.S. Canadian Numeral found.		
		5.	"	"	U.B.S.		
		6	"	"	U.B.S.		
		7	"	"	U.B.S.		
		8	"	"	U.B.S.		
		9	"	"	U.B.S.		
		10	"	"	U.B.S.		
		11	"	"	U.B.S.		
		12	"	"	U.B.S.		
		13	"	"	U.B.S.		
		14	"	"	U.B.S.		
		15	"	"	U.B.S.		
		16	G.25.D.1.3.	"	U.B.S.		
		17	"	"	U.B.S.		
		18	"	"	U.B.S.		
		19	A.28.B.9.5.	"	U.B.S.		
		20	"	"	U.B.S.		

(Sgd) A.H. Domaille. 2/Lieut.
for Lieut. O.C. 18th Labour Coy.

11. Burial return sheet 2. 23 September 1919. Note 'G' map reference and Irish Guards identification.

12. Headstones at St. Mary's A.D.S. *Left:* A Lieutenant of the Irish Guards; the original headstone. *Right:* Lieutenant John Kipling, Irish Guards; the replacement headstone.

13. Headstone of Private Blaber, Civil Service Rifles.

14. An Irish Guards Soldier's 'star' which could readily have been mistaken for an officer's 'pip'.

'MY BOY JACK?'

The Search for Kipling's Only Son

Additional photographs for the 3rd edition

15. Puits 14 in 1905

16. How John Kipling would have seen the top of Puits 14 as he approached, seen across the Chalk Pit.

17. The front view of Puits 14 today. The winding gear has now been dismantled.

18. The name of Lieutenant A.L.H. Jacob, 1/18th London (Irish) Regiment on the Memorial Wall at Dud Corner.

19. The path leading to the Chalk Pit and Puits 14 today. The 2nd Irish Guards attacked along this route.

20. The 'Lone Tree' at le Rutoir, replanted on 25 September 1995.

Scots or 2nd Irish Guards in them', and questioned the wisdom of the orders that had sent her son so far forward 'with what is described as a "few men".' With some bitterness she concluded, 'There is very much to be explained and <u>paid for</u> at the end of this awful war.'

In enclosing a copy of this letter to Lady Edward, Carrie commented, '[it] adds confusion to confusion. I think she must have invented the idea that Captain Cuthbert went into the building to see John, because if they were fighting hard and Captain Cuthbert was the only officer, I do not see how he could have left his men. I think the more probable solution is that he went into the building when he retired through it. The value of her letter is that we shall now hunt for 1st Scots Guards as well as 2nd Irish wounded.' She told her mother that she had actually met Captain Cuthbert's 'wife (or widow)' at one of her Committee Meetings, probably for the Red Cross. 'He also went into a building to tie up a wound . . . (close to John's building on the map) . . . We hope he and John may have been together when the Germans fought our men back. One takes comfort from small things and we feel so glad to think John may possibly not have had to face that onrush alone.' As mentioned in John's letter of 17 September, although Cuthbert (known as Harold, but first name James) was serving with the Scots Guards on 27 September, he was in fact an Irish Guards officer, had been Adjutant of the Reserve Battalion at Warley and obviously knew John. It is quite probable, therefore, that he would have wanted to help the lad when he saw him wounded. Like John, his body disappeared and he too is commemorated on the Loos Memorial at Dud Corner.

After this raising and dampening of hopes, Carrie was again buoyed by a letter from a young Coldstreamer, C.P. Blacker, who wrote that he had met John on a ship coming back from Engelberg with Oscar Hornung and that 'his death is deeply felt out here by all who knew him. Everyone admired him, and everyone liked him, officers and men alike.' 'These boys are so nice,' she wrote at the foot of the letter. 'Could anything be more delightful than this.'

On 12 October Captain John Bird, who commanded No 2 Company, wrote the Kiplings the expected formal notification of John's probable situation, headed 'In trenches'. He described the attack of 26/27 September and how John, leading his platoon, advanced with the Grenadiers and the Scots on Puits 14 and a 'Red Brick House'. 'There were machine guns in these buildings and although they had been heavily shelled they opened from them a considerable fire and also from another wood just beyond. Two of my men say they saw your son limping just by the Red House and one saw him fall and somebody run to his assistance, probably his orderly who is also missing . . . I am very hopeful that he is a prisoner. This could be, I presume, confirmed by getting the American Embassy to ascertain. Your son behaved with great gallantry and coolness and handled his men splendidly. I trust that your great anxiety may be allayed by definite news of his safety soon. Please accept my most heartfelt sympathy. I had a great affection for him.'

This window of hope was kept open by a letter dated 14 October from Frank Witts, an officer in John's company. He reiterated how well John had led his men that afternoon 'without any hesitation or faltering though it was his first time in action. What that means I know for I have been out here many months, myself. I was close behind and saw his platoon crossing the open for nearly a mile under shell and machine gun fire without a break or bend in the line, it was a grand sight . . . After he reached the wood I did not see him again, but with the greatest pluck and courage he led his men further and was in fact mixed up with Scotts [sic] Guards when he was last seen. It is my earnest hope that he will still be found alive.'

Lieutenant Colonel Butler wrote a statement which confirmed that John's platoon had reached 'just beyond PUITS 14. While there Kipling was seen to hobble back to the buildings of PUITS 14 apparently shot in the leg, and to lean against a wall of PUITS 14. Shortly after this our troops fell back from PUITS 14. Kipling has not been heard of since. Presumably he was left wounded in PUITS 14 and fell into German hands.'

The Kiplings would have taken comfort not only for the consistency of the story that he was wounded in the leg and had probably been taken prisoner, but also from the many expressions of praise for John's bravery. All Rudyard's hopes and aspirations for John, from his very birth, were that he should pursue a naval or military career, the ultimate concluding glory of which is, of course, an heroic and glorious sacrificial death in the service of King and Country. Commanding Officers' letters of sympathy to bereaved parents of widows were often of a steriotypical nature and naturally tended to enhance the qualities of the deceased. Yet through all the letters about John shines a genuine affection and admiration for a likeable young officer, who was lost doing an extremely good job. He was obviously capable of inspiring much affection. Even the staff at Brown's Hotel were 'desolated' at his loss.

About this time came some light relief in the form of a visit from their favourite nephew, Oliver Baldwin. 'He has left school and has a tutor until Spring when he goes into the Army. He was born the Spring of the year Rud was ill in America and will be 17 the Spring of 1916. A nice boy and a great delight to see a boy about,' Carrie wrote to her mother. Still reeling from the thought that John might be dead, she could not bring herself to say 'the year Josephine died', but rather 'the year Rud was ill'. For the next few years Oliver, who was not at all deterred from his burning desire to get to the front by the news about John, would be the nearest thing to a son they had.

Lady Edward, only too pleased to help the Kiplings in their hour of need, as they had helped her, had been extremely active. Carrie returned a wire that Clemenceau had sent and remarked, 'The letter you send about Lord Edmund Talbot seems to prove that Mr Gwynne is quite wrong in his idea that he has been able to and could help. What I cling to as a second line is old Goschen. [British Ambassador in Berlin when war broke out] . . . Your writing to the Crown Princess of Sweden is a stroke of genius. Her German mother-in-law has expressed admiration always for R.K. who . . . once met her in Sweden [when receiving the Nobel Prize] and later in Italy, and there is a chance she may be moved to help. I myself believe that Rud is correct and that the Germans if they have got John will not be slow to advertise it.' Pathetically she added, 'Rafter said of John that he was "never downhearted", which makes one not so downhearted oneself'

Rudyard was indeed so convinced that the Germans would make propaganda use of the capture of a famous author's son that he arranged for a leaflet, asking for news of John, to be dropped by aeroplane over the German lines. In his Introduction to the 1977 reprint of Kipling's *History of the Second Battalion of the Irish Guards,* George Webb, Editor of the *Kipling Journal,* says the leaflet, written in German, asks for news of the son of the world-famous author [*Sohn des weltberühmten Schriftstellers*] and whether he is dead or alive. One would assume that this was done quite soon after John's disappearance, but Rider Haggard's diary does not record the leaflet drop until 17 March 1917. In any event there was no response. Haggard, too, was keeping an eye on the news. On 16 October he noted that the agent he shared with Kipling, A.P. Watt, had sent him an extract from a letter Carrie had written them about John. It described Bird's account and Haggard commented, 'He was in advance of his men at the time and up to last Tuesday nothing more had been heard of him. Still he may be captured and alive. It is terribly anxious work for his family. If perchance he is dead, it would be better to know the worst at once. Yet his is only one of hundreds of similar cases which excites my particular interest because I happen to know him and his parents.' Two days later he saw that 'John Kipling is included in the list of missing only, not among the "missing and wounded", or "missing believed killed", so there is good hope that he has been taken prisoner.'

As for Princess Margaret, she was prompt to respond to Lady Edward's plea. On 19 October she wrote from Stockholm on her royal crested paper, with an 'M' surmounted by a crown, 'Dear Lady Edward, Thank you so much for your letter. I am only too glad to help the poor Kiplings. I have written to two different people in Germany at once and should I get any news I will telegraph straight to the Kiplings, the sooner it is possible to relieve their anxiety the better. It sounds as if he ought to be a prisoner but even if he is and the other officers too the Germans are always slow in answering and sometimes those who have been missing and wounded for months past have turned up. It seems they keep no proper lists of those in hospitals or cottages in Belgium. I suppose on purpose! Will you give the Kiplings my kind message from me and say that as far as I am concerned I will do all I can and wish it were more.' She was obviously a Kipling fan. 'I wonder if Kipling is going to bring out a book with what he has seen at the front? How interesting it would be . . . Yours, Margaret.' But despite her willingness to help, Princess Margaret could find out little. On 2 November she wrote again to Lady Edward, enclosing two cards in reply to her questions about John and a Lieutenant Medley, both drawing a blank. 'The only ray of hope is that they say *"noch nichts"*. It may be that they are in hospitals in Belgium and of those who are there they always refuse to send lists. I am so sorry. Please tell the Kiplings I have done all I could. I will make another effort about Belgium.' As a thankyou for her efforts, Rudyard sent Princess Margaret one of his books which she told Lady Edward she 'thought most kind of him'.

Rudyard had written to the U.S. Minister in Holland, Mr Van Dyke, to see if he could dredge up some news from the Germans. He and Carrie had met him at the Depews' Château near Compiègne at Christmas of 1913. It had been a jolly time, with Van Dyke's two children joining the festivities. Julia Depew later wrote, 'You can imagine what a Christmas that was. One not easily forgotten by old or young.' Van Dyke had an interesting background. He was a clergyman, had been professor of English literature at Princeton, lectured at the Sorbonne in 1908/9, and was Minister to Holland and Luxembourg 1913–1916. In 1917 he became chaplain to the US Navy. But Carrie was not confident that he would be able to achieve much, as 'the Germans will not trouble and in fact try and give pain and rejoice in it. The best way to find out is by a sort of secret service and this is all at work. Sometimes the uncertainty drives me nearly off my head.' Carrie now, and ever more bitterly, had begun to share Rudyard's hatred for 'the Hun', vividly manifested in the story *Mary Postgate*, written before John was posted missing, but published in that very month of September, leading many people to believe, mistakenly, that it was written in a frenzy of hatred because of his son's loss.

It is the story of a 44-year-old spinster, Mary Postgate, and there is a great deal both of Carrie and of Rudyard in her character. She was engaged as a companion to a 60-year-old spinster (Miss Fowler) who was suddenly given charge of her orphaned 11-year-old nephew, Wyndham. It soon fell to Mary to see to all the boy's needs: getting him off to school with all the correct kit, playing with him during the holidays, acting as his intermediary with Miss Fowler. An affectionate relationship built up between the two otherwise unloved human beings. When the war broke out Wynn 'announced on a postcard that he had joined the Flying Corps'. When he demanded an increase in his allowance (shades of John),

Kipling prophetically put into Miss Fowler's mouth the words, 'He must have it. The chances are he won't live long to draw it.' Indeed, before he had completed his training the lad was killed 'during a trial flight'.

Mary's reaction had interesting comparisons to the Kiplings' on hearing the news of John being posted missing. She outwardly contained her feelings while 'the room was whirling' round her as she read the 'announcement in an official envelope' and simply said, 'It's a pity he didn't die in action after he had killed somebody.' John's almost certain death was more acceptable because he probably had. Miss Fowler decided to give away all Wynn's clothes. They would keep only his cap and belt – a memento for each of them – and as for his toys, books and other possessions 'burn every single thing . . . so that no one can handle them afterwards.' His books – the Hentys and Marryats and other boys' favourite reading – his gramophone and cracked records, his OTC and sports team photos, his model ships and jigsaw puzzles – all were listed in such detail that one can imagine Rudyard making a careful inventory of the contents of John's bedroom. In particular there was 'a packet of all the letters that she [Mary] and Miss Fowler had ever written to him' – much as John had carefully preserved all his family's letters, which would be returned to them.

Mary burnt all these well-loved remnants of a young and unfulfilled life on an open-air furnace. Just as she was emerging from the village shop with a bottle of paraffin there was a loud crack which she interpreted as a bomb dropped from a German plane. In the wreckage of a 'cart-lodge' a nine-year-old girl was killed. The local doctor, who tended the little girl's shocked mother, later told Mary that the accident was simply caused by the dangerously rotten beams in the stable collapsing and warned her not to spread rumours in the village about any other possible cause. Significantly, however, Miss Fowler then told her that she had heard a couple of aeroplanes passing half an hour before.

Mary carried on with her fire when she became aware of the body of a man in uniform pinned by a branch to the foot of an oak tree. He had hair 'so closely cropped that she could see the disgustingly pinky skin beneath'. There was no doubt as to his nationality. It made her so angry that she rushed back to the house to get the revolver that the two spinsters had acquired on hearing of 'certain Belgian reports' [obviously of German atrocities]. It fired 'flat-nosed bullets, which . . . Wynn said, were forbidden by the rules of war to be used against civilized enemies.'

The mesmerisingly appalling climax to the story has been much discussed – how Mary ignored the wounded German's pleas for help, whipping herself into a frenzy of hatred by recalling what had happened to the little village girl, to her own Wynn, as she jabbed at the funeral pyre of his belongings, humming unaccustomedly to herself and with 'a glow which seemed to reach to the marrow of her bones'. She decided that her strength of will in simply allowing the man to die was '*her* work – work which no man . . . would ever have done' [For was not the female of the species more deadly than the male?] Then 'the end came very distinctly in a lull between two rain-gusts. Mary Postgate drew her breath short between her teeth and shivered from head to foot.' At home afterwards Miss Fowler saw her 'lying all relaxed on the other sofa, quite handsome'. It was explicitly shocking stuff, but, the sexual connotations aside, the element of revenge was perfectly acceptable to most readers at the time it was published.

Reactions to the story would have helped to occupy Rudyard's mind, although he and Carrie were still frantically rushing from hospital to hospital interviewing the wounded of the Loos battle. They had obviously compiled a minute-by-minute chart of John's last movements and marked up a map. These always accompanied them on their interviews, and information was carefully checked against them. Already more inconsistencies had been thrown up. The comforting thought that John was merely wounded in the leg was already shaken by another eye witness who said he saw John shot in the neck. On 26 October Rudyard went to the Eastern General Hospital in Brighton and took a statement from Private Troy of the 2nd Bn Irish Guards who had been in No 3 Coy, 9th Platoon, who offered a clear and detailed memory of the afternoon of 27 September. 'His account of the fight squares exactly with the geography of the ground as reported to me by various wounded, and is confirmed by the map,' said Rudyard in his report. 'He states that in their first advance they came on through Chalk Pit Wood, and from Chalk Pit Wood charged in the direction of a house on their left and some mining buildings on their right. The house was a two-storeyed one, full of Germans with machine-guns. This house they took, and Troy noticed John firing into the windows of it with his revolver.' Unlike Wynn Fowler, John had the opportunity to kill Germans. This news would have delighted Rudyard. That was the last Troy saw of John, but he ended his account with another pleasing bit of information, 'He says that John was good to his men, and in France used to buy them bread and tea, and note-paper to write home with.'

The thought that John had not just been wounded in the leg but in the head caused Carrie to write in despair to Lady Edward, 'If he was captured he might from the nature of the wound have lost his mind; I often think I shall do the same.' As each new piece of the jigsaw came in, Carrie reported the findings both to Lady Edward and to her mother, noting the contradictions ('This story does not fit with Colonel Butler's account.' Another report was 'not satisfactory by a long way'.) Only to these two women did she freely express the fears that she hid from the outside world. At the end of October she wrote, 'We hear today from Berlin the letter coming via the American Ambassador here sent of course in his bag that if John is alive wounded and a prisoner it may well be 2 months before the Germans will give them any information. The wounded are kept in Belgium and they never report until they are well enough to go to Prisoner Camp in Germany. Of course we send them word at once. So there is nothing for it but to sit out our trial and be turned from side to side hunting here for confirmation and waiting to hear from Germany. The recent murder of Nurse Cavell does not exactly make one feel easy.' [She had been executed on 12 October.] Some days later Carrie continued on the same theme, 'You realize of course this waiting for news of wounded and prisoners is quite unnecessary. The Hague Convention provided machinery for the officers and both England and France send word at once of all theirs buried by us, wounded and prisoners. Every officer and man wears a disc around his neck giving his name rank regiment and religion. The Germans have never sent us a list of dead and delay the information for months and months . . . One must go on, but it's pretty difficult,' she admitted. She was beginning to feel it was 'impossible they should find John's body if he has been killed'. At this time of year she and Rudyard always walked round the Bateman's estate, marking the trees to be chopped down for firewood for the winter. This year she found 'It is rather heart-rending to go about and realize how doubtful it is that there is a son to inherit and carry on the place. He took the keenest interest in every detail and often made excellent suggestions. I particularly looked forward to the time when he would take an active part in the management of things. He was practical and knew how to manage men who liked him always.'

On 26 October a bundle of John's papers was sent to his bank, Messrs Cox & Co, by a Lieutenant Brooke Murray at G.H.Q., B.E.F. It comprised letters contained in a wallet, which had been forwarded to the regiment by the Mayor of the village (probably Acquin) in which the 2nd Battalion had been billeted. Rudyard had great difficulty in obtaining this package and on 14 December he wrote to the War Office asking for 'the proper papers to fill in so that I may obtain my son's effects'. Significantly he added, 'His rank was Second Lieutenant then, but the Gazette of November 9th announced his promotion to Lieutenant under date of June 7th.' He was, he concluded, 'particularly anxious to have my son's effects'. [P.R.O.] As the package had been left before the battle, their return had no bearing on whether John was still alive or not.

November had brought more shattering news. Sir Louis Mallet, who headed the 'Inquiry Department for Wounded and Missing' of the British Red Cross and St John Ambulance, started in Béthune under Major Fabian Ware in October 1914, wrote telling them of a report dated 5 November from a Sergeant Kinnelly [actually Kinneally] of No 4 Coy, 2nd Irish Guards who was in the Guards Camp in Harfleur. Kinneally stated that 'I came on Mr Law [2nd Lieutenant Pakenham-Law] who was dead and then met Sergt. Cole No. 4 Coy, now back at the front. He said "Poor

115

Mr Kipling is killed." Then I came on Mr Kipling myself. He was lying on his face and his head was covered with blood. I am sure he was then dead. This must have been about an hour after he was hit. It would not have been possible for Mr Kipling to have been taken prisoner. The whole Guards' Division was between the Germans and the place where he lay, and we have held the ground ever since.' In the margin at this point Carrie wrote 'quite incorrect'. But Kinneally had more bad news to tell: 'I can easily explain his body not being found and brought in. The ground where he lay was very heavily shelled from the big guns; and men lying there might be buried in a crater. It was impossible to bring in even all the wounded men.'

Sir Louis had asked Fabian Ware to send him the lists of all the graves that had been registered, and if anyone was likely to have news of John's grave it was he. He tried to soften the blow by adding, 'It is of course to be noted that this is the report of one man only, and so possibly confirmation should be awaited,' but finished on a pessimistic note, 'but we fear it leaves but little room for hope.' They could not accept the seeming finality, and on 9 November went to the Guards' HQ to see de Vesci. That day Carrie wrote to her mother, 'All these days we are busy collecting information from wounded soldiers.' They were not taking Kinneally's report as final. They submitted it to Lord Kerry for verification. He thankfully said, 'I do not think that Sergeant Kinnealley's evidence can be accurate. For one thing Pakenham-Law, though I believe he never recovered consciousness after he was wounded, died not on the field but in the dressing station.' He also said that everything he had heard indicated that John had been hit during the advance of 5th Platoon with Scots Guards, whereas the main Irish Guards contingent never got to Puits 14. 'I feel quite certain if the Guards Division, or any part of them, had got between the Germans and the place where he lay as stated, someone would have known of it at the time and his body would have been recovered by now.'

They then tracked down the Sergeant Cole mentioned by Kinneally. He too wrote a summary of his memories of the day. Though his platoon 'was on the extreme right of the line and your son's on the extreme left' he had spoken to a 'Sergeant M Henahan who was in charge of the platoon next to your son's'. Henahan distinctly remembered seeing John's platoon '50 yards in advance of our lines and the time was 4.30 . . . and he was unwounded' as they reached a house. By the time Henahan's platoon reached it there were some Grenadiers and Scots Guards, but he 'saw no sign of Mr Kipling.' Cole raised the possibility that John had advanced beyond the house 'into the second wood'. But a Mrs Kennard, 'presumably in charge of the Hospital where Sergeant Kinneally was treated', sent an amplified version of his report to Landon, who was also doing all he could to help, in which he repeated that 'Mr Kipling . . . was killed about 5 o'clock on the afternoon of the 27th September. I was only 5 or 6 yards away ... Mr Kipling was about 50 yards in front of his platoon and was shouting "Come on boys". He was about the bravest officer I ever saw, and would I believe have won the V.C. A couple of shrapnel burst over his head and I saw him fall. We did not stop.' Kinneally was then 'wounded and gassed in the wood and got no further. I came to in half an hour or so and started with the help of a stick for the dressing station.' He then repeated his story about coming across John's dead body. [Kinneally's, and the other personal accounts quoted here, are reproduced in John's P.R.O. file.]

Carrie would not accept it. On 15 November she wrote to Lady Edward, 'I think from a letter that Rudyard had from Lord Kerry that the Battalion now thinks that John was killed, but that again does not move me much, because I do not think they can be keeping back any news they had, and we probably have had the evidence of as many people as they have, but the interesting thing that he does say is that we have not even now regained the bit of ground where John fell.' In the same letter she acknowledged Lady Manners' message of sympathy sent via Lady Edward and reported that Elsie was going up to London to stay with Lady Bland-Sutton 'in order to work at the Red Cross, and I think that the change will do her good.'

Lord Milner wrote them a belated letter of sympathy, 'I have not written to you in these days of special sorrow and anxiety not because I was not thinking of you, but fearing that even well-meant words of sympathy would only add to your pain. But I think you realise that for any number of reasons, not only personal friendship but the sense of what we all owe to your inspiring patriotism, the blow which has fallen upon you has hit us all very hard and no-one more than myself.' What Kipling would have found of especial solace was the fact that in the letter Milner also asked for his help and advice. 'I am in a very isolated position just now, anxious to do what little I can to help the country, but often very perplexed as to the best course. I still like to talk it over with an understanding friend ... Don't answer this, but do come and see me if you can.' Milner was being wooed by Lloyd George, with whose politics he violently disagreed, to become part of the government the latter had ambitions to lead once Asquith's administration crumbled. This he would eventually decide to do, both men putting aside their previous enmity in view of the crisis facing the nation.

Meanwhile Oliver Baldwin was still chafing at the bit to emulate John. 'My cousin, John Kipling, was commissioned into the newly formed second battalion of the Irish Guards very soon after the declaration, and I was rather jealous of him. He had a gold-braided cap, too, which made things even worse,' he confessed in *The Questing Beast*. He also felt that his father did not understand him. Naturally he wrote to his Uncle Rud. Rudyard wrote him a calming reply on 20 November, very much in the style he used to John. 'The check that you say has been laid upon you is the first part of your burden as a man and it must be met with patience and dignity – both of which you have. I will do all I can to help you by developing the military point of view to your father which is the point I am most competent to speak about. You on your part must promise me not to sulk or storm. I ask this,' he continued poignantly, 'because the relations between a man and his father are the most precious in the world and depend quite as much upon the son as on the father. Once injured they are awfully hard to re-establish. Your father is trying to do what he thinks best for you and if you show any uncontrolled signs of disappointment at his action [Kipling knew his impetuous nephew only too well] you will only be justifying his idea that you are too young to go forward into training.' Stanley Baldwin was well aware of the fate that had befallen his nephew and was doing his utmost to deter his son from following him. 'So remember that you are a man and must meet this situation as a man,' continued the wise Uncle Rud. 'I can't tell you how thoroughly we sympathize in and understand your feelings and I believe your father will later on realize them too and will then release you from the indignities to which your size rather than your age exposes you daily.' Kipling may well have been referring to the changing minimum chest size requirements for recruits and it appeared that Baldwin was not prepared to get the rules stretched for his son as Rudyard had been in regard to John's deficient eyesight. 'I know my advice is hard, but I depend upon you to follow it – as a test.' exhorted Rudyard, as he had often done to John. His trump card was to refer to Oliver's hero cousin; 'Though John often blustered and swore about at large when I gave him advice as a man to a man I can't recall any time when he did not in the long run follow it. And that, I think, gave him the start of the discipline that made him so good a young officer. I'll tell you about it some day. Believe me, managing a son isn't all beer and skittles. Now go on and sit tight and shut your mouth and above all things keep yourself fit.' There is little doubt that Kipling gratefully seized upon the opportunity to lecture Oliver in this paternal fashion now that there was little chance that he would ever again be able to give such advice to his own son.

Rupert Grayson, too, was enlisted to play the role of son. He was encouraged to visit Bateman's as soon as he was fit enough and was immediately roped in to compile 'R.K. scrapbooks'. He had amusing memories of these wartime interludes with the Kiplings and loved to hear Rudyard recount the story of a convalescent Rupert being found asleep one night 'under a roof of his heavy manuscripts'. Rupert's explanation was 'that at that time I was walking in my sleep and I believed that if I had to move a great weight I would wake up.' Kipling would always end the tale, 'And then I knew that for all the years of writing I hadn't laboured in vain.' Another time, during one evening session on the scrapbooks they were 'sitting in front of the great log-fire in the hall – the ashes used to be kept for about a month and formed a bed on which lay the sweet-smelling timber,' recalled Grayson. 'Suddenly I saw something glitter. With a pair of tongs I fished out a diamond bracelet. Mrs Kipling was both delighted and embarrassed, because she had already claimed on the insurance for its loss.' She deserved this bit of luck, for despite the apparent light-heartedness, Rupert, who was very fond of both the Kiplings, noticed the sorrow beneath. 'He kept alive for a long time the hope that John might still be living, but it was not to be. Losing him was a crushing blow from which he never entirely recovered,' he remarked. 'At this time Kipling seldom went to London. He spent long hours at his work-table.' One of the poems he was working on was *A Nativity* published in 1916. In it, Rupert felt, 'he expressed his overwhelming loss and the barren content of his life.' Two verses in particular struck him as moving expressions of the parents' grief for John:

> *The Cross was raised on high;*
> *The Mother grieved beside –*
> But the Mother saw Him die
> And took Him when he died . . .'

> 'Is it well with the child, is it well?'
> The watching mother prayed.
> For I knew not how he fell
> And I know not where he is laid . . .'

Rupert, who already knew that he wanted to write himself, was fascinated to be able to watch the master at work. He was amused that he 'never saw a page of manuscript that he had not decorated with little pictures down the wide margin. "Something my forebears bequeathed to me," he said one day, for his father, Lockwood Kipling, was a fine draughtsman.' Carrie would have approved that 'It was my task to burn the contents of the waste-paper basket. He had an intense dislike of his fame being exploited and took every precaution that none of his manuscripts should fall into the hands of people who would sell them to collectors, nor did he write to anyone who would be likely to sell his letters.' This was a rule that Rudyard was persuaded to break for his cheeky nephew, Oliver. Earlier that year, when he was still at Eton, Ollie had wheedled some valuable Kipling signatures out of Uncle Rud. On 10 March Rudyard sent him 'half a dozen of 'em – beautifully written', and demanded to know the 'S.P.R.' (the selling rate). Ollie obviously overdid it, killing the goose that laid the golden egg. 'Sorry again but I really haven't anything suitable for the young – even the young at Eton – anonymous or signed. I've been rather busy lately and have neglected the claims of pure literature. Ever your affec. Uncle Ruddy.'

His relationship with the more mature Rupert was quite different. 'He would talk on every kind of subject in his unique way, a spicy mixture of biblical invocation and barrack-room slang. He would take a volume from the shelves and read passages that appealed to him, but his favourite reading was The Book, and his knowledge of it was tremendous.' Although Kipling was not religious in the traditional manner that would have made him turn to God or even to a priest for comfort, nevertheless the familiar, resonant words of the King James Bible would have offered some reassurance at this painful time. As was manifest in *A Nativity* and other works written in his grief for John, he often identified with God who had also lost a Son in a cruel manner.

The search continued. Rudyard received a long statement dated 6 November from John Cochrane, who had been Second Sergeant of 6 Platoon and was now in Springburn Red Cross Hospital. It was the most detailed and personal they had yet heard. Cochrane confirmed that his platoon was to the left of John's, No 5. The two platoons got mixed up in the advance which started at about 4 o' clock and Cochrane remembered, 'Mr Kipling took charge of both. He came to us and gave us the range and direction. He directed us to fire at the ground story of some pit head buildings . . . It was about 4.45 by this time, and Sergeant Peters having been hit, I as second sergeant was in charge of Platoon 6. Mr Kipling was walking to and fro along the line, and I said to him that he had better lie down and share my sandbag, but he laughed and said, "Oh, this is nothing, Sergeant." The German machine gun fire was then cutting up the ground about us and I said, "For goodness sake, sir, lie down, you'll get struck," but he did not lie down till I caught him by the sleeve and pulled him down. A bullet just then struck the sandbag we were behind, and he said, "This is a fairly hot place, Sergeant." We then got the order to charge and he got in front and led to the pit head buildings. We got through a gap in the yard wall, and by dodging among the rubbish heaps in the yard, he and I got close up to the window from which the machine gun was firing. He got so close under the wall that the Germans could not hit him without exposing themselves. [At this point Carrie, obviously cross-checking with her charts, inserted an asterisk and the comment, "confirmed by Pt J Martin No 7 Platoon Pt Troy No. 9 Platoon".] He used his revolver and others of our men smashed in the door and we cleared out the Germans about 25 of them. We killed them.' The two proud and anxious parents would have followed this description as if they were with John second by second and Rudyard's heart must have almost burst with exultation at this last statement. His boy had fulfilled all his hopes: he had learned from his training, carried out his orders more than bravely and killed a substantial number of the enemy.

Sergeant Cochrane was then wounded twice, but said, 'I did not feel this in the excitement. When we had finished the Germans in the pit build-ings, Mr Kipling called, "Come on boys," and we rushed round the right of the house where others of our men were and went on to the first German trench, which ran along a line about 30 to 40 yards behind the Pit building.' Cochrane was again wounded and grazed by a shrapnel ball. 'I then fell and the others went on with Mr Kipling into another wood behind the German trench and that is the last I saw of him. Nor have I heard from any of our men what happened to him afterwards . . . Our Regiment and Coldstreams cleared out this wood behind the German trench next day and found our dead in it, and, as they did not find Mr Kipling I think it is quite possible that he may have been wounded and taken prisoner. Otherwise I should have expected his body to be found. As an officer he was more or less conspicuous. He had leather Sam Browne belt not webbing, and had an officer's cap.' Cochrane lay out for 24 hours in the path of the German counter-attack, shells falling around him. By some miracle he survived and got back to his own lines by rolling himself along the ground. He was then taken to a dressing station 'somewhere in rear of Hulluch'. Cochrane's clear and rational account, which has a ring of authenticity, was accompanied by a sketch map and the words, 'I should be very glad if I could be of any further use to Mr Kipling's family as I thought a good deal of him. He was very brave and was much liked by the men whose spirits he kept up by his own cheerfulness.'

Rudyard and Carrie were briefly sustained by this confirmation of what every parent of their age would wish to hear of their soldier son's last moments, with its perpetuation of the dwindling hope that John may have been taken prisoner. Kipling was realistic, however, and on 12 November he wrote to Brigadier Dunsterville, telling him that since receiving the initial report that John was 'wounded and missing' they had heard 'nothing official. But all we can pick up from the men points to the fact that he is dead and probably wiped out by the shell fire.' He was talking to an old friend, and a military man at that, and proudly recounted that John 'had his heart's desire and he didn't have a long time in trenches. The Guards advanced on a front of two platoons for each battalion. He led the right platoon over a mile of open ground in face of shell and machine-gun fire, after having emptied his pistol into a house full of German m.g.'s. His C.O. and his Company Commander told me how he led 'em and the wounded have confirmed it. He was senior ensign tho' only 18 years and six weeks, worked like the devil for a year at Warley and knew his Irish to the ground. He was reported on as one of the best of the subalterns and was gym instructor and signaller.' One senses how Rudyard would have loved to have shared this experience with his son. 'It was a short life,' he continued with controlled understatement, 'I'm sorry all the years' work ended in that one afternoon but – lots of people are in our position – and it's something to have bred a man. The wife is standing it wonderfully tho' she, of course, clings to the bare hope of his being a prisoner. I've seen what shells can do, and don't.'

Rudyard's other male confidant, Rider Haggard, saw him in town on 22 December and wrote in his diary, 'He has heard nothing of John and evidently has practically lost hope. He says that from all the accounts he can gather, the boy made a good end in his first action, that he liked his men and was liked by them. Poor lad! He added that he was very fond of me and asked me what I had done to make his children so fond of me. I answered I didn't know except that young people like those who like them.' One reason for John's affection may have been the gift of a copy of *The Yellow God*, inscribed 'To John Kipling from his antique friend, H Rider Haggard. Ditchingham September 1913'. It was one of John's prized possession. Despite his worries over John, Kipling, according to Haggard, 'expressed his opinion of the Government and individual members thereof in language too strong to write down even in a private diary. His vigour on the subject was amazing.'

Julia Depew also came to London in December and visited the Kiplings at Brown's. Their stoical façade was firmly in place. 'One could never imagine that a tragedy had occurred in their lives. They seemed absolutely cheery and evidently had not allowed themselves to believe that they would not see John again.' The façade cracked, however, when Rudyard, out of Carrie's sight, accompanied Julia to her car. Then he 'took hold of my arm, and pressing it so that it almost hurt, said, "Down on your knees Julia, and thank God that you have not a son." I knew then that he knew. Rud was never the same in any shape or manner after John's death.'

It was maintaining appearances that helped him to keep going. Somehow the Kiplings got through Christmas of 1915. In her diary Carrie called it a Christmas day 'in name only'. Teddy Price, the next best thing to a son, who was then in the OTC and would be commissioned later in the year, was with them on New Year's Day. January started busily again on the trail. Haggard was also still on it. On 27 December he had 'interviewed a young wounded soldier of the Irish Guards, named Bowe. He was near to John Kipling (within forty yards) when they entered the wood near Givenchy [they were actually nowhere near Givenchy] where the latter vanished. What became of him remains a mystery. He may have rushed ahead in charging the German Maxims and been captured. If he fell it is a marvel that he was not picked up as the wood remained in our hands for days. Bowe and another man named Frankland who was with him were of the opinion that he was either blown absolutely to bits by a large shell, which they had seen happen several times, or taken and murdered in the German lines during the two hours that elapsed before they finally rushed the wood. These possibilities, however, I did not put down in the signed statement which I sent to Rudyard Kipling. There is still a faint hope that he is a prisoner. He has just vanished. Bowe said that the poor boy was much liked.' The next day Haggard's daughter, Lilias, received a letter from Frankland, the soldier who had accompanied Bowe – 'a very well educated man', commented Haggard. 'He writes that Bowe, who is a very nervous youth and shy, now remembers certain other things about John Kipling. "Bowe did see Lieut. Kipling after the wood was taken under the following circumstances. The Irish Guards had dug themselves in on the edge of the wood when they heard a loud shouting from a body of men in their rear. The Sergeant in charge, thinking the Germans were making a flank or rear attack, ordered them to retire from the wood. This they did and found the noise to be the cheers of the Grenadier Guards who had come up to support the Irish. Bowe now says that as they left this wood he saw an officer who *he could swear* was Mr Kipling leaving the wood on his way to the rear and trying to fasten a field dressing round his mouth which was badly shattered by a piece of shell. Bowe would have helped him but for the fact that the officer was crying with the pain of the wound and he did not want to humiliate him by offering assistance.' Such was the respect with which the Irish Guards men regarded their officers. It may have killed young John. No wonder Haggard decided, 'I shall not send this on to Rudyard Kipling – it is too painful, but, I fear, true. Still it makes J. Kipling's disappearance still more of a mystery. A shell must have buried him, I think.' It was a highly probable deduction.

Ann Lay then visited the Kiplings from the American Consulate in Berlin with information that Carrie preferred to tell Lady Edward in person rather than to include it in her letter of 7 January 1916. Elsie was packed off to stay with the Astors at Cliveden for some light relief. Before the war the whole family had enjoyed happy times there. In her *Epilogue* to Carrington's biography, Elsie recalled how, after she had come out in 1914 and 'went to the stately London balls of that last summer of the old world, my father would often come with me, talking to chaperones and eating late suppers with other parents of his generation. Invitations to the large week-end parties of those days would be accepted by my parents if I wanted to go. There was an evening at one of these gatherings at Cliveden when my father, acting in charades with convincing horror, made his fellow guests' flesh creep.' There were no such games now. Elsie was as involved as her parents in the quest for news of John and spent some time talking to a Mr Lowry, 'the American who investigates the condition of the German prison in England and the English prisoners in Germany', as Carrie put it. But she was disappointed that 'even Elsie was able to tell him several things about the treatment of our prisoners in Germany which he did not know. All the prisoner side of the business seems very hopeless, so it would be a wonderful help if this Swiss business could be put through, and we could get even a portion of our prisoners out of their clutches, but I am afraid they will never let them go.' News had come about a man supposed to be John's orderly found in a hospital and still, on 11 December, only partly recovering consciousness after his severe wounds, but there had been 'silence ever since'. Elsie, with typical Kipling concern, had visited the hospital at Cliveden, where she had met 'a very nice Irish Guardsman' who sadly knew nothing of John's fate.

On 24 January Rudyard had to remind the War Office that, despite filling in the requisite papers in December, he still had not received John's personal effects. Then on 28 January they eventually arrived. There is a dreadful finality about this act of sending back to the bereaved the sad reminders of their loved one. The receiving of just such a parcel, of her fiancé Roland Leighton's effects, was harrowingly described by Vera Brittain in her *Chronicle of Youth* in a scene that must have been remarkably like the one to greet John's. 'It was terrible,' she wrote. 'Mrs Leighton and Clare [his sister] were both crying as bitterly as on the day we heard of His death . . . All that was left of his toilet luxuries came back – a regular chemist's shop – scented soap, solidified Eau-de-Cologne etc. We no longer wondered why he wanted them. One wants the most expensive things money can buy to combat that corruption . . . Mrs Leighton remarked almost with awe how very openly one has to live at the Front, when any moment one's most private personal belongings become the property of one's nearest relations.' Handling the intimate items of clothing so lovingly sewn and marked, the small comforts they too had been asked for and which they so happily scurried out to supply, these last possessions which John would have touched, must have caused a torrent of emotion to well up. Tears would inevitably have been shed at Bateman's as well as the Leighton home at Keymer. Did this mean the end of hope? As these were not effects taken from a body a glimmer of hope still remained. In some ways it would have been a blessed relief to let go: the endless searches, interviews, sifting of evidence, with the constant see-saw of raised and dashed hopes, were wearing, wearying and harrowing beyond description. Carrie was so overcome that on 1 February Rudyard took her for the old favourite cure at Bath while he visited soldiers in nearby hospitals.

Princess Margaret of Sweden had not given up. She offered more help through Lady Edward and Carrie was delighted to accept. 'I feel somehow the Princess, who through your kindness offers help, may be able to get some news. We have seen and heard from over 20 wounded 2nd Battn men now and we are more at sea than ever. They all agree he was wounded, severely wounded some as you know say killed but we have not found the man who was near him; he was killed perhaps too.' Lady Edward had persuaded Rudyard to open a commemorative rifle range at George's old school, Winchester, and had proudly sent a copy of his speech to his fan, Princess Margaret. She wrote on 16 February thanking Lady Edward for the speech and to admit, finally, that 'all my efforts to find something out about poor young Kipling have been in vain, they seem to have no record of him in Germany or at least that is what all the authorities say and I feel pretty sure Prince Max of Baden who was the last person I turned to about it has done his best, as he knew Rudyard Kipling so well by reputation and had had so much pleasure and interest in reading his books that he was most keen to do all he could. The only chance still left is that he may be in some cottage in Belgium and the Germans simply won't let anyone know who they have there. I can't say how dreadfully, dreadfully sad I feel to have to say this but now having heard from Prince Max I was bound to let you know the truth. Will you kindly let the Kiplings know. Prince Max said he would not tho forget about Lieutenant Kipling so should he be found he is sure to wire at once.'

Carrie wrote to Lady Edward asking her to send on messages to Princess Margaret. Her latest letter, Carrie felt, reached 'just another deadlock or rather the same one. But by now we both realize if John is alive he is in one of those cottage hospitals in Belgium or France and until he is well enough to be moved we shan't hear – but [and here is a long, long line] _____ it's a pretty serious wound that keeps one five months!'

Another panic from Ollie, chomping at the bit at yet a new setback just as his 17th birthday approached, was a diversion. 'Your letter just in. Keep calm be vaccinated and give us time to think,' wrote fond yet practical Aunt Carrie, seizing at the opportunity to fuss over a well-loved boy once more. 'It's a new regulation just out; but since they have changed once they may change again. One thing Uncle Rud says is quite certain we must "lie low" until you are 17. Sandhurst is one way out and the Inns of Court another – in both you would get part of your training before you were 18. We go to London from here. Uncle Rud will ask questions and discover what – if any thing can be done and will try and do it. Only you must go on quietly marking time. We are sorry for your disappointment and there will be a way out.' Rudyard added, 'I'm awfully sorry for your news but I don't think that it is necessarily final but it is final till after you are Seventeen. As Aunt Carrie says nothing in time of war continues long: and I can't for the life of me see where the officers for the new armies are coming from and I think you'll find that they'll quietly lower the age for officers once again. Meantime I'll find out what I can and I'll let you know. Go on steadily with your life: for this, after all, is part of a soldier's duty. I don't pretend it's cosy but there's lots that you can learn that will help you and German will help you horrendously when you get to Berlin.'

Intellectual stimulation came for Rudyard from visits to Bateman's by personalities such as the Dutch artist, Louis Raemakers, who arrived in April. His powerfully bitter anti-German 'cartoons' did much to whip up hatred against 'the beastly hun' whose *Kultur* consisted of rape, pillage, torture and attrocities against 'Poor Little Belgium'. He showed Rudyard his portfolio and asked for advice about exhibiting his drawings in the U.S. His escape from Holland had been dramatic. An excited Carrie told her mother how he had pretended to sail on a particular boat, but, hearing of a plot by the Dutch Secret Service to kill him, had secretly slipped off and, not even telling his wife, had hidden up and sailed several days later.

About that time the Kiplings had managed to lay their hands on an account of a German prison. 'It's the same prison where the soldier we met at Bath spent nearly a year and of which he wrote an account,' Carrie explained to her mother on 12 April. 'When one imagines one's son in such a prison its best by far to believe him dead. And,' wrote this anglicized American, 'when one knows the state of things went for 18 months before the American Ambassador took any steps to reprove the German Government one realizes how helpless we feel having the welfare of our prisoners in his hands.' The war had begun to impact on Rudyard's overseas royalties and Carrie finished her letter crying poverty as 'Income tax has gone up to 8s in the £ so everything is more expensive and I can only manage Aunt Kitty [her mother's sister whom she and Rud were maintaining in a home] out of principal and I do think Josephine [her sister] ought to help.'

Her depression deepened and on 19 May she wrote to Lady Edward thanking her for writing an 'Echo' of John which had greatly pleased her. Nevertheless, 'For no particular reason these have been very hard days for us both and I should like to bolt into a cave and tear off and out and down all the carefully built up commitments and just be a broken-hearted mother for a little bit. What a dreadful place all earth would be if we were able to do such things.' Only to Violet Cecil, who understood from personal experience how she was feeling, did Carrie allow herself to voice her primitive, bereaved mother's despair. Not even to her daughter, the loyal and supportive Elsie, did she let the façade of calm acceptance crumble. 'The two great sorrows of their lives, my parents bore bravely and silently, perhaps too silently for their own good. My mother hardly ever spoke of her two lost children,' she wrote, her hurt apparent at her mother's seeming coldness and distancing from her. 'But sometimes my father would talk of them to me. There is no doubt that little Josephine had been his greatest joy during her short life,' she noted, describing her elder sister's charm, beauty and personality in an extraordinarily unselfish way, understanding that 'She belonged to his early, happy days, and his life was never the same after her death; a light had gone out that could never be rekindled.' She was equally aware that her adored father then turned most of his attention on to her brother. 'My father was devoted to him, and his pride and interest in his son's short time as a soldier were intense. The long-drawn-out agony of the years during which his fate was uncertain left its mark on both my parents though outwardly they remained calm.' Aunt Georgie, 'the beloved Aunt', also understood the bitter pain beneath the accepting exterior. On first seeing Rudyard after the dreadful news had reached him, she felt 'greatly touched by his look. Quite well, he seemed, and younger and stronger than before, as if he had died and been buried and risen again, and had the keys of hell and of death.' But the effort to project an air of physical and mental strength was not sustainable and his health rapidly declined.

On 4 July 1916 the War Office asked the Officer Commanding the Guards Depot for information about John because 'an unofficial report had been received that the officer was killed, and informant saw him buried in a wood near Loos'. The informant was '6419 Pte P Fitzgibbon according to 6959 Pte J Martin'. As a result of that enquiry Rudyard received a letter on 14 September saying that as 'no further report has been received concerning Second Lieutenant J. Kipling . . . it is regretted that it will consequently be necessary for the Army Council to consider whether they must not now conclude that this officer is dead'. Rudyard was asked if any further news of John had reached him and that, if not, 'the official action taken as a result of the decision would consist in the winding up of the officer's accounts, and the removal of his name from the Army List.' Rudyard was appalled. This would mean the giving up of all hope that John might yet be found. On 18 September he replied, 'I should be glad if you would postpone taking the course you suggest in regard to my son Lieutenant John Kipling. All the information I have gathered is to the effect that he was wounded and left behind near Puits 14 at the Battle of Loos on September 27th 1915. I have interviewed a great many people and heard from many others, and can find no one who saw him killed, and his wound being a leg wound would be more disabling than fatal.' He then pointed out that John was in fact a 'Lieutenant', not a '2nd Lieutenant' [in view of the November 1915 'Gazetting' of the promotion] and that 'he was incorrectly reported as "Missing" instead of "Wounded and missing".' The next day came a letter from the C.2. Casualties department apologizing for the errors and saying that 'the Army Council do not desire to proceed with the official acceptance of death in opposition to the next-of-kin, and consequently in deference to your wishes, no further action will be taken at present.' [P.R.O.]

Life continued through the summer, with Rudyard's writing interspersed with occasional visits to London so that he could keep abreast of events both at the war front and behind the scenes on the political front. 1 September saw the second anniversary of George Cecil's death and Carrie wrote to her friend Violet, 'My thoughts have been with you every hour of this day and its only because I know no one can say or do anything to help that I have made no attempt.' Despite all the news to the contrary, she persisted in clinging on to the hope that somewhere, somehow, *her* boy might still be found alive. 'I enclose with this a letter,' she continued, 'sent me by Mrs Cuthbert. You will see what Hells one lives in knowing that there are these secret camps and that our Govt will not take one step to help the men in them. All day and every day I cry for some confirmation some real proof that John is dead and there are thousands of mothers who feel as I do.' To take her mind off the continuing anguish she worked tirelessly for the Red Cross, and when they turned down some of the supplies she sent them, she offered them to Violet for the hospital at Villers Cotterets. She shared Rudyard's pleasure in the company of young visitors and was delighted when, on 6 September, six Naval officers turned up at Bateman's on their motor bikes. They had taken Rudyard's casual 'Do come and see me' invitation at face value. 'Such a nice lot,' Carrie enthused.

Without John's softening influence, Rudyard and Elsie sometimes found Carrie's bossiness hard to take. In one of his affectionate letters to his mother-in-law Rudyard wrote on 8 September, 'I told Elsie that the only living thing her mother went in fear of was you, which I believe is true! and I described to her how when C used to argue with you or suggest plans you just went on taking no notice whatsoever. This cheers Elsie and when C is laying down the law to us both or administering us with a severe hand, Elsie says to me, "Tell me again how Grandmummy sits on Mummy. She wouldn't dare behave like this if her Mother were here".' As often happens with fathers and their daughters, Rudyard was far more demonstrative with Elsie than was her mother. 'Elsie is absolutely one of the two dearest things that God ever made,' Rudyard enthused to his mother-in-law. 'The war has deepened and strengthened my small daughter's character most wonderful. She has many chores to do in the way of looking after people . . . She is also our chauffeuse . . . and her little car which she washes herself is our only neans of communication with the outside world. Then she helps housekeep and sews and knits and packs for the wounded. Now that she is a woman too you can imagine that between her and C I am very well governed and corrected.'

Carrie had been stung on the face by wasps that were attacking her homemade jam and had to wear a patch over her eye. She felt she resembled 'a learned pig or a pig-faced lady' and a somewhat mischievous Rudyard decided that he would tell the five wounded officers who were coming to lunch that 'it was shrapnel picked up in the last Zeppelin raid'.

Nephew Ollie (sometimes known as 'Beloved Buttons') was getting nearer to his heart's desire and was starting at the Royal Military Academy at Sandhurst. 'Is there anything that there is at Bateman's that we can send you?' asked Rudyard on 3 October, 'Rough socks, mitts etc. etc. are plentiful just now.' The following month he wrote, 'Your room [was it John's old room?] has been carefully cleaned and disinfected and we expect the Board of Health to pass it in a very few weeks . . . I tell you frankly that I expect rather big things of you and to begin with a good place at entering Sandhurst. Herein disappoint me at your peril.' On the

19th Ollie arrived at Bateman's and Carrie started to think of the approaching holiday. Teddy Price, now a 2nd Lieutenant, also spent a couple of days (9–10 December) with them. 'Xmas can never be anything to Rud and me again but a day of repression of sorrow for the sake of those about us and we mean to start this year and do a very little for Elsie's sake,' she wrote to her mother. Once again they managed it and went bleakly into another New Year.

Chapter 8

I WILL MAKE THEE A NAME:

The History of the Irish Guards. Rudyard's Work with
the War Graves Commission. The Kings Pilgrimage
and Other Travels.

Thy line is at end . . . but at least I have saved its name.
Rudyard Kipling, *The Favour.*

By 1917 Rudyard Kipling was respected and famous not only in Britain but around the world, for his literary achievements and as a public figure with strong opinions, most of which were in tune with the mood of the moment. As a result he was besieged by requests for him to take honours, awards, official positions and public engagements. Most of them, other than those which represented recognition of his writing achievement, he had steadfastly refused. Hilton Brown, in his 1945 *New Appreciation*, wrote, 'A sonless man has no use for titles,' and Elsie Kipling in her *Epilogue* to Carrington's biography of her father said, 'Though great honours were offered to him, he refused to accept any but literary or academic ones, holding that accepted honours would mean the loss of that complete independence to say, in prose or verse, what he thought should be said.' As early as 1899 he had turned down a knighthood (but accepted an honorary Doctorate of Literature from McGill University in Montreal). In 1903 he again refused a knighthood (this time a KCMG) and an invitation to join the Prince of Wales on his tour of India. In 1907 he received the Nobel Prize for Literature and honorary degrees from Durham and Oxford. The following year he received an honorary Doctorate of Literature, this time from Cambridge. Although Carrington dubbed him 'the people's laureate', and T.S. Eliot called him 'a laureate without laurels', he never became official poet laureate. After Tennyson's death in 1892, he was recognized as a minor contender and Carrington describes the attempts of Arthur Balfour, nephew of the Prime Minister, to promote his candidature in 1895, again rebuffed by Kipling himself. When the inadequate Alfred Austin died in 1913, Kipling seemed the obvious choice to replace him, but Asquith, then Prime Minister, was well aware of Kipling's antipathy to writing 'to order' and did not even ask him. In 1910 Kipling had not wished to join the British Academy, nor the

American Academy of Arts and Sciences. He had an antipathy to biographies which he described as 'the Higher Cannibalism'. In 1917 he declined to write the biography of his good companion Dr Jameson, as he did of other South African friends, Cecil Rhodes in 1902, and, despite the pleas of Lady Milner, a personal friend with whom he had closely shared the grief of losing a son, Lord Milner in 1925. On 14 April 1914 Kipling wrote to Sir J.R. Dunlop-Smith to ask him to get 'a Pottinger – grand nephew of Eldred . . . he comes out of Sandhurst at the end of this term' a commission in the Indian Army. Dunlop-Smith obliged and in 1916 he asked Kipling to return the favour by writing a foreword to a book about the Indians in the war. This Kipling declined to do. In 1915 he had been asked by the War Office to write a History of the Battle of Ypres. This too he refused. Perhaps most surprising of all was his refusal to write a biography of 'the beloved Aunt', Lady Georgiana Burne-Jones, when she died in 1920, as he did not wish to 'share my feelings with *any* public' [Letter to Sir Sydney Cockerell quoted by Carrington].

Other requests on his time and support were more mundane, but showed the catholic nature of his interests. On 28 February 1925 he wrote to Rider Haggard, 'Oh, here's a chaste selection from my mail . . . (1) Request to put 20 stories into "literary style" for a mercantile marine captain on his uppers. Would you like the job? (2) Join Committee for International Memorial to Byron and help us get 10, or 15, thousand quid out of the public. Nice, alluring job! (3) Give away prizes at a modern and progressive girls' school (*Just* your style.) (4) Write text-book for Schools on "overseas settlement." D'you know it's vulgar to talk of emigration, these days? (5) *Ditto, ditto* to appeal (Allah knows why!) to the natural ideals of the young. (6) Write "poem" rebuking lazy bricklayers. (7) Take up two or three perfectly impossible scandals about the price of bread and the importation of motor parts . . . *Isn't* it just the same old world, and the same old mail-bag!' Kipling went on to admit to Haggard that 'I've done a deuce of a lot of thinking – the sum and the substance of which is that I wish I had as straight and high a record as you have of work done. But I never took on Commissions and now I rather regret it.' Haggard served on several Commissions, such as those on Imperial Communication, the National Birth Rate and the East African Inquiry and complained that 'Some fifteen years solid of it I have put in as one of the great unpaid on these accursed Commissions, etc, which really are trying because of the small minds that often you have to fight in them.' But in his letter to his esteemed colleague Kipling was forgetting (or having one of his modest moments) the great commitment he was making to one of the most challenging Commissions ever constituted in this country.

For, despite declining all these other commitments, Kipling had, in 1917, undertaken two monumental tasks, into which he would pour his feelings of love, grief and, perhaps, remorse and guilt, for his son John's death. As we have seen, that death aged and debilitated Rudyard, yet the work he would undertake was exhausting and draining of his declining energy. There is no doubt that he was building his own memorial to John in what may have been an act of expiation comparable to that generally attributed to Earl Haig in his work for the British Legion and other ex-Servicemen's organizations. Haig had, deservedly or undeservedly (and the debate still rages), earned the accusatory epithet 'Butcher' for the thousands of casualties for which he was deemed responsible during the Great War. His untiring work for these organizations was perceived by many as being motivated by guilt. Lady Haig, in *The Man I Knew*, describes how Haig, like Kipling, 'shunned publicity and would only attend functions when he was obliged to' and how in his last years 'Practically all his time was devoted to the work of the British Legion and of the formation of the British Empire Service League.' So it was with Kipling and the *History of the Irish Guards* and his work with the Imperial War Graves Commission.

First came a request, on 8 January 1917, from Colonel Douglas Proby, then in command of the Irish Guards Headquarters at Buckingham Gate: 'All the Guards' Regiments are writing Regimental Histories of this War and we want to do the same. It has been suggested to me that you might be willing to undertake this for us, not as a business matter, but as a memento of your son's service in the Regiment.' Proby knew how to pierce Kipling's soft underbelly and on the 16th he was writing to thank Rudyard for his letter of acceptance which read, 'There is nothing I should like more than to try to write the war record of the Regiment though I am afraid it is work that is a little outside my line of country.' Rudyard immediately started work. Given, as we have seen, his attitude towards 'the Irish question', and the turbulent situation in Ireland at the time, this was not without a measure of irony and sensitivity; yet he threw himself into the research with diligence and thoroughness. By the end of the month registered parcels were winging their way to Burwash containing maps and battalion diaries, meticulously acknowledged and charted by the current secretary.

On 3 March Carrie recorded, 'Rud settles down to Irish Guards History'. She also attributes the writing of *The Irish Guards* to this date, although it was not published until *The Times* carried it on 11 March 1918. Written as a *Prologue* to the *History*, but not printed as such in the original edition, it begins,

> We're not so old in the Army List,
> But we're not so young at our trade,
> For we had the honour at Fontenoy
>   Of meeting the Guards' Brigade.
> 'Twas Lally, Dillon, Bulkeley, Clare,
>   And Lee that led us then,

132

> After a hundred and seventy years
> We're fighting for France again!

and has the refrain,

> *Old Days! the wild geese* are ranging,*
> *Head to the storm as they faced it before!*
> *For where there are Irish their hearts are unchanging,*
> *And when they are changed, it is Ireland no more!*
> *Ireland no more!*

[*'Wild geese' was the name for 18th Century Irish Mercenaries who had fought for the French.]

The verses were Rudyard's apologia to the southern Irish Catholics whom he had so vociferously attacked before the war. They were set to music by that most English of composers (second only to Elgar) Edward German, who had visited Bateman's to discuss the project on 4 February. It was performed in concerts throughout 1918 to stirring effect. Rupert Grayson had visited Bateman's when the idea of making the verses into a song was mooted and had suggested that Elgar be invited to compose the music. 'No,' he said abruptly, 'Edward German will set my verses to music.' Grayson commented, 'German's music was melodious and charming, but I was disappointed it was not to be Elgar – a great composer with a superb sense of pageantry. I said nothing because I had learned to keep my mouth shut whenever Carrie shot me one of her warning glances. I would dearly have liked to know what Elgar had done to offend Kipling . . . If Kipling was the leading poet of that period, Elgar was surely the leading composer.'

Kipling wrote to many of the regiment's officers for clarification on tricky military points or for their personal memories. On his behalf Lieutenant Colonel the Hon T.E. Vesey sent out a round robin with three questions. One related to the blowing up of the Bridge at Beautur between 28 and 30 August 1914, the second requested details of the Rest Camp at le Havre in August 1914 and the third asked what were the first bombs used in the war and where was the first Bombing School. Some replied with detailed sketches, one recalled the villa at le Havre lent them by a M Alexandre who had 'seven charming daughters', another wondered modestly if his account would give the impression that 'the writer was quite a "chap" with many soldierly virtues', in which case 'the narrative is a gross deception and I deplore it'. Eric Greer, who commanded the 2nd Battalion from 13 January 1917, felt that his memory was fallible but that if he and 'Alex' [Alexander] could 'get together we'll be able to work it all out so as not to miss an hour'.

Kipling then began sifting through the battalion diaries and the personal accounts. It was a painful and gruelling exercise. Time and again it would seem like rubbing salt into the open wound of John's disappearance. In *Rudyard Kipling at Home and Work* Dorothy Ponton, Elsie and John's governess and then Rudyard's secretary from 1919 to 1924, described the history as 'a work of two volumes written as a memorial to his son. It was a work of poignant memories; for he knew many of the men who had been killed in action. Some of the material for the book was collected from the diaries of officers – mere scraps of paper stained with the mud of trenches – or even flecked with blood.' Despite periods when Rudyard attempted to relax, or involve himself in other matters of concern, 'Mr Kipling bent his whole genius to completing this masterpiece of the Great War. "This will be my great work," he once said, and at another time, "It is being done with agony and bloody sweat".' It was also being done for no profit to Kipling personally. On 18 March 1918 the charitable 'Kipling Fund' was set up for the benefit of the Irish Guards, Prisoners of War, Widows and Orphans, into which went all the earnings from the book. A great PR drive was put into action to publicize the event. A Press Release, headed 'KIPLING FUND' was sent out to all the national papers – from *The Times* to the *Sporting Life*. It reported Mr Rudyard Kipling's gift, during the matinee organized by Lady Paget at the Empire Theatre, of £300 to the fund, plus 100 signed copies of his poem *The Irish Guards*, together with all copyright attaching thereto. Edward German donated his original manuscript and all his rights connected with the setting of the poem to music. A.P. Watt's literary agents gave their services free. By 17 April the fund had swelled to £700 which was to be invested in National War Bonds, repayable in 1927.

When the Irish Guards were disbanded in 1919 Dorothy recalled, 'Some of the officers spent weekends at Bateman's, when they doubtless gave the author first-hand information of certain engagements at the front, which he skilfully wove into the fabric of the whole story. Often Mr Kipling would take his visitors along the banks of the Dudwell to fish. "It's a strange thing," he said, "these war-worn youngsters, who didn't mind killing Huns, will blanch and squirm when the moment arrives to attach a worm to the end of a hook. "Please, would you mind doing it?" they will plead and look the other way.'

These visits by young Irish Guards officers must have been painful and pleasurable in almost equal proportion. They filled a small part of the void left by John, providing youthful chatter, acting as the playmates Kipling always craved, the objects of the fussing over that Carrie missed. But they were alive and John was dead. A frequent visitor was Oliver, demobilized on 31 May with the rank of full Lieutenant. He was feeling rudderless, his personality disturbed, and was experiencing a growing hatred of the 'British Class System'. This he must have hidden from Rudyard at this stage, for he was still welcomed joyfully at Bateman's. Oliver clung to his old army comrades for security and companionship and Carrie recorded in her diary for 10 August 1919 that he was bringing George Bambridge, also of the Irish Guards, 'to help about the history' and that their help was 'most effective.' Captain G.L.St.C. Bambridge of the 1st Battalion gradually became closer to the entire family. His 'exploits (he was several times wounded, won the M.C., and was mentioned in despatches) are duly noted in the history. His friendship with us continued when peace came in 1918, and he often visited "Bateman's",' wrote Elsie in the *Epilogue* to Carrington's biography. After the visit to Bateman's, George and Oliver (who had been appointed Vice-Consul in Boulogne, and who hinted importantly about 'Secret Service' work) spent an intimate month together in Algeria.

Kipling had been filling in details and gaps, and wrote to Captain A.F. Gordon, DSO, MC, the last wartime commanding officer of the 2nd Battalion, at the Regimental Headquarters at Buckingham Gate for a number of maps for 1915 and 1916 and for the number of regimental losses, killed and wounded, for each month. He knew he was asking a great deal, and justified his demand. 'The more I go into the history, the more clearly do I see the difficulties, and I am quite sure that you must be overworked but the main thing is to get the History as full and accurate as possible, so I hope very much to see you when I am next in Town and to make you further trouble. You must forgive me and, if possible, pass the burden on to the office.' When the first draft was finished Rudyard enlisted the then Colonel Alexander to help him revise it and he stayed at Bateman's from 18–20 December 1920.

Miss Ponton provided a human insight into Kipling's working methods. 'He worked at it methodically and with the utmost care to get all details correct. His usual method of procedure was to study the subject closely and then set down, in his own inimitable style, the result of this study. This formed the original manuscript. When the typewritten copy was presented to him, he pruned or expanded it, and the next copy would be subjected to the same process till – perhaps not until four or five copies had been carefully revised – the finished article would be laid aside till a final revision of the whole was made just before publication.' Rudyard's inconsistent handwriting was sometimes a stumbling block. 'He sometimes accused me of making "pot shots" at an undecipherable phrase,' she recalled. But Rudyard's own attempts with a typewriter were 'much more undecipherable than the other. "The beastly thing won't spell," he complained.'

Rudyard was notoriously careless with his manuscripts, and there were panic stations when 'a whole chapter of the Irish Guards history, which had been sent for a fourth revision, disappeared'. Eventually 'it turned up inside another book in Mr Kipling's study.' Dorothy Ponton gave a revealing glimpse into Carrie's suspicious guardianship of every scrap of Rudyard's written work when a page of manuscript went astray. When Dorothy denied having received the missing page, 'Mrs Kipling looked very suspiciously at me,' she recalled, 'whereupon Mr Kipling went off humming, as was his wont when bothered,' only to return 'with a broad smile' clutching the offending sheet. 'Sorry,' he said, having forgotten to tear it off his pad. Fearing that anything written in the great man's hand could be sold for profit or otherwise exploited (and obviously ignorant of Rudyard's indulgence of young Oliver), Carrie made it a firm rule that nothing in his handwriting 'must leave the house'.

The final ms of the history was just about to be handed over to be despatched to the printers when Carrie's eagle eye spotted a few hand-corrected sentences. Nothing would suffice but that Dorothy had to retype all the pages bearing such corrections. 'Mr Kipling raised his eyes to Heaven in despair and then glanced quickly at me,' wrote Dorothy, who had to retype the ms 'at high pressure'. It was delivered in time for the Kiplings to take a hard-earned break in Spain and Gibraltar in March 1922. On the 21st Kipling wrote to a Mr Calmont at the Irish Guards HQ, 'The History has passed out of my hands now . . . It will be on sale at all booksellers . . . On the day the book comes out, a cheque for £500 will be sent you which, subject to your approval I should be glad to have sent in as a contribution from the Regiment to the Guards Memorial. In this way, the written history of the Regiment will contribute towards a permanent memorial to its dead.'

Despite the holiday, Kipling's health continued to deteriorate. Although on 27 July Carrie's diary exults, 'The Irish Guards finished,' she adds that Rud was exhausted, 'yellow and shrunken'. Dorothy Ponton was genuinely fond of her master and she too worried at his physical condition. 'In August [of 1922] Mr Kipling, whose health had been troubling him for some time, suddenly became desperately ill and was rushed to London for an X-ray examination.' He was in great pain, although his doctors assured him that 'all was well'. Seymour-Smith accused Kipling of suffering from 'one of the most terrible and misunderstood of illnesses . . . hypochondria', claiming he was 'as ill with his terrified anticipations of cancer, and madness, perhaps, as with anything else'. There is no doubting the reality, however, of the stomach ulcer that was failed to be diagnosed at this time. He was in severe pain which was only relieved by a strict diet. Dorothy remembers that 'During the autumn the proofs of the Irish Guards history were corrected by dint of sheer will-power.' The book was finally published on 16 April 1923 and on the 18th Carrie delights in her diary in an 'excellent review in *The Times*' of the previous day. It was written by John Buchan who said, 'No other book can ever be written exactly like this, and it seems likely to endure as the fullest document of the war-life of a British regiment, compiled by a man of genius who brings to his task not only a quick eye to observe and a sure hand to portray, but a rare spirit of reverence and understanding.' *The Commonwealth* felt that it evoked the war with such force and directness that 'one could almost believe Mr Kipling had seen everything at first hand'. Though there was a note of criticism in that Kipling 'does not berate the Germans, nor does he openly mention the hopeless incompetence of British Staff Officers, but by ironical implication he shows them to be what they were – full of the confidence and credulity of ignorance.' Nevertheless, it added that 'we can be deeply grateful to Mr Kipling for this monument he has raised to his son's memory.'

There have been many other claims by Kipling enthusiasts that this was a regimental history like no other; that it is uniquely full of human anecdotes and personal experiences. Cross found it to have 'a curious light-hearted quality about it all. Every few pages there is an account of a humorous incident.' But the habitual reader of regimental histories would find none of this unusual. That was the nature of the genre, where an interested historian (often an officer of the regiment) strove to present his beloved regiment in the best possible and most human light. None of them, however, were professional writers of Kipling's stature and few would have been so involved as to have lost their only sons fighting for the regiment. Seymour-Smith swung to the other side of the pendulum in his reaction to the Irish Guards History and was somewhat arrogantly dismissive: 'Few have read the military work, and it is not distinguished even among its kind – the laureate of force did not understand much about its practical application. But it is conscientiously done.' Kipling tried very hard to understand the military background of the events and anecdotes he was describing; many did indeed 'read the work' and the fact that it was considered worthy of reproduction in 1997 surely bears witness to its enduring qualities as a work of literature as well as a meticulous record of a regiment's part in the Great War.

Rudyard tried to distance himself from his personal loss when writing the history. In the Introduction, however, he lowered his guard to the extent of saying, 'And there were, too, many, almost children, of whom no record remains. They came out from Warley with the constantly renewed drafts, lived the span of a Second Lieutenant's life and were spent. Their intimates might preserve, perhaps, memories of a promise cut short, recollections of a phrase that stuck, a chance-seen act of bravery or of kindness. The Diaries give their names and fates with the conventional expressions of regret. In most instances, the compiler has let the mere fact suffice; since, to his mind, it did not seem fit to heap words on the doom.' It takes no great powers of perception to read the personal pain between the written lines. Many Kipling biographers make much of his scant direct referral to John's part in the Battle of Loos. In *The Great War and Modern Memory* Paul Fussell misses it completely and maintains that, in being 'honorable and decent', Kipling 'performs the whole job without mentioning his son, who appears only in the list of dead, wounded, and missing at the end, together with hundreds of others.' John certainly does appear in that sad section, when Kipling correctly lists him under the Lieutenants (the 'gazetting' of his promotion having taken place on 11 November 1915), but when talking about the action of the 1st Scots Guards near Chalk Pit Wood on 27 September 1915, Kipling says, 'Their rush took with them "some few Irish Guardsmen," with 2nd Lieutenants W.F.J. Clifford and J. Kipling of No. 2 Company who went forward not less willingly because Captain Cuthbert commanding the Scots Guards party had been Adjutant to the Reserve Battalion ere the 2nd Battalion was formed, and they all knew him. Together, this rush reached a line beyond the Puits, well under machine-gun fire [out of the Bois Hugo across the Lens-la Bassée road]. Here 2nd Lieutenant Clifford was hit and wounded or killed – the body was found later – and 2nd Lieutenant Kipling was wounded and missing.' He later summarizes, 'The number of known dead is set down officially as not more than 25, which must be below the mark. Of their officers, 2nd Lieutenant Pakenham-Law had died of wounds; 2nd Lieutenants Clifford and Kipling were missing.' This is a highly significant description, not least in the designation of John as a '2nd Lieutenant' on 27 September and the fact that he was part of a small group advancing with the Scots Guards, to which we will return in the last chapter of this book.

After listing other officer casualties, Kipling sparingly comments, 'It was a fair average for the day of a debut, and taught them somewhat for their future guidance.' His bitterness shows through when he finishes the section, 'So, while the Press was explaining to a puzzled public what a far-reaching success had been achieved, "the greatest battle in the history of the world" simmered down to picking up the pieces on both sides of the line, and a return to autumnal trench-work until more and heavier guns could be designed and manufactured in England. Meanwhile, men died.'

The *Irish Guards History* was as well received by members of the regiment and the relatives of their fallen sons as it was by the critics. One dissenting voice was that of the soldier poet, Edmund Blunden. In the *National and Athenaeum* he wrote, 'The fact is that Mr Kipling appears not perfectly to understand the pandemonium and nerve-strain of war; . . . He makes constant stern attempts at actuality; he constantly falls short, in expressions merely strained, in sheer want of comprehension. To those who were in the line, his technical phraseology will seem incongruous now and then . . . the Irish Guards have been chronicled with decision and skill, but as to the multitudinous enigma of war atmosphere, Mr Kipling has not written much that convinces us.' Blunden's own personal account of the war, *Undertones of War*, would not appear until 1929, and he seems to resent anyone who had not personally experienced the 'appalling misery' of war trying to document it; Kipling did not belong to that large, but exclusive, club of war veterans.

From most other quarters Kipling received many letters of praise – and some begging letters as well. On 16 April Ex-Guardsman Michael Goode wrote saying that he saw John 'leading his men bravely with revolver drawn'. He went on to ask for a free copy of the History as he could not afford the £2 to buy it. A similar ploy was tried by George Francis Dowling of the 2nd Battalion who said he was John's orderly until the night before Loos and could he have a book at 'trade rates'. Others wrote pointing out errors in the entry relating to their sons. Typical was a Mrs Emily Baldwin (who, despite the name, does not appear to be a relative) who pointed out that her son, Lieutenant H.R. Baldwin, had been mentioned as a *2nd* Lieutenant, joining in June *1918*, whereas he 'had long been a *Lieutenant* at that date' and he had joined on 12 June *1917*. Mrs Baldwin asked, 'Can it be that the mistake has been made at the HQ of the Irish Guards?' This, too, is significant in relation to the confusion over John Kipling's rank. Other letters were of simple gratitude to Kipling for paying such a magnificent tribute to the Irish Guards and for bringing back such vivid memories. One, from a Mrs Lola Law, whose son Francis, known as 'Pokey', was a good friend of John's, must have made bitter-sweet reading for Rudyard. She described 'those terrible snatched leaves, one in particular just before the September fighting, when we sat looking out over the serene beauty of that Donegal Bay on a perfect blue and gold August afternoon and spoke of some bit of work which was to have been finished for him to see during the leave – a wall a-building. It will be finished in a fortnight, I said. I could see the unsaid "and I shall likely to never see it" in the child's eyes as they devoured the quiet beauty as if for the last time.' Mrs Law's son's premonition was, thankfully for her, unfounded; Francis won the MC on 5 June 1917 and, though wounded on 1 August 1917, survived the war.

Kipling's other great gesture of dedication to his son's memory was to accept Fabian Ware's invitation to become one of the Commissioners of the Imperial War Graves Commission. Ware had gone out to the western front as a Major with the Red Cross at the outbreak of war. Aged 45, he had already had a varied and distinguished career as a teacher with a strong interest in educational reform, an administrator under Lord Milner in South Africa, editor of *The Morning Post* and as an adviser to the Rio Tinto Company. He was a liberal with a small 'l' (a breed normally abominated by Kipling) with a strong desire to improve any situation with which he was involved. 'Energetic' is an adjective invariably used to describe him. His Red Cross 'flying unit' at first concerned themselves with picking up the wounded in the wake of the British retreat from Mons. Gradually they became involved in the recording of the dead and their burial sites and thence in maintaining the graves. All this was done on a voluntary basis, with no government support or financial help and Ware realized that there was no official mechanism in place for the recording of graves. At first Ware persuaded the Red Cross to pay for his Mobile Unit's work, which involved 'considerable patience and some skill as an amateur detective', as a member of the team called Broadley recorded. Requests from bereaved relatives flooded in for information about the location of their loved ones' graves. Local people were interviewed, children being of particular help. Gradually the Unit started a systematic marking and recording of the graves they found, encouraged by the head of the Paris Red Cross Office, Lord Robert Cecil. But without official status they could only achieve limited and spasmodic success. Eventually a frustrated Ware 'looking rather dishevelled and with his hair awry . . . burst into the office of General Macready, Adjutant-General to the British Expeditionary Force, to persuade him of the importance of registering and marking British graves,' [*The Unending Vigil*, 1967, Philip Longworth.] Macready lent a favourable ear and the result (on 2 March 1915) was the Graves Registration Commission, officially recognized by General Haig. Ware was now forced to give up his normal Red Cross work to concentrate on the work on the graves.

On 26 April 1915 Cecil wrote to Ware on Red Cross notepaper subheaded 'Enquiry Department for Wounded and Missing' confirming the arrangement with Macready that the Department 'is communicating information as to graves to relatives' and that Ware should be 'prepared to receive from us special enquiries as to particular graves'. The sending of wreaths was to be discouraged as 'the result will probably not be such as they would desire' but Curés and other local dignitaries should be encouraged to give help in the maintenance of graves, and photographs would be taken where possible.

Cecil went on to discuss a particular case. 'I notice that Gladstone's body has been sent home, and I understand that this was done in obedience to pressure from a very high quarter. It is from the point of view of administration perhaps a little unfortunate.' He invited Ware's comments. The case concerned an officer who was the grandson of W.E. Gladstone. 'I entirely agree with your remark about Gladstone's body,' replied Ware. 'Incidentally the exhumation was carried out by British soldiers under fire. Fortunately nobody was hit. The impression it has created among the soldiers out here is to be regretted. The one point of view that seems to me to be often overlooked in this matter is that of the officers themselves, who in ninety-nine cases out of a hundred will tell you that if they are killed would wish to lie among their men. [A case in point is that of General George Patton who lies at the head of his men in the American Cemetery in Luxemburg.] To return to Gladstone, the administrative difficulty is met by the fact that permission was granted in his case because he was a Lord-Lieutenant. I am talking seriously.' This is a highly significant letter. The exhumation and repatriation of Gladstone's body contravened all Ware's firmly held beliefs that there should be equality in the burial and marking of war graves. In addition, in March 1915 Marshal Joffre had expressly banned exhumation and Ware was anxious that his men – all declared unfit for active service – should not expose themselves to danger. In May he issued a circular to that effect when one was killed working in Ypres.

All these factors contributed to Fabian Ware agitating for a formal organization with further-reaching powers and a wider organization that would continue after the war and encompass all the forces of the Empire. The Prince of Wales, a serving officer with the Grenadier Guards, acted as Ware's ambassador to the Prime Minister, Lloyd George, to suggest a Commission to be constituted under Royal Charter. The idea was well received and, despite opposition from Sir Alfred Mond, the First Commissioner of Works, on 27 March 1917 Lloyd George called a meeting of all those who had expressed interest and who might be involved. They decided to establish an Imperial War Graves Commission. The Royal Charter was finally agreed on 17 April, approved by the King on 10 May and executed on 21 May. Its main brief was to acquire land for cemeteries; 'to make fit provision for the burial of officers and men of Our said forces and the care of all graves in such cemeteries, to erect buildings and permanent memorials therein, and generally to provide for the maintenance and upkeep of such cemeteries, buildings and memorials to complete and maintain records and registers of all graves with such cemeteries.' There would be a President (the Prince of Wales), a Chairman, Vice-Chairman and 'Such other persons, not exceeding the number of eight in all, as may from time to time be appointed Members of the Commission by Royal Warrant.'

This is where Rudyard Kipling came in. Already he had become interested in the concept and on 14 August Carrie recorded in her diary, 'Rud and H Baker [one of the Commission's chief architects] discuss plans for War graves', and on 6 September that Fabian Ware had asked him to join the Graves Commission 'on behalf of Lord Derby'. With his 'Confidential' letter of the previous day, Ware, in his then capacity of 'Director of Graves, Registration and Enquiries, War Office', enclosed an official letter asking Rudyard if he would become one of the eight 'other Members' required by the Imperial War Graves Commission Charter, which was also enclosed. Seven had already been chosen, of whom most had agreed. They were the Adjutant-General, Sir Nevil Macready, General Sir Herbert Plumer (then commanding Second Army in France), Sir William Garstin of the Red Cross and Fabian Ware himself. 'An Admiral' had also been asked, as had the somewhat surprising but enterprising choice, Mr Herbert Gosling, the Labour MP and strong trades unionist. 'Lord Derby,' wrote Ware, 'very much hopes that you will see your way to helping us in this work,' and he went on to describe the enthusiasm of the Prince of Wales for the work of the Commission. Rudyard was offered the chance (which he took) to talk things over with Ware, who put pressure on him by saying that he had to go to France the following week but that he must 'get this matter fixed up first'.

Rudyard didn't take long to make up his mind. This was another chance to achieve something significant in John's memory. That his old friend from Africa days, Lord Milner, whom he much admired, was the Commission's Chairman may have helped his decision. On the official letter of 5 September from Fabian Ware asking Rudyard to serve Carrie noted, 'Fabian Ware comes for the night. Reports Rud's name the idea of Lord Derby [who had lost his son-in-law in the war] who "wanted a man of imagination and one who knew the soldier".' On 21 September Lord Derby wrote expressing his gladness that Kipling was to serve on the Board, and on 27 October came the formal letter of appointment, enclosing the Royal Warrant under the 'Sign Manual of His Majesty' (George V). Kipling served on the Commission with an almost driven dedication. The extent of his involvement was summarized in a detailed letter of 14 July 1960 from the then Director-General Mr W.J. Chalmers, CBE, to an enquirer called J.S.I McGregor in South Africa:

'I am not sure whether you know that Rudyard Kipling was a member of the Commission from 1917 until his death on 18 January, 1936. I think the following Resolution which was passed by the Commission at their 191st Meeting will best give you an idea of the part he played in their work:-

"The Commission place on record their deep and abiding sense of the loss which they have sustained in the death of their colleague and friend, Mr Rudyard Kipling. They feel that an association of no ordinary official nature has been broken; and they know that this feeling is shared by their staff to whom, in consultation in London or on frequent visits to the cemeteries abroad, he gave encouragement, inspiration and a sense of personal interest in their work and welfare. As an original member of the Commission, he helped to build the work from its foundations. He first, in 1918, in a pamphlet entitled *The Graves of the Fallen*, interpreted their policy to the people in every part of the Empire; he spoke to the British and French nations at the Unveiling of the Loos Memorial, the perpetual testimony of his personal sacrifice; the inscriptions on the memorials erected by the Commission throughout the world were written, approved or selected by himself, and it may be said that this counsel and his active support have helped them in all their undertakings."

As you may know, his only son, Lieutenant John Kipling of the 2nd Bn. Irish Guards, who was killed on the 27th September, 1915, aged 18, is commemorated on the Loos Memorial in the Pas-de-Calais, in France.'

The Director-General continued by quoting from *The Immortal Heritage*, published in 1937:

> 'Among those who have held appointments as unofficial members and are now dead, were William Garstin, Rudyard Kipling, Harry Gosling and Robert Hudson. The two first of these lost their only sons in the War. Rudyard Kipling gave of his genius freely and whole-heartedly in the service of the commemoration of the dead; every inscription approved by the Commission was his in conception or in its final form, and his poem on the King's Pilgrimage in 1922 has a lasting place in the literature of our language.'

He finished this letter, written in the thoughtful and helpful style which had characterized the Commission from its origins and which still exists today:

> 'Apart from the many inscriptions for the great memorials which he composed, you may like to know that there is to this day a certain type of memorial headstone for which he made the general inscription and which is known to the office as a Kipling Memorial. It commemorates men who were originally buried in a known cemetery but whose graves were later lost. At the foot of this stone are carved the words "Their glory shall not be blotted out".'

During this time Kipling gradually developed a close relationship with the Commission's inspiration and driving force, Fabian Ware, and on 1 November 1917 he responded to Lord Derby's suggestion that Ware should become 'permanent vice-chairman' of the Commission: 'I entirely agree. This strikes me as the obvious and workmanlike solution of the question.' The collaboration was not without its prickly moments, however. Ware was an extraordinary man whose philosophy was quite different to Kipling's. But an examination of their correspondence shows the progression of their friendship in their mutual modes of address. 'Dear Mr Kipling' gives way to 'My dear Kipling' and finally by 1926 'Dear Rudyard'; and 'Dear General Ware' becomes 'My dear Ware' and finally 'Dear Fabian'. Yet there was some friction in 1922 when, on 19 June, a disgruntled Ware complained to Rudyard, 'Why have you given my autograph copy of the poem [*The King's Pilgrimage*] to the Imperial War Museum?' From the tone of the letter it seems an act of revenge by Kipling for a supposed misdemeanour of Ware's but sadly no other correspondence about the matter survives in the Commission's archives. Carrie noted in her diary, on 11 September 1928, 'A bothering letter from F Ware annoys Rud'. But for the most part they confided their frustrations and even some extraordinarily intimate comments to each other, as when Kipling, in a letter to Ware written in February 1919 from the Grand Pump Room Hotel (where Carrie was taking the waters) about the advantages of a headstone over a cross on the war graves, suddenly interjected, a propos of nothing. 'This is a foul town, full of wet and saddenly demorilized prostitutes [sic]'. Then in July 1926 Ware complained that the French had decided that 'they had no money whatever to put up memorials'. He suggested that on the large memorials the British were erecting there should be an inscription 'in good French' dedicating them to the 'Armées Françaises et Britanniques'. Kipling of course had to come up with a tactful version. In November Ware wrote again after a visit to France with Sir Edwin Lutyens (the Commission's chief architect), General de Castelnau and French architects to try to sort out 'certain difficulties known to the Commission which have arisen between us and the French with regard to the "Missing Memorials".' Ware the diplomat succeeded, and Kipling replied thanking him for 'the news of the successful issue of your intrigue with the French and Lutyens. It isn't an Embassy that I would care to have chaperoned! The lot of the Professional Undertaker is hard.' His inscription for the Anglo-French cemetery that was built behind the resulting memorial to the missing at Thiépval was worked over many times – words altered, scored out, insertions made – before he was happy with the final version: 'Here are laid soldiers of France and of the British Empire that their peoples and the world may remember the common sacrifice of two and a half million dead'. General de Castlenau was thrilled: *'Je vous félicite d'avoir demandé à l'illustre et génial Rudyard Kipling, son concours pour l'inscription qui nous préoccupe.'* [I congratulate you on having asked the illustrious and genial Rudyard Kipling for his assistance on the inscription that preoccupies us.]

This attention to the smallest detail was typical of Kipling. When Rudyard joined the Commission John had not yet been officially declared dead, but the anguish of rising and failing hopes was still raw. He found it hard to stand back from too close an involvement and identification with the bereaved. When his 'advertisement' and booklet about the aims of the Commission were published, they took the invitation to make suggestions as an opportunity to communicate directly with the great man who understood their grief as a result of his personal loss. On 22 February 1919 he replied to Ware's advice to send on all correspondence to the Commission; 'I'll send the correspondence on where it needs an official answer: but these damned mothers are too heartbreaking sometimes, not to answer.' Not only did he answer many of the letters, but he also took practical steps to help. On 10 August 1920 he received a typical letter from a Mr and Mrs Weller of Southfields who begged to tender their 'sincerest thanks for the kindness and trouble you have taken regarding the additional inscription on the headstone of our son's grave. It has been a great comfort to us to see the care and attention that is being so nobly rendered to assuage a little the many broken hearts. We feel proud Sir of having had the honour and pleasure of meeting you and wish you every reward for your unselfish and humanising labour.'

In March 1919 the Foreign Office had published the agreement signed with the French the previous November concerning British war graves in France. The Imperial War Graves Commission was acknowledged as the sole authority responsible for preserving British graves in France and for erecting monuments within the cemeteries on land purchased and donated by the French government. Rudyard, as a Commissioner, would have been privy to all the negotiations concerning the graves, yet he had no known grave for his own son. It must have been difficult for him to remain objective. The controversy over whether headstones or crosses should mark the graves and whether bodies could be brought home was in full flight and Lord Wolmer suggested that the views of the bereaved were not represented on the Commission. *The Times* commented on 4 May that the bereaved were represented: 'To name only one, does he forget Mr Kipling, than whom none of its members is a more ardent supporter of the principal of uniformity?' Rudyard had duty and dedication to shield him, planks whose value he would later acknowledge in the tale *In the Interests of the Brethren.*

But the emotional pressure proved too much and in February 1921 Kipling asked to be released from sitting on the Memorials Committee. 'I don't at all like the idea of your retiring from this Committee,' wrote Ware on 8 February 1921, 'as I personally shall not be satisfied with any decision on this special matter which has not been arrived at after placing all the facts and arguments before you.' But Kipling was not to be moved. It did not, however, prevent him from labouring long and hard to produce the moving and memorable inscriptions that are carved on each headstone of an unidentified body – 'A soldier [sailor, airman or whatever appropriate cognomen] of the Great War. Known Unto God'. For Sir Edwin Lutyens' sarcophagus-like Stone of Remembrance he chose the words 'Their Name Liveth For Evermore', and on the 'Kipling Memorials' 'Their Glory Shall Not Be Blotted Out'. The inscriptions were from Kipling's eternal source of comfort, Ecclesiasticus, Chapter 44, Verses 13 and 14. (This book from the Apocrypha does not appear in every copy of the Authorised Version of the Bible and should not be confused with Ecclesiastes, which does.) There were dissenters, however. The Kipling Memorial inscription caused one next-of-kin to write to the Commission that he felt the words to be 'ugly' and proposed 'Their Glory Shall Abide For Ever'.

Even the choice of the inscriptions for standard headstones and memorials had not been without an element of controversy. Other suggestions were proposed, such as "Then shall the dust return to the earth as it was: and the spirit shall return unto God who gave it,' from a mother, Mrs Amelia Sowell, on 24 January 1920. She also proposed that on the Stone of Remembrance should be depicted 'fragments of destroyed wire entanglements. In bottom left corner foreground a large shell hole containing one or more deceased soldiers partly buried by fallen debris shell bursting overhead and on ground a township under bombardment and afire or similar battle scene in top left hand corner. The stone would be surmounted by the figure of an Angel'! 'Greater Love Hath No Man than This' was another suggestion, as were a sundial and a path using stones from the Giant's Causeway, a symbol of the Path of Duty and the inscription *'Ave Imperator, morituri te salutamus'* (Hail Caesar, we are who about to die salute you), the Dove of Peace with the Rose of England in its beak and the words 'For King and Country'. How appropriate and dignified Kipling's chosen words seem in comparison. The Commission had made a wise choice in his appointment.

Viewed from today, the task that lay ahead of them – to negotiate the acquisition of land from the host country (not always thrilled at the prospect, despite the tactful propaganda to the contrary), to design (with architects and sculptors who often behaved like prima donnas) and build cemeteries, re-inter the dead, record and mark each burial, landscape the cemeteries, design and build the memorials to the missing, with all the problems attendant on hiring and employing such a huge and diverse workforce, to placate and communicate with relatives – seems so immense as to be impossible to complete. The question of the form of the grave marker and the memorials raised strong and sometimes bitter feelings. On 2 May 1920 the MP W. Burdett-Coutts gave a speech in the House of Commons on behalf of the Commission outlining their policy of Equality of Treatment and uniformity of the design of the memorial stones. Opposition to the concept was led by Colonel Sir J. Remnant who put down a motion saying, 'That in the opinion of this House the relatives of those fell in the War should be allowed to erect monuments of their own choosing'. There was vociferous opposition, but even if the idea of uniformity was accepted, what should that uniform marker be? Many mothers favoured the religious symbol of the cross. Kipling favoured a flat stone. 'As far as inscriptions and lettering go [here he drew a cross] is not equal to [and here a headstone] for advertisement purposes.' An extract from a letter from Kipling ('who kindly came down to the House the other day and made a most convincing speech to a meeting of hon. Members') was reproduced in the pamphlet of Burdett-Coutts' speech that was afterwards distributed: 'You see we shall never have any grave to go to. Our boy was missing at Loos. The ground is, of course, battered and mined past all hope of any trace being recovered. I wish some of the people who are making this trouble realised how more than fortunate they are to have a name on a headstone in a known place.' Eventually the headstone prevailed.

Rudyard combined the regular holidays to France that he had long enjoyed with work for the Commission and his continuing, but, as he knew, virtually useless, search for John. On 21 July 1920 Carrie accompanied him on the crossing from Southampton to le Havre to make a tour of the battlefields. One of their ports of call was Villers Cotterets, where they saw George Cecil's grave. On 25 July they went to Loos and, no doubt armed with the maps they had made during the period of their intensive interviews with Irish Guardsmen, identified Chalk Pit Wood and the area where John had last been seen, cleared the previous year by the Commission's battlefield clearance teams. There was no thought of finding his body.

The year saw much activity in the identification of graves. The Germans had at long last begun to supply lists of burials and the Commission had been formally recognized by the German Government. The 'Widows' Counsellors Organisation', an arm of the Salvation Army, had been writing to the Commission asking for information on POW graves and in May questions on the subject were asked in the House. Even though John was now formally listed as killed, the tide of hopeful enquiries of which Rudyard was only too aware must have raised flickering hopes from time to time.

One lighter note in this otherwise sombre year was Rudyard's entry in the Bateman's Visitors' Book for 4 August, 'MOTHER F.I.P. about 6.30 p.m.' – in other words Carrie fell in the pond. Rudyard would have probably known better than to have laughed at the actual time.

In 1921 a further systematic search for bodies was made by the Imperial War Graves Commission in the Loos area – another slight window of hope opening for Rudyard and Carrie that by some miracle John might yet be found. In May the *Liverpool Courier* reported that some 5,000 British soldiers were buried in the unoccupied section of Germany and that up to a quarter had yet to be identified. If their original fear that the badly wounded John had been taken prisoner and had perhaps died in captivity was correct, he could be among them. During the year the responsibility for searching the old battlefields passed from the Directorate of Graves Registration and Enquiry to the Commission, which took over complete responsibility from 10 September and the Directorate formally closed the following year. All British forces were evacuated from France that month and the Headquarters British Troops France and Flanders closed in October. Many of the bereaved felt that, without the soldiers to help, the Commission's small staff would be unable to continue to search with sufficient thoroughness: in 1920 Brigadier General E. Gibb, Commanding British Troops in France and Flanders, had reported that

8,559 men were working on exhumation. The poet John Oxenham protested at the change and the *People* newspaper ran an article entitled, 'The Soldiers' Graves Scandal'. In the process of handover various initial statistics were produced: total B.E.F. casualties were estimated at approximately 739,000. 80,000 were unaccounted for and 42,000 more had been found and were then lost during the war; 5,179 British POWs died in Germany and 7,452 in Occupied Territory. All these figures Rudyard would have seen, with the inevitable question, 'Where did John fit in to these statistics?' It was not the sort of information he would have bothered Carrie with; no need to re-open her wound.

Increasingly he travelled further afield on Commission work and in March 1922 he went to Gibraltar and Malta, preceded by a letter from Ware to the Governor and Commander-in-Chief, General Sir Horace Smith-Dorrien, GCMG, DSO – 'Mr Rudyard Kipling who is, as you probably know, one of the unofficial members of the Commission sails for Gibraltar tomorrow . . . You will perhaps remember that he lost his boy (who is among the "Missing") in the Irish Guards at Loos, and he one of the hardest working of the unofficial members of the Commission.'

Perhaps the apogée of Kipling's association with the Commission came in May 1922, when he accompanied King George and Queen Mary on what became known as 'The King's Pilgrimage'. The organization of it was a mammoth task for Ware, who consulted Kipling from the outset of the planning. 'The visit is for May 11–13 inclusive. <u>Absolutely secret</u> at present. But it's splendid and I must let you alone know at once. I said he was very grateful to you for having suggested it,' wrote an excited Ware in a hand-written <u>'Personal and Confidential'</u> letter on 9 March 1922. In a P.S. Ware conveyed his disappointment that Kipling had turned down the Order of Merit. In his next letter of 28 March Ware asked Kipling if he would write a draft for the speech the King would deliver at Terlincthun. 'Whatever we send they will probably knock about, but we may be able to get in something that really matters,' he says in what was becoming his habitual unguarded frankness with Rudyard. Kipling's love of the motor car was renowned and he could always be relied on to provide a suitably impressive vehicle to transport VIPs. His current Rolls was familiarly known as 'The Duchess', but she was not always as reliable as she was handsome – particularly with regard to punctures. On Kipling's annual tour of the previous year she had sometimes had as many as two a day. Ware asked him to give a lift to the Hon P.C. Larkin, the High Commissioner for Canada, to the main ceremony at Terlincthun and to show him some Canadian graves. 'The pace is quickening,' exclaimed Ware, the administrative adrenalin flowing. Then there was delightful news for Kipling, 'With altogether minor alterations the speech is approved [by the Palace] – they can hardly find enough words to say how beautiful they think it is.' With typical precision, Ware's next letter of 1 May stated that the 'official time at Vlamertinghe is 15.59' and asked Kipling if he could 'pick up one or two other H Cs' [High Commissioners]. Kipling said he could 'take four (including Canada)' and then worried as to 'what clothes should be worn'. A secretary added a P.S. after Ware's next letter of 5 May to the effect that 'the General had forgotten to mention the order regarding clothes to be worn. Palace says "top hats".' Kipling asked for a ticket to the main ceremony for Carrie, but not for Elsie who had also been invited. Ever conscientious, he summarized his duties on 8 May: 'My plan would be to sleep Larkin the night of the 11th at Lille and get him back to Folkestone to sleep the night of the 12th and the motor will be available at 8 a.m. on Saturday morning for the place that you suggest and if you will give instructions that I am to be sent word of the hour of the visit to the Meerut Cemetery [Indian and Egyptian cemetery near Boulogne] I will arrange to join Lord Arthur Browne and the India Office Representative there as suggested . . . We shall be staying at the Bellevue Hotel at Lille.'

Ware's meticulous planning paid dividends. The Pilgrimage was a resounding success. It was recorded by Kipling in the Hodder and Stoughton publication, *The King's Pilgrimage*, to which the King wrote a foreword saying that all the profits would go to 'the philanthropic organizations which for some time have been assisting relatives to visit the cemeteries abroad'. Kipling started the book (as he did with many of his short stories) with a related poem of the same name:

> Our King went forth on Pilgrimage
> His prayer and vows to pay
> To them that saved our Heritage
> And cast their own away.

Two verses, both in brackets and italics, show his own sense of loss and his longing for a grave at which to mourn himself:

> (All that they had they gave – they gave;
> and they shall not return,
> For these are those that have no grave
> where any heart may mourn.)

and:

> (Father and Mother they put aside, and
> the nearer love also –
> An hundred thousand men who died, whose
> graves shall no man know.)

The line above indicates his secret resignation to never finding John's grave and the fact that the book, and the poem, were yet another tribute to his son.

The illustrated booklet charts the King's progress around the battle-fields after a State Visit to Brussels. He arrived in the Royal Train (a source of some aggravation for Ware as some VIPs were allowed to ride on it – General Haig, Ware himself and one or two others who were unwell or old and infirm – causing several others to complain bitterly that this honour had been refused them) wearing army service uniform. The first stop was Zeebrugge Churchyard. Then it was on to the great cemetery at Tyne Cot, where the King suggested that the Cross of Sacrifice should be erected on one of the German pillboxes which gave the cemetery its name (as they resembled Tyneside cottages) and in the taking of which many lives were lost. Before visiting the Menin Gate at Ypres the King requested a visit to Ypres Town Cemetery, where he visited the grave of his cousin, Prince Maurice of Battenberg. Next it was Vlamertinghe Military Cemetery, where Kipling was introduced to the King for the first time. Rudyard was doing his best to avoid permanent attachment to the offi-cial party and recorded in relief that the affair at Vlamertinghe lasted only 'half an hour from first to last'. He had heeded the dress code instruction, however, and changed into his formal wear in a cottage beside the ceme-tery. The King continued to Hop Store Cemetery, Brandhoek Old Military Cemetery, Poperinghe Communal Cemetery and Lijssenthoek Cemetery. At every stop he met local dignitaries and children, IWGC officials and gardeners and many relatives visiting the graves. Passing from Belgium into France, the King went first to Vimy Ridge, where he spent the night of 11 May. The next morning he visited the huge French cemetery at Notre Dame de Lorette. There he joined with Haig in a ceremony with Marshal Foch and General Weygand. There followed a quick tour of the Somme battlefield cemeteries at Warlencourt, Warloy-Baillon, Forceville, Louvencourt, Picquigny, Crouy and Longpré-les-Corps-Saint. That night was spent at Etaples and the next morning he visited Lutyens' graceful cemetery on the site of the great Bull Ring training and base hospital area. The Queen had not yet joined the party and she entrusted him with a task that a mother had requested of her – to lay a spray of forget-me-nots on the grave of her son, Sergeant Matthews. This the King reverently did.

Meanwhile Rudyard drove on southwards, down the la Bassée to Lens road, 'a most awful stretch of road and the countryside so altered that we passed where John had disappeared. Red House, Chalk Pit wood and all smoothed out.' That the ground had so changed since their visit to the spot the previous year made their tangible link with John more tenuous and perhaps marked the end of any hope of finding his grave.

On 13 May, on his way to join up with the official party in the final ceremony of the Pilgrimage at Terlincthun, Rudyard visited the Indian

Cemetery called Meerut, in an act of homage to the troops he so admired from the land he still longed for. There he found the grave of a bearer called 'Ganga Din' ('Ganga' being a version of 'Gunga') who had died of pneumonia in March 1915. He was reminded of the hero of his famous poem, *Gunga Din*, written twenty-six years earlier, who also died for his monarch, 'A-servin' of 'Er Majesty the Queen'.

At Terlincthun Cemetery, 'set at the foot of Napoleon's column', the King delivered the speech that Kipling had written. It included a paragraph that encompassed all Fabian Ware's ideals:

> 'Standing beneath this Cross of Sacrifice, facing the great Stone of Remembrance, and encompassed by these sternly simple headstones, we remember and must charge our children to remember, that, as our dead were equal in sacrifice, so are they equal in honour.'

Kipling's pride was complete when he and the other 'unofficial' commissioners were formally presented to His Majesty. King George took the opportunity to have a few private words not only with Rudyard, but with Carrie too: he talked to her about John. The much-reproduced photograph of Rudyard walking beside the King was taken here. It was somewhat of an anticlimax when the dear Duchess broke down on the last leg of the journey at Zeebrugge.

The book of the Pilgrimage was a best seller, 25,000 copies being printed, despite Kipling's own criticism at the proof-reading stage that 'Hodder and Stoughton might have made the book's typographical appearance more attractive and interesting'. His suggestion that the King's speech should be indented was taken up. Writing from the Privy Purse Office at the Palace, Sir Frederick Ponsonby made a more serious criticism to Ware, 'which the King did not make, and which I therefore pass on only for your private information, and that is that not enough is made of the fact of Lord Haig accompanying the King. After all, he was in command of the whole British Army, and the mere fact of his going out should be brought into prominence.' Nevertheless, the public and the staff of the IWGC were eager purchasers and Princess Alice of Athlone wrote asking for a copy.

In August Kipling paid as much attention to the inscriptions for the isolated R.E. Grave on Railway Hill, above the Menin Road in the Ypres Salient, as he did to the great national memorials. A Cross of Sacrifice was to be erected over the bodies of an officer, three NCOs and nine men of 177th Tunnelling Company killed in the underground mining of November 1915–August 1917 and Rudyard's draft shows much crossing out and altering of words. Each task of commemoration was important him, be it in the highly visible sites of Ypres or the Somme or in far-flung battle sites such as Gallipoli, East Africa and Mesopotamia.

The next high-profile task for Commissioner Kipling was the composing of inscriptions for the Commemorative Tablets to be erected in Cathedrals in Belgium, France and the UK. The tablets were designed by Lieutenant Colonel H.P. Cart de Lafontaine, OBE, FRIBA and executed by Mr Reginald Hallward. The handsome plaques, cast in gesso, painted, gilded and coloured, were set in stone. They summarized the sacrifice of the British and, where they did not have their own separate Cathedral memorials, her Dominion Forces. 'As you know,' Ware wrote to Kipling, in what had become his habitual confidential style, on 13 October 1922, 'the Dominions have all their own tablets up in Amiens and it is high time that we reminded the French that these islands also did something . . . We cannot overlook the propaganda purposes and that is why we think the numbers of the United Kingdom losses ought to be mentioned.' Ever the professional, Kipling summarized, in the required 191 characters, the components of the enlistments (total 8,818,896), the killed or died of wounds (908,371) of the Royal Navy and the British Army and, including the Royal Air Force, the total 'Dead for the Empire' calculated as 1,069,825.

Other tablets were erected in Notre Dame Cathedral in Paris (which was unveiled by the Prince of Wales on 7 July 1924 with impressive pomp), other Cathedrals in France and Belgium (including Ypres) where troops had been quartered, and on 19 October the Prince of Wales unveiled a similar tablet in Westminster Abbey. There are replicas of the Amiens and standard French plaques flanking the entrance hall of the Commission's Head Office at Maidenhead. Kipling took a particular interest in these tablets and always tried to include a visit to them on his extensive travels for the Commission and his Continental holidays. Each one, in its reference to the Missing or Dead, was a memorial to John.

In September 1923 plans for the main memorial to the missing of the Ypres Salient were well under way by the architect, Sir Reginald Blomfield. In his draft design Blomfield indicated an inscription over the arch. An indignant Ware wrote to Rudyard on the 18th, 'Blomfield had no right, when we gave him permission to publish the picture of the Menin Gate Arch, to write in his own inscription and as soon as I spotted it in the published picture I remonstrated with him about it. I think I can manage to get hold of Mackenzie King as soon as he arrives in England so as to stop any trouble about this, but I am a little bit uneasy, because I was under the impression that you had been officially asked to consider this inscription and have said so in these letters, but I can find no trace of any letter to you to this effect. In that case I imagine that nothing but my conscience is wounded, as you always do settle these inscriptions for us and I cannot think that you will not also do so in this case.' A placating Kipling replied on 20 September, 'It is a bit awkward just on the eve of the Conference, but what remains of your conscience is all right, for, of course, I always considered that all inscriptions came my way sooner or later, and the Menin Gate one is specially an inscription to be thought over. I expect Blomfield, as you say, put the words in for the look of his sketch.'

The great memorial arch was finally unveiled by Field-Marshal Plumer on 24 July 1927. The speech this popular old soldier gave came from the heart, particularly his reference to each of the dead whose names are engraved on the gateway – 'He is not missing. He is here.' They were words, well-reported in the press and on the BBC, that must have meant a great deal to Rudyard and Carrie Kipling. The finale of the ceremony was the reverberant sounding of the Last Post under the great arch. It made such an impression that the citizens of Ypres decided that this tribute to the British and Dominion forces who lost their lives in the defence of the Ypres Salient should be a nightly occurrence. A Last Post Committee was formed and from Armistice Day 1929 the bugle call has been played nightly, with only a break during the WW2 German occupation, when it was sounded at Brookwood Cemetery.

Almost a year later Kipling was asked to suggest an inscription for the Cross of Sacrifice which was to be erected near Sir Douglas Haig's grave at Dryburgh Abbey. After his being accused of not giving Haig enough exposure in *The King's Pilgrimage* Book, Kipling did little to make amends with the non-committal inscription he wrote: 'This Cross of Sacrifice is identical with those which stand above the dead of Lord Haig's Armies in France and Flanders. 10 July 1929'. Haig had been the commander of the 1st Army with which John was serving when he was killed at Loos. It had been an ineptly commanded battle and perhaps Kipling could never find it in his heart to forgive Haig. He was much warmer in his tribute to his fellow commissioner, Harry Gosling, when on 24 October 1930 he wrote, 'Write him as one that loved his fellow men' – a variation on a line in Leigh Hunt's poem *Abou Ben Adhem*.

On 4 August 1930 had come what was perhaps the culmination of Rudyard's work for the Commission: the unveiling of his own boy's name carved in stone on the Loos Memorial at Dud Corner (so called because of all the unexploded British shells which had once been collected there). All hope of finding a grave had long since died. The ceremony was performed by General Sir Nevil Macready, Adjutant-General to the B.E.F. in 1914 and, because of his experiences of the chaotic treatment of graves in the Boer War, a great supporter of Fabian Ware in the setting up firstly of the Graves Registrations Commission and then of the Imperial War Graves Commission itself in 1917 when he became, with Rudyard Kipling, one of the 'unofficial members'. Inspired by the haunting playing of the Last Post at the Menin Gate, from 25 September 1930, Rudyard and Carrie instigated the nightly sounding, initially for one year only, of the Last Post here at the Loos Memorial where John's name was inscribed.

The memorial, designed by Sir Herbert Baker, with sculptor Sir Charles Wheeler (who had sculpted John's memorial plaque for Burwash Church), had originally been planned for Béthune, but in 1926 the French intimated that they had become 'disquieted by the number and scale of the Memorials which the Commission proposed to erect'. A drastic reduction, from the planned twelve to four, followed. Sites for Soissons, La Ferté and Neuve-Chapelle had already been acquired, the fourth memorial was destined to be on the Somme (Thiépval), so the names originally to be inscribed on memorials at Cambrai, St Quentin, Lille, Pozières and Béthune had to be contained on walls within the land allocated for cemeteries in the area. Dud Corner Cemetery was built on the site of an old German stronghold known as the Lens Road Redoubt, captured by the 15th (Scottish) Division on the first day of the Battle of Loos. The Loos Memorial occupies the side and back walls of the cemetery. Its inscription was adapted from the words Kipling wrote for the Menin Gate Memorial and it records the names of nearly 21,000 officers and men. The register notes that the remains of 44 men have subsequently been identified and their names removed. The deletion of John Kipling's name would have made it 45.

Chapter 9

THE GREAT WAR ENDS

*The Search for John Ceases. The Effect of John's Death
on Rudyard's Work. The Armistice.*

'When the storm is ended'
Rudyard Kipling, *Mesopotamia*, 1917

Apart from the work with the Commission and the *Irish Guards History*, life – and work – had to go on. One sad piece of news in January 1917 was of the divorce of the Kiplings' friend of many years, Julia, from her husband Chauncey Depew. The war had hit the Depew couple hard at their château at Annel, which they turned into a hospital. In August 1914 they had had to evacuate it as the Germans swept towards Paris, then in September of 1916 an English Battery had been installed in the nearby grounds, which, according to Carrie, fired incessantly. The strain on their relationship seems to have been too much. Julia, however, later found consolation and a new husband in the form of General Taufflieb, who became Commissioner of Alsace after the war.

On 2 February Elsie was 21, 'and all the coming of age we shall have in the family now'. Losses which hit them personally continued and were duly reported to Carrie's mother. On 2 March they had been 'very upset . . . over the loss of a young friend of John's and ours' and on 29 April she reported, 'Poor Elsie has lost another boy friend, Charlie Bonar Law, who was reported missing and wounded in Egypt. If by luck he is alive and a prisoner of course he is in better hands with the Turks than if he were with the Germans. She knew how anxious his family would be 'until and if they are able to get further news'. The Bonar Laws' case would have brought back memories of their own 'POW phase' ending in ultimate disappointment. She and Rudyard had been to 'a postponed St Patrick's Day Sports Day' at Warley and met a lot of John's friends. Though it was a long hard day they were 'pleased to have done it'. During the day they made some enquiries on an impatient Oliver's behalf. 'It appears the Regiment has a number of Ensigns under age (19) for going out but we are going to Warley on St Patrick's Day,' Rudyard promised on 12 March, when he would get more confirmation. 'Meantime, every dam thing you do and say and are counts, as the Regiment is acutely aware that most of

155

the new staff was lately C.S.Ms. or Q.M.Ss. After all there is a limited supply of the old material.' Had Rudyard been feeling a sense of guilt and responsibility for John's death, it is inconceivable that he would have worked so hard to ease Oliver's under-age entry into the war.

On 1 May 1917 Kipling made a little publicized visit with Perceval Landon to the Italian Front, which is well-documented in Peter Lewis's booklet *The War in the Mountains* and in Rudyard's almost daily letters to Carrie. She was not best pleased at being left and complained to her mother about it. It was a tiring tour, starting with a frustrating bureacratic delay in Paris. Then it was on to Rome, where he met an adoring Gilbert Frankau (who claimed to know Kipling's entire poetic output by heart). After suffering from shell shock, Frankau had wangled himself to Italy in the guise of an Intelligence Officer making a propaganda film. He managed to get Kipling to attend a viewing. The film was of a highly fanciful nature and Rudyard asked Frankau, 'How did you come to think of that fiction?' Finally he chuckled, 'Superb. But you will be slain for this my friend.' Frankau was, indeed, hauled over the coals for his colourful imagination. From Rome Kipling's journey took him to Udine, Gradisca, the Isonzo River, Gorizia and the Dolomite and Trentino Fronts and Carrie sent him out orange-coloured glasses for protection against the glare of the snow and the sun. The results were five articles which appeared in the *Daily Telegraph* and the *New York Tribune* between 6 and 20 June, the first one Kipling wrote, on Rome in wartime, being censored by the War Office and never published.

Back at Burwash, Carrie still couldn't let go of John and the investigations continued. On 23 May, by which time Rudyard had returned and was 'finishing his Italian work', she had heard from Mrs Cuthbert and was livid with the War Office who, as she wrote to Lady Edward, 'has excelled itself in its hopeless stupidity, and announced her [Mrs Cuthbert's] husband's death not to her . . . but to the Public Trustee, with whom he was connected as a trustee in some small property . . . [who] forwarded the news to her.' Lady Edward had come up with another suggestion, enlisting Lord Northcliffe's help, that Rudyard should publicly take up the case of missing prisoners, which Carrie declined, supposing that only the War Office or the Foreign Office could help and she was convinced they wouldn't, 'until one day they discover they must get into dreadful trouble if the war ends and thousands of prisoners are found who have never been returned and they can not show they have brought one little gram of promise to the weight against the Germans'. It was an unrealistic flight of fancy, and she continued in a more down to earth vein, considering the case of Mrs Cuthbert on whose behalf the President of the USA, the King of Spain, the US Minister to Holland and all the regular societies had been written to with no results 'and now they announce the man's death on the 27th September 1915 and no one cares, no one in authority is anything but bored to death at the woman wanting to know why they did not get her the news sooner. I don't often lash out but there it is and there it will remain.' When Carrie had had time to discuss Lady Edward's idea with Rudyard, she wrote again thanking her for her thoughts and understanding sympathy, which 'through all these months has been such a rock of strength that I am sure you will understand why he feel he can not take up this matter'. As Rudyard was personally involved he did not feel he could 'go into it on general principles. It is this that has kept him from printing out [she means writing up for publication in the press] the heartless and disgraceful laziness with which the whole question of Prisoners and missing has been treated from the top.' Their wound had been re-opened. 'You will have realized how the coming of this news of Captain Cuthbert's death – with no reason or excuse for the delay of 19 or 20 months in its announcement and not coupled with any word about John has shaken and shattered us afresh.' In her bitterness and growing hatred not only of the Germans but of the Establishment she saw it as 'an organized piece of work on the part of the Germans, but the people who have us in their power here can't be expected to see that, since if they did they would have to meet the fact. The game is to be generous to the Germans at the expense of our own people – after the war, if one can keep going to the end, things must be done.' In the light of her greater experience she pitied 'the poor Bonar Laws [who] don't in the least realize about their boy yet, and write "others of his regiment who were missing, have been reported as wounded and of course Charlie will be soon". Why never give credit to the enemy for skill we do not use and pretend we are above doing it.'

On 27 June, their nephew and protégé Oliver at last got his wish. He was commissioned into the 3rd (Reserve) Battalion of the Irish Guards, nearly four months after his 18th birthday on 1 March. The life of yet another young man they were intimate with was in jeopardy. Then came another milestone, another hurdle to surmount – John's birthday. On 17 August his parents were staying at Brown's 'in the rooms we had when we came here after we were married', as she told her mother and reported that yesterday's news from the Front was of the retaking of the Bois Hugo, 'which was the wood from which they shelled John and his men nearly 2 years ago and today comes the news of the Germans big counter-attacks at Hill 70 and that they were killed by us in their thousands. So it makes not a bad birthday for our John,' she commented in an understandable wave of revengeful satisfaction. The date was also noted by Mrs Roosevelt (Rudyard was in frequent correspondence with her husband) who sent a 'very nice and kind' letter. On that day Rudyard wrote to Oliver, who was on a Lewis gun course at Tidworth: 'It's the old boy's 20th birthday today – so not too cheerful a time.' Rudyard applied his usual antidote – work.

His mind was also occupied by another visit by his sister Trix to the farm cottage at Bateman's. Carrie had little sympathy for her and told her mother on 23 September that she 'just has hysteria' and she hoped she would be better 'after the change'. On the 27th – '<u>John's day</u>', she reported even more sad news for the Bonar Laws. Their other son Jim had been reported missing. 'He was here the last time he had leave June 13 I see by the visitors book and was so happy and gay because then they had news that the other boy who was fighting the Turks was a prisoner. Since it has been denied – a little mistake made by the Pope who investigated the matter.' In fact both boys were dead. Lieutenant Charles John Bonar Law, age 20, of the 3rd Bn, att'd 115th Bn the KOSB, was later posted as killed in action on 19 April. He is buried in Gaza War Cemetery. Captain James Kidston Bonar Law of the Royal Fusiliers, age 24, serving with 30 Sqn the RFC, was reported missing on 21 September after an air accident and has no known grave. He is commemorated on the RFC/RAF Memorial at Arras.

On 2 September had come a poignant moment. C.E. Stanford, a master at John's old school at Rottingdean, wrote to Rudyard explaining that one of his boys had found a note which had fallen behind a board in his locker. 'It was the locker dear John had and this letter must have slipped behind when he had it and remained there ever since.' Stanford didn't know which was kinder, 'to burn it or send it to you but I think I ought to send it on, tho' I'd gladly have spared you the pain'. Sadly the note, which sounds as if it contained a home-sick plea, has not survived.

That ever more of their friends were, like them, losing their sons only reinforced Rudyard and Carrie's conviction that they could have done no less. However, the question as to whether Rudyard felt in any way responsible for John's death and, consequently, guilt and remorse, is a matter of keen debate. Biographers (the present ones included) are divided in their opinion. Marghanita Laski feels the Kipling parents each bore a burden of responsibility for the death of a child. 'The Kiplings must have been aware that here were two deaths that their own actions had helped to bring about. If only Carrie had listened to her mother-in-law on the risks of taking the children to America in mid-winter – if only Rudyard had put his foot down – If only they had left John to discover his own right place in war work suited to his physical disabilities.' Thomas Cross tackles the question head on: 'Is it possible Kipling felt a twinge of guilt over his son's death? . . . Did Kipling feel any remote sense of responsibility?' He wonders whether the writing of the *Irish Guards History* was 'an act of penance' for interceding with Lord Roberts to get his 'pleasant, not-too-bright schoolboy with poor eyesight' a commission. He categorically answers his own question: 'I think that all evidence points to the fact that it was not, and that Kipling felt no guilt whatsoever over John's death.' Hilton Brown, on the other hand, felt that 'in the case of John . . . he had the dreadful knowledge that he was himself partly to blame. John was short-sighted like his father; he had varicose veins [the source for this statement is not stated], he need not have been a soldier; but Kipling had been so soldier-possessed, had moved so closely with Roberts in his campaign for universal service, that neither father nor son was left with any honourable retreat. That must have been a grim thought for Kipling during many hours between 1915 and 1936.' Hilton Brown misses the point that John had spent two years at Wellington, a school whose whole purpose was to prepare boys for commissioned life in the Army, had been a member of the OTC and had himself made strenuous efforts to enlist, as so many of his friends had done. It was their culture.

During the lonely years of 1916 and 1917 Kipling worked on several poems, some of which were completed and quickly published, others not till later. One of them, *The Question*, is generally interpreted (as by Angus Wilson) as 'a remonstrance to neutrals'. As with all Kipling's writings, it is dangerous to assume there is only one interpretation, or that he adhered strictly to the facts as he developed a theme. It must be remembered that Rudyard Kipling was a *creative* writer. He interpreted the facts – autobiographical, political or whatever – to suit the thread or the rhythm of his story or poem. Critics who do not understand this complain that *Baa Baa, Black Sheep*, for example, is not 'accurate'. The point that they are missing is that it is a work of *fiction*. Kipling had every right to take elements of his personal experience and then to weave them into his writings. There is little that he wrote after John's death that was not in some way influenced by that trauma in his life: allusions to his loss, overt or covert, are legion. Yet there is virtually nothing which prosaically and accurately recounts his son's death and his reaction to it. Thus one can interpret *The Question*, 'If it be proven that I am he For whom a world has died . . . Then how shall I live with myself through the years' as a cry of guilt for John's death. The poem *My Boy Jack* (see page xii) is probably the nearest Rudyard allowed himself to get to a factual reference to the dreadful situation he faced with the declaration of John being 'missing'. Yet he transposes the loss to a naval context, and this is perhaps why he refers to the boy as 'Jack' (as in 'Jack Tar') rather than 'John'. The great truth in the poem is the comfort in the fact that 'he did not shame his kind.'

The Sons of Martha can also be read as having allusions to John and other junior officers of the Great War. Kipling contrasts the carefree 'Sons of Mary' with Martha's caring sons, who wait upon them by smoothing their path with their efforts, much as the keen young subaltern, John, did for his men. The verse,

They finger death at their gloves' end where they
   piece and repiece the living wires.
He rears against the gates they tend: they feed him hungry behind their fires.

Early at dawn, ere men see clear, they stumble into his terrible stall
And hale him forth like a haltered steer, and goad
    and turn him till evenfall

seems to be referring to a brave young officer cutting the enemy wire before a dawn attack on the trenches. Martha, 'of the careful soul and the troubled heart', who 'lost her temper once', sounds much like Carrie.

Natural Theology, which follows the course of religion through the Primitive, the Pagan, the Medieval and the Material to the Progressive, mocks so-called religious folk who blame their God or Gods for all the misfortunes that befall them. So the Progressive man declares,

Money spent on an Army or Fleet
    Is homicidal lunacy . . .
My son has been killed in the Mons retreat.
    Why is the Lord afflicting me?

Kipling's answer was

This was none of the good Lord's pleasure,
    For the Spirit He breathed in Man is free
But what comes after is measure for measure,
    And not a God that afflicteth thee.
As was the sowing so the reaping
    Is now and evermore shall be.
Thou art delivered to thy own keeping.
    Only Thyself hath afflicted thee!

Not for Kipling the traditional comfort of blaming it all on God. He knew he only had himself to blame for the harvest of John's death. He sowed its seeds by encouraging him from a small child to want to pursue an army or naval career. It is important here to differentiate between responsibility and guilt. Certainly Rudyard knew that he was 'responsible' for John's death. He admits it – 'Only Thyself hath afflicted thee!' – but he made no expressions of 'guilt'. The whole culture of the Empire, the White Man's Burden, the public school ethos of *Dulce et Decorum est Pro Patria Mori*, developed the acceptance that it was proper for the British ruling classes to lead by example, proudly and from the front. Family after family had given their sons to Moloch. The Kiplings' turn simply came. There could not be guilt attached to answering the call of duty even if it resulted in sacrifice. Army training crystallized the ethos of selfless leadership in its instructions to young officers: 'First feed the horses, then the men, then yourself.'

Gethsemane is a strong identification with a soldier who prayed that his 'cup might pass', but who 'drank it when it we met the gas Beyond Gethsemane'. Perhaps Rudyard was thinking of John, who, in the terrifying hours before the Battle of Loos, might also have hoped that his cup might pass.

Of the stories of this period, *On the Gate*, subtitled *A Tale of '16*, was not published until 1918, when Kipling read it to Rider Haggard, who called it 'a quaint story about Death and St Peter, written in modern language, almost in slang, which his wife would not let him publish. It would have been caviare to the General if he had, because the keynote of it is infinite mercy extending even to the case of Judas.' It describes in a curiously light-hearted way the overtime St Peter had to put in at the Heavenly Gate (which is like a cross between a modern office staffed by rule-bound clerks and a pedantic Army Department) to deal with the flood of would-be entries as a result of the War casualties. 'Thanks to khaki everywhere, the scene was not unlike that which one might have seen on earth any evening of the old days outside the refreshment-room by the Arch at Victoria Station, when the army trains started,' is a typical word picture. It is little wonder that Carrie, so soon after John's death, found it hard to take its note of flippancy at the attempts of soldiers to enter heaven.

She, as always, dreaded the onset of winter and the long dark nights which left too much time for thought. 'Trix is going to be a heavy additional burden,' she moaned to her mother on 30 September. 'There is nothing in the world the matter with her except selfishness and self-centredness carried to the nth degree.' One is tempted to murmur about pots calling kettles black.

Oliver Baldwin, now with the Irish Guards, was conducting his own investigations about John. In May he had spent his embarkation leave at Bateman's and 'when the telegram [posting him overseas] arrived I capered round the lawn with joy, for the last great adventure had begun. One of the family [John] had fallen. I was the avenger,' he wrote. He saw several months of active service, notably in the assault on the Canal du Nord in September, when he freely admitted to his father that his nerves were 'in none too good a state' and that 'It's about time I got wounded; it seems to be the best way of getting home these days.' On 4 October he reported that he had discovered a Sergeant Farrell of No 12 Platoon who claimed to have seen John being shot. Rudyard immediately wrote back inviting Oliver to Bateman's so that he could tell them more details 'about where Farrell was in the action. Meantime I have said nothing about this to Elsie and I'd rather you didn't tell her until we've investigated a little further.' On 20 October, after interviewing the man, Oliver wrote a report to his 'dear Uncle'. 'This is his story:- Apparently in the heat of the advance on the 27th, Sergt. Farrell found four or five men and John trying to capture the farm building we have heard such a lot about. The men were at the door and John was calmly emptying his revolver into the 12 Huns and machine gun that were in the house. As Sergt. Farrell came up, John was hit through the temple and fell back into his arms. Farrell bound up his head as best he could, John was quite quiet, his eyes were closed. The Irish retired, Farrell carried John back with them. He placed him in a shell-hole and saw he was dead. Sergt. Farrell further adds that he was probably killed instantaneously. However, he never suffered and was probably buried by a shell afterwards. Farrell seems very clear about it all. It seems to clear a lot up, doesn't it?' So here was yet another clear, emphatic and quite different account of John's final moments. Farrell followed up Oliver's report with a letter of his own, corroborating the story and firmly stating that he would never have left John had he not been convinced that he was dead and 'beyond any further help'. Farrell was then interviewed by Colonel Vesey who confirmed that Farrell had carried John '50 yards to the left edge of the wood and about 15 yards from it' and left him in a shell hole as he was dead. He added that a Lance Corporal Scanlon had seen John in the shell hole at about 6.30 p.m. 'shot very badly across the temples. He was just breathing at the time. He could not get him in.' Again, a slightly different version. Vesey went on to say, 'I cannot understand why these two N.C.Os. have never said anything about it before. They are both excellent N.C.Os. and reliable men. Perhaps you would like to see them and talk to them. Their stories agree in the main essentials. But in the confusion of battle the actual details given by people afterward seldom agree. The only reason I can put forward why they have not come forward before is that N.C.Os and men hardly ever discuss any events in France when they get back here. It is an extraordinary thing but it is so. I feel so sorry that these details should not have come to light before.'

At the time Rudyard was busy with the Burwash Village War Memorial, on whose committee he served. But on 12 December Carrie noted in her diary that Rudyard went to London and was convinced by Sergeant Farrell that 'John was shot through the head and carried to a shell hole at 6.30 on 27 September on the left edge of Chalk Pit Wood'. They seemed to have accepted it as the end of the matter. There were no more interviews, no more reports. Trying to put on a brave face for Elsie that Christmas must have been more difficult than ever. Yet there was probably a certain sense of relief as well. What they now needed was to find John's body, and to have a grave and a focus for their grief.

In April Rudyard began working on his powerful *Epitaphs of the War*. In the 1941 essay which introduced his choice of Kipling's verse, T.S. Eliot talked of Kipling's gift for two kinds of verse in which he excelled: the epigram and the hymn (of which he felt *Recessional* was a supreme example). 'Good epigrams in English are very few; and the great hymn writer is very rare. Both are extremely objective types of verse; they can and should be charged with intense feeling, but it must be a feeling that can be completely shared. They are possible to a writer so impersonal as Kipling: and I should like the reader to look attentively at the *Epitaphs of the War*.' Most of Kipling's work can be read at several levels, and Eliot was obviously completely missing one when he judged the *Epitaphs* to be 'objective' and 'impersonal'. So many echoes of John, direct and indirect, can be found in them, for instance:'

An Only Son

I have slain none except my Mother. She
(Blessing her slayer) died of grief for me

Shows Rudyard's sympathy with Carrie who had lost her most treasured possession in John.

The Beginner

On the first hour of my first day
In the front trench I fell

reminds us that John was killed in his first action. More difficult to interpret, for no source for this incident can be found is

A Son

My son was killed while laughing at some jest. I would I knew
What it was, and it might serve me in a time when jests are few.

Perhaps it was wishful thinking. Angus Wilson remarked that it is 'grimly ironic' to place Rider Haggard's discovery that John had last been 'crying with pain from a mouth wound' against this epitaph.

The one most often quoted is

Common Form

If any question why we died,
Tell them because our fathers lied.

The accepted meaning of 'fathers' is in the general, Establishment/ Government sense of the mismanagement of the conduct of the war. If Kipling did indeed feel that he had, at the least, been economical with the truth about the seriousness of John's myopia, and thus eventually was responsible for his death, this could be a public admission of guilt.

There is no doubt that, even if Rudyard had not used his influence to get John a commission at the outbreak of the war, the boy, determined for his own and for his father's sake, to get himself into the war, would have done so unaided. There is some basis of truth in the apocryphal tales of Recruiting Sergeants asking 16-year-olds to run round the block and come back when they were 18, of perfunctory medical examinations. Had he enlisted as a private soldier, John Kipling's OTC experience and his general background would inevitably, finally have led to a commission. Had he gone out to France still in the ranks, he would probably have survived longer. He may have been killed on the Somme in July 1916 or, if lucky, at Passchendaele in July 1917, rather than at Loos in September 1915. If Kipling *did* feel guilty, it should in all reality only be because he was instrumental in accelerating the death of his son.

For Rudyard there was the consolation that Rider Haggard had decided to over-winter in Sussex and had taken a house at St Leonards. The friends saw each other often, and at a time of great uncertainty for each of them – Haggard about his work and Kipling about his beliefs in the aftermath of John's death – found their long discussions extremely therapeutic. 'He is a very shy bird,' noted Haggard in his diary, 'and as he remarked, has no friends, except I think myself, for whom he has always entertained affection, and no acquaintance with literary people' He continued, 'There are two men left living in the world with whom I am in supreme sympathy, Theodore Roosevelt and Rudyard Kipling.' Rudyard could well have said the same. Their mutual sympathy and understanding was further strengthened when, on 14 July 1918, Roosevelt, too, lost a beloved son, Quentin.

Haggard was tempted back to spiritualism by the writings of Sir Oliver Lodge and Sir Arthur Conan Doyle. At the age of eighteen, like the young Kipling newly returned from India, he had found himself in the exciting world of a London full of the temptations of the flesh and the current fad for spiritualism. Andrew Lang, also interested in the paranormal, encouraged his curiosity. Although at first scoffing at the seances held by the aristocratic ladies at whose salons he was welcome, he attended one seance at which the physical manifestations of 'some existent but unknown force' [Pocock] were all too real. He was terrified and vowed to attend no more. Yet he kept an open mind and was prepared to examine the findings of the Society for Psychical Research. Kipling, however, still nervous of the Society's influence on his sister, steadfastly refused to listen. During one particular long debate on 22 May (when Haggard pronounced Kipling to be 'thin and aged and worn', suffering from the mysterious intestinal disorder which gave him great pain) they talked about 'the soul and the fate of man'. Haggard asked him 'if he wished for extinction and could contemplate without dismay, separation from all he loved – John for instance. He replied that he was never happier than when he knew that as a child his boy was asleep in the next room. Why therefore should he mind it in the grave, or words to that effect . . . Poor old boy,' Haggard sympathized, 'John's death has hit him very hard. He said today that I was lucky to have lost my son early, when I still had youth to help me to bear up against the shock and time in which to recover from it . . . Mayhap he is right: Often I think so myself. I pointed out that this love of ours for our lost sons was a case of what is called "inordinate affection" in the Prayer Book which somehow is always bereaved. "Perhaps," he answered, "but I don't care for 'ordinate' affection and nor do you".' They also discussed reincarnation and the fact that 'every year which passes draws back a curtain . . . and shows us to ourselves in yet completer nakedness.' Haggard strongly believed this, while Kipling thought 'that there are many to whom this did not happen: "little" men who are increasingly pleased with themselves.' At the end of this baring of souls, Haggard concluded, 'Altogether I had a very pleasant afternoon. A long talk with Kipling is now one of the greatest pleasures I have left in life – but I don't think he talks like this with anyone else, indeed he said as much to me.'

As Carrie could talk to Violet Cecil because they shared the tragedy of the loss of a son, so Kipling could talk to Haggard. Did they, one wonders, talk to each other in such a frank way about their pain?

The Kiplings continued to derive pleasure in the company of the nearest thing that they had to a son – Oliver Baldwin. On 24 May Carrie must have experienced a sense of *déjà vu* as Ollie stayed with them during his embarkation leave. 'He and Elsie and Rud are very happy together,' she wrote, distancing herself from their carefree appearance as she dreaded yet another close loss. He came to stay again whilst on leave in October and Rudyard took him to see *As You Like It*.

But Rudyard's mind was still fixed on John and yet more poems expressed his unhealable wound. *The Song of the Lathes*, for instance, written to the tune hummed by a munition worker as she operates the 'fans and the beltings' to make shells for 'Guns in Flanders', contains a verse that might have been sung by Carrie,

> Once I was a woman, but that's by with me.
> All I loved and looked for, it must die with me;

Most moving of all is *The Children*. Its language is simple and direct; there is no obscurity here; it rings true and heartrendingly personal:

> These were our children who died for our lands: they were dear in
> our sight.
> We have only the memory left of their home-treasured sayings and
> laughter.
> The price of our loss shall be paid to our hands, not another's
> hereafter.
> Neither Alien nor Priest shall decide on it. That is our right.
> *But who shall return us the children?*

Kipling's oft-used device of italicizing a line to give it greater meaning has never been used to more searing effect than in this baying plea. He then returns to the theme of *Common Form*,

> They believed us and perished for it. Our statecraft, our learning
> Delivered them bound to the Pit and alive to the burning.

In the last verse, and in particular the penultimate two lines, it is as if Kipling is playing a horror film in his mind of John's end:

> That flesh we had nursed from the first in all cleanness was given . . .
> To be senselessly tossed and retossed in stale mutilation
> From crater to crater. For this we shall take expiation.

Expiation – it was one of Victor Hugo's great themes – implies guilt and perhaps this emotion crept into Kipling's mind at times, only to be overwhelmed by his belief in the greater cause of defeating Germany and saving the Empire.

Many of the concepts expressed in *The Children* are returned to in *Mesopotamia*, but in a more bitter, anti-politician/anti-staff fashion. This is a poem triggered by a specific event – the sending of a Brigade led by

Brigadier Townshend to drive the Turks out of Basra. Townshend succeeded, but then moved inland towards Baghdad, where his force was surrounded in the old fort of Kut-el-Amara, surrendering after a five-month seige. While Townshend and his officers were interned or imprisoned, many of the men were brutally tortured and murdered:

> They shall not return to us, the resolute, the young,
>> The eager and whole-hearted whom we gave . . .

The phrase 'we gave' implies a deliberate sacrifice by 'their fathers' [the Establishment], who are further castigated:

> But the men who left them thriftily to die in their own dung,
>> Shall they come with years and honour to the grave? . . .
> Our dead shall not return to us while Day and Night divide –
>> Never while the bars of sunset hold.
> But the idle-minded overlings who quibbled while they died,
>> Shall they thrust for high employment as of old?

>> . . . .

> Shall we only threaten and be angry for an hour?
>> When the storm is ended shall we find
> How softly but how swiftly they have sidled back to power
>> By the favour and contrivance of their kind?

The storm was indeed soon to end.

On 11 November 1918 Carrie wrote, 'A quiet beautiful day; all waiting for news'. The longed-for news – of the Armistice – did not in fact reach Burwash until the next day, when the ringing of the local church bells celebrated the end of four years of hell. 'A world to be remade without a son,' said Carrie.

Chapter 10

THE TWILIGHT YEARS:

*Life Without Children. Rudyard's Death. The Surrogate
Son's Attack. Carrie's Death.*

'Then how shall I live with myself through the years . . . ?'
Rudyard Kipling, *The Question*, 1916

The war was over, but what was peace going to bring? Rider Haggard
went to visit the Kiplings on 15 November to mull over the good news
and found them both looking much better. Then a great feeling of uncertainty fell upon the trio of friends: Haggard, Kipling and Roosevelt. The
latter wrote to Haggard, 'Like you, I am not at all sure about the future.'
In the first week of the new year he died, never having got over the shock
of the death of his son Quentin.

As well as his general unease with the current political scene, Kipling's
prejudices seemed to increase rather than decrease in the aftermath of the
War. America was a perpetual target for his scorn and hatred. First there
had been her refusal to come into the war on the allied side, and when she
did he was angry with her that it was so late. He was scathing about
Woodrow Wilson: 'I am sorry that there is a schoolmaster, instead of a
man at the head of the U.S. today,' he had written to Roosevelt. Rupert
Grayson, still a frequent visitor to Bateman's, was staying there when
Kipling was writing *The Vineyard* (which accompanied the story *Sea
Constables*), 'the poem that gave so much offence to the Americans'.

> At the eleventh hour he came
> But his wages were the same
> As ours who all day long had trod
> The wine-press of the wrath of God.

Grayson compared Kipling's attitude to the Americans with William
Randolph Hearst's to the English: 'He was charming to me and his many
other English friends, but he thoroughly disliked us as a nation.'

Kipling felt no pity for the defeated enemy either, and one of his most
terrifyingly vicious poems, *A Death-Bed*, was written this year. It was in
response to a rumour (which was untrue) that the Kaiser was dying of

cancer of the throat. The poem intersperses the doctor's comments – that he had observed 'a gland at the back of the jaw And an answering lump by the collar-bone', that the cancer was 'rather too late for the knife, All we can do is to mask the pain', that if necessary a 'triple dose' of painkiller should be administered and that the patient should die 'while the effects of the drug endure' – with the dying Kaiser's own mad ramblings about the way in which victims of the war died:

> Some die shouting in gas or fire;
> Some die silent by shell and shot.
> Some die desperate, caught on the wire;
> Some die suddenly. This will not.

Angus Wilson found the poem 'more revolting to me than anything Kipling ever wrote'. But then Wilson's son had not been killed in a war in which the Kaiser had led the enemy.

In March another bitter blow hit Carrie. Her mother, to whom she remained emotionally close despite their physical distance from each other, to whom she had poured out all her fears and grief about John, died. Later Carrie was to write to her Aunt Kitty, 'She and I wrote twice a week for all the 27 years of our separation and I think were more closer and more intimate than most mothers and daughters who live in the same town or village.' On the very day she died, and unaware of the tragic event, Carrie wrote her last letter to her mother. She told her that she and Rud had had to refuse an invitation to Princess Pat's (Patricia, daughter of the Duke of Connaught) wedding, but that they had been to see the Guards Division, '8 thousand strong who are marching past the King and through the city and so back 8 miles in all'. They thought it a wonderful show; 'The Irish Guards quite splendid. It is the last tribute. How proud John would have been to have marched with his Regiment.'

At the end of his History of the 2nd Battalion Rudyard movingly describes this same event. 'In the Spring of '19 came the release, and the return of the Guards to England, and, on a grey March day, the Division, for the last time, was massed and moved through London, their wounded accompanying them on foot, or in the crowded lorries, while their mascots [Irish wolf-hounds] walked statelily in the intervals . . . The stream of troops seemed scanty between the multitudes that banked it. Their faces, too, told nothing, and least of all the faces of the veterans – the Sergeants of twenty-three, and the Commanding Officers of twenty-eight, who, by miracle or the mercy of severe wounds, had come through it all since that first hot August evening, at the milestone near Harmignies [the 1st Battalion at Mons], when the first bullet fell on the turf, and men said, "This is The War?"' [Kipling, like most Britishers, regarded the battle at Mons on 23 August 1914 as the first of the war. It was – but only for the

British. The French and Belgians had already sustained thousands of casualties.] The 2nd Battalion was now due to be disbanded; for them nothing but the memory of the war would remain, 'And, as they moved – little more than a Company strong – in the wake of their seniors, one saw, here and there among the wounded in civil kit, young men with eyes which did not match their age, shaken beyond speech or tears by the splendour and the grief of that memory.' How piercingly Kipling must have examined these battle-worn faces and longed to have seen the missing face that meant so much to him.

Finally, on 30 April, Rudyard admitted he would never see that face again. He instructed his solicitors, Herbert Smith, Goss, King & Gregory, to write to the War Office about John saying that 'the search in Germany for missing men has not revealed any trace of him' and that they should 'issue a certificate evidencing this'. John had left no will and his bankers, Messrs Cox & Co, released to Rudyard, Caroline and Elsie [their ages were wrongly later filled in in pencil as Rudyard being 53, Carrie 50 and Elsie 23], as his next of kin, the pitiful sum of £64 0s 4d – his accumulated pay. He had been paid whilst in France at the rate of 8s/6d per day, with 'Guards Pay' of £70 pa. Sergeant J.A. Corcoran of the War Office replied to Herbert Smith on 10 June that, in view of 'the length of time that elapsed since the Officer was officially reported missing' and 'the fact that his name has not appeared in any list of prisoners of war received from the German Government, the Army council are regretfully constrained to conclude, for official purposes, that Lieutenant Kipling is dead, and that his death occurred on, or since, the 27th day of September, 1915' [P.R.O. papers].

It was a chillingly final act in John's short life. The War Office wrote on John's Record of Service: 'Death accepted for official purposes, 27 Sept 1915'. There is pitifully little information on the sheet: 'Date of Birth: 17.8.1897. Height: 5ft 6½ins. Single. Name and Address of nearest relative (stating relationship): Rudyard Kipling, Batemans Burwash Sussex (Father). Periods of Employment: At Home: From 15.8.14 To 15.8.15. Abroad (Specifying Stations) 2nd Bn France From 16.8.'15. Missing 2-10-15. Lieut 7.6.'15 (Gaz. 11.11.'15).' So there it was, in black and white. John was officially dead. When the news was made public, a letter came from Buckingham Palace, dated 4 July 1919. 'Dear Mr Kipling,' it read, 'The King and Queen have during the War invariably sent messages of sympathy to the nearest relative of those who have lost their lives in the service of their Country. In case of doubt, however, Their Majesties have refrained from sending any message, always hoping that the report might not be true.' Now that they had heard the news, they sent the expression of their sympathy and wished to assure Rudyard 'that during the long months of uncertainty Their Majesties' thoughts have been constantly with you and those who have been called upon to endure this exceptional burden of anxiety.'

Oliver, the substitute son, continued to be a comfort. He came to stay at Bateman's on 10 August and when he left, three days later, Carrie moaned, 'We all love to have him and deplore his leaving. A hint of a son about the house always crosses with his visits.'

Then, in September, the battlefield clearance team of the Imperial War Graves Commission began working on the Loos battlefield. Knowing Kipling's personal interest in that area, and the recent news of the confirmation of John's death, it is highly probable that Fabian Ware would have informed him. When the team exhumed a body that they identified as a Lieutenant of the Irish Guards, surely Kipling would have been invited to view the remains? Apparently [according to Norm Christie] other bereaved fathers did so. No record has been found showing that Kipling travelled to Loos to identify a body. One can only assume that if he was given the opportunity he asked specific questions about the remains, the answers to which convinced him that this was not the body of his son.

Kipling was reminded about the area of Loos when, on 18 October, Gilbert Frankau, recalling his wartime meeting with Rudyard in Rome, sent a story which he felt he should have been recounted at that time. 'When my Brigade – the 107th, RA – was billeted in the little village of ACQUIN, some miles behind St Omer for rest (X'mas 1915/16) our "hostess" – a very ordinary French peasant woman [Frankau was a fearful snob] – hearing that one of our officers was *homme de lettres* [he was also vain], came to me & asked if I knew "M. Kipling". I said I did not, & inquired why she asked. She said: "Because once his son lived in this house & he was such a *gentil garçon*. Therefore, I thought that if I could find one who knew his father, I could let him know that we remembered him." If I have unduly trespassed in writing you after so many months of doubting please forgive me. But somehow I felt that both you and Mrs Kipling will be glad to know that in a village of France "it is well with the child".' [A quotation from *A Nativity*]. Carrie, certainly, would have been pleased that someone had maternal feelings for her boy in the days before his death.

In December 1919 Ollie was in Germany with the Army of Occupation and his ever-inquisitive Uncle wrote to him, 'What I want to know is, how the Hun behaves and how you all behave to the Hun . . . As far as one can make out from the papers the Hun is grossly ignorant of the fact that he has not come out of the war with flying colours and, up to date, very little seems to have been done for his education in that respect.' He had no place for the Christian concept of forgiveness of one's enemy.

1919 drew to an end: mercifully it had been a busy year. Julia Depew was now married to the French General Taufflieb and during the year her new husband had taken Rudyard, Carrie and Elsie on a tour of the Verdun battlefield. After the tour Rudyard said, 'For the first time in my life I have come to the place where I feel that if anyone gave me another idea my head would not stand it – it would burst.' Taufflieb had lived through some tumultuous events during the war, notably the army riots in Soissons in May 1917, when he had been fired upon by his own men, and which spilled into nearby Villers Cotterets. As commander of XXXVIIth Army Corps he was commended by Pétain for his firm suppression of this and subsequent mutinies (he ordered four company commanders to select five men each for punishment – i.e. probable execution – and then said, 'And now, tonight, you *will* move up to the trenches.') Rudyard quickly perceived the General to be a kindred spirit. A son of Alsace, he had dedicated his life to the restoration of what he considered to be France's lost provinces and was an implacable Germanophobe. The following year he was appointed Governor of Alsace and from then on, each year until his death, Rudyard, with Carrie, either visited the Tauffliebs in Strasbourg, shared joint holidays with them in Cannes or received them as guests at Bateman's.

The year had included the publication of a collection of poems, *The Years Between*, and Kipling was working on more short stories. There had been some light entertainment, such as a visit to a lecture by the wartime cartoonist, Bruce Bairnsfather, touring the country with a 'chalk and talk' show on his popular creation, 'Old Bill'. In June, mainly to give Elsie some diversion, they had attended the wedding of the year when Diana Manners had married her one surviving suitor, Duff Cooper.

Kipling and Haggard started the year of 1920 with a new fear – Bolshevism. They joined the Liberty League, an anti-Bolshevik movement promoted by Northcliffe, in the spring. It was ill-conceived, ill-run and short-lived and is mostly remembered for the lampoon,

> Every Bolsh is a blackguard
> Said Kipling to Haggard.
> That's just what I say
> Said the author of "They".
> I agree, I agree
> Said the author of "She".

In February 1920 Rudyard did an extraordinary thing. He took Carrie to show her the 'House of Desolation'. She described the event in her diary on the 25th, 'Rud takes me to see Lorne Lodge . . . where he was so misused and forlorn and desperately unhappy as a child – and talked of it all with horror.' Memories of John's happy childhood were still strong and he may have felt the need to contrast them with his own sad ones. It is a measure of his closeness to Carrie that he should feel the need to unburden himself to her in this way. John was at the forefront of their thoughts at this time (was he ever far away?) as they had recently commissioned a bronze memorial to him. They chose Charles Wheeler (later Sir Charles, who went on to become a President of the Royal Academy of Arts), then a struggling young sculptor, to execute it. Wheeler, in his autobiography *High Relief*, described how, when opening the door to his Justice Walk studio to an unexpected knock, he 'saw a short man standing in morning dress and wearing a silk hat. My first thought was – here is someone selling encyclopaedias, and then he handed me his card. On looking at it I was so astounded that I handed it back to him. It read "Rudyard Kipling".' Wheeler ever after regretted his stupidity in handing back this highly prized visiting card. It was his colleague Sir Herbert Baker (who had visited Bateman's the previous August to discuss the memorial with them) who had sent the Kiplings to Wheeler. The latter had designed some details for Baker on the Harrow School War Memorial which had obviously pleased him. Kipling explained that he wanted a bronze plaque to John to hang in Burwash Church. The inscription was to read, '*To the memory of John Kipling Lieutenant Second Battalion Irish Guards the only son of Rudyard and Caroline Kipling of Bateman's who fell at the battle of Loos the 27th September 1915 aged eighteen years and six weeks: Qui ante diem periit*' (who perished before his day). He came with Carrie (Wheeler wrongly calls her 'Clemmie') to monitor the progress and 'When any point of detail arose he always demurred to her opinion. The Kiplings were well pleased with the clay design. The only criticism was, I recall, his questioning a slackness in the ribbon binding the wreath of laurel. "John would not have liked a loose strap," he said; and so I tightened it up.' There were more problems with the casting. Wheeler used 'A very skilled, but in some ways not altogether reliable, founder (recommended by my professor) [who] delayed and delayed until, the time being short, he was obliged to carry out hurriedly his contract to supply the bronze casting by the agreed date. The hurry was considerable and the casting consequently disastrous. Since I was committed to show the memorial tablet to my client, a large hole, which had appeared in the plaque, had to be patched, again hurriedly of course and again of course badly. Kipling spotted it at once, turned and enquired who was my bronze founder. "An Italian named —," I replied "I don't know his lingo," Rudyard said, 'but tell him from me it's bloody".' With unusual restraint Carrie noted in her diary on 18 April, 'John's memorial is a great failure – to be done again.' The poor young sculptor was mortified and immediately ordered a new cast. This was obviously to the Kiplings' liking as they then asked Wheeler to make a bust of John from photographs. When Wheeler wrote asking them to come and see the result, he received no reply, nor to a second letter sent some weeks later. 'In a third letter, guessing the reason, I suggested that perhaps they found it hard to face up to the sculptured image and if that were so I would destroy the work and call the whole thing off. This proved to be the case. Poor Kipling was utterly undone by his son's loss and never got over it.'

Despite the hiccups with John's memorial, Wheeler went on to become one of the Imperial War Graves Commission's most important sculptors and often met Rudyard again in his capacity of Commissioner. The last meeting was at the unveiling of the Indian Memorial at Neuve Chapelle in 1927 – he carved the two splendid tigers which guard the base of the tall column. Everyone present was 'eager to see the poet and became entranced – we all did – by the words of Rudyard who, though not on the Speech List, was called to his feet and spoke without notes briefly and movingly about the bravery of Indian soldiers fighting on European soil. His earnest words silenced the restless feet and impatient murmurings so that you could hear the proverbial pin drop till he sat down to tumultuous applause.' Neuve Chapelle is barely 10 miles from where John was last seen and there was a long-believed story that Kipling had asked for John's name to be included on the memorial of the Indian troops with whom he so warmly identified. This is even confidently stated in the May 1982 issue of the *Piffer*, the journal of the Punjab Frontier Force Association. A recent search by the Commonwealth War Graves Commission at Maidenhead in the Neuve Chapelle Memorial register confirms that John Kipling's name is *not* on the Indian Memorial.

Wheeler's most poignant memory of Kipling concerned his own son. 'A portrait bust of my son, Robin, aged nine months, seemed to give him particular pleasure and he looked closely one day to see if I had put in the crease at the back of the neck which he said was such a lovely thing in a child's head.' Kipling continued to take a strong interest in Robin's progress.

On 24 March Rudyard and Carrie set off on the continental motor tour that was to become again an annual feature. This first post-war tour must have brought back many memories. On their last tour before the war, in March 1914, John had been with them and it had been a light-hearted trip. John, overwhelmed by his parents' many visits to cathedrals, had opted out of Chartres, but his interest would have been re-awoken when the party did the last 37½ miles to Amiens in 62 minutes, a fact delight-edly recorded by Rudyard. Even now, in 1920, Rudyard still found release and entertainment in travelling and recorded, 'At Bordeaux C [Carrie] and E [Elsie] saw woman at street door in chemise and hat only. Was arrested by police and put into a cab. I alas! missed it.' The tour had started with cemetery visits in St Omer and Rouen with Colonel Goodland, Deputy Controller, France and Flanders of the Imperial War Graves Commission.

July saw Rudyard presented with an honorary degree at Edinburgh University. He described the event to his revered old friend, Colonel Feilden, 'I strictly remembered your injunction about my speech, eschewed prolixity and the Scotch accent and got a good reception.' He was secretly amused when the Moderator ('*such* a Scot') showed pride in 'having annexed an Englishman', only to discover that Kipling's mother was a Macdonald.

As their son's birthday approached, Carrie went through his possessions and gave many of his books to the village school library. The village War Memorial was completed, and although Rudyard had sat on the committee he refused, 'though pressed', to unveil it. Perhaps this was because John's name, which was, of course, among those inscribed upon it, was followed by an incorrect date for his death – 29th instead of 27th September. On 24 August Lord Home performed the ceremony and was then invited to Bateman's for tea.

An attack on Kipling appeared in an article in the *Morning Post* of 28 August by the young President of the Oxford Union Society, a certain Beverley Nichols [who later went on to gain some fame as a columnist and broadcaster]. He sneered at the 'elderly poets' who wrote sonnets about 'the happy warrior' and maintained that, 'They have had their day, and a long day and a bloody day it has been. If you wish to see what young men think of war today . . . you will not find it in the flamboyant insolence of Rudyard Kipling, you will not even find it in the poems of Rupert Brooke. You will find it in the verse of Siegfried Sassoon.' Haggard commented on this in his diary, 'I am not fortunate enough to be acquainted with the works of Siegfried Sassoon, who, from his name, I presume is a Jew of the advanced school.' A footnote then adds, 'Since I wrote this I have read these verses. They are feeble and depressing rubbish.' It is as well that Haggard did not have to earn his living by writing literary criticism. Kipling would have been little touched by Nichols' youthful outburst and in *Palm* to *Pine* Marghanita Laski listed the great war poets – including Sassoon – and concluded that 'Rudyard Kipling, nearly fifty when the war began, was too old to fight, and he is not usually thought of as one of the war poets of the Great War. But he was a war poet and at times a painfully fine one.'

As each Christmas loomed, the pain got slightly duller and Carrie recorded that Christmas Day of 1920 had 'been kept in the old style at Bateman's [with] much pleasure and no joy'. That the beloved aunt, Georgina Burne-Jones, had died that year would have added to the joylessness.

The next few years were very much taken up with Rudyard's War Graves work. He and Carrie had started to travel frequently again, often adding holidays on to the cemetery tours, especially in France where Rudyard felt so at home. 'Rud had always loved France since his father took him as a small boy to the Exposition of 1879,' wrote Julia Taufflieb [*Kipling Journal*]. 'He spoke French fairly well; fluently but not always correctly. He was more beloved by the French people than any English writer. I know of one French general who carried some of Rud's books with him all through the four years of war. One day Rud showed me a paper-covered copy of *The Light That Failed* translated into French. It had a bullet hole right through. A young French soldier had sent it to Rud with the words, "You have saved my life, so I think this book belong to you".'

In November 1921 he was honoured and feted with honorary degrees in France, both at the University of Strasbourg (when the President and Mme Poincaré were present) and at the Sorbonne, much to Julia Taufflieb's pride and delight. The theme of his acceptance speeches was Anglo-French co-operation. The trip ended with a holiday in Cannes, where Bonar Law was convalescing and the two enjoyed several discussions. On the return to Bateman's nephew Oliver again came to stay and, as there was still a deficit on the Burwash Village War Memorial, Rudyard paid the necessary £10. Politics were still engaging his mind. Kipling was dubbed a 'die-hard' because of his attitude to the new Irish Treaty, and to the terms for German reparation, and Carrie noted in her diary, 'Rud more depressed over the terms of South Ireland than he ever was during the War'. He even went to see Admiral 'Blinker' Hall, the Director of Naval Intelligence, to discuss his fears about the fate of the Loyalists and he and Lady Hall became frequent visitors to Bateman's.

In March 1922, the *Irish Guards History* finally completed, the family visited Spain, though Carrie grumbled to her diary, 'I am worn out and can't do these continual journeys doing the work, their arranging, plus the usual work but can't get Rud to realize it.' Then came the memorable King's Pilgrimage in May, described above. On 19 July Carrie accompanied Rudyard to see the Unknown Soldier's Tomb at Westminster Abbey and then the two of them went to 'hunt for Phil Burne-Jones's portrait of Rud in the National Portrait Gallery'. They were unable to find it! After this series of travels Rudyard's mysterious intestinal problem became acute. A period of hospitalization, consultations with Bland-Sutton and even X-rays all failed to diagnose the cause. The only consolation was that it was deemed that Kipling did not have the cancer he had always feared.

In October Bonar Law became Prime Minister and Stanley Baldwin his Chancellor of the Exchequer. Rudyard went to London and was visited by his cousin Stan en route to Buckingham Palace to receive his seal of office. Then he suffered a relapse and on 15 November was operated upon by Bland-Sutton. Rudyard was extremely ill; even the King and Queen sent a message of sympathy.

He obviously still secretly feared he had cancer and this fear was expressed in several stories of this period. One of them, *The Wish House*, is widely regarded as one of his most accomplished stories. It belies the frequent claim that he was unable to portray women convincingly. The whole story unfolds during a perfectly naturally written conversation between two old working-class women. One of them, Grace Ashcroft, has, by the supernatural intervention of a friend's young daughter, been able to visit the Wish House of the title where she succeeded in taking on the illness that is killing her erstwhile lover, 'Arry Mockler. It manifests itself in her body as a cancerous ulcer and during her visit to her old friend, Liz Fettley, she confesses not only her relationship with 'Arry but the fact that the wound had 'turned'. Mrs Fettley understood. 'Human nature seldom walks up to the word "cancer".' It is a story of selfless love and is a tribute to the gratitude Rudyard felt towards Carrie for her devotion to him which, he was convinced, pulled him through his illness. The poem which accompanies the story, *Late Came the God*, almost sacriligiously ends,

What is God beside Woman? Dust and derision!

A Madonna of the Trenches is generally interpreted as a ghost story in which one of the characters, Auntie Armine, dies of 'a bit of a gatherin' in 'er breast' – a euphemism for cancer. There is another reading, however, of this powerful story which transports the reader straight into the unspeakable filth and degradation of Western Front life, where the walls of the trenches are built up with corpses, which also lie several deep under the wooden duckboards and creak terrifyingly when frozen. The main character, Strangwick, is mentally unbalanced by his experiences, but gradually one of Kipling's deliberately onion-skinned layered stories reveals that his state is not caused, as he maintains, by his job as a Runner through these horrifying trenches, but by an event that he is trying to hide. Strangwick served in the platoon of a sergeant who back at home had been such a friend of his family that Strangwick called him 'Uncle John'. On Strangwick's last leave, his Aunt had given him a note for Uncle John to say 'that I expect to be through with my little trouble by the twenty-first of next month, an' I'm dyin' to see him as soon as possible after that date'. After receiving the message, John, who was due to go on leave on that very date, shaved, cleaned himself up and proceeded with two braziers full of charcoal to a deserted dugout. There Strangwick claimed to see a frighteningly lifelike vision of his Aunt Armine and he was devastated to observe that, although she was 'nearer fifty than forty', there is obviously a strong, passionate, carnal relationship between her and the Sergeant. According to Strangwick's later account, the lovers – the very real Sergeant and his ghostly Aunt – retreat into the dugout and the Sergeant wedges it shut behind them. The next day Strangwick receives a telegram to say that his Aunt is dead and the Sergeant is found frozen to death in the dugout. It is the knowledge of this suicide pact in the next world ('I'm dying to see him') that caused Strangwick's breakdown. Or so he says.

But there are two major clues that point to a quite different interpretation. Firstly the title of the story is *A Madonna*, i.e. Mother of *The*

Trenches. The conventional explanation of the story ignores this fact. Secondly, at the very end, when Strangwick's sponsor for Lodge membership is revealed as Auntie Armine's widower, Brother Keede, a local doctor and a former officer in Strangwick's battalion, exclaims, 'That's all I wanted,' a curious reaction usually unexplained. If one re-reads the story as being that of a woman made pregnant by Uncle John and planning to have an abortion on a precise date, her message to him that 'I expect to be through with my little trouble by the twenty-first of next month' has that clear meaning. The title now makes sense too. Further proof of the 'abortion theory' is that when Uncle John gets the news about the 'twenty-first' he starts to hum a hymn and smartens himself up, the actions of a man suddenly relieved of a burden – the pregnancy. He can now go on leave to meet his lover with a light heart. The tale can also be read as a murder story. Strangwick was extremely fond of his Aunt and respected Uncle John. He was horrified at learning of their illicit liaison – which he must have done while on leave, not during the 'ghostly' meeting as he pretends. That episode is simply a fictional cover up and what ails him is not only what he did, but also that he might be found out. He keeps harping on at the inappropriateness of the affair at Auntie Armine's age – 'An' she nearer fifty than forty' – even more surprising if she was pregnant. Keede's attitude towards Strangwick suggests that he does not believe the man's story. Strangwick actually says, 'You don't think I did him in, do you?' The suicide theory is based on the evidence that the door of the dugout in which John suffocated was closed from the inside. But that, and other evidence that would corroborate a suicide, was not first hand. It was provided by Strangwick. An extension of the murder theory is that Auntie Armine's husband knew about the affair and he and Strangwick planned the murder together. After the dreadful deed Strangwick began to have fits and Mr Armine felt duty bound to look after him, if only for his own protection. Dr Keede clearly has his own suspicions that Uncle John's death was murder and when he learns that Strangwick's protector is Mr Armine, that for him is proof and he makes his 'That's all that's wanted' remark as the jigsaw falls into place for him. Another skin of the onion is unpeeled. But the reader can read it at whichever layer he or she chooses.

In the story Kipling also returns to one of his favourite themes – Freemasonry – as the story is set in a Lodge. Kipling had been initiated into the Hope and Perseverance Lodge in Lahore at the age of 20, dispensation having been granted for the admission of a minor because the Lodge badly needed a secretary. It was a racially mixed Lodge and Kipling saw his membership as a passport – 'So yet another world opened to me which I needed'. His advancement to 'the degree of Royal Ark Mariner' came in on 13 April 1887. He then joined the Independence with Philanthropy Lodge in Allahabad. Much taken with the new fraternity he had joined – Hilton Brown is assured that 'he could not *not* have been a

Mason' – Kipling wrote *The Mother-Lodge* (from *The Seven Seas*, 1896), which illustrated its class and rank-free nature:

> Outside – "Sergeant! Sir! Salute! Salaam!"
> Inside – "Brother", an' it doesn't do no 'arm.
> We met upon the Level an' we parted on the Square
> An' I was Junior Deacon in my Mother-Lodge out there!

After his return to London in 1889, Kipling joined the Authors' Lodge but there is little evidence of regular, active involvement with Freemasonry once he had left India. There were, however, many other references to masonry in his works, the *envoi* to his collection of stories *Life's Handicap* (1891), *My New-Cut Ashlar*, is a favourite with Freemasons, as it ends with the words

> Help me to need no aid from men
> That I may help such men as need!

which epitomize the masonic philosophy. It refers to the Masons' symbolic hewn stone, or 'ashlar'. The sharp-eyed will also notice that the illuminated initial letter 'T' drawn by Kipling for *The Butterfly that Stamped* shows King Solomon reclining on his throne, wearing a Master's apron, a collar with significant letters upon it and a bracelet with a square and compasses pendant. There are also references to Freemasonry in the poems *The Press, The Song of the Dead* and *The Merchantmen*. Although it does not contain any overt references to Freemasonry, *Recessional* is thought to exemplify masonic principles and is often sung at lodges. Even *The Widow at Windsor* compares Victoria's Empire to a Masonic Lodge;

> Then 'ere's to the Lodge o' the Widow,
> From the Pole to the Tropics it runs –
> To the Lodge that we tile with the rank an' the file
> An' open in form with the guns.

This was the element in the poem considered (wrongly) by many as being in such poor taste that it lost him his chance to become poet laureate.

After the war Kipling was convinced that the comradeship and mutual support offered by Freemasonry would be the ideal environment to heal men broken physically and mentally by the war and deprived of the one element that had meant so much to them during that horrific time – the bonding with other men who had shared their experiences. He had no interest in the British Legion. It was a club for old soldiers whose figure-head was Haig, whom he despised, and he was not himself a soldier: he was, however, a Mason. For the ex-Service Imperial War Graves Commission workers in France and Belgium he helped to found a Lodge in Lille called 'The Builders of the Silent Cities' and in 1927 he was a founder of a Lodge of the same name in London for Commission workers who had completed their work on the cemeteries. Haig was atoning for the thousands of men who died under his command in the war, Kipling for the one who meant everything to him.

Another post-war story with masonic connections is *In the Interests of the Brethren* into which Kipling weaves the rules of the code that steadied him after the deaths of Josephine and John. At the beginning of the story the narrator recognizes his tobacconist as a fellow Mason when 'We shook hands'. The tobacconist, Mr Burges, is much patronized by ex-soldiers whom he encourages to come to his Lodge of Instruction (described by Kipling as 'mainly a parade-ground for Ritual. It cannot initiate or confer degrees'), the Faith and Works Lodge, which welcomed any visiting veterans in town, many of whom are shell-shocked or physically wounded. It is magnificently decorated with prized masonic art. (Burges is actually a wealthy merchant, as are other members of the Lodge.) It is, in fact, the same Lodge in which *A Madonna of the Trenches* is set and the character of Keede first appears here; many of the members are recruited from the hospital in which he works. The story places great emphasis on the comforting importance and beauty of Ritual and the need to conform to it, yet the Lodge infringes masonic regulations by admitting all and sundry and by being open for down-and-out ex-servicemen at many unauthorized hours. A Clergyman Brother disapproves and it is feared that 'he'll inform on us one of these days'. The story ends with the narrator 'speculating how soon I could steal a march on the Clergyman and inform against "Faith and Works No. 5837 E.C".' [Incidentally the name was used for a real Lodge founded in Wolverhampton in 1928.] It is a complete volte face. As the story unfolds the reader is encouraged to be favourably inclined towards the 'misconduct' of the Lodge because it is doing good work. However, the narrator (Kipling) is going to 'inform' on the offending Brothers. His message is that ritual and routine in themselves are comforting, but only if they are adhered to. Keeping up appearances and conforming to what is required by a society (in this case a masonic one) is what he and Carrie also had to do after John's death in the more general society of their milieu and the story is justifying that requirement. Kipling is also saying that rules are made to be obeyed, whatever the consequence, just as John had done in following military discipline though it lost him his life. After their meetings the Brethren enjoy a simple banquet, for which visitors are not allowed to pay. This aspect of the proceedings is picked up in the poem which accompanies the story, *Banquet Night*.

A Friend of the Family is a third story set in the Faith and Works Lodge. It too spells out in detail that some found nauseating stories of the Brethrens' wartime experiences – a feature of several of the realistic stories in *Debits and Credits* which led to a certain amount of adverse criticism. Kipling may not have served in the war, but he spent many hours during his search for John and in his research for the *History of the Irish Guards* talking to wounded men. His stories of fearful war experiences ring true and are in no way exaggerated, but, again, there was resentment – by those who were there of one who was not – writing about *their* war.

These war stories, written in the wake of John's death, were carthartic but painful to compose. And they were written during a period when he was seriously ill and in great pain. As always, Carrie pulled him through and a cheerful event occurred at the end of 1922 to aid the convalescence. She and Rudyard remained close to the Bonar Law family. Kipling had always thought that their daughter Isabel reminded him of his precious Josephine and he and Bonar Law had grown closer over their mutual loss of sons after Charlie and Jim Law had also been killed in the war. Isabel Law had married Major-General Sir Frederick Sykes (one of the founders of the RAF) and on 22 December Rudyard had the pleasure of congratulating them 'on the birth of a manchild'. He would 'joyfully accept appointment as godfather and could hardly wait for him to be old enough to be able to kick about on the slope of Keylands grass and to learn his swimming in Bateman's pond [Bonar Sykes, *Kipling Journal* March 1996].

However, on 20 March the next year (1923) Rider Haggard visited him and found him still 'looking drawn and considerably aged . . . It struck me that we were a pretty pair of old crocks [Haggard had gout]. As to the future of our country he was despondent.' He feared a Labour Government which he was convinced would 'produce a terrible financial crash, and he asked whether all those that we lost in the war, his boy John and the rest, died to bring about such a state of affairs as we see today.'

By April he was fit enough to go to Cannes to convalesce. The route home was strenuous – Grenoble, Aix, Annecy, Lausanne, Evian, Bourges, Dijon and Troyes. Rudyard constantly sought 'substitute Johns. In Lausanne he met 'a young Cavendish Bentinck of the FO with unlimited possibilities of impudence' who had been at school with John. By 21 May they were once again at Villers Cotterets where they were to investigate the possibility of erecting a memorial stone to the 1st Irish Guards. Naturally they went to the cemetery to pay their respects to George Cecil. Rudyard wrote, 'I seem to have seen it all my life. It was as usual – tore the heart out.' The Cecils had a grave to weep over; the Kiplings had not. Rudyard balanced his sadness by his delight in his motoring, exhilarating, like Toad, in speeding. The Duchess, despite 'lying down' from time to time, 'broke all our modest records . . . first 16m in 25 min.' A 'light-blue two seater with lots of luggage behind' had the temerity to overtake them at 46 mph and, with a surge of early road rage, Kipling urged his chauffeur to give chase. 'We got up to fifty but even then we could not see him,' he commented dejectedly. The long tour finally returned to Bateman's by way of Compiègne, Dieppe and finally Newhaven.

Relations with Oliver were still good and on John's birthday (17 August) Carrie wrote, 'It is a help to me to have only Oliver in the house.' It was probably his last visit. The storm that caused a bitter rift was about to break.

On Armistice Day, 11 November 1923, Rudyard wrote a poem called *London Stone* which describes laying wreaths at the Cenotaph and observing the Two Minutes' Silence. During those quiet minutes it is permitted to let the feeling of grief and even bitterness flood in:

> For those minutes, tell no lie;
> (Grieving – grieving!)
> "Grave, this is thy victory;
> And the sting of death is grieving."

Even Rudyard, who normally never let his mask of acceptance slip, allows himself, in the company of others who shared his pain, to show his grief:

> *"As I suffer; so do you."*

That may ease the grieving.

But the wound was gradually healing and Carrie confessed at the end of the year that it had been the 'best Christmas since 1914'.

1924 was to bring some cruel losses to the Kiplings. In the spring the family visited Madrid where George Bambridge, who had been of such help in the writing of the *Irish Guards History*, was Honorary Attaché at the Embassy. During the visit Elsie and George became engaged. She recognized that, 'Though my father was delighted by my obvious happiness and was fond of George, something like despair filled him as he looked forward to life at Bateman's without his only remaining child. The years since John's death had brought us very close together and he had come to depend on my constant companionship.' Obviously not suspecting that George's close friendship with her cousin Oliver was anything more than the natural comradeship of fellow officers of the same regiment, Elsie wrote, 'Oliver my dear, I do hope you'll be pleased with my news; George and I are engaged and most gloriously happy! but also *most* sensible and nice!' With innocent irony she continued, 'I can only wish that some day you will find as completely the right person as I have.' In fact Oliver had already found his lifetime companion, John Parke Boyle, known as 'Johnnie', and had set up home with him in the summer of 1923 at Watlington Farm, Shirburn. Did Rudyard, ever-alert against 'beastliness,' sense his nephew's homosexual nature and suspect that his future son-in-law might share it? Seymour-Smith, with no declared source, maintained that Rudyard 'suddenly developed a mad jealousy of Bambridge – but the details of all this have been suppressed'. Carrie was thrown into despair at the idea. She depended on Elsie for much more than daughterly affection and companionship – the girl had gradually taken more and more administrative functions from her shoulders. Nevertheless she threw herself into a flurry of trousseau and furnishing buying. It was to be a big wedding. On 2 August Elsie wrote to 'My dear old Olly' that she hoped it would take place 'in the middle of October', and that she wanted Oliver to come and have a meal with her and George as 'Somehow I feel you would bring John's special blessing with you.'

Before embarking on the final arrangements the Kiplings set off on their annual tour, visiting cemetery after cemetery, with Rudyard writing careful notes at each stop. On 31 August they visited St Mary's ADS Cemetery where, sixty-eight years later, the Commonwealth War Graves Commission would change the inscription on a grave marked 'A Lieutenant of the Irish Guards' to that of 'Lieutenant John Kipling'. Given the Kiplings' connection with the regiment, there cannot be any doubt that they would have visited this grave, probably guided to it by the gardener, as Helen Turrell was guided to her son's grave in the story that Rudyard wrote a few months later, *The Gardener*. That there was no hint of a suspicion that he might have been standing at his son's grave is indicated by the emotionless comment that Rudyard made about the cemetery; 'Spoilt by Gardener's shed – but otherwise very good'. The tour also included visits to see the Cathedral tablets for which Rudyard wrote the inscription at Notre Dame in Paris and in Amiens.

On their return 700 invitations were sent out for the wedding. It was held at fashionable St Margaret's in Westminster on 22 October. There were nearly 1,000 people in the church, 500 at the reception, and 400 presents. After the ceremony Carrie wrote, 'We sadly return to face an empty side to our life and for the present are too weary to meet it.' The newly weds immediately left for Brussels, where George was now posted. And now Oliver was no consolation or comfort to them. Not only was he in an open relationship with another man but he had committed the further unthinkable and unpardonable sin of standing as *Labour* candidate for Dudley. He was also at times completely mentally unbalanced, perhaps because of his harrowing experiences in Armenia in the Armeno-Turkish War of 1920 and the Armeno-Russian War of 1921, when he was imprisoned and tortured by the Bolsheviks and the Turks and witnessed the Armenian Massacre. His mother Lucy wrote an extraordinarily frank letter to Oliver's lover, Johnnie Boyle, in which she said, 'It is only those who really love him who know how ill he really is, mentally and physically – & who understand the mental suffering that he endures sometimes since his dreadful experiences in the East . . . It is as though a devil sometimes got possession and . . .[he takes] a devilish delight in saying and doing things that hurt.' She ended by thanking Boyle 'for loving my Oliver'. His aunt and uncle were not so broad-minded, nor so forgiving. Oliver became *persona non grata* in the house where he had been treated for so many years as a son. 'That winter was a dreary one at Bateman's,' commented Elsie, 'the house seemed "very large and quiet", my father wrote me.' Of course there were floods of letters and even visits. 'His abiding interest was now to be everything that concerned my new life.' Birkenhead maintained that 'Caroline was never able to reconcile herself to it [the marriage] and could not refrain from making constant dangerous and uncalled-for interferences in her daughter's married life, which were strongly resented.' Bambridge is often described in Kipling biographies as 'wealthy', but in the Kipling Papers there are several references to Rudyard slipping the odd £300 or £400 to Elsie when she was hard up.

By the end of the year Rider Haggard had also been taken ill: first with 'a most fearful attack of indigestions' on 5 November and then in December with a bladder infection, which remained with him until February of the following year, 1925. Rudyard wrote him encouraging letters, to which Haggard replied with the gift of a ring with the seal of the Egyptian king, Akhenaton. Kipling replied, 'I value old Akhenaton's thumbpiece but more than that I value your exceedingly cock-eyed p.c. (No I won't sell it for an autograph!)' and kept up the encouraging flow of letters. February was a busy time for visitors at Bateman's. Gwynne of the *Morning Post* came to stay, as did Lorna Baldwin, now Lady Howard, 'practically my child since her babydom', as Rudyard told Rider Haggard, with her husband Sir Arthur Howard and their friends Donald and Diana Palmer. He also told Haggard that Elsie had 'been really enjoying life' and she sent Haggard her 'special love. D'you know that kid's very fond of you? Always was (and so was John)'. He advised his friend to 'be glad you're in bed – even if those damnable nights are long and even Ecclesiasticus who is my refuge, doesn't always help.' Haggard replied, 'What you say about Elsie touches me. Please tell the dear girl so when you write. Also about John.'

In March Rudyard persuaded Carrie to undertake another of the marathon journeys he loved. They sailed from Southampton on the RMSS *Normannia* and Rudyard was touched when 'stumbling up the gangplank in the half-light an aged care-taker hailed us, who had been a Steward on the old *Kinfauns Castle* when the children were little and remembered not only them, but the Stewards whom they affected and got things out of.' Their first stop was Rouen ('Rud to a cemetery,' grumbled Carrie), then to Chartres where he visited the cathedral. The vibrant stained glass windows inspired a sonnet which starts, 'Colour fulfils where Music has no power': and he started work on the story that was to be called *The Gardener*. On the 16th they were at Angers, on the 17th at La Rochelle, on the 18th Poitiers, the 19th Angoulême and on the 22nd arrived at Pau via Lourdes. Work on *The Gardener* continued as they moved on to San Sebastian where, on the 27th, Carrie reported that *The Gardener* was finished. It appears to have been the visit to the war graves cemetery at Rouen which triggered this tender story. He wrote to Haggard, 'Went off at once to Rouen Cemetery (11,000 graves) and collogued with the Head Gardener and contractors. One never gets over the shock of this Dead Sea of arrested lives – from V.C's and Hospital Nurses to coolies of the Chinese Labour Corps. By one grave of a coolie some pious old Frenchwoman (bet she was an old maid) had deposited a yellow porcelain crucifix!! Somehow that almost drew tears.' In fact St Sever cemetery at Rouen, created to bury the casualties from the great Base Hospitals and General HQ, contains 3,083 burials. An extension had to be started in September 1916 and it contains a further 8,356 burials, including forty-four members of the Chinese Labour Corps and one of the war's best-known VCs, the Rev Theodore Bayley Hardy, Chaplain to the Lincolnshire Regiment, an exceptionally courageous and well-loved man. No wonder Kipling was so overcome with emotion.

The setting for *The Gardener* is actually transposed to a Belgian cemetery with the fictional name of Hagenzeele. This could be a compilation of two cemetery names in the Ypres Salient, each having the word 'Dump' in their title – *Hagle* Dump and Oak Dump Cemetery, Voorme*zeele*. Or he may have been influenced by the fact that he was writing to *Hagg*ard at the time. This is a story which overbrims with personal references, although the heroine is female. Helen Turrell is the *alter ego* of Mary Postgate. In common is the fact that they are spinsters who had a deep maternal love for a young boy who is killed in the war. But where Mary is cruelly revengeful for the death of Wynn, Helen mourns Michael with quiet acceptance. The opening paragraph of the story tells the reader, in veiled talk, that Helen is the unmarried mother of Michael, whom she passes off as the orphaned child of her dead 'black sheep' of the family brother, George. She preserves the myth, only allowing herself the indulgence of letting the child call her 'Mummy' at bedtime. It was their secret pet-name and there is something of the young angry Ruddy in the description of Michael's outburst when he hears that Helen has betrayed that trust. Nevertheless a close and loving relationship, so like that of Rudyard's to his children – 'variegated and glorious as jewels on a string' – grew between them as the boy progressed through prep and public school. When war broke out Michael, like John before him, tried to enlist, but as Rudyard aided John into the new 2nd Battalion of the Irish Guards, so the captain of Michael's OTC 'headed him off and steered him directly to a commission in a battalion so new that half of it still wore the old Army red'.

Ironically Michael gets his wish to go to the front when his battalion is called 'to help make good the wastage of Loos' – the battle in which John was killed. After experiencing several weeks in the relatively quiet sectors of Armentières and Laventie, Michael was killed by a shell-splinter.

What happened subsequently is in all probability what Kipling believed had happened to John's body: 'The next shell uprooted and laid down over the body what had been the foundation of a barn wall so neatly that none but an expert would have guessed that anything unpleasant had happened.' Like the Kiplings, Helen received an official telegram informing her that Michael was missing. She too went into automatic mode, 'pulling down the house-blinds one after one with great care, and saying earnestly to each: "Missing *always* means dead". Then she took her place in the dreary procession that was impelled to go through an inevitable series of unprofitable emotions.' The next section is pure personal experience: 'The Rector, of course, preached hope and prophesied word, very soon, from a prison camp. Several friends, too, told her perfectly truthful tales, but always about other women, to whom, after months and months of silence, their missing had been miraculously restored. Other people urged her to communicate with infallible Secretaries of organizations who could communicate with benevolent neutrals, who could extract accurate information from the most secretive Hun prison commandants. Helen did and wrote and signed everything that was suggested or put before her.' Of course no trace of Michael can be found and Helen gets through the rest of the war in a state of numbness. After the Armistice she even gets involved in the village Memorial, just as Rudyard had done. Then came the extraordinary news – the news that Rudyard and Carrie longed in vain to hear – that Michael's body had been identified and re-interred in 'Hagenzeele Third Military Cemetery'. 'So Helen found herself moved on . . . to a world full of exultant or broken relatives, now strong in the certainty that there was an altar upon earth where they might lay their love.' How important it was for the bereaved to have that focal point, that 'altar'. The Kiplings were never to experience that comfort. Helen joins the hundreds of relatives who made their way to their loved ones' graves in France and Belgium and Kipling's description of her pilgrimage has the ring of realism – the 'razed city full of whirling lime-dust and blown papers' (obviously Ypres), the officer from the 'Central Authority' (the War Graves Commission) who helped her to locate her cemetery, the embarrassingly emotional mother who fell on her breast, the woman who professes to be making regular visits to cemeteries to take photographs for friends who then confesses to Helen that she is actually visiting someone very special to her – obviously a lover. Then Helen reaches the cemetery, one of the Silent Cities, as Kipling called them, still being landscaped and still with its temporary wooden crosses with tin inscriptions. A feeling of hopelessness overcomes her after her initial shock at the sheer numbers and the magnitude of her task in locating Michael's grave amongst the 21,000 buried there. [In fact the largest Commonwealth War Graves Commission cemetery, Tyne Cot in the Ypres Salient, has only just over 11,000.] Then she sees a man kneeling 'behind a line of headstones – evidently a gardener, for he was firming a young plant in the soft earth'. He asks her who she is looking for and Helen replies, 'Lieutenant Michael Turrell – my nephew . . . as she had many thousands of times in her life.' The man is not taken in by her habitual lie. 'Come with me', he said, 'and I will show you where your son lies.' The final words of the story, 'and she went away, supposing him to be the gardener', give rise to the usual interpretation that the man is actually Jesus, for they are almost identical to parts of St John, Chapter 20, which describes Mary Magdalene's visit to Jesus's empty sepulchre after his resurrection. Jesus then materializes, but she 'knew not that it was Jesus. Jesus saith unto her, Woman, why weepest thou? whom seekest thou? She, *supposing him to be the gardener* saith unto him, Sir, if thou have bore him hence, tell me where thou hast laid him.' It has, however, always been the custom for gardeners in the war cemeteries – be they Belgian, French or, as the majority after the war and for many years thereafter, British ex-soldiers who worked with the Commission – to be as helpful to pilgrims as possible. At that time most cemeteries were tended regularly by the same people, who came to know who was buried where. So perhaps the unidentified man actually was a mortal gardener, acting in a Christ, or Saviour-like way to Helen in her hour of need, as the gardener may well have guided Rudyard to the Irish Guards Lieutenant's grave at St Mary's ADS the previous year.

The poem that accompanies this moving story, beautiful in its simplicity and its empathy with Helen Turrell's feelings, is called *The Burden*. It continues the theme hinted at in *The Gardener* of Mary Magdalene, to whom

> One grave to me was given –
> To guard till Judgement Day –
> But God looked down from Heaven
> And rolled the Stone away!

But there was no resurrection miracle for Helen Turrell or for Rudyard and Carrie Kipling.

Carrie reported in her diary for 21 April, 'We have never returned so sad, depressed and hopeless.' The sight of so many graves, when they still didn't have one on which to focus the grief which never diminished, made these cemetery visits dreadful for her to bear and there was no relief in childless Bateman's. The depression was compounded when, on 14 May, Rider Haggard died, Kipling's one male soulmate, the fellow creative writer whose intellect sufficiently matched his own so that their satisfying and stimulating discussions could free-wheel from practical issues such as agrarian policies and Bolshevism through concepts like religion, theosophy, resurrection, reincarnation and spiritualism. In 1912 Haggard had confided a sealed parcel to his publisher, Charles Longman, not to be opened until his death. It was the manuscript of his autobiography with the words, 'I dedicate this record of my days to my dear Wife and to the memory of our son, whom now I seek.' At last Haggard's belief in the life hereafter was revealed. If Rudyard was shown this dedication it would surely have re-awakened his hope that he, too, would be reunited with his son in the next world.

Carrie was more concerned with the miseries of this life. On 17 August she wrote, 'John's birthday was never easy for me to face, or the days between now and September 27th.' On that date she simply wrote, 'John's day'. On 3 October they went to Winchester College to visit the war memorial, designed by Rudyard's War Graves Commission colleague, Sir Herbert Baker, and on which George Cecil's name was inscribed. On the 22nd of the month Carrie recorded, 'Our Elsie has been married a year – so sad and lonely for me'. A year later they attended the opening of the Guards Memorial, which she described as 'a wonderful ceremony and the close of the war for so many of us'. Could she now accept John's death as final, that chapter of her life closed for ever? Hardly: because of Rudyard's position with the War graves Commission, their attendance was more or less compulsory at all the official openings and commemorations they could manage. On 19 October it was the 'Opening of the Memorial to the million dead' at the Abbey and on 11 November they went 'to the Home Office for the Armistice Service'. The war and its aftermath still dominated their lives.

Another serious illness hit Rudyard in December, this time pneumonia, and it was so severe that reports of it appeared in the press. On 31 December Elsie called to say goodbye before she and George left for Madrid where George was to be Honorary Attaché at the British Embassy. 'So ends the year,' was Carrie's final diary entry for 1925: 'A very sad year for me with nothing ahead for the other years but the job of living.'

Rudyard slowly recovered and Fabian Ware wrote on 26 January 1926 that, during a recent visit to Canada, a Mrs Smillie, 'Regent of the Ottawa Municipal Chapter, Imperial Order of the Daughters of the Empire', sent her best wishes for an improvement in Rudyard Kipling's health. Ware cheered him up by telling him, 'I always began my lectures with a quotation from your poem on the King's Pilgrimage with other references to your work for the commission, with the result that the more imaginative reporters generally referred to you and me as the pen and sword respectively of the Commission.'

That year Rudyard took a long time to convalesce in France, thus missing the events of the General Strike back at home. After his return the bleak existence at Bateman's continued, interspersed with visits to friends and relatives in the UK, such as the Baldwins at Astleys or Chequers (although he now mistrusted the politics of his cousin Stanley, currently Prime Minister), to Elsie in Madrid, to the Tauffliebs in Strasbourg and to Imperial War Graves Cemeteries and Memorials around the world. There were more ambitious, perhaps unwisely so, travels, too, like the trip to South America in 1927, which took them to Rio de Janeiro, returning through Lisbon and Biarritz. Carrington remarked that these long journeys 'usually ended in illness for one of the two, since the changes of diet ... usually upset his digestion', and they exhausted Carrie. But the desire to escape the cold and dark of the English winters in their gloomy house was as strong as ever and to 'roll to Rio' had long been an ambition. The literary result of the tour was a series of *Brazilian Sketches* for the *Morning Post*. On their return a highlight was a visit to Buckingham Palace on 28 April where the King gave new colours to the Irish Guards. John would have been present with them in spirit at this moment of glory for his regiment and one can imagine the turmoil of emotions – pride mingled with longing and regret – that his ageing parents experienced.

During this year the Kipling Society was formed by an ardent fan called J.H.C. Brooking who had been trying to get it underway since 1922. He received no encouragement from Kipling who viewed the whole idea with horror because of all the possibilities it entailed of invading his jealously-kept privacy. 'They could at least have waited until I was dead,' he complained. That one of his old school pals, Dunsterville, was the Society's first president and another, Beresford, was a founder member, allayed no fears, for the former had already started writing reminiscences of his schooldays with the famous author.

1928 opened with the death of another great English author, Thomas Hardy, and Kipling acted as one of his pallbearers. Another honour was an invitation to stay at Balmoral, a real friendship having developed between King George and the Bard of the War Graves Commission. The year saw no long voyages, but much work at home with the Commission. In June he helped with the arrangements of the Prince of Wales's pilgrimage to the war graves and in September was working on what Carrie called 'an article on the Unknown Dead', and also drafted a letter of the Queen for publication by the Commission.

The principal trip of 1929 was a war graves tour to Egypt and Jerusalem. He and Carrie left Tilbury on 1 February sailing via Gibraltar and Naples to Alexandria. On the 15th Rudyard was visiting cemeteries at Cairo and on the 25th he drove 250 miles to inspect other outlying cemeteries. One was the cemetery at Gaza, where he and Carrie visited the grave of Bonar Law's son, Charlie. Carrie wrote to the family [Bonar Sykes, *Kipling Journal*], 'the cemetery is now the most perfect site . . . I can feel content with it and how much more it would mean to you . . . We send you this bit from the headstone, and all our loving thoughts and remembrances of Charlie.' Rudyard added that Charlie 'has a soldier of his own battalion on either side of him. I liked that specially.' Once again they were standing at the grave of a friend's son and the longing for one of their own would have welled up anew. On their return they sent photographs of the cemetery to the Bonar Laws.

Such was Kipling's devotion that he travelled all the way to Assuan [Aswan] to see just one war grave buried near the great dam. Then it was on to Jerusalem where they arrived on 21 March. There there were more graves to visit.

In 1930 they sailed to the West Indies. Carrie was at this time the greater invalid, suffering from diabetes and rheumatism and she was advised to seek the sun as a possible cure. Helen Cecil, now Helen Hardinge, travelled with them in a surrogate Elsie role, not a successful idea according to Professor Pinney, (*Kipling Journal*, December 1998) but was unable to stay on when Carrie, after developing appendicitis, collapsed when the party reached Bermuda and was hospitalized for three months. Rudyard was frankly terrified. She was his mainstay, his nurse, his travel agent, his general manager. And now he was alone to look after and worry about her and to take care of all the day-to-day arrangements and decisions. While she was separated from him in hospital, he wrote, as he had done after all the tragedies in his life, as occupational therapy. The outcome was the story *A Naval Mutiny*. But Rudyard felt he had to get Carrie out of the somewhat primitive medical care that was available in Bermuda and eventually, at the beginning of June, managed to get them a passage to Halifax, Nova Scotia, America being totally out of the question for them both.

Incredible as it may seem, the intrepid globetrotters took off again on 25 February 1931 to Port Said, Assuan and Cairo, meeting Fabian Ware there in March. They returned via Naples, Toulon, Aix and Nevers to Amiens and Paris. On 14 May a French delegation came to the War Graves Commission offices in London headed by General Castlenau and Rudyard proudly gave an address in his best French. On 29 June he was off to Paris again, to make a speech to the France-Grande-Bretagne Association, having, somewhat pointedly, declined an invitation to the unveiling of General Haig's memorial at Montreuil the previous day (which he could well have attended), the only Commissioner to refuse. On 11 November, Armistice Day, Carrie wrote in her diary, 'We stand in the street at the Cenotaph; a deeper feeling this year than ever before.' There were times when she felt that time was working its clichéd healing process, then the hurt broke through, as sharp as ever.

Later that month came a delightful interlude. Rudyard and Carrie had a visit from their two little American nieces, Josephine and Beatrice, the daughters of Carrie's sister Josephine and her husband Theodore Dunham. It must on the one hand have brought back painful memories of their own Josephine but on the other it was a joyful experience to have two adoring, well-behaved children in the silent house where there was now no one to frolic with. The years temporarily dropped off Rudyard. 'Uncle Rud was setting out a new book of a dozen tales. It is to be called *Limits and Renewals*,' wrote Josephine to her parents. 'He read us two of the stories sitting by the fire with his feet up against the wall. And with such expression! It was as if the scenes were alive before you!! Every now and then he'd stop and say, "Savez?"' At long last he had again his preferred audience to try out his stories upon: children. Josephine was most impressed with a 'very Indian' story, about devotion to the King

Emperor, which Rudyard told her was based on his own experience of having seen the King during a cold visit to a war cemetery tell an English Colonel to put his overcoat back on as 'Good men are scarce'. 'It is a masterpiece,' the young fan declared. The story that so impressed her was *The Debt*. In it Kipling not only draws on his knowledge of the War Graves Cemeteries, but also returns to his Indian childhood as the story is seen through the eyes of a young Sahib, six-year-old William, son of the Doctor of the Gaol. Like the young Rudyard, William is told tales by his *ayah* and Indian servants. One of them is a convict, 'One Two Three', who served in the war in 'Frangistan'. Rudyard had actually seen the episode with the King and the Colonel (actually a General) in what sounds like the Indian Cemetery at Neuve Chapelle: 'A narrow cemetery, walled with high walls, entered by one door in a corner'. While waiting for the King, the General, who had been sick, huddled for warmth in his '*Baritish Warrum*', but took it off to meet his sovereign in his 'medalled uniform'. Afterwards he told his Colonel that the King's act saved his life: 'For an hour coatless in that chill would have slain me.' It is a simple, touching story, full of the tenderness Kipling felt for these loyal men of the Empire who so willingly served their 'Padishah'.

Her sister Beatrice was more impressed by the story *Beauty Spots*, which she pronounced 'very funny'. This un-Kipling-like farce is about the revenge the son of a director of 'The Jannockshire and Chemical Manure Works' and his best friend wreak on a stuffy old Major who pettily reacts to his precious village being infiltrated by vulgar tradesmen who would, he feared, wish to thrust themselves 'into local society'. During his son's absence in France to see a specialist to treat his long-standing reaction to being gassed in the war, the father inadvertently causes an alarming rash to break out on visitors to his property by over-chemically-manuring his land. The son, James, affectionately known as Jemmie or Jem, and his friend Kit paint the family's gross pet pig, Angelique, in the most lurid spots, produce her to the pesky Major, who was duly convinced that she was 'infected to the marrow. She's rotting alive'. He high-tails it to the village to spread the alarming news, where-upon Jem and Kit hose down Angelique and restore her to her normal pinkish-white hue. When the Major returns to proceed with his complaint about the infected pig (with most of the village present to witness the drama) and is met with an unblemished sow, the lads convince everyone that he must have been hallucinating as a result of over-indulgence in alcohol the previous night. He retreats with his tail metaphorically between his legs, and, as Kipling repeats in his end of story poem, *The Expert*, 'Youth . . . in mirth more dread than wrath, Wipes the nuisance from his path.'

When making an over-sized sow the heroine of his story, Kipling may well have been recalling a hilarious anecdote recounted in one of John's last letters, written from France on 26 August 1915: 'In the billets where my platoon sleep there is a great big sow which wanders around the yard. The men sleep in a corn shed just next to the stye. The old sow is always ravenously hungry & I suddenly heard a tremendous row & shouting & out of the yard gate onto the mainroad rushed the sow with a man's emergency ration bag in its mouth. The bag was full of biscuit and bully beef. After her rushed all the billet with clubbed rifles, sticks, stones etc. But the sow ran much faster than they did & they chased it for about 150 yds till it was turned back by some men coming down the road. She never let go the ration bag but rushed back.' Eventually, after much beating, the sow relinquished the bag and collapsed exhausted on a dung heap. 'I don't think I have ever laughed so much in my life.' Two days later Rudyard replied, 'Your letter of the 26th with the joyous tale of the Emergency Ration sow just came in this evening: and Mums and I howled over it.' One has a clear mental picture of the anxious parents, relaxing their fears for once as they were brought closer to the lighter side of their son's life in France, a bright moment that was recalled all these years later when the story was gestating. Another link with John in this light story is the description of the relationship between the industrialist, Mr Gravell, and his soldier son. There are intimate touches when Kipling is obviously drawing on his own very physically affectionate relationship with John. When Jemmy is 'bleaching out' from the effects of gas in France, Gravell drives up to London by himself 'with the padded arm-rest down, which was never the case when his Jemmy came along'. When Jemmy returns, the father says, '"Oh, but I'm glad you're back, Jemmy! I've wanted you desperate." "Me, too, Dad." The hug was returned . . . "Then, run along and get up the champagne. Your tie's crooked, my dear." He put up his hand tenderly, as a widower may who has had to wash and dress a year-old baby.' Though not, of course, a widower himself, Rudyard had always had an extremely 'hands-on' attitude to his children.

When the small nieces moved on in their European tour in January 1932 Josephine wrote to her 'Dear Uncle Rud' (her Aunt Carrie was, predictably, away on one of her treatments in Bath) 'I feel as if the magic of Bateman's were clinging to me still'. Though now old and very frail, Kipling had not lost his Pied Piper touch with children and continued to derive much pleasure from their company. Another gratifying feature of these later years was his continuing rapport with the King. On 6 December came wonderful evidence of the esteem in which George V held Rudyard Kipling – he asked him to write the Christmas speech that was to be broadcast for the first time. On the 13th he took the draft for the King's approval and Carrie noted in her diary that he was pleased with it. Two days later he accepted the final draft and on Christmas Day the Kiplings sat beside their radio in Bateman's and listened to the broadcast. Carrie wrote, 'A wonderful thing for Rud to hear the King speak his words to

the people of the Empire and to have the song of the cities come true.'
Rudyard had foreseen the importance of broadcasting in *With the Night Mail* written as early as 1905 and in *As Easy as A.B.C.*, written in 1912.

Limits and Renewals was published the next year. In it Kipling's hatred, bitterness and feelings of revenge had abated to produce a collection of stories that, although their main inspiration was still the Great War, shows that, despite the bereavements, the broken bodies and minds, life must be continued, renewed. Where the revenge motif still occurs, as in *Dayspring Mishandled* (acknowledged to be one of his finest stories), it is often tinged with humour, hoax or farce, as in *Beauty Spots, Aunt Ellen* and *The Tie*. Some of the descriptions of what the horrors of war inflicted on those who fought it are explicit and harrowing – in *The Woman in His Life, Fairy-Kist* and *The Tender Achilles*, for example, of which there was not universal approval from veterans of the war. As usual the stories are accompanied by verses and the poem that accompanies *Fairy-Kist, The Mother's Son*, returns to a subject treated by many of the younger war poets – Owen, Sassoon, Gibson, Tennant – a soldier driven mad by 'the noise, and fear of death, Waking and wounds and cold', burdens laid upon the subject which were 'More than a man could bear'. Kipling deals with it with sensitivity and lack of histrionics in a skilful exercise in empathy.

> I have a dream – a dreadful dream –
> A dream that is never done,
> I watch a man go out of his mind
> And he is My Mother's Son.
>
> . . . .
>
> And no-one knows when he'll get well –
> So there he'll have to be:
> And, 'spite of the beard in the looking glass,
> I know that man is me!

Limits and Renewals is often dismissed as the writing of an old, sick and tired man, obsessed with disease, doctors and medicines. Certainly, in many respects, Kipling fitted this bill. He was 67. He was suffering from the years of pain caused by the duodenal ulcers which had not yet been diagnosed. The tragedies in his life had exhausted him. The poem that accompanies *The Tender Achilles* is entitled *Hymn to Physical Pain*. It is often interpreted as a personal statement, a description of Kipling's own sleepless nights and a longing for the Forgetfulness that will keep 'The Pains of Hell at bay!' Yet he could still sparkle, still find notes of originality, of a new compassion. The collection is, without doubt, still the interesting work of a versatile and original genius.

From now on, however, his failing health and his concern with politics seemed to take over his life to the detriment of his once prolific creativity. He was worried by the rise of National Socialism and wrote a poem called *The Storm Cone*, in which he warned,

> Stand by! the lull 'twixt blast and blast
> Signals the storm is near, not past;

which Elsie says 'was criticized as being "exaggerated and gloomy"'. Stanley Baldwin's apparent move to the left was also a matter of increasing concern. Kipling began to look inward and started work on the curiously unrevealing autobiography, *Something of Myself*, not to be published until after his death. Winter was spent in Monte Carlo where, as usual, he was looked after by Dr Bres and then, at last, the Parisian Dr Roux diagnosed the seriousness of his duodenal ulcer. Treatment was changed accordingly and there seemed to be a resultant improvement in Rudyard's condition. At last he could be confident that he did not have cancer. One wonders how the long list of distinguished physicians and surgeons, listed by Birkenhead and headed by the distinguished Sir John Bland-Sutton, had failed to realize the root cause of his long-standing, painful and miserable ailment. It is interesting to note that the last recorded visit by Bland-Sutton in the Bateman's Visitor's Book is on 11 January 1933, before Rudyard's trip to Monte Carlo and consultation with the French doctors. It was as if, after all these years (he first appeared in the Visitor's Book in 1906 and some years came with Lady Bland-Sutton several times for lunch and tea), Kipling had now lost confidence in him.

A reason to be happy in 1933 was the fact that Elsie and George Bambridge moved back to England, well within easy motoring reach in Hampshire. Their marriage, though outwardly happy, was childless. Christopher Walker, who is writing Oliver Baldwin's biography, has a letter, signed 'George' and in writing that strongly resembles Bambridge's, written in the early '30s (therefore long after the break between Oliver and the Kiplings) which is a thankyou for what could well be interpreted as an extremely intimate afternoon spent together. Walker believes that it was well-known in certain circles that the Bambridges' was a *mariage blanc*. It is not beyond the bounds of credibility that Elsie might have accepted a non-physical marriage to escape the suffocating atmosphere of post-war Bateman's. Whether her intuitive father was aware of this situation, if it did indeed exist, we shall never know.

On 5 October Kipling's *Collected Verse, 1885–1932* was published, after a vast amount of work in 'correcting the proofs of this vast mass of print, classifying the verses, indexing them, and arranging them in chronological order', a task which he undertook single-handedly.

1934 followed the usual pattern of overwintering in the South of France and back at home Rudyard continued to preach preparedness, even advocating, way ahead of his time, that air-raid shelters should be built. 1935 brought an interesting new project and a new medium. Alexander Korda the film maker offered him a contract for *Toomai of the Elephants*. Then, uncharacteristically, Kipling decided to speak out publicly on his strongly held views about the dangers of drifting unprotected into the jaws of another onslaught by the old enemy. It was the King's Silver Jubilee year and Rudyard chose as his forum the Royal Society of St George on 6 May. He made a powerful speech, appealing to the emotions rather than to reason and began with words guaranteed to shock, 'Great Britain's quota of dead in the War was over eight hundred thousand when the books were closed in '21 or '22 . . . Furthermore, a large but unknown number died in the next few years from wounds or disease directly due to the War. There is a third category of men incapacitated from effort by the effects of shock, gassing, tubercle and the like. These carry a high death-rate because many of them burned out half a life's vitality in three or four years. They, too, have ceased to count. All these were men of average physique, and, but that they died without issue, would have continued our race.' As always, in the general, the pain of the particular shone through. His own line had come to an end with John. The impassioned exhortation ended with the warning that anticipated the *Blitzkrieg*, that 'if the attack of the future is to be on the same swift "all-in" lines as our opponents' domestic administrations – it is possible that before we are aware, our country may have joined those submerged races of history who passed their children through fire to Moloch in order to win credit with their Gods.' All the old feistiness was still there and the speech, according to Elsie, 'was resented as being "unsuitable for Jubilee Year" and was hardly reported in the press.'

It was also election year, and Baldwin became Prime Minister for the third time. Rudyard was out of tune with his policies and his political agitation continued. The Tauffliebs visited Bateman's in November and Julia found Rudyard 'better than he had been for a long time'. She commented on the eternal cheerfulness and bravery with which he met the pain that he had lived with for so many years. But intimations of mortality were beginning to press on him. He had a mystic belief in the biblical concept of man's allotted span being three score years and ten and was totally surprised when his 70th birthday, on 30 December 1935, drew worldwide tributes such as he hadn't enjoyed for many a year. Letters and telegrams flowed in, including one from his friend the King.

On 8 January 1936 Rudyard wrote to his brother-in-law Theodore Dunham that 'man's life is 25,000 days'. He had now exceeded that expectation and obviously considered himself to be living on borrowed time. It would not be for long.

The annual trip to Cannes was planned and en route Rudyard and

Carrie went to Brown's in January. From there they visited their son-in-law George, suffering from bronchitis in Hampstead. Early the next day Elsie received a phone call from the Middlesex Hospital to which her father had been rushed with a violent haemorrhage, his duodenum finally having perforated. A major operation was undertaken, but, despite signs of some rallies, Rudyard Kipling died in the early hours of 18 January, gone to be reunited with the children whom he had missed so terribly from the moments of their deaths in 1899 and 1915. Carrie and Elsie were distraught and exhausted, having stayed with the dying man through his final hours. There had been as much public concern and interest in his condition as there had been during his illness in New York in 1899. Now, on the news of his death, Carrie, herself ill and in a stage of collapse, rallied to receive the barrage of press. It was her 44th wedding anniversary.

Rudyard's coffin, covered, as befitted the unofficial laureate of the Empire, with the Union flag on which lay a bunch of violets sent by Stanley Baldwin's wife Lucy, lay in the Hospital's Chapel before being transported to Golders Green Crematorium. Elsie pointed out to Carrington the irony of its arrival to the strains of the Red Flag, as the cremation that preceded Rudyard's was that of Saklatvala, the Indian Communist. On 23 January there was a moving and impressive service in Westminster Abbey before his ashes were buried in Poets' Corner. His pall-bearers reflected his stature, his status and his interests: his cousin Stanley Baldwin, the Prime Minister, Admiral of the Fleet Sir Roger Keyes, Field-Marshal Sir Archibald Montgomery-Massingberd, Professor J.W. Mackail, O.M., Sir Fabian Ware, the Master of Magdalene College, Cambridge, Mr H.A. Gwynne and Mr A.S. Watt (son of Kipling's agent, A.P. Watt). James Barrie (now Sir James) was due to have been among them, but was sadly not well enough to attend. The list of mourners reported in *The Times* reads like an extract from *Who's Who*, reflecting the catholic nature of his interests and the admiration with which he was regarded. Surprisingly, in view of his long estrangement from his aunt and uncle, Oliver Baldwin was among the family members. *Recessional*, now generally accepted as a hymn, and *Abide With Me* (Kipling's own choice for his funeral) were sung as a procession wended its way past the grave, on the edge of which Carrie had stood throughout the ceremony, her swaying controlled by the firm arms of her daughter on one side and her son-in-law on the other. The report of the funeral ends, 'Among the floral tributes was one composed of foliage and flowers from the British War Cemeteries in the vicinity of the Loos battlefield. The wreath, which was from the staff of the Imperial War Graves Commission in France and Flanders, was brought to London by Mr Prynn, the head gardener in charge of the Loos cemetery, in which Kipling's son is commemorated.' These flowers, nurtured in the soil where John's unfound body lay, would have meant more to Carrie and Elsie than all the others. A memorial service had already been held (on the 20th) at Dud Corner Cemetery on the Loos battlefield, attended by the Préfet of the Pas de Calais and many other French dignitaries, together with representatives of the War Graves Commission. A beautiful wreath was placed against the wall bearing John Kipling's name, then, before he set off to London bearing the Commission's wreath, gardener Prynn played the Last Post as he or one of his assistants had done every night for the past two years in the ceremony funded by Kipling in memory of John. There was also a memorial service at Burwash Parish Church at which Colonel Feilden was one of the principal mourners.

The obituaries took up many column inches in the papers of the day. *The Times'* piece was headed 'MR RUDYARD KIPLING STORY-TELLER AND POET AN INTERPRETER OF EMPIRE' and started with the appropriate words, 'One of the most forcible minds of our time has ceased to work, with the death early this morning of Rudyard Kipling.' The tributes poured in: from 'Stalky', Bernard Shaw, the Queen (despite the fact that the King lay dying she made the time to write of the sadness she felt at the loss of a personal friend), the Prince of Wales, the Duke of Connaught, Winston Churchill, John Masefield, John Buchan (now Lord Tweedsmuir), General Sir Ian Hamilton, and many members of the War Graves Commission. The Masonic Lodge that he helped found for the Commission's members, 'Builders of the Silent Cities' paid a special tribute, quoting the lines

> We reckon not with those
> Whom the mere fates ordain
> The power that wrought on us, and goes
> Back to the Power again.

There were also moving testimonies to Kipling's humanity, his warmth and wit, his Peter-Pan-like qualities, his love and respect for children, his flashes of humour, his sparkle – all of which added up to what would now be called charisma. Winston Churchill wrote, 'There has never been anyone like him. No-one has ever written like Kipling before, and his work has been successfully imitated by none. He was unique and irreplaceable.'

Perhaps the reaction would have been even greater to the death of this 'story-teller of genius, who took the world by storm, and for a whole generation remained the most popular, the most humorous and, in some ways, the most romantic writer using our tongue,' as John Masefield, then Poet Laureate, described him, had not the good friend of his later years, King George V, also died. As Kipling's ashes were being buried in the Abbey, the King's body was lying in state at nearby Westminster Hall. 'The King has gone taking his trumpeter with him.'

From his widow, Carrie, had been taken her very *raison d'être*.

For 44 years her whole life had been utterly devoted to the genius she knew she had married and to the children she bore him. Despite her abrasiveness, her obsession to control, her often domineering and demanding behaviour, her over-protectiveness, her hypochondria that matched and sometimes exceeded her husband's, there is no doubt that Rudyard absolutely adored her and depended upon her entirely: there are innumerable tender and loving references to and about her in his letters to his children, his other relations and his friends. He admired her business acumen and organizational skills. Now he, her eldest daughter and her son were all dead, her youngest daughter married and concerned with her own life. She was old (three years older than Rudyard) and she was ill, but somehow she found the strength to cope with the aftermath of such a famous man's death. So often in accounts of Rudyard Kipling's life Carrie appears as the villain in the story. Even her own daughter, in her *Epilogue* to Carrington's biography, criticized her vehemently. 'My mother introduced into everything she did, and even permeated the life of her family, with a sense of strain and worry amounting sometimes to hysteria. Her possessive and rather jealous nature, both with regard to my father and to us children made our lives very difficult, while her uncertain moods kept us apprehensively on the alert for possible storms. There is no doubt that her difficult temperament sometimes reacted adversely on my father and exhausted him, but his kindly nature, patience, and utter loyalty to her prevented his ever questioning this bondage, and they were seldom apart.' The other side of the coin was expressed by her godson, Bonar Sykes, in the *Kipling Journal* of March 1996, 'The bad press she sometimes received was, I think, incomprehensible to my mother [Isabel Bonar Law], who had the warmest regard for her, and received from her many special kindnesses.' Above all, the two important men in her life, Rudyard and John, were never in any doubt of her exceptional love for them.

Bereft of them both, she must at first have felt that life had no further point for her. But by 4 March she felt strong enough to go to Cannes to recuperate. From the California Palace Hotel she wrote to her old friend Violet (now Lady Milner) that she was dreading coming back to 'take up the endless work of settling up Rudyard's affairs but first I must go to London for a little but never again to Brown's. There are things one can spare oneself and this is one.' There were hints of other troubles, too. 'I think of it all vaguely – the dreadfulness we have got ourselves into and am thankful he is spared it all. He would have hated the humiliation and the knowing we brought it on ourselves.' Perhaps this was a personal reference, but it could have been an observation on the 7 March reoccupation of the Rhineland by Germany, unopposed by the League of Nations, France or Britain, something Rudyard would have abhorred.

Whatever this mysterious trouble was, there was worse to come. On 29 July 1936 a hurtful bombshell burst in the press. The *Daily Telegraph*, the *Daily Express*, the *Daily Mirror* and other papers reported in detail a speech given by the once favourite nephew, Oliver Baldwin. Of all the unlikely audiences to whom to make such a controversial lecture, Baldwin chose the elocution teachers at the summer course of the London Academy of Music to address on the subject of 'Rudyard Kipling the Man'. It sounded an innocuous enough subject, but the teachers were soon aware that they were listening to a vicious personal attack on a man who, at the time of his recent death, had regained much of the early respect and admiration he had enjoyed at the beginning of his career.

Baldwin started by presenting his credentials, stating that he was only five when he first remembered his uncle and that 'there is nobody living who knew Kipling in certain moods as I knew him'. He condescendingly, and somewhat inaccurately, said that Kipling had been successful in the early stages 'because he was the first artist known in Anglo-India – a world where art and literature had been entirely unknown'. Kipling was not liked by those in authority in India, he continued, and 'He developed a kind of inferiority complex, and, on his return to England began to interest himself in Anglo-Indian politics. He wrote his verses to attack and sneer at people who had different political views from his own. From 1910 to 1914 he wrote a whole series of anti-democratic poems, all in the defence of force and of hatred and in connection with the Ulster question.' Of course there was an element of truth in this description of the early poems from the collection *The Years Between*, but the key to the bitter note can be traced to the phrase 'people who had different political views from his own'. The political chasm between Kipling and the Baldwins had become unbreachable. Oliver was now firmly in the Labour camp, having stood as their parliamentary candidate for Dudley in 1924, served as its Labour MP 1929–31, was their candidate for Chatham in 1931 and Paisley in 1935. He and the arch-conservative could no longer see eye to eye, but it is hard to understand the depth of the hatred that comes through Baldwin's speech. 'In 1914,' he continued 'came the war, and to him it was the answer to "the maiden's prayer". He had preached that this was coming. He had tried to lead people to join the Army to prevent it.' From one who had beseeched Kipling to help him get into the war under-age this is the most extraordinary ingratitude. 'He was proud his son had joined the Army at the age of 17. Here his inferiority complex had come out – he was not able to be a soldier himself, but his son was in uniform.' Again a grain of truth is twisted spitefully. 'In September, 1915,' he went on, 'his son was posted as missing at the battle of Loos. From that date Kipling became an entirely different man. He was stopped dead from his urge of war. Imperialism stopped dead for him. There was that awful bug at the back of his mind saying: "After all, didn't you want this war? didn't you urge it on? didn't you want people to go and wave flags and beat drums? and have you not paid for it?"'

It is difficult to comprehend that this was written by the same Oliver who had so proudly followed his cousin John into the Irish Guards and who had gladly offered help with the writing of their History. He knew how much pleasure he and other young officers gave both the Kiplings during their visits; how the grieving couple tried to hide their grief to make these stays enjoyable, yet Oliver maintained, 'It broke him completely. He shut up like a clam. He was not interested in anything new. All the lovely side of his nature – all the "jungle book", all the playing with children, all the love for people – went like that.' This certainly does not tally with the loving Uncle Rud who had so recently read his amusing stories to his young American nieces. The idea that Kipling never saw anybody can easily be dispelled by glancing through the Bateman's Visitors' Book. The last time Oliver appears in it is a long stay from 11–18 August 1923, but the list of those who stayed the night or who came for a meal (Kipling kept two separate lists and specified 'lunch', 'tea' and 'dinner' on the 'Meals' list for each year) is as full as ever from that date until just before his death. It includes the usual regular family visitors, now often with children in tow; as many as 'five' or even 'seven', complete with 'nurses' and/or maids, are sometimes specified. On 5 August 1931 Rudyard recorded that '28 scouts' had come for the day! Rupert Grayson brought his bride, Kermit Roosevelt came with his young family. Mrs Cuthbert, whose husband had been lost with John, remarried and, as Lady Rayleigh, she often brought her children to see the Kiplings. So did Julia Taufflieb's daughter, married to the English Dr Stanley and Kipling wrote delightful letters to their daughter Jane. There was the usual mix of the distinguished and the famous: Lord Dunsany, patron of Frances Ledwidge and himself a poet, with his wife, Lord and Lady Edward Gleichen, Sir Fabian and Lady Ware and Colonel Goodland of the War Graves Commission, R.C. Sheriff who wrote *Journey's End*, and a sprinkling of publishers and 'royals'. There were also the frequent and well-documented travels to the continent.

Yet Oliver had even more darts to fire. 'He concentrated himself in revenge. He looked upon me to be the one to revenge his son against the German people. That, to me and to you, is a horrible and unpleasant and sad state to get into. He felt like that. Here were the Germans who killed his son, and he wanted to see the end of Germany.' That Kipling pushed Oliver into the war solely to revenge John is cruelly untrue: Oliver couldn't wait to go. And now he comes to the crescendo of this hymn of hate; the section which gave him all the publicity. Kipling, he maintained, 'wrote the wickedest short story ever written in the history of the world – the story of Mary Postgate.' Many newspapers boxed a brief summary of the story over their report of the speech in general, but without in any way attempting to describe the main character's orgasmic reaction to the German pilot's death. Nor did the report of Oliver's speech indicate that he had in any way justified this sensational claim for the story. Finally he said, 'In 1923 he realized there was a new world entirely, and he could not keep pace with it. The result was he was very much wrapped up with himself in his home and never saw anybody.' The date is significant as it obviously marks the occasion of the final rift between himself and his Uncle Rud. The idea that the Kiplings pulled up the metaphorical drawbridge of gloomy Bateman's and moped is absurd. The diatrabe finished by repeating that Kipling looked to Baldwin 'to revenge his son. He wanted me to take his son's place, so that he would have somebody connected with him fighting.' That there were times when Rudyard looked to Oliver 'to take his son's place' had an element of truth, but it was more in a pathetic attempt to fill the void left by the death of an adored son than to appoint a champion to fight for him. Indeed Oliver had appointed himself John's 'avenger' when he was called for overseas service in June 1918.

Knowing just how close Oliver had been to both Rudyard and Carrie, how fond they were of him, it is difficult to comprehend the virulent nature of the feud that arose between them. Certainly Rudyard abhorred Baldwin's politics. Rupert Grayson felt that after the war Kipling 'believed that it would not be long before England and France . . . would be dragged into another war. In many ways he had become less tolerant. He was always an imperialist and a die-hard Tory, and he never forgave my old friend Oliver Baldwin, son of the Prime Minister who was Kipling's cousin, for sitting in the House of Commons as a socialist.' And there was the shocking (to someone of Kipling's self-confessed homophobia) and far more personal reason for the sudden break with Oliver – his relationship with Johnnie Boyle. His reaction to that would certainly have been something that Carrie and Elsie would have excised from the Kipling Papers.

Elsie was appalled at the newspaper articles. She rushed to her adored father's defence with hurt and angry letters to the Editor of the *Daily Telegraph* and others. Kipling's faithful secretary, Dorothy Ponton, also flew to her old master's defence. She wrote a supportive article entitled 'KIPLING DID NOT CHANGE' and sent it to the Editor of the *Morning Post*, H.A. Gwynne. His secretary replied, 'With regard to your article . . . it may have escaped your notice that the MORNING POST did not publish any reference whatever to the original lecture by Mr Oliver Baldwin, the publication of which the Editor deprecated very much.' It says much for Gwynne's continuing loyalty to Kipling that the paper made the uncommercial decision not to report this speech. It was hot stuff and they were missing out to all the papers that gleefully carried long reports and comments upon it. 'As an old friend of the late Mr Kipling, the Editor thinks that the less reference to this deplorable affair the better,' the secretary continued. 'He, however, from his personal knowledge of Mr Kipling, endorses all that you say in your article.'

What Dorothy did say was that 'From 1911 till 1914 I taught Mr Kipling's daughter entirely, and his son occasionally in the holidays. In these pre-war days Mr Kipling was a man with a strong sense of duty, a deep love of his country and a divine sense of humour. In the summer holidays of 1911 Oliver Baldwin (then an Etonian) and his sister Margot, were at Bateman's, the Sussex residence of the author. Mr Oliver Baldwin's recollections of his "Uncle Rud" in those days must be very happy.' She went on to describe how when war broke out and 'his young friends were scattered – and many of the killed in action – Mr Kipling's spirit remained unbroken'. She had met Rudyard a few days after John was posted 'wounded and missing' and recalled, 'Only those who have been through the agony of that grief can understand what these words mean to the parents of an only son. But Mr Kipling had no inclination to appeal for sympathy. All he said was "The boy had reached the supreme moment of his life, what would it avail him to outlive that?"' She felt that the father 'concentrated himself <u>not</u> on revenge, but on writing words that would comfort the bereaved and warn the world against making too easy conditions with a ruthless enemy. This showed [Mr] Kipling with a strong sense of duty and a deep love of his country.' She next described working with Rudyard on his History of the Irish Guards. 'Though he had lost his buoyant step,' she said, 'and was beginning to suffer from gastric trouble, he was as young in spirit as ever – always ready to make, or enjoy, a good joke; a prodigious worker; a cheerful and sympathetic friend.' She felt that the History was 'a memorial to his son', but that 'heart-rending as it must have been for him to write of young men whom he had known so intimately and who were now dead – he never omitted a chance of relating some comic event or anecdote that relieved the tragedy of war.' Finally, Dorothy wrote, 'Those who agree with Mr Oliver Baldwin's explanation of the writing of "Mary Postgate" should read "Janeites". "The United Idolaters", "Propagation of Knowledge", and some of the verses written after 1919. I think these conclusively contradict Mr Oliver Baldwin's statement that Rudyard Kipling was embittered by the war and that all the lovely side of his nature died with him.'

Dorothy Ponton was by no means alone in wishing to refute Baldwin's attack. The letters pages of all the main newspapers were full of supportive statements by a diverse array of Kipling devotees: a Canadian ex-soldier, J.W. Barry, who had long corresponded with Kipling and who had had a memorable visit to Bateman's in August 1933, happened to be staying at the Kenilworth Hotel when the story broke. He wrote that the address was 'unfair and unkind'; that Kipling 'was very much the boy who had never grown up. He laughed and joked with much abandon – and he did it on soup and prune-whip, for even then his stomach was acting badly.' J.H.C. Brooking, the founder of the Kipling Society, described the statement as 'absurd'. Captain Ernest Preston, RNVR, 'Organizer of the

Kipling Society', wondered 'how Mr Oliver Baldwin can seek publicity by belittling Rudyard Kipling'. G. Roberts 'of London' defended *Mary Postgate* as illustrating 'truthfully the extreme passion of hatred which is generated in the women of an invaded country when they see their men or their children killed before their eyes,' and in a telling barb continued, 'It might flash across the mind of Mr Oliver Baldwin that if England in general, and the Baldwin family in particular, had heeded the solemn warning against German rearmament delivered in the great patriot's last speech to the people of this country, which he made at the Authors' dinner in 1935, there might be today fair prospect of that peace in Europe which is not desired only by pacifists.' 'E.V.' felt that 'two of Baldwin's statements' were 'grotesquely untrue', and went on to quote 'Beauty Spots', 'The Eye of the Allah', 'speeches at the Sorbonne and in Strasburg' as being proof that all Kipling's creation had certainly not gone. And as for *Mary Postgate*, it was 'not a pleasant story . . . But it is not wicked; it is merely true to life.'

The *Daily Telegraph* published some powerful defences of Kipling. The first was from none other than Stalky himself – Major-General L.C. Dunsterville. He took up the accusation of Kipling suffering from an inferiority complex and quoted his own experiences in the Punjab from 1885 onwards when he 'saw a good deal of the young writer who was amusing the Anglo-Indian world with his bitter satires on men in high places. The knowledge that the great ones of the earth were quailing before the shafts of his wit filled him with an almost excessive "superiority complex", and this subconscious feeling of superiority persisted with him throughout his life,' wrote his old school pal with refreshing honesty. He movingly recalled Rudyard's reply to his letter of sympathy about the death of John, 'I have lost what I treasured most on earth, but I can only fold my hands and bow my head. When I look round and see what others have suffered I am silent.'

Another school friend, General Sir Alexander Godley, quoted the Irish Guards History as proof that the writer was not 'a broken man' and that 'all the lovely side of his nature' had not gone. And Viola Apsley described how, over tea in the autumn of 1934, Kipling chatted to her 7-year-old son, Henry, who pronounced that 'the little man with bushy eyebrows was extremely intelligent about motor-lorries'. Rudyard followed up with a letter to Young Henry enclosing 'a small Kodak which is very good and quick for snapshots' so that he could take shots of cars of different makes, or aeroplanes. As he had done when writing to his own 7-year-old boy he had 'written this in print because my own handwriting is not very easy to read'. Viola Apsley's final dig was, 'Would anyone seriously attend to Mr Oliver Baldwin's criticism did the latter not own his father's name? I think most of the Labour party agree with [me].' Edward Shanks perceptively observed that *Mary Postgate* could not have been written as a result of

John's death as it was first published in *Nash's Magazine* for September 1915 and that John did not die until the 27th.

In the next wave of reaction, on 7 August the *Star*, dubbed by Elsie 'the Socialist Evening paper', under the heading 'Just Over a Week Ago', printed a summary of Baldwin's statement, and under the heading 'Today', a summary of Elsie's reply. A *Star* reporter then interviewed Oliver, who had obviously been unprepared for the tidal wave of reaction his address would invoke. 'The whole matter is dead and finished. I hate arguing, and I am not going to reopen the matter now.' But it wouldn't go away.

On 8 August the *Sphere* concluded from Baldwin's speech that 'he has the material for a desperately interesting book on Rudyard Kipling . . . the story of a wizard who helped to set going by his skill a gyroscope which proved a juggernaut, and spinning on its inexorable way, obliterated all that the wizard held dearest . . . It came and killed his dearest and his pride was pricked. He shut himself away and the virtue was gone out of him. Mr Oliver Baldwin said some very intimate things about the relationship between himself and Mr Kipling, things which most people had been shy of saying. If truth is best, pleasant or unpleasant, he was justified in saying them.' There was no doubt as to where the magazine's sympathies lay. Elsie wrote indignantly, 'With the supposed intimate knowledge of my Father (Mr Rudyard Kipling) by Mr Oliver Baldwin I should like to point out that my Father had not seen or spoken to him for certainly . . .' and here she wrote the figure '13' in her draft and crossed it out to replace it with '10 years prior to his Death. It is therefore clear that Mr Oliver Baldwin's statements about my Father and his feelings in his latter years are of little value.' The Editor of the *Sphere* replied on 11 August that he would publish 'the essential detail of your letter in next week's issue of the *Sphere*,' but that he would only publish 'statements of fact', not the 'statement of personal opinion with which you conclude'.

The following week 'the Old Stager' printed Elsie's letter 'without comment' in his column, saying defensively, 'It was with aloofness and impartiality that I made the reference to Mr Baldwin's recorded utterances on the subject. It was a matter of interest of an hour, but in my view by no means one on which to join issue or to take sides'!

And so the story fizzled out, as all sensational stories eventually do. But the harm inflicted on the frail Carrie was incalculable. However, the coolness that had grown up between the Kiplings and Oliver's father, Stanley, was forgotten in the sorrow of Rudyard's death. On 3 March Carrie had written to Violet saying, 'It was a kind and gracious gesture on Stan Baldwin's part to take Rud's place on the War Graves Commission, and I am deeply grateful to him for it.' (In fact Rudyard's value to the War Graves Commission was such that it was thought that he could not be replaced by one man alone. Stanley Baldwin was considered an appropriate choice to fulfil part of Rudyard's functions as he was 'a cousin of Mr Kipling. He is also a master of the English language.' [Fabian Ware] But Kipling's old critic, Edmund Blunden, had also been asked to serve 'in an advisory capacity', to which he agreed on 29 February.) But then came this unexpected blow from a Baldwin. Perhaps the most hurtful factor in the whole sorry tale was the cowardly way in which Oliver waited until Rudyard had died to launch his attack.

There now only remained the curious self-appointed task of censoring Rudyard's papers for posterity. The process started by Carrie and continued after her death on 19 December 1939 by Elsie Bambridge is fully described in all the main biographies of Rudyard Kipling (e.g. Birkenhead, Carrington, Angus Wilson), as is the incredible *volte face* performed by Elsie towards Birkenhead in sanctioning and then in banning his book, which could not then be published until after both their deaths – Birkenhead's in 1975 and Elsie's in 1976. What these two women allowed to be perpetuated was the image of Kipling as a loving father. So many letters from Rudyard to John and to Elsie, and a selection of John's replies (though, sadly, not Elsie's) were carefully preserved that we are able to share the extraordinary depth of his love for his children. The letters that remained outside of Carrie and Elsie's jurisdiction complete the picture of a man devoted to and devastated by the premature deaths of two of those children. He may well have counted it as his greatest achievement to have sired a manchild who nobly acquitted his duty and laid down his life for God, King, Country and Father.

EPILOGUE

Is It Really Jack?

In March 1992 Norm Christie, the Records Officer at the Commonwealth War Graves Commission, submitted a paper that argued that a grave in St Mary's ADS (Advanced Dressing Station) Cemetery near Loos in France, then marked by a headstone that read 'A Lieutenant [not Second Lieutenant] of the Irish Guards', did in fact contain the body of John Kipling. The submission went as high as the then Director of the Commission and was approved.

Thus, apparently, ended a search that had started almost eighty years earlier when John Kipling was posted missing during the battle of Loos in September 1915 and when, in September 1919 during battlefield clearance near Loos, a body found on the battlefield was identified as 'UBS (Unidentified British Soldier) Lieut. Irish Guards' and reburied in St Mary's ADS Commission cemetery. On 9 June 1992 Miss Beverley Webb, then Information Officer of the Commission, wrote to the Records Office of the Irish Guards to say 'Our Records Officer has been successful in establishing beyond reasonable doubt that the Lieutenant (John Kipling) is actually buried in Plot 7, Row 3, Grave 2 in St Mary's ADS Cemetery, France.'

On 9 July 1992 Major A.J.D. Sheridan wrote from the Regimental Headquarters of the Irish Guards at Birdcage Walk to Mrs Peter Lumsden, 'As the closest remaining relative of Lieutenant John Kipling Irish Guards, it is my duty to inform you that the Commonwealth War Graves Commission have established beyond doubt that Lieutenant Kipling is buried in Plot 7, Row D, Grave 2 in St Mary's ADS Cemetery France. His name will be removed from the Loos Memorial to the Missing and a headstone recording Lieutenant Kipling's details will be erected on his grave.' Efforts to trace Mrs Lumsden five years on have failed. She is not known to members of the Kipling Society and the current staff at Regimental Headquarters of the Irish Guards are unable to discover why Major Sheridan believed her to be related to Kipling.

At this date, March 1998, a new headstone has been erected to replace the old one but John Kipling's name has not been removed from the List of the Missing on the Loos Memorial. Is there then some doubt about the identification?

When an army officer is faced with a tactical situation in the face of the enemy that requires some action on his part he is trained to use a method of analysis which is known as 'Appreciating the Situation'. By assessing in a logical manner all the factors relevant to the situation (such as the aim of any action, the strength of the enemy, the strength of friendly forces, the supplies available, the ground etc) and thence drawing conclusions, he is able to come up with a 'Course of Action' that should achieve the aim. However, in real life what often happens is that the officer is unable to face the tedium of the intellectual rigour needed to identify and to examine the factors affecting the possible courses of action, and he intuitively decides upon a course of action and then sets about finding factors and conclusions that confirm his choice. That process is known as 'Situating the Appreciation'. In examining the case given for the identification of the body of John Kipling it is tempting to situate the appreciation in order to confirm the identification or to refute it according to one's feelings, and in order to 'appreciate' rather than to 'situate' the case it is necessary to start at the very beginning of the process that led to the erection of the new headstone and to examine all of the relevant factors one by one.

The identification of the body by Norm Christie was the result of a process of detection and deduction that calls for admiration, but the process was by no means unique to the search for John Kipling. The Commonwealth War Graves Commission is charged in its charter to strive to give a name to all the burials in its care and that effort is continuous, although as the First War recedes into history the number of opportunities to name an unknown soldier inevitably grow fewer.

The initiative that leads to an identification can arise in a number of ways. A private request from a member of the family or an interested member of the general public can prompt research that leads to success. Such a case is that of 2nd Lieutenant H.W. Mann of the 6th Loyal North Lancs. He and his brother, Captain H.G. Mann, were both killed on 10 August 1915 in Gallipoli. Second Lieutenant Mann was overlooked when the lists of the missing were compiled, it having been assumed that there was only one officer named Mann, but inspection of the Regimental History following the enquiry to the Commission revealed the error and on 5 December 1996 an order was issued to add his name to the Addenda Panel on the Helles Memorial.

Another way in which an enquiry can start is via examination of the records of the Commission at Maidenhead or via the attention of an enquiring mind and subsequent logical deduction. This next case is one of the latter. During a visit to the Western Front, Roy Hemington, an Executive Officer of the Commission, went to Hooge Crater Cemetery in the Ypres Salient in Belgium. He noticed that one headstone showed the burial of an unidentified Lieutenant of the Queen's (Royal West Surrey Regiment) and that the Lieutenant had both the MM and the MC. Thinking this to be unusual, on his return Hemington examined the regimental records of the Queen's and discovered that only one officer matched the rank, the regiment and the awards – Lieutenant T. Darlington MC MM – and therefore the grave that he had seen was Darlington's. In March 1997 an order was issued to have Darlington's name placed on the headstone.

Yet another way is via routine maintenance. In 1995, while replacing a headstone in Pargny Cemetery in France, the record documents were examined and it was found that during an exhumation in 1921 two bodies had been identified but for some reason the information was not acted upon at the time. Now, however, the names of Captain S. Mountford and 2nd Lieutenant J. MacMillan, both of the Royal Scots, have been removed from the list of the Missing on the Pozières Memorial and engraved on headstones at Pargny.

The identification of John Kipling involved elements of all of the above – an enquiring mind, logical deduction, the interest of the general public and, additionally, a supposed dramatic mistake. But was it a correct deduction that the unknown officer, whose body was found in September 1919 during battlefield clearance and identified as a Lieutenant of the Irish Guards, and reburied in St Mary's ADS Cemetery, was actually John Kipling?

The case put forward by Norm Christie was founded upon the supposition that John Kipling had been a Lieutenant on the day that he had gone missing and that all Irish Guards Lieutenants except one can be accounted for, leaving just John and the unknown – hence they must be one and the same. But was John Kipling a full Lieutenant on the day that he went missing and, more importantly, was he wearing that rank?

A further prop to the identification was the suggestion that the recorded map reference, G25, of where the body was found in 1919 (6,000 yards from the front line) was incorrectly noted and should have been H25 (in the area where John Kipling disappeared). The first aspect to examine, however, is that of rank. Since the body was identified in 1919 as a full Lieutenant and not a 2nd Lieutenant, if John Kipling had not been wearing the uniform of a full Lieutenant when he died then the body cannot be his – if the identification is correct.

The lowest officer rank is that of Second Lieutenant and that was indicated in the Irish Guards by a single pip on each shoulder, the next rank above that is Lieutenant with two pips on each shoulder (these are actually known as 'stars' in the Guards). Promotion in peacetime from one rank to the next could be anticipated, that is to say the officer would know that promotion was going to take place at some particular date in the future. If that date was, say, 27 September, it would seem certain to the layman that when 27 September arrived, the officer could, in his own time, change his badges of rank from Second Lieutenant to Lieutenant by adding an extra pip to each shoulder. Not so. The official notification of an officer's promotion is published in the *London Gazette* and that generally takes place after the actual date of promotion – the process is known as 'being Gazetted'. In most regiments it would be highly unlikely that an officer would 'put up his rank', ie alter the rank badges on his uniform, until he had been Gazetted. It was not 'done'. This view is reinforced by a letter written on 10 July 1915 by Lady Manners, mother of John Manners, Grenadier Guards, killed at Villers Cotterets in 1914) to Lady Edward (mother of George Cecil, Grenadier Guards, killed with John Manners) in which she talks about a young mutual friend who had recently joined his regiment, 'but', she says, 'he is not gazetted yet and untill (sic) he is which may not be for another week does not wear uniform'. Although in this case Lady Manners is talking about commissioning rather than promotion, the principle is clear – the key to action is the announcement in the *London Gazette*. High profile confirmation of this is the case of the poet Wilfred Owen who was killed on 4 November 1918 and whose notification of the award of the MC for an action in October describes him as '2nd/Lieutenant W.E.S. Owen'. The day after his death the *London Gazette* announced that Owen had been promoted to full Lieutenant with effect from 4 December 1917, a year earlier, but Philip W Guest, Honorary Treasurer of the Wilfred Owen Association, has seen a 1920's photograph of the original wooden cross placed over the grave and the rank is marked as Second Lieutenant. Clearly Owen had not known about his promotion or, if he had, had not worn the rank on the day that he was killed – he had not been 'Gazetted'.

John Kipling was a Second Lieutenant in the 2nd Battalion when the Irish Guards sailed for France on 16 August 1915, and he went missing and was probably killed on 27 September 1915, barely six weeks later. He was Gazetted on 11 November 1915, ie after he was killed, with the date of his promotion shown as 7 June 1915, ie before he was killed. Thus the researcher working on records some time after the event, or using the memorial records of the Imperial/Commonwealth War Graves Commission, in looking up the rank of John Kipling, would correctly conclude that he was a full Lieutenant and not a Second Lieutenant when he died. But was he wearing the rank for it to be found in 1919 during a search of the battlefields? Did John Kipling know in advance that he was to be promoted and had he put up his rank, bearing in mind that at the time of his death he had not been Gazetted? The answer to the first part of the question is 'almost certainly not' and that is clear from two of his letters home.

The first was on 16 July, when, still excited by the prospect of going to war, he wrote home, 'In case you have forgotten my position,

John. 2nd Lieutenant
Irish Guards
Brigade of Guards
2nd (res) Battln
Warley Barracks
Brentwood. Essex. O.H.M.S.'

The second was written on Sunday 19 September 1915 while John was in the area of Béthune, some 8 miles north-west of Loos. He wrote to his father asking for a new 'aluminium Disc with a string through it like this . . .' and he drew a picture –

2nd Lieutenant
John Kipling
C of E
Irish Guards

He clearly and deliberately asked for his rank to be shown as a '2nd Lt'. It is possible for someone in the heat of the moment to forget a recent change in circumstance, even a promotion, but here John Kipling drew a picture of what he wanted and that was a considered action. There cannot be any argument that on 19 September 1915, eight days before he went missing, John Kipling considered himself to be a 2nd Lieutenant and that he would have been wearing that rank. Could he have learned of his impending Gazetting with its backdated promotion in the next few days before the battle and added the extra pips? Two later letters suggest not.

On Thursday 23 September he wrote home again and did so once more at 5.30pm on Saturday 25 September. It was, he said, 'a hurried line as we start off tonight . . . the front line trenches are nine miles off from here.' It was, however, a letter of over 200 words (his last) and if John had learned that he was to be promoted there is no doubt that he would have proudly told his parents that fact in one of his last two letters. He reported that they were being shelled in the open and that the rain was intense. In the extremely unlikely event that he learned of his promotion between writing the last letter and moving up into battle the following day, the conditions for putting up a new rank, let alone finding the pips that were needed to do it, were such that he would not have attempted it. If he had done so it would have been recorded.

During wartime, regiments keep a daily record of events known as the

'War Diary'. Theoretically it is written daily and records everything of note that happens during every day, including the casualties. In practice the War Diary is not written every day because the realities of warfare do not allow it, but it is certainly written soon after the event and provides the most contemporary official record of what happened when. The War Diary of the 2nd Battalion was written possibly within hours of the action – certainly within days. In describing the attack of the 1st Scots Guards and the capture of Puits 14 (see Map 1, the area where John disappeared) on 27 September 1915, the War Diary recounts: 'the 1st Scots Guards had come up partly round, and partly through the right flank of the 2nd Irish Guards, and had captured PUITS 14 BIS. 2nd Lieutenants CLIFFORD and KIPLING, and some few Irish Guardsmen had also gone forward with this party.' The officer writing the diary (probably the adjutant or assistant adjutant, whose normal duties would make him aware of all promotions in the battalion) was clear that John Kipling was a 2nd Lieutenant and not a Lieutenant at the time that he disappeared and this also rules out the possibility that John had been promoted in the field by the Commanding Officer in the hours before the battle. Such a promotion would have been recorded in the War Diary. In Rudyard's official history of the Irish Guards there is even more substantial confirmation of John's effective rank on 27 September as that of a 2nd Lieutenant.

In the search for his son and the research for his *History of the Irish Guards*, Rudyard Kipling talked or wrote to every member of the regiment who had information to offer. He was painstaking in his efforts to be accurate in what he recorded. In a letter [RHQ Irish Guards] written from Bateman's on 16 May 1919 and addressed to Captain A.F. Gordon at the Regimental Headquarters of the Irish Guards, in which he thanks Captain Gordon for various maps (including Map 44, the area around Loos), he explained that he wanted to give the losses for 'every month' as 'it would enormously add to the interest and help to give the picture of the Regiment in the war.' He apologized for the extra work that he was asking Headquarters to undertake, 'but the main thing is to get the History as full and accurate as possible'. In his determination to be accurate there cannot be any doubt that if his only son had been holding and displaying the rank of full Lieutenant at the time of his death then Rudyard would have found out and said so in his History. In fact what he wrote about the action with the Scots Guards around Puits 14 on 27 September was 'Their rush took with them "some few Irish Guardsmen", with 2nd Lieutenants W.F.J. Clifford and J. Kipling . . . 2nd Lieutenant Kipling was wounded and missing.' Was Rudyard just copying from the entry in the War Diary? No, because among the other documents that he would have examined was John's AB 83, his record of Service, and under the 'War Service' column is the entry noting John's promotion – 'Lieut 7.6.'15 (Gaz. 11.11.15)'. Rudyard's history takes full account of John's

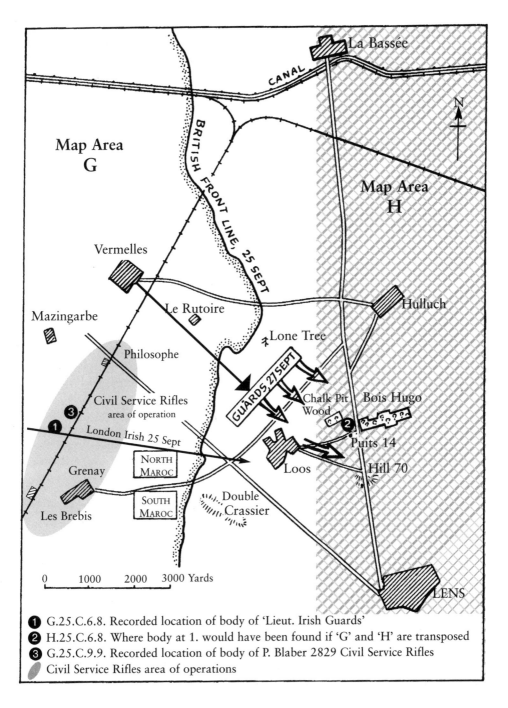

Map Area G

La Bassée

CANAL

BRITISH FRONT LINE, 25 SEPT

N

Map Area H

Vermelles

Le Rutoire

Hulluch

Mazingarbe

Lone Tree

Philosophe

GUARDS, 27 SEPT

Chalk Pit Wood

Bois Hugo

Civil Service Rifles
area of operation

❸

❶

London Irish 25 Sept

❷ Puits 14

Grenay

NORTH MAROC

Loos

Hill 70

SOUTH MAROC

Double Crassier

Les Brebis

0   1000   2000   3000 Yards

LENS

❶ G.25.C.6.8. Recorded location of body of 'Lieut. Irish Guards'
❷ H.25.C.6.8. Where body at 1. would have been found if 'G' and 'H' are transposed
❸ G.25.C.9.9. Recorded location of body of P. Blaber 2829 Civil Service Rifles
  Civil Service Rifles area of operations

Map 1   The Loos Battlefield

211

promotion, for in Appendix A of the history of the 2nd Battalion, in the list of *Lieutenants* 'Killed in Action or Died of Wounds', is 'J Kipling, 27.9.15'. Thus as far as Rudyard was concerned John's promotion had not come through at the time that he was killed, hence he described him as 2nd Lieutenant for that moment, but the *Gazette* entry of November backdated the promotion to before his death so that historically speaking John *was* a Lieutenant when he disappeared, a fact taken account of by Rudyard in his listing of John as a full Lieutenant in the 'killed in action' list.

There is even earlier evidence of Rudyard's total conviction that his son was a 2nd Lieutenant at the time of his death. During the anxious days following John's disappearance Rudyard pulled every string at his command in order to find out what had happened to his son. In his letter of 14 October 1915 to Mr Van Dyke, American Minister at the Hague, Rudyard expressed the hope that through neutral channels some information might be found and said, 'He [John] was a 2nd Lieutenant in the Second Battalion Irish Guards and I have reason to fear that he had lost his identification disk before he went into action and so could only be identified by his clothes, all of which were marked. He wore a small gold signet ring with monogram J.K. and though he would have been wearing spectacles in action the mark of pince-nez which he usually wears is very distinct on both sides of his nose.' [University of Princeton Library.]

There is yet another letter that confirms the rank. On 12 November 1915 Rudyard wrote to 'Stalky', Brigadier Dunsterville, bringing him up to date with the news of John. Proudly he said, 'He was senior ensign tho' only 18 years and six weeks'. After John's disappearance Carrie visited Guards HQ in the hope of getting news and saw de Vesci who told her, 'John was his best ensign'. An ensign was a *Second* Lieutenant.

If then it is now certain that John Kipling was wearing the uniform of a 2nd Lieutenant when he died does that rule out the 1992 identification of the body said to be 'UBS Lieutenant Irish Guards' as being his? Probably, but not totally. The 1919 'unknown' identification could have been incorrect in either rank, regiment or both. After all, in part of the supporting argument for the identification of the body as being that of John Kipling, Norm Christie supposed that a mistake had been made in the map reference showing where the body had been found. He suggested that the reference G.25.C.6.8. should have been H.25.C.6.8. (Map 1, Points 1 and 2). Once the possibility of a mistake is admitted it calls into question all aspects of the records made at the same time. It is sensible, therefore, before coming to any conclusion, to examine the process by which the battlefields were cleared, the bodies exhumed, identified and reburied.

As described in Chapter 8, attempts to identify the dead and to mark

212

their place of burial were made as early as October 1914 by a Red Cross Mobile Unit commanded by Major Fabian Ware. His efforts led to the creation of a *Graves Registration Commission* in 1915 which he directed, and then to the *Imperial* (now *Commonwealth*) *War Graves Commission*. At the end of the war, however, and until the British forces were withdrawn from the continent in September 1921 and the Imperial War Graves Commission took over, the searching of the old battlefields and the exhumation of bodies for the purpose of identification and re-burial, was done by the *Directorate of Graves Registration and Enquiries* under the War Office.

The work on the ground was carried out by Labour Companies, often made up of Chinese, Russian, Egyptian and other nationalities, but commanded by British Officers. Using map squares to define the areas in which they were working, the Labour Companies worked systematically across the ground in long lines (see Plate 8) rather as modern police forces do looking for evidence at the scene of a serious crime. When remains were found a standard form known as a *Burial Return* had to be completed on which the precise location of the remains was marked using a map reference, and the reasons for any identification given. Each day's Burial Return was signed as accurate by an officer.

The returns made in the field, probably originally written in indelible pencil on the spot, were taken to an office facility where they were collated and typed on to formal sheets, each sheet listing some twenty or so bodies. Returns were filed together under the name of the cemetery to which the reburials were made and it was on 23 September 1919 that 18 Labour Company's Burial Return recorded the reburial in St Mary's ADS of the body of 'U.B.S. (Unknown British Soldier) Officer Lieut. Irish Guards' (see Plate 10). However, the map reference given for the spot where the body was found was in the area. 'G.25' some 6,000 yards behind the Loos fighting of 27 September 1915 which had been in area 'H 25' (see map) and part of Christie's case was that the place where the body was found had been wrongly recorded as 'G25' when it should have been 'H25'. The area of Loos around Hill 70, Bois Hugo and Puits 14 where John Kipling was last seen is in block 'H 25', not 'G 25', and the letter change to 'H', if accepted, would put the body exactly at the scene of action, adding to the argument that it was that of John Kipling. The argument appears to be reinforced when considering whether it was possible that a badly wounded officer, probably without his glasses upon which he depended in order to see more than a few feet in front of him, could have gone back some 6,000 yards from 'H25' where he was wounded to 'G25'. It is possible, of course, but is it probable? In the rush of the Irish Guards back from Chalk Pit Wood to the Loos–Hulluch road he might have become separated from the regiment, been picked up by a motor ambulance and taken back to a medical facility, but that is very unlikely. Does that then

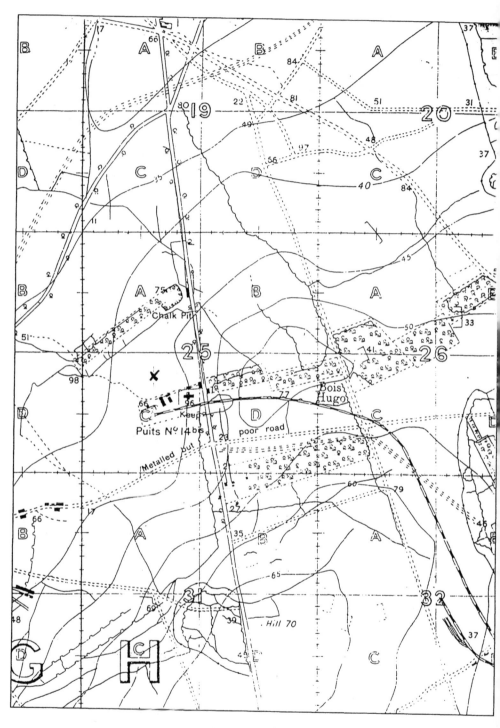

Map 2   Note the large letters 'G' and 'H' in the bottom left-hand corner and the reference H.25.C.6.8. on this 1915 map.

lead to the final conclusion that the recorded map reference of 'G25' must be wrong? Not at all.

In supplementing the proposition that the reference *was* wrong Norm Christie argued that the body could not have been found in 'G25' because 'at no time during the war were British units in action at . . . "G25".' That statement suggests a misunderstanding of the realities of the war being fought, because while it may be correct to say that at no time during the war were trench battles fought in the area of 'G25', the area was very much within range of the German guns and was heavily shelled, causing many casualties among rear-echelon troops or fighting units moving up to or back from the front. There were, in fact, three Irish Guardsmen found in the 'G25' area on 23 September 1919 as will be seen later. They cannot all have been wrongly recorded. Perhaps the 'Lieut. Irish Guards' was not wrongly located but wrongly identified as such. The 'mistaken' map reference is not vital to Christie's submission. It merely supports it. How then was the 'Lieut. Irish Guards' identified?

There are two elements to the identification – first that the body was that of an officer, a Lieutenant, and second that he was of the Irish Guards. Officers could be identified by their rank badge, the type of uniform, including the hat, marked clothing, perhaps a Sam Browne belt, though some Warrant Officers wore them, and by their button arrangement – the Irish Guards officers wore their jacket buttons in groups of four (being the fourth Guards Regiment in order of seniority). It is probable that since neither uniform nor buttons would differentiate between 2nd Lieutenant, Lieutenant or Captain, the officer identification as a Lieutenant was made from the pips. The pips worn by the Irish Guards at that time did not include the shamrock or any other means of identifying the holder as belonging to the Irish Guards, therefore the second part of the identification as being of the Irish Guards could not have come from the pips but must have come from the uniform or the button arrangement. Or could the officer have been mistakenly recorded as being of the Irish Guards when he was not, because a numeral or regimental button was found and attributed to him? Irish Guards officers did not wear numerals. Irish Guards soldiers did. They intermittently wore on their shoulders a brass 'I.G.' (actually two separate letters) and/or a brass 'star' bearing a shamrock which could have been mistaken for an officer's pip (Plate 15). Buttons might have been regimental, bearing a harp and a crown, or they might have been general service as worn by almost every regiment in the army. Would the search party have known these fine distinctions? As the Burial Return shows (Plate 10), three bodies were found at the same location, given as G.25. C.6.8., and, while this reference could cover a 50-yard square, it could also mean a common grave, in which case the numeral or button could have been that of one of the other bodies and not from the officer. If so, the officer could have been from any number of other regiments or corps and not from the Irish Guards. What is more, if the star had been mistaken for a pip then the body might not have been that of an officer at all but that of a soldier. After all two other Irish Guards soldiers were found in the area on that same day (Plates 10 and 11). [David Horn, Curator of the Guards Museum, offered a further option: 'The brass letters I.G. and the regimental star would have been punctured through the material. Suppose in the grave there was just a star halfway up the shoulder strap on only one shoulder. An observant "digger" or "intelligent officer" in charge might assume that the lower holes in the strap had been for a second rank star. If three bodies were found in the same area perhaps they were all soldiers.'] Although those doing the battlefield clearance would have been experienced and no doubt equipped with reference material for identifying regiments and ranks, there are so many idiosyncracies in dress and customs between regiments that it is quite possible that if all three bodies were found in the same grave that the officer identification was mistakenly linked with the Irish Guards identification which actually belonged to one of the soldiers' bodies, or that a star had been mistaken for a pip and that none of the bodies was that of an officer at all.

The Commission's case for naming the unknown burial as that of John Kipling rests upon the 1919 identification of the body as being that of the only full Lieutenant of the Irish Guards unaccounted for, ie John Kipling. The fact that it now seems certain that John Kipling was not wearing the rank of a Lieutenant when he was killed does not negate that case, but it does mean that for the case to remain valid the identification of the body as a Lieutenant and not a 2nd Lieutenant must have been a mistake on the part of 18 Labour Company. The Burial Return at Plate 10 gives no information as to how the identification was made. Colonel Goodland, Deputy Controller of the IWGC in France and Flanders at that time, wrote, 'About 17% of . . . bodies were identified by buttons, badges, tags if of metal – not the composition ones – boots bearing regtl numbers – teeth – odds and ends in pockets, letters etc – all sent to London for the special branch to examine' [CWGC archives]. If anything substantial had been found to confirm the body's rank as 'Lieutenant', surely it would have been recorded. It looks as if the rank was arrived at by deduction.

A supporting argument for the identification of Kipling's body was that a mistake in the map reference of where it had been found had been made by 18 Labour Company. What they had recorded as G.25.C.6.8. was said to have actually been H.25.C.6.8. (Map 1, Points 1 and 2). This latter reference is within the area where Kipling was last seen, while the earlier one is 6,000 yards behind it. How, then, were 18 Labour Company carrying out their work and could their records have been wrong? If there is a mistake or mistakes they could have happened either during the exhumation process and recording in the field or at the 'office' when the Burial Returns were typed. First the work in the field. Could the exhumation teams have believed themselves to be in area G when they were actually in H?

Examination of the Burial Return records for St Mary's ADS which are held at the Commission's headquarters at Maidenhead show that reburials began in early September 1919. The earliest record held is for 2 September when bodies were found in G11 and G10 but the records may not be complete. What is clear is that the four sheets covering the work done on 4 September record exhumations of some 100 bodies of which around 80 were found in area G23, an area around 'Lone Tree' (see Map1) that was in the direct line of the advance of the 2nd Battalion of the Irish Guards to Loos. On the 8th the area worked is A, with one body found in G, on the 9th it is all G, on the 11th it is all G, on the 12th it is all G, on the 16th nine bodies were found in M3, on the 17th thirty-three bodies were found in G4 and on the 23rd, of the fifty-nine bodies recorded, thirty-eight were found in G, the remainder in A. This was the day, 23 September 1919, on which the body described as 'U.B.S. Officer Lieut. Irish Guards' was found, the body later identified as that of John Kipling. 18 Labour Company had been working in the area G for at least two weeks, surely long enough to know where they were on the 23rd. Is it feasible that they could have mistaken H25 for G25? Perhaps.

Map 2 shows the lettering system for the maps that would have been used at the time. Area G, a large square, contains thirty-six smaller 1,000-yard squares numbered from 1 to 36, (each confusingly quartered into further squares lettered with small capitals, A,B,C and D) as does the adjacent area H in which H.25.C.6.8. is marked. The large identification letters G and H for the thirty-six square lots are close together (in the bottom left-hand corner) and it is possible that, while actually working in area H.25.C., a cursory glance at the map to establish a map reference might lead to the assumption that it was actually G.25.C. But on the previous day, 22 September, one of the Burial Returns records that they *were* working in H25 and found over sixty bodies there. It is not credible that on the following day, when working some 6,000 yards further west, they believed that they were in the same place as on the 22nd. A mistake in the field record is extremely unlikely and examination of the typed records supports this view.

The typed records held at the Commonwealth War Graves Commission show three burial returns were submitted by 2nd Lieutenant A.H. Domaille of 18 Labour Company for 23 September 1919, the day that the unknown Irish Guards Lieutenant was exhumed. Two are shown at Plates 10 and 11. There may have been more but they do not now exist. However, the three that are illustrated bear examination for what they reveal about the field entries.

Plate 10 shows that *all* the exhumations were in the area 'G'. Thus, in supposing that the first on the page, ie the Irish Guards Lieutenant, should have been 'H', does that imply that the mistake is singular and applies only to the first entry or are all the entries on that page incorrect? Certainly the large letters 'G' and 'H' on the 1915 battlefield map 36c (Map 2) are side by side and an inexperienced or careless officer might use the incorrect letter for the day's work, but while an officer with a map is said to be the most dangerous thing in the British Army it stretches the imagination to believe that an experienced team, knowing the importance of recording where they had searched in order properly to cover the battlefield, would make such an error. In addition, it is quite inconceivable that one entry on the page would be made as 'H' and all the others, including two more bodies found in the same place as the first, as 'G', when covering the same piece of ground on the same day. Additionally a second member of the Irish Guards, identified by his numeral, is listed on the same page as having been found at G.25.C.9.4. If the first is wrong then so is the second. It is highly likely that the way in which the exhumation process worked was that the pencil entries in the field records were made, or directly supervised, by the officer in charge of the search party. If he had mistakenly read the map area as 'G' instead of 'H' then *all* the entries for that day would have been wrong, not just the ones for the two Irish Guards.

Plate 11 has its first entry a 'U.B.S. Irish Guards' who was identified by his numeral. Tellingly it records that the body was found at 'G.25.C.2.5.', very close to where the Lieutenant was found. If the Lieutenant's original burial was recorded as being in G.25 when it should have been in H.25 – part of Norm Christie's argument was that no Irish Guards had been in the area of G.25 – then the unknown Irish soldiers on Plates 10 and 11 must also have been wrongly recorded. It is stretching imagination too far to suggest that three singular mistakes took place, on different sheets, each to an Irish Guard and each a transposition of the letter 'H' for the letter 'G'. Therefore a mistake in the field is quite improbable and the process of transcription from the field records to the typed records must now be examined. Perhaps mistakes were made there.

Supposing that the typist was transcribing from indelible pencil records made in the field, it is conceivable that, having misread and typed a run of incorrect 'G' entries on Plate 10, he or she could have continued on to the second sheet. However, at the bottom of Plate 11 and the top of the third sheet are entries for area 'A' and at that point the typist would inevitably have paused, perhaps moving on to a different set of field records, and surely would have reflected upon what had been typed to date. The third return (not shown here) deals with exhumations that are entirely in area 'A'. Furthermore, closer examination of Plate 10 shows that the lower case letter 's' does not print correctly while on the second two sheets it does. Hence it is likely that two different typists were working from the field records produced on 23 September 1919. The typewriter that produced Sheet 1 (Plate 10) and the entry for the 'Officer Lieut. Irish Guards' is a different machine from that used for Sheet 2 (Plate 11) and the entry for the second Irish Guards soldier. It is quite impossible that each typist would have incorrectly read the field record in the same way and only for the Irish Guards entries.

Therefore, although already seen to be highly improbable, if there *was* a mistake in recording the 1919 exhumation it was made in the field on the original 'indelible pencil' field records and not in the transcription and it applied to *all* the records made in the area 'G' for that day. If one is wrong then they are all wrong. But they are not: the fourth entry on Plate 10 is that for '2829 BLABER. P. 15th London Reg. Civil Service Rifs. K.I.A. 9.11.15.' His body is recorded as having been found at G.25.C.9.9. (Map 1. Point 3) and if the 'Kipling' entry (the first entry on the same sheet) is wrong then Blaber's is too. The bodies were reburied, two head-stones apart, confirming that they were found at the same time in the same area and reburied simultaneously. So where was Blaber killed?

The 1st Battalion Civil Service Rifles, Blaber's regiment, arrived at trenches at Maroc (Map 1 – a sprawling area synonymous on many maps with Grenay) on 1 September 1915 firmly in the map area 'G'. Its Regimental History records that the battalion was involved in support duties, 'carrying gas cylinders, digging assembly trenches and bridging trenches', and 'with the exception of two platoons of B Company, the whole battalion looked on from the reserve trenches' during the Battle of Loos. The history goes on to record that following the battle 'towards the end of the period . . . Companies in turn occupying the 'Spinney' trenches . . . had their nerves sorely tried by the eccentricities of enfilade fire . . . There were as many as thirty casualties a day.' These and the Maroc trenches were the ones occupied by the battalion when it was relieved on the night of 13 November by the 1st Cameron Highlanders, ie four days after Private Blaber was killed. Maroc is in square G26, adjacent to G25 and nearer to the front line. They marched back through Mazingarbe (see Map 1). They never went to area H25. Maroc is 4,500 yards due west of H25.

Thus it is probable that Blaber was one of the 'thirty casualties' on 9 November and was wounded in the area of Maroc in G26 and was evac-uated to a Regimental Aid Post or Field Ambulance facility some way behind the trenches. The map reference given on the Burial Return (Plate 10) as the place where Blaber's body was found is 'G.25.C.9.9.' (Map 1. Point 3) and that is on a direct line between Maroc and Mazingarbe, the withdrawal route (Map 1 shows it) used by the battalion and a line on which a Regimental Aid Post would most likely be sited. It is therefore absolutely certain that the reference given for Blaber is correct, that all the entries on the Burial Return are correct and therefore so is that for the body found some 350 yards from Blaber and identified as the unknown 'Lieut. Irish Guards', ie 'G' not 'H'.

Therefore no mistakes were made in the field with the map references on 23 September 1919 and no mistakes were made in the transcriptions from the 'indelible' entries to the typed pages. The body *was* found in G.25.C.6.8. Does that mean that the identification of the unknown Lieutenant's body as that of John Kipling was absolutely wrong? No, but it weakens the case and it is time to review the Commission's arguments and the evidence.

The body found in 1919 was identified at that time as Lieutenant. The arguments above establish beyond reasonable doubt that John Kipling was wearing the uniform of a 2nd Lieutenant when he died. Therefore the body is not that of John Kipling if the 1919 identification is correct. The supporting argument that the letter 'G' had been mistakenly used instead of 'H' in the map reference for where the body was found has been seen to be wrong. So if the body is not that of John Kipling then whose is it? There are a number of possibilities and integral to each is that a mistake was made in the 1919 identification, because, now that it is clear that John Kipling was not wearing two pips when he died, there is no longer a full Lieutenant of the Irish Guards unaccounted for and hence the description 'UBS Lieut. Irish Guards' must be inaccurate. But in what way?

There are three possibilities. One is that the description 'Lieut.' is wrong in the 1919 identification. If the identification of rank was made as a result of finding a single pip (2nd Lieutenant) instead of two pips (Lieutenant) but the description 'Irish Guards' is correct, then who are the candidates? Examination of the records of the Commonwealth War Graves Commission shows that in the case of the 1st Battalion (this battalion must be considered because it manoeuvred in the Mazingarbe 'G' area before Loos) four Lieutenants and one 2nd Lieutenant are listed as missing but they were lost in the Ypres area and so they are excluded. As for the 2nd Battalion (John's) Lieutenant John Kipling and 2nd Lieutenants T. Pakenham-Law and W.F.J. Clifford are the only officers listed as missing. Thus any one of the three could be the 'U.B.S'. Interestingly, Pakenham-Law is listed in the 1919 official HMSO publication 'Officers who Died in the Great War' as having died on '27/8/15' (a month previously) and presumably because of that he is listed amongst the Missing on the memorial at le Touret which covers the period before the battle of Loos. But on a flimsy piece of paper and written in indelible pencil, Lieutenant Colonel Butler, commanding the 2nd Battalion wrote from France to 'My Dear Tom' on 29 September, 'A hasty scrawl to tell you we made an attack on 27th – it was successful and we have been at grips with the Bosch ever since. Our casualties in officers are–

27th Wynter – wounded

    Clifford – missing – I have very little doubt he is really dead. He was hit but I have no authoritative news yet as to whether he is actually dead.

Stephens – wounded

Kipling – missing – no evidence as to whether he is dead or not

Pakenham-Law – wounded and has since died

Grayson – wounded' [RHQ Irish Guards].

The War Diary gives the time (4pm) and date (27 September) of Pakenham-Law's wounding and therefore the 'Officers who Died in the Great War' is wrong, further evidence that mistakes in records are all too possible. Additionally, because he was killed in September, Pakenham-Law's name should not be on the le Touret memorial but on the one at Dud Corner which commemorates the missing from the battle of Loos. According to *Du Rivigny's Roll of Honour* Pakenham-Law was 'buried in a garden at Loos', but this does not exclude him from being the 'U.B.S', although it may suggest that Clifford and Kipling are the more likely candidates.

The second possibility is that the identification of 'Irish Guards' was wrong because an Irish Guards numeral from another body was wrongly attributed to an officer. In that case there is no possibility of identifying the body but it would not be that of John Kipling.

The third is that an Irish Guards 'star' was wrongly taken to be an officer's pip, in which case the body was not that of an officer and therefore not that of John Kipling.

Given the evidence for the identification as presented to the Commission by Norm Christie (which omitted all reference to Kipling's request for an identity disc showing him as a 2nd Lieutenant) it was a reasonable conclusion that the grave was that of John Kipling. Further and wider examination of the possibilities as above must cast doubt on that conclusion and there is one more, perhaps even more powerful, argument, that casts doubt on the identification and that comes from Rudyard Kipling himself.

When the body 'U.B.S. Lieut. Irish Guards' was identified in September 1919 Rudyard had been working on the *History of the Irish Guards* for two years and would continue as long again with careful and painstaking research to establish every detail of the Regiment's part in the war. He was also an active and dedicated Commissioner on the Board of the Imperial War Graves Commission, making frequent visits to the battlefields and knew well Fabian Ware, its Vice-Chairman, and Lord Milner, its Chairman. What is more he had strong links with the British Red Cross Society via his friendship with Robert Cecil, who, before Sir Louis Mallet, had led the combined Red Cross and St John Ambulance organization and whose nephew, George, had been lost at Villers Cotterets and for whose body Rudyard had searched in 1914. By March 1919 the British Red

Cross was compiling lists of burials in France and Belgium, and by August it had been estimated that there were over 16,000 graves distributed between 600 cemeteries in Germany and the Imperial War Graves Commission was working on producing certified lists. Rudyard would have been scrutinizing these in detail looking for information about John, particularly in August and September as the fourth anniversaries of both John's birthday and disappearance approached. Barely a month after the finding of the 'U.B.S. Lieut. Irish Guards' Rudyard wrote to Lord Derby [CWGC] at the War Office agreeing to the suggestion that General Fabian Ware should be appointed as 'the permanent Vice-Chairman of the Imperial War Graves Committee' and expressing the view that, whatever design was accepted for the headstones of the dead, it should enable the deceased regiment to be clearly indicated. He went on, 'What knowledge I have of the feeling among officers and men, dead and alive, convinces me that their chief desire would be for distinctive regimental headstones . . . After all, whatever his individual position as a civilian may have been, when a man is once in the Service, it is for his regiment that he works, with his regiment that he dies, and in his death he wishes to be remembered as one of that regiment . . . [we should] . . . as far as possible, . . . carry out a regiment's wish as to the headstone to be placed over their dead.' Surely there cannot be any doubt that with Rudyard's connections, his public image, his frequent visits to France, his involvement with the smallest details of the Commission's work and his concern to establish the fate of all members of the Irish Guards, and one in particular, in order to write his 'accurate' history, that he would have been told by the Controller on the spot, Colonel Goodland (who was well known to him) about the 23 September finding of the grave of an 'unknown' Irish Guards officer. If so, then he must have dismissed the possibility that it could have been John. He certainly did when he visited St Mary's ADS in 1924, because it is inconceivable that he would not have seen the grave of the 'unknown Lieutenant, Irish Guards'. There are many references in his work to the sadness of not having a grave at which to mourn. Rudyard and his wife Carrie made extensive and exhaustive efforts to locate John's.

If Rudyard was not convinced, and he would desperately have wanted to be, then we cannot be either.

The critical analyses above need no further comment. It is now up to the reader to decide if the body in St Mary's ADS is that of John Kipling or not, but on page 224 some experts give their opinions.

POSTSCRIPT TO 2001 EDITION

Prior to the publication of this edition we wrote to the Commonwealth War Graves Commission, suggesting that, in the light of the new evidence presented in this book, they might wish to review their decision to change the headstone in St Mary's ADS from that of 'A Lieutenant of the Irish Guards' to 'Lieutenant John Kipling Irish Guards'.

On 14 September 2001 we received a letter from the Secretary and Director-General, Mr Richard Kellaway, which stated,

GRAVE 7.D.2 – ST MARY'S A D S CEMETERY, FRANCE. LIEUTENANT JOHN KIPLING

I promised to write back to you about the identification of this grave.

I have read with great interest the additional material you have submitted and it certainly raises questions.

I am also conscious that ultimately the Commission's member governments are necessarily responsible for matters relating to the identity of their respective war casualties. In all the circumstances I propose referring to the British government (Ministry of Defence) not only for its views in relation to the Commission's original research and the additional material which you have supplied subsequently, but also for any other information which perhaps it may now be able to add with the benefit of all this.

I hope this will help lead to a situation satisfactory for all concerned.

We are hopeful that the correct decision will ultimately be made. Perhaps the only way the mystery could indisputably be solved would be for a DNA test to be made on 'John' and his sister Elsie Bambridge's remains (both his parents were cremated). Elsie is buried with her husband in the Parish Churchyard of Arrington in Cambridgeshire which adjoins Wimpole Hall, their last home, now a National Trust Property.

This is, however, an action which we would never dream of seriously suggesting as they both deserve to rest undisturbed.

WHAT THE EXPERTS SAID
ABOUT THE IDENTIFICATION

In order to reach as fair a conclusion as possible concerning the veracity of the identification of John Kipling's grave we asked four people, whose professional or other-time activities require an analytical mind, to give their opinion based on the evidence assembled in this book.

Each wrote an account of their reading and conclusions. Here we extract the summary findings of each –

Anthony Babington
Former Circuit Judge, decorated soldier and author
When the existing evidence is carefully assessed it fails to establish that the 'U.B.S. Officer Lieut. Irish Guards' was the body of John Kipling.

Captain David Horn MISM
Ex-Grenadier Guards, Curator the Guards Museum
In my opinion the body is not that of Lieutenant (then 2nd Lieutenant) John Kipling.

Michael A Johnstone
Metropolitan Stipendary Magistrate and Military Historian
. . . a heavy burden of proof lies on him who asserts that this (the location at which the body was found) *was 6,000 yards out and I do not consider that this burden has been discharged . . . what is really being said is . . . an argumentum ad hominem.*

Howell Griffiths M.A.
Justice of the Peace, former Headmaster
I cannot agree with the statement made by the Commonwealth War Graves Commission that '. . . our records Officer has been successful in establishing beyond reasonable doubt that the Lieutenant (John Kipling) *is actually buried in Plot 7, Row D, Grave 2 of St. Mary's ADS Cemetery.'*

SELECT BIBLIOGRAPHY

Amis, Kingsley, *Rudyard Kipling and His World*, Thames & Hudson, 1975

Baldwin, Oliver, *The Questing Beast*, Grayson & Grayson, 1932

Birkenhead, Lord, *Rudyard Kipling*, Weidenfeld & Nicolson, 1978

Brown, Hilton, *Rudyard Kipling. A New Appreciation*, Hamish Hamilton, 1985

Carrington, Charles, *Rudyard Kipling. His Life and Work*, Macmillan, 1955

Cohen, Morton, *Rudyard Kipling to Rider Haggard*, Hutchinson, 1965

Cross, Thomas, *East and West*, Luckystone Press, 1991

Eliot, T.S., *A Choice of Kipling's Verse*, Faber & Faber, 1941

Gilbert, Elliot L. *"O Beloved Kids"*, Weidenfeld & Nicolson, 1983

Green, Roger Lancelyn, *Kipling: The Critical Heritage*, Routledge & Kegan Paul, 1971

Higgins, D.S., *The Private Diaries of Sir Henry Rider Haggard*, Cassell, 1980

Imperial War Graves Commission, *The King's Pilgrimage*, Hodder & Stoughton, 1922

Kipling, Rudyard,

    Debits and Credits, Penguin Books, 1987

    Just So Stories, World's Classics, 1987

    Kim, Oxford University Press, 1987

    The New Army in Training, Macmillan and Co Ltd, 1915

    Plain Tales from the Hills, Wordsworth Editions Ltd, 1993

    Puck of Pook's Hill and Rewards and Fairies, Oxford University Press, 1993

    Selected Stories, Penguin Books, 1987

    Something of Myself, Penguin Books, 1987

    The Complete Stalky and Co., World's Classics, 1987

    The Definitive Edition of Rudyard Kipling's Verse, Hodder and Stoughton, 1940

    The Five Nations, Methuen and Co, 1903

    The Irish Guards in the Great War Vols 1 and 2, 1923

    The Irish Guards in the Great War: The First Battalion/The Second

    Battalion. Spellmount Ltd, 1997

    The Jungle Book, Macmillan & Co, 1951

    The Light That Failed, Macmillan & Co, 1891

    Limits & Renewals, Penguin Books, 1987

    The Years Between, The Dominions Edition, 1919

    Twenty Poems, Methuen & Co, 1918

    The Kipling Journal, various editions

Laski, Marghanita, *From Palm to Pine,* Sidgwick & Jackson

Lewis, Peter, *The War in the Mountains by Rudyard Kipling*

Longworth, Philip, *The Unending Vigil,* Constable, 1967

Orel, Harold, *Kipling Interviews and Recollections Vols 1 and 2,* Macmillan Press Ltd, 1983

Orwell, George, *Essay on Kipling,* in *The Works of Rudyard Kipling,* Wordsworth Poetry Library, 1994

Page, Norman, *A Kipling Companion,* Macmillan Press Ltd, 1984

Pinney, Professor T., *The Letters of Rudyard Kipling,* Vols I, II 1990, Vol III 1995, Vol IV in preparation, Macmillan

Pocock, Tom, *Rider Haggard and the Lost Empire,* Weidenfeld & Nicolson, 1993

Ponton, Dorothy, *Rudyard Kipling at Home and at Work,* privately printed

Seymour-Smith, Martin, *Rudyard Kipling,* Queen Anne Press, 1989

Simkins, Peter, *Kitchener's Army,* Manchester University Press, 1988

Smith, Michael, *The Rottingdean Years,* Brownleaf, 1989

Thirkell, Angela, *Three Houses,* Oxford University Press, 1931

Walker, Christopher, *Oliver Baldwin,* In preparation

Wheeler, Sir Charles, *High Relief,* Country Life Books, 1968

Wilson, Angus, *The Strange Ride of Rudyard Kipling,* Secker & Warburg, 1977

Young, W. Arthur & McGivering, John H., *A Kipling Dictionary,* Macmillan, 1967

APPENDIX TO 2007 EDITION

Why Re-examine the supposed 'Identification' of John Kipling?

In 2007 ITV1 showed a two hour drama for television entitled 'My Boy Jack', an adaptation of a play about John Kipling by David Haig produced by Ecosse Films. David played Rudyard Kipling and John Kipling was played by Daniel Radcliffe, best known for the Harry Potter films.

In conjunction with the drama the Imperial War Museum staged a small Exhibition also entitled 'My Boy Jack' for which we acted as consultants. Thus considerable interest was generated anew in the story of John Kipling and in working with the Museum on the Exhibition we decided to re-examine the supposed 'identification' of an Unknown Officer's body as that of John Kipling.

When the 'identification' was first made it prompted us to write this book – the first biography of John Kipling, and in the First Edition in 1998 we argued that the 'identification' was unsafe, a view which sparked much discussion.

Following the presentation of our views to the Commission, the Director General, Mr Richard Kellaway, wrote, 'I have read with great interest the additional material you have submitted and it certainly raises questions'.

In 2001 Mr Kellaway passed the matter to the MOD PS4(A), the department then charged with establishing the identification of discovered battlefield remains. We met MOD and outlined our doubts about the 'identification', but while accepting that there were flaws in the Commission's case for naming the Unknown Officer's body as that of John, PS4 declined to reverse the naming. At that point we decided to let the matter rest.

Now, six years later, with the matter raised again because of the Haig drama and the IWM Exhibition, we have written this Appendix to the Third Edition in which we approach the 'identification' from a different direction, and for previous and new readers alike we feel that a concise explanation of the structure of our arguments is needed and that is what follows.

Clearly it is senseless to repeat in detail arguments already presented in the first two editions, but to ease the path of the reader we have summarised them in the progression of our explanation below with page references to the main text. No changes have been made either to the main story or the Postscript as they appear in the Second Edition.

Interestingly, when recently we asked the Joint Casualty and Compassionate Centre at RAF Innsworth (who have now taken over the

227

responsibility of identifying battlefield remains from MOD PS4(A)) for their view on the 'identification', they said that they had no record of the case.

Why the Commission Decided to Name the 'U.B.S. Officer Lieut. Irish Guards' as John Kipling

In 1919 18th Labour Company, a battlefield clearance unit looking for bodies in the Loos area, discovered remains which they recorded to be in an area whose main map reference was G.25. Amongst those remains were 'U.B.S. (Unknown British Soldier) Lieut. Irish Guards' and '2829 BLABER. P. 15th London Reg. Civil Service Rifs. K.I.A. 9.11.15.'.

These bodies were discovered in the 500 yards by 500 yards map square G.25.c. just under 160 yards apart. [See 18th Labour Company's 23 September 1919 Burial Return on page 108.]

On 27 September 1915 John Kipling had disappeared during the battle of Loos near a minehead known as Puits 14 and in an area whose main map reference was H.25. This is over three miles away from the area known as G.25. He was claimed to be the only full 'Lieutenant' of the three Irish Guards 'Lieutenants' that were killed that day who remained unaccounted for after the battle.

The proposition put to the Commission by an internal researcher was both deductive and seductive. It was :–

'If John Kipling is the only Irish Guards full 'Lieutenant' unaccounted for in the Loos area then the 'U.B.S. Officer Lieut. Irish Guards' must be him.'

But how could this be when the U.B.S. was found in area G.25 over 3 miles from where John Kipling was last seen alive in H.25?

The proposition's answer was: '18th Labour Company made a mistake in the map reference when they found the body. The main reference was not G.25. but H.25.' i.e. the area around Puits 14 where John was last seen.

The Commission accepted the argument and the headstone was renamed.

Our First Reaction

Our first reaction was that of admiration for the deductive reasoning that had led to the 'identification' and as background for our biography of John we asked for a copy of the proposition that had been made to the Commission.

However it then became clear that two mistakes on the part of 18th Labour Company were needed for the 'identification' to be accepted as being 'beyond reasonable doubt'. One was that they had wrongly recorded the map square where they had found the body as 'G' and not 'H', and secondly that they had wrongly identified the U.B.S. as a 'Lieut' when Kipling had been wearing the rank of a 2nd Lieutenant. This seemed to us to be two mistakes too far, almost the 'fitting' of the evidence to suit a particular conclusion, and we decided to examine the evidence concerning each of them.

The Map Reference 'Mistake'

When bodies were found while searching battlefields the details supporting any identification, and the map reference where the remains were found, were recorded in indelible pencil in a record book. These details were later typed out onto a BURIAL RETURN which was signed by an officer as being correct. [See page 108 for 18th Labour Company's Return].

Thus, if there had been a mistake with the map reference then it could have happened in two ways :–

1.   18th Labour Company wrongly recorded in indelible pencil in their record book the map reference as G.25 instead of H.25 at the time that the remains were found OR

2.   The reference was wrongly copied from the record book at a later date onto the BURIAL RETURN as G.25 instead of H.25.

How likely was either of these two events?
Both are very unlikely.

Firstly, 18th Labour Company had been working in the 'G' area for two weeks before the date of the BURIAL RETURN. [See page 217]. They were very unlikely to have recorded their activities as being in 'H'. In any case the 'G' area is one of railway lines and sidings while the 'H' area of Puits 14 is of woods and open country. It cannot be reasonable to suppose that 18th Labour Company did not know where they were.

Secondly, could the map reference have been wrongly copied from the record book? Yes it could but it wasn't. Here is the reason why:-

All the bodies listed on the 23 September BURIAL RETURN are shown as being found in 'G'.   The body of '2829 BLABER.P 15TH London Reg. Civil Service Rifs' was found less than 160 yards from the 'U.B.S. Officer'. If the reference for the latter is wrong then so is the one for nearby BLABER. But Blaber's regiment was not in area H. It moved in area G. [See map page 211]. Thus, since Blaber must have been in area 'G', the body now named as that of John Kipling must also have been in area 'G' as recorded by 18th Labour Company and not in area 'H' as the proposition to the Commonwealth War Graves Commission supposed.

Therefore there was no mistake with the map reference, either in the field or later with the typing.

[This is covered in detail in pages 216 - 220].
What about John Kipling's rank?

The Rank 'Mistake'

There is a clear distinction between a Second Lieutenant and a Lieutenant. The latter is senior to the former and wears two pips on each shoulder while the former has one.

The BURIAL RETURN states quite clearly that the 'U.B.S. Officer' is a 'Lieut.' although no reason is given in the column, 'Means of Identification', for that conclusion, nor for his identification as 'Irish Guards'.

18th Labour Company would have been sensitive to the distinction between a Second Lieutenant and a Lieutenant as the signatures at the bottom of their BURIAL RETURN show:-

'A.H. Domaille. 2/Lt.
For Lieut.O.C. 18th Labour Coy.'

They would not have mistaken a 2/Lt for a Lieut.

Since the BURIAL RETURN states the rank clearly as 'Lieut.' it must be assumed that rank insignia were found i.e. two pips or an Identity Disc.

So if John Kipling was wearing only one pip the body cannot be his.

But was John Kipling wearing the insignia of a '2/Lt?'

The answer is 'Yes' and it is confirmed by evidence that was not given to the Commission in the original submission for the change of name.

On the 19th of September, just 8 days before he was to be killed in the battle of Loos, John wrote horne. He had lost his identity disc and asked his father to get him a new one. He drew a picture of what he wanted. [See page 209].

It said:-

'2nd Lieutenant
John Kipling
C ofE
Irish Guards'

So at that time he clearly wore the rank of a 2nd Lieutenant.

To the civilian researcher there appears to be one avenue yet to be explored which is the possibility that John 'put up' the rank of a full Lieutenant after that letter, sometime in the 8 days before he was killed.

This notion is prompted by the fact that on 11 November 1915 (i.e. after he was killed) he was 'Gazetted' as having been promoted to Lieutenant on 7 June 1915 (i.e. before he was killed). 'Gazetting' is the publication in the London Gazette of a promotion and it might seem to the non-military person that as John's promotion date was 7 June he would have known that at that time and would have put up the new rank immediately. That he did not do so is evident from his letter of 19 July. In any case at that time, even if he knew of it, an officer would not assume his new rank until the promotion had been published in the London Gazette. We examine this situation in greater detail on pages 207 – 212. A further confirmation that John Kipling was wearing the rank of a 2nd Lieutenant on 27 September comes from the Irish Guards war diary for that day, which refers to '.... 2nd Lieutenants CLIFFORD and KIPLING ...'. The war diary is probably the most authentic source of information about daily regimental activities during battle.

It seems to us that it is not unreasonable to suppose that had the Commission been aware of John's letter of 19 September, clearly stating that his rank was that of a '2nd Lieutenant', then they would not have sanctioned the change of name of the headstone in St Mary's ADS Cemetery because, that rank accepted as 2nd Lieutenant, meant that three Irish Guards 2nd Lieutenants were missing and the U.B.S. might be any one of them. It would certainly have meant that the grave could not be identified as that of John Kipling.

Rudyard's Search

Rudyard Kipling was distraught at the loss of his son. Convinced at first that John was 'Missing' rather than dead, he called upon influential friends, including the Prince of Wales, to try to get news of him from the Germans. [We look at these efforts in pages 98 – 104]. It is said that he even arranged for leaflets to be dropped over the German lines asking for information about John.

Rudyard set about finding members of the Irish Guards who might be able to tell him exactly what happened in the area of Puits 14 where John was last seen. He interviewed or corresponded with more than 20 soldiers including John's Company Commander and Battalion Commander. They all had first or second hand accounts to give but, as is inevitable in warfare, they differed in some details (not surprising since the prime motive on a battlefield is survival rather than observation). However they mostly agreed on one thing – that John was last seen alive in the area of Puits 14. After months of research Rudyard himself in 1916 in a letter to the War Office summed up his conclusions as:–

'All the information I have gathered is to the effect that he was wounded and left behind near Puits 14 at the Battle of Loos on September 27th 1915.'

The search however did not stop there.

In 1917 Rudyard began work on the Regimental History of the Irish Guards [see pages 132 – 139] and within his search for detail and accuracy lay the hope that he might find out more about John. When the work was published he dedicated it to his son. That same year, 1917, Rudyard became a Commissioner of the Imperial War Graves Commission, an appointment that he took very seriously and which gave him access to the latest news from the battlefield search teams who were looking for bodies. If a body were to be found that by any measure might be that of his son he had a hot line to the news. He never got any.

St Mary's ADS (Advanced Dressing Station) Cemetery

This is the Commonwealth War Graves' Commission cemetery where 18th Labour Company re-buried the 'U.B.S. Officer Lieut. Irish Guards' and '2829 BLABER.P.

On the 31st of August 1924, on their annual motoring tour, Commissioner Rudyard Kipling and his wife Carrie, visited the cemetery. There cannot be any doubt that Rudyard, with his usual fixation on detail, would have examined the Cemetery Register and certainly would have sought out any Irish Guards grave. It is not far fetched to assume that he stood in front of the grave of 'U.B.S. Officer Lieut. Irish Guards'.

Here then was a father who had spent years searching for his beloved son. Here was a father who as a Commissioner of the Imperial War Graves Commission could not have been in a better place to examine every scrap of evidence concerning the identification of bodies. Here was an author who had written an acclaimed history of the Irish Guards. Here were a mother and father desperate for a 'name on a headstone at a known place' at which to mourn (their desperation for a place at which to mourn is expressed in Rudyard's story *The Gardener*. [See pages 184 – 186]).

Yet Rudyard and Carrie did not think that the grave was John's. If they didn't, after all their searching, how could anyone else think it to be so 'beyond reasonable doubt'?

If the Grave is not John's then whose is it?

Almost half of the casualties of the Great War have no known grave. While the Commission strives to name as many graves as possible as new evidence emerges, no new evidence has appeared concerning John Kipling. What we know today, Rudyard Kipling knew on the 31st August 1924. He did not identify the grave as that of his son.

However, if the grave is not that of John Kipling then who is the 'Lieut. Irish Guards'? Clearly, given that John was wearing the rank of 2nd

Lieutenant then the U.B.S. if actually a 2nd Lt, could be Clifford or Kipling or Pakenham-Law, all three 2Lts of the Irish Guards and missing during the battle of Loos and without a known grave.

As we have shown, in order for the grave to be taken as that of John two mistakes had to be admitted – the map reference and the rank. Equally, if the grave is not John's then since no 'Lieut.' of the Irish Guards is unaccounted for at least one mistake must have been made in that description i.e. he wasn't Irish Guards or he wasn't a 'Lieut' or both.

Is there then another candidate other than an officer of the Irish Guards?

Yes there is.

On the 25th September, the opening day of the battle, the 1/18th London Irish attacked the German lines in the area of the Double Crassier (map page 211) more than a mile and a half south west of where the Irish Guards would attack two days later. They had moved forward from the village of Noeux-les-Mines, a route that took them through the middle of the 'G' area where the unknown Lieutenant's body was found.

Three of the Regiment's officers were killed that day. Two have known graves. One is missing and his name is on the Memorial at Dud Corner, Loos. He is:–

Lieutenant Arthur Leslie Hamilton Jacob.

If the one and only mistake that 18 Labour Company made was to confuse 'Irish Guards' with 'London Irish' then Jacob is certainly 'beyond reasonable doubt' the UBS. He is of the right rank and he would have been in the 'G' area where 18 Labour Company said that they found the body.

The badges of the two regiments are quite different but no detail of why the 'Lieut' was thought to be of the Irish Guards is recorded on the BURIAL RETURN in the 'Means of Identification' column. If there had been simple confusion, either in the field or in the office, between the names of the regiments, then it also solves another mystery left untouched by the 'identification' and in so doing adds weight to the identification of Jacob as the Officer UBS.

The mystery is how any Irish Guards came to be in the G.25 map square over three miles away from their Regiment's area. On the same Burial Return as the UBS Officer is a UBS soldier also shown as Irish Guards and on the other sheet for that day is another 'U.B.S. Irish Guards'. [See page 109].

However that mystery is solved if 18 Labour Company mistook the London Irish bodies for Irish Guards – the UBS officer and the UBS soldiers were not Irish Guards but London Irish, whose Regiment was in the

233

G.25 area.

Thus the UBS Officer would not be John Kipling but could be Lieutenant Jacob – or perhaps neither.

What do you think?

The Experts' Views

Following the publication of the First Edition of this book we asked four people whose professional lives demanded an analytical approach to evidence, to examine the arguments in it and to give their opinion on the 'identification'.

In the Second Edition we published their summary findings. All agreed that the 'identification' was unsafe.

Here we publish in full their conclusions given following the first book.

Anthony Babington. QC.
Former Circuit Judge, decorated soldier and author

In 1992 the Information Officer at the Commonwealth War Graves Commission expressed the opinion that it had been established 'beyond reasonable doubt' that a body found in the vicinity of Loos on 23 September 1919 and described as 'U.BS. Officer Lieut. Irish Guards' was that of John Kipling.

It is difficult to understand where she discovered the evidential facts to justify such a conclusion. The unidentified body is that of a full Lieutenant: it seems clear that when John went missing he was still a 2nd Lieutenant. Admittedly his promotion had been authorised but he would not have been entitled to wear his pips until it had been gazetted.

The War Diary of his battalion records that when he was last seen he was a 2nd Lieutenant, and eight days earlier he had written to his father asking for a new identity disc in the name of 2nd Lt. John Kipling: Rudyard obviously believed that his son had only been a 2nd Lieutenant when he went missing as was shown by his letter to Mr Van Dyke and the account of the action on 27 September 1915 which he wrote subsequently in his history of the Irish Guards.

Norm Christie's reasoning is unconvincing. The principal ground for his belief that the unidentified body was John Kipling's appears to have been that all other Irish Guards Lieutenants were accounted for after the fighting on 27 September 1915. He offered no explanation for the fact that the dead officer was a full Lieutenant and Kipling would almost certainly have been wearing the badges of rank of a 2nd Lieutenant. Further, Christie seeks to support his theory by suggesting that the relevant Burial Return showed the place where the body was found incorrectly and that in reality it had been discovered much closer to the locality where Kipling had last been seen alive. However this Return was signed by an officer whose party had been searching this particular area for the previous two weeks and it is most unlikely that he could make such an error. It is a pity that the Return does not reveal how the dead Lieutenant was known to belong to the Irish Guards. As it is, we cannot be absolutely certain that was so.

When the existing evidence is carefully assessed it fails to establish that the 'U.B.S. Officer Lieut. Irish Guards' was the body of John Kipling.

Captain David Horn MISM
Ex-Grenadier Guards, Curator The Guards Museum

In my opinion the body is not that of Lieutenant (then 2nd Lieutenant) John Kipling.

It would appear that had the position where the bodies of the UBS Lieutenant Irish Guards and the other two UBS Irish Guards had been incorrectly annotated then so too would the other bodies including that of Blaber P.

I am not convinced by the Means of Identification 'Numeral Found'. So far as can be ascertained the Irish Guards did not wear 'numerals' on their uniform. They did wear small single brass roman letters I.G. on their shoulder straps under a small brass Star of St Patrick. I suspect this is what is meant by numeral.

The UBS Lieutenant Irish Guards therefore could only have been identified in three ways. His Irish Guards jacket, having its buttons in groups of four, would have been a 'positive'. His identity disc would likewise have been positive, however we know he had lost it and required a replacement from his family. The third could have been his rank badges – had they been in place. The identification would then have been clearly wrong as Kipling was not dressed correctly as a Lieutenant when he disappeared, only as a 2nd Lieutenant and his shoulder straps were unlikely to have been 'punched out' for future promotions. I think that the three bodies 'Irish Guards' were all soldiers. The two shown as 'numeral identified' obviously were, and the third, having no numerals in his shoulder straps, but only the punched holes where they had been, giving to the untrained finder the impression of rank.

Michael A. Johnstone
Metropolitan Stipendiary Magistrate and Military Historian

I am satisfied beyond reasonable doubt that when Jack Kipling went into action at the battle of Loos on or about 27 September 1915, he was, and believed himself to be, a Second Lieutenant or Subaltern and would presumably have been wearing the appropriate uniform with one pip only.

It follows therefore that if in his return Second Lieutenant Domaille was referring to a first Lieutenant when he said 'Officer, Lieut Irish Guards' then the body found at G.25.C.6.8 and buried in row D plot 2 of the cemetery cannot be that of Jack Kipling. However, it is my civilian experience that sometimes First Lieutenants and Second Lieutenants are indiscriminately and incorrectly referred to as 'Lieutenant'. The possibility is alluded to by the authors. As previously noted Second Lieutenant Domaille, unsurprisingly for an officer, punctiliously signed himself as such. I think that this fact alone provides some evidence, although not conclusive, if in other returns of his he referred to officers as 'Second Lieutenant'. The conclusion must then be inevitable whether or not a mistake was made as to the original point of exhumation.

I do not propose in detail to review the arguments about the point of exhumation but it does seem to me that a heavy burden of proof lies on him who asserts that this was 6000 yards out and I do not consider that this burden has been discharged by the arguments put forward by Norm Christie. It seems to me that what is really being said is 'the body is John Kipling's but he could have been at G.25 so there must have been a mistake' i.e. an argumentum ad hominem or, as has been said, situating the appreciation.

Howell Griffiths M.A.
Justice of the Peace. Former Headmaster

Having read the paper on the identification of Lieutenant John Kipling, and based only upon information given in it, I cannot agree that the evidence of identity meets the standard that would be required in a criminal court of law, i.e. that the identification 'is beyond reasonable doubt'.

Therefore I cannot agree with the statement made by the Commonwealth War Graves Commission that '... our records Officer has been successful in establishing beyond reasonable doubt that the Lieutenant (John Kipling) is actually buried in Plot 7, Row D, Grave 2 of St Mary's ADS Cemetery'.

In order to be certain that the body identified was that of John Kipling, on the basis of what is circumstantial evidence, the body would need to have been found, undeniably, in the area in which Kipling was operating at the time he went missing. This was not the case. Again, there would need to be clear physical evidence identifying the body as that of Kipling, e.g. an identity disc, a ring with a monogram J.K., labelled clothing, an unusual physical characteristic, or, at least, a confirmation that at the time he went missing, Kipling definitely wore the uniform of a full Lieutenant and that the U.B.S. in question was undeniably a full Lieutenant and that the regiment was undeniably the Irish Guards. This was not the case either.

However I do believe that it is possible that the body is that of Lt Kipling, because substituting the map reference H25 for G25 does place the body in the area in which Kipling disappeared, and because the only Lieutenant missing from his battalion during the period we are concerned with was Kipling who was, after all, a full Lieutenant from 7th June 1915. Who can tell what badge of rank he wore on the day he died? Who can be sure that a mistake in recording the map reference in question did not take place? Who knows what evidence was available to 18 Labour Company when the U.B.S. was found? Again, I did not find that the arguments against the body being that of Kipling, based on assumptions about the way in which the records might have been collated, excluded the possibility of this being Kipling. I have not found that the way that people are supposed to carry out a task necessarily matches the way they actually carry it out. If the body was that of a Lieutenant in the Irish Guards, but was not in the expected location, who knows what strange things occur in battle that might explain it? It is not, I believe, beyond credibility that Kipling could have ended up in sector G.

Nevertheless, even examining the evidence against the 'balance of probabilities' measure as required in a civil court, rather than 'beyond reasonable doubt' of the criminal court, I found it difficult to agree that the body is that of John Kipling. There is still the doubt about the badges of rank worn by Kipling at the time. There is no evidence of his personal possessions being found on or near the body, the ring with the monogram J.K., or the marked clothing mentioned, or the spectacles he wore etc. The actual map reference recorded, not the suggested alternative, does not put Kipling in the area he might have expected to have been in at the time he went missing. Then, if he was wearing a 2nd Lieutenant's uniform and a mistake was made about the exact rank of the U.B.S., there were three 2nd Lieutenants missing from Kipling's battalion. It could have been any one of these.

Our Personal View
The body of the 'U.B.S. Lieut Irish Guards' may be that of John Kipling, but it is not so 'beyond reasonable doubt'.

Addendum - an extraordinary co-incidence
While working with the IWM on their exhibition 'My Boy Jack' we came across badges in the museum's collection labelled 'Irish Guards'. One of these showed a wreathed harp with similarities to that of the London Irish or the Royal Irish Rifles. Someone at the IWM had mistaken a 'harped' badge for that of the Irish Guards. Is that what the 18th Labour Company did (as we suggest above) thus leading them to the wrong regimental identification?

So, reader it is now up to you. Do you believe that, 'beyond reasonable doubt', the body is that of John Kipling?

INDEX